Evil in the Western Philosophical Tradition

# Evil in the Western Philosophical Tradition

Gavin Rae

EDINBURGH
University Press

Edinburgh University Press is one of the leading university presses in the UK. We publish academic books and journals in our selected subject areas across the humanities and social sciences, combining cutting-edge scholarship with high editorial and production values to produce academic works of lasting importance. For more information visit our website: edinburghuniversitypress.com

© Gavin Rae, 2019, 2021

First published in hardback by Edinburgh University Press 2019

Edinburgh University Press Ltd
The Tun – Holyrood Road
12(2f) Jackson's Entry
Edinburgh EH8 8PJ

Typeset in 10/12 Goudy Old Style by
Servis Filmsetting Ltd, Stockport, Cheshire

A CIP record for this book is available from the British Library

ISBN 978 1 4744 4532 0 (hardback)
ISBN 978 1 4744 4533 7 (paperback)
ISBN 978 1 4744 4534 4 (webready PDF)
ISBN 978 1 4744 4535 1 (epub)

The right of Gavin Rae to be identified as the author of this work has been asserted in accordance with the Copyright, Designs and Patents Act 1988, and the Copyright and Related Rights Regulations 2003 (SI No. 2498).

# Contents

Preface vii

Introduction 1

## PART I Theological Foundations

1. The Rise of the Problem of Evil 21
2. Augustine, Free Will, and Evil 39
3. Aquinas, Privation, and Original Sin 55
4. Descartes and the Evil of Error 77
5. Leibniz and Theodicy: Evil as the Good 96

## PART II From Autonomous Reason to History

6. Kant on Radical Evil 117
7. Schelling and the Metaphysics of Evil 138
8. Nietzsche and the Genealogy of Evil 163

## PART III Socialisation and Psychoanalysis

9. Arendt on Evil: From the Radical to the Banal 189
10. Lacan and the Symbolic Function of Evil 208
11. Castoriadis: Evil and the Social Imaginary 236

## PART IV  The Subjects of Evil

12. The Perpetrators of Evil — 261
13. Remembering the Victims — 286

Conclusion — 319

Bibliography — 323
Index — 341

# Preface

This book aims to provide a conceptual history of the ways in which evil has been thought in the Western philosophical tradition. In so doing, it defends four different, but ultimately related, points: (1) while the conceptual problem of evil – how to reconcile the existence of evil with a God who is understood to be omnipotent, all-knowing, and supremely good – arose with and from the advent of Judaism and its movement to a monotheistic metaphysical system, it was with the rise of Christianity that it became *the* problem par excellence. Much ink was spilt trying to resolve this issue *within* an explicitly Christian framework, before Western thinking sought to abandon that framework for alternatives. Far from dissolving the problem of evil, these changes exacerbated it and, indeed, stimulated significant conceptual development, in relation to both the concept 'evil' and the metaphysical, ontological, and epistemological premises subtending it. (2) Contrary to popular belief, the meaning of evil is far from obvious or agreed upon; it is the almost complete lack of agreement about its meaning and what it refers to that is most striking, with this being because (3) each conception of evil is premised on different metaphysical, ontological, and epistemological assumptions. On first appearance, this might lead to the conclusion that Western philosophical thinking about evil is defined by a fundamental cleavage between pre- and post-Kantian thinking on the topic: the former basing itself explicitly on theological Christian doctrine which the latter abandoned. (4) I call into question any notion of a strict division between theologically (pre-Kantian) and secular (post-Kantian-)orientated analyses by showing that the latter often continue to employ theological language, concepts, motifs, or figures.

With this, the book contributes to the so-called theological (re)turn that has marked contemporary theory and specifically the line of critique that disrupts the notion that there exists a straightforward binary opposition between the theological and secular. While it has increasingly abandoned any explicit link to Judaeo-Christian theology, Western thinking on evil continues to be shaped and framed, often in implicit and subtle ways, by the theological framework from which it originated as a conceptual problem.

These arguments will be more fully worked out in the text, but, at this stage, I am pleased to acknowledge that the book forms part of the activities for the Conex Marie Skłodowska-Curie Research Project 'Sovereignty and Law: Between Ethics and Politics' (2013–00415–026), co-funded by the Universidad Carlos III de Madrid, the European Union's Seventh Framework Program for Research, Technological Development and Demonstration under Grant Agreement 600371, the Spanish Ministry of the Economy and Competitivity (COFUND2013–40258), the Spanish Ministry for Education, Culture, and Sport (CEI-15-17), and Banco Santander. Information about the project can be found at https://sovereigntyandlaw.wordpress.com

Aspects of Chapter 7 were originally published as 'The Problem of Grounding: Schelling on the Metaphysics of Evil', *Sophia*, 57:2, 2018, pp. 233–48; I thank the publishers for permission to include them here. Material from a number of chapters was presented to audiences at Uppsala University and the Universidad Carlos III de Madrid; I am grateful to those who attended for comments and queries. I would also like to acknowledge the staff at the Doe Library at the University of California, Berkeley, who helped me to locate materials for the chapters on Descartes and Leibniz. At Edinburgh University Press, I thank Carol Macdonald for her support for the project and, along with her assistant Kirsty Woods, help in bringing it to publication, the anonymous reviewers for their comments on an earlier draft, and Fiona Sewell for her keen eye and insightful suggestions during the copy-editing stage. Lastly, but by no means least, I once again acknowledge the input and presence of Emma throughout this project. Her unwavering support and willingness to listen as I stumbled through the labyrinth made it all possible: *gracias totales*.

# Introduction

While Western moral, philosophical, and theological thought has historically privileged the good,[1] this privileging has been accompanied by profound, if subterranean, interest in evil. In what follows, I set out to chart a history of evil as it has been thought within this tradition. A number of studies have recently traced different conceptions of evil from the eighteenth century onwards.[2] They re-enforce my point that 'evil' has been an important concept within Western philosophical thinking, but by confining themselves to the last three hundred or so years, they fail to appreciate that the problem of evil has a much longer history; one that goes back to the inter-Testament years. Indeed, the largely 'secular' approach to the problem of evil that has dominated since the eighteenth century is not only a reaction to the theological one that dominated prior to this period, but, as we will see, continues to be influenced, often in subtle ways, by it.

To understand Western thinking on 'evil' we need then to return to its theological origins, specifically the inter-Testament years (300 BC to AD 300) when developments within monotheistic thought created questions and problems that had not been troubling for the polytheism previously dominant until, with the rise of Christianity, evil became *the* problem to be accounted for and overcome. The purpose of this study is to trace how thinking on evil developed from this problematic, both within theologically inspired premises, and latterly within supposed 'secular' ones. Doing so will reveal the breadth and depth that have marked thinking about evil. Rather than being clear and obvious as common-sense, everyday intuition tends to hold, the meaning of evil has been remarkably contested. There has been complete lack of agreement about what evil entails, how to think about 'it', and what can be done, if anything, to avoid 'it'. While opponents of philosophy may point to this as proof of its inability to tackle 'real-world' issues, of which 'evil' might be considered one of the most pressing, the history of evil points to a different conclusion: 'evil' is far from simplistic and obvious; 'it' is a remarkably complex concept that entails and depends upon the answers given to a range of metaphysical, epistemological, ontological, and normative questions.

The history of evil offered is *a* history, not *the* history. I do not claim that it is the only one available or even that it is the definitive version. The thinkers and approaches engaged with do, however, elucidate a fascinating and often ignored aspect of Western thought. My selections are guided by the contention that Western thinking has been marked by a number of fundamental changes that delineate various crossroads leading in several directions. In charting this history, the aim is not to argue for one position over others, but to identify major milestones that have constituted Western thinking on the topic. I focus on those that have either significantly developed already existing conceptual frameworks or decisively broken with previous ones to offer alternatives. This is bound to entail a somewhat controversial selection. Not only have some thinkers been omitted who rightly have a justifiable claim to be included, but limiting the analysis of each thinker to a single chapter risks provoking the ire of specialists who would like a fuller treatment. The need to balance breadth and depth is, of course, a problem that accompanies every attempt to offer a history of a topic. Other figures could have been incorporated, but I think those chosen are relatively uncontroversial and capture the major trajectories that define Western thought on the topic.

Importantly, I note that this history appears to be marked by one fundamental division above all others: that between theologically orientated approaches that explicitly ground the problem of evil in Judaeo-Christian doctrine, and secular or post-Christian efforts that account for evil without explicitly grounding their explanations in the Judaeo-Christian tradition; indeed, they more often than not explicitly distance themselves from that tradition. The key figure for this argument is Kant: pre-Kantian thinkers tend to adopt the theological approach, while post-Kantian ones are prone to affirm the secular or post-Christian one. Such a division supports the conclusion that Western thinking generally and on evil specifically has undergone a historical process of secularisation.

The literature on secularisation is enormous, but, in one of the most sophisticated recent analysis of the topic, Steve Bruce remarks that 'the secularisation paradigm aims to explain one of the greatest changes in social structure and culture: the displacement of religion from the centre of human life'.[3] On this understanding, it describes

> the decay of religious institutions; the displacement, in matters of behaviour, of religious rules and principles by demands that accord with strictly

technical criteria; the sequestration by political powers of the property and facilities of religious agencies; the replacement of a specifically religious consciousness (which might range from dependence on charms, rites, spells, or prayers, to a broadly spiritually inspired ethical concern) by an empirical, rational, instrumental orientation; the shift from religious to secular control of a variety of social activities and functions; the decline in the proportion of their time, energy, and resources that people devote to supernatural concerns.[4]

Bruce's analysis is a sociological one and so combines two methodologies: a historical investigation that he takes to show that 'the peoples of preindustrial Europe were deeply religious'[5] and an empirical inquiry rooted in statistical reporting. To undertake the latter, he focuses on 'demand for religion'[6] as a proxy for religious belief, claims that church attendance reveals levels of religious belief, and, by citing reports that show that religious attendance has decreased rapidly across Western Europe,[7] concludes that this reveals that a process of secularisation has taken and is taking place. While noting that this process could be altered, he thinks it highly unlikely, with the consequence that 'secularisation must be seen as irreversible'.[8]

This, however, can take stronger or weaker versions: in the former, this process eventually leads to a completely secular culture with no religious element; in the latter, it entails the decay of religiosity without completely abolishing it. Bruce seems to vacillate on this issue: in his description of secularisation, he talks of the decay, displacement, and transference of religious to secular sentiment, thereby appearing to affirm the weaker version. However, at other times, he makes statements that seem to confirm the stronger claim; for example, that 'it is reasonable to assume that the trend we have seen for a century will continue',[9] which can only mean that the declining trend will eventually hit zero religiosity or full secularity. This vacillation brings to the fore the question: does secularisation describe a process whereby theological-religious motifs are displaced from their previously dominant and foundational role but continue to be expressed in society, or does it entail a process whereby theological-religious motifs are gradually completely eliminated from society?

This book defends the former by showing that supposedly secular analyses of evil often continue to depend upon theological motifs, concepts, figures, or ideas. Despite what many of the authors examined explicitly claim, their great theological refusal continues to *implicitly* make use of or point to that which it rejects. In so doing, this book contributes to the (re)turn to theology that has marked recent critical theory.[10] While various commentators have undertaken analyses of Western thinking's conception of modernity,[11] epistemology,[12] social imaginaries,[13] political theology,[14] and phenomenological philosophy,[15] to disrupt any straightforward binary opposition between the theological and secular or linear movement from the former to the latter, I complement and extend this line of critique by examining this issue through the lens of philosophical studies of *evil*, one of the key moral concepts in Western thought. To reiterate, the claim is not that secular analyses of evil are actually theological in disguise or that they are determined by their theological heritage; it is that their explicit rejection of theology continues to implicitly and often quite subtly make use of the language, logic, figures, and motifs of the paradigm that they reject.

To give one example of what this might look like, Bruce claims that through secularisation, 'evil and sin have been turned into alienation and unhappiness'.[16] This, however, ignores the fact that 'alienation' is an inherently theological concept, first being used to describe the evil that arose from separation from God.[17] Even if the way in which alienation is understood to occur is not grounded explicitly in a relationship to God, to describe evil as entailing any form of alienation is to continue to implicitly depend upon a theological language, motif, relation, and concept. We cannot then simply think in terms of a binary opposition between explicitly theological and secular analyses; the movement to the latter does not simply replace the former. The secular continues to *implicitly* depend upon the theological narrative and so is engaged in a far more entwined, tangled, difficult, and complex conceptual relationship to that which it originated from and often explicitly rejects.

## Structure of the Book

Part I looks to the origins that brought forth the *conceptual* problem of evil, showing that it arose with the rise of monotheism, before outlining the main ways in which this tradition, specifically its Christian trajectory, has dealt with it. To this end, Chapter 1 identifies that, while polytheistic metaphysical systems could account for evil relatively easily – by locating evil across numerous Gods or in one opposed to a good deity – the rise of monotheism altered the parameters of the debate and meant that evil had to be accounted for within the constraints of a singular deity who was held to be responsible for all.

Initially, monotheistic thought insisted that God was a complex of opposites, meaning that He was both good and evil. Any evil that existed was a consequence of God's wrath, done in His name by figures sent by Him.

The figure of *the satan* in the Book of Job is the most obvious and famous example of this. Gradually, however, the tensions resulting from this understanding in combination with splits within the nascent Hebrew community led to conceptual alterations in the understanding of God that contributed to the development of an implicit dualism within monotheism. As a consequence of the movement from the Old to New Testaments and Judaism to Christianity, God was no longer understood to be a complex of opposites, but was associated with supreme goodness. Evil, in contrast, was located in another cosmic figure and realm: *Satan* and *Hell*.

While this saved God's goodness, it did so by appearing to undermine His power. After all, if God was all-powerful, why did He not simply annihilate Satan and, by extension, evil? That He did not appeared to indicate that He either sanctioned Satan's and evil's continued existence or was powerless to stop them. This was obviously troubling. Indeed, it threatened the monotheistic principles upon which Judaic-Christian thinking is based. The easiest solution was to adopt a straightforward dualism, a position most explicitly seen with the rise of Manichaeism in the third century. While highly seductive, the challenge brought forth by Manichaeism galvanised Christian thinkers to offer a response, one that would account for the existence of evil within monotheistic parameters. Initially, this led to the study of Scripture, but when that was found to give multiple and sometimes contradictory responses, Christian thinkers realised that *they* would have to develop the conceptual resources to reconcile God's omnipotent, all-knowing, supreme goodness with the undoubted existence of evil.

The challenge was most brilliantly taken up in the late fourth and early fifth centuries by Augustine (Chapter 2), who based his account on three questions: what is evil? Who is responsible for evil? And why does not God prevent individuals from committing evil? First establishing that God creates *ex nihilo*, Augustine links God to the good and the good to being to conclude that what God creates has being which, because it emanates from Him, is good. Because evil is the opposite of good, it must lack being. Crucially, Augustine distinguishes between *privation*, entailing a lack of that which an entity should have based on its universal form, and *negation*, describing the differences and hence natural inequalities that exist between beings, to conclude that evil is a privation not a negation. As a privation, evil does not have substantial being and could not have been created by God. This, however, brings forth the question of who is responsible for evil.

Augustine responds by distinguishing between evils suffered (*malum poenae*), which will come to be known as 'natural evils', and evils committed (*malum culpae*), which will become 'moral evils'. To account for the latter, Augustine develops the free-will argument: God provides humans with the capacity of free choice, which they can use to affirm His goodness or turn away from Him towards their own particular, bodily desires. Moral evil results from the latter. Natural evils are committed by God to punish moral evils. The important point about natural evils is that they aim to correct individual behaviour so that it accords with the right path of God. With this, Augustine appears to account for the existence of evil, exculpate God from responsibility for it, and secure His goodness. This 'solution' did, however, lead to the third question: why does not God prevent individuals from committing evil? Augustine's responds by pointing to an underdeveloped theodicy wherein any evils that are committed and suffered ultimately contribute to the good.

While Augustine's account reinvigorated Christian thinking, it was suggestive rather than fully thought out and called for revision and extension. As Christianity cemented its dominance throughout Western Europe, it came into contact with alternative doctrines. This interaction stimulated intense debate within Christianity, which led to substantial doctrinal changes, and, ultimately, confusion over what was official doctrine regarding evil.

In the thirteenth century, Thomas Aquinas (Chapter 3) responded by both systematising and developing Church dogma. Incorporating Aristotelian insights that had come to Christianity from its interaction with Islam, Aquinas took over the free-will and privation arguments outlined by Augustine and made them more conceptually nuanced and logically rigorous. His real innovation, however, was to account for the problematic doctrine of Original Sin – the notion that since the Fall of Man in the Garden of Eden, human ontology has been marked by sin – by turning to a naturalist explanation whereby the evil of Original Sin is understood to reside in semen that is passed on through the procreative act. With his incorporation of the naturalist perspective, Aquinas not only substantially developed Christian doctrine, but also laid the foundations for the incorporation of naturalist premises that marked subsequent Western thought as we move from the thirteenth to seventeenth centuries.

This transitional period of around four hundred years was dominated by two trends, both of which would noticeably alter thinking on evil. The Christian Church became increasingly concerned about the impact that the figure of Satan was having on Western civilisation. This led to demonologies and greater attention being paid than ever before to the role that Satan was playing in the world, concern that was most infamously manifested through the Spanish Inquisition.[18] This was accompanied and, to a degree, undermined by a gradual epistemological shift away from conclusions based on theological speculation and Scripture to those that could be justified through rational analysis grounded in naturalist premises. Rather than looking to God or the Heavens for answers, reason and the natural realm became the foundations of thought.

A key milestone in this process was René Descartes's *Meditations on First Philosophy*[19] (Chapter 4), which aimed to demonstrate, through sceptical, rational analysis, the existence of an omnipotent, all-knowing, supremely good God. In so doing, Descartes linked evil to human error to undermine the Christian notion that evil was an effect of a malevolent cosmic being. In contrast, Descartes held that evil emanates from the improper use of human cognition; namely when the infinite will oversteps the finite knowledge that properly belongs to human judgement. Because the latter is given by God, departing from it is to depart from God, which re-enforces one of the central meanings that evil had for the Judaeo-Christian tradition.

Descartes's account of evil is important because he links it to epistemological questions, while his focus on the relationship between human will and evil develops the Augustinian approach in a way that lays the groundwork for Kant's thinking on the topic. Descartes's conception of God was, however, subject to sustained attack. The insistence that God creates according to His will seemed to make His actions arbitrary. By affirming God's power, manifested through His unconstrained will, Descartes appeared to call into question His goodness. It is perhaps not surprising that this led to a counter-proposal, most famously defended by Gottfried Leibniz, that privileged God's goodness, expressed in His perfect knowledge, over His power.

Chapter 5 shows that Leibniz agreed with Descartes that God's creation is linked to His will, but claimed that His will is an effect of His knowledge. This is not arbitrary, which would call into question the notion of 'truth', but is based on the Idea that defines the unchanging essence of each thing. God must, then, create in accordance with the Idea of each particular thing, meaning that there is determinacy to His actions. God is further constrained in what He can create by virtue of His goodness: He must create the best of all possible worlds. Because of this, we can be assured that the world we live in, including all the evil in it, is the best that could have been made.

Leibniz supports this through the introduction of a number of conceptual innovations, namely the distinction between natural, moral, and metaphysical evils and that between God's antecedent and consequential wills. With this, he develops Augustine's privation account of evil by claiming that evil does not have real being but only exists from the limited and flawed perspective of human being. What humans consider to be an evil is, as a consequence of God's supreme goodness and perfection, the least amount of evil required for God to create the best of all possible worlds.

The basic upshot of Leibniz's conclusion is that evil is nothing to worry about; it ultimately contributes to the greatest good. This was meant to be comforting: God is with us throughout all the trials and tribulations suffered. However, informing everyone who suffers an evil that it is nothing to worry about or is needed for the greater good was always going to elicit a reaction. It is perhaps not surprising that Leibniz's theodicy was almost immediately subject to remorseless critique, most famously captured in Voltaire's *Candide*.[20] It is, however, crucial to historical studies of evil because it lies on an important crossroads entailing something of a culmination for thinking about evil from strictly theological premises and being the impetus that brought forth secular accounts.

To outline these, Part II moves beyond theologically inspired analyses of evil to those that marked the hundred years or so from the end of the eighteenth century to the end of the nineteenth century, specifically Kant's *Religion without the Boundaries of Mere Reason*,[21] published in 1793; Schelling's *Philosophical Investigations into the Essence of Human Freedom*,[22] published in 1809; and Nietzsche's *On the Genealogy of Morals*,[23] published in 1887. This period was marked by increasingly radical critiques of the metaphysics underpinning Christian thinking and, by extension, its understanding of evil.

Chapter 6 examines Kant's attempt to understand evil within the boundaries of autonomous reason. Rejecting Leibnizian-inspired theodicies because of their unjustified metaphysical assumptions, Kant follows the parameters established by his critique of pure reason to limit the application of human knowledge to the phenomenal realm. Evil cannot be understood through reference to God, but only by reference to that which is phenomenally experienced; a methodological innovation that brought Kant to focus on the actions of individuals. Rejecting the long-standing concept of 'natural evil' and the notion of 'diabolical evil', often associated with the figure of Satan, Kant focuses on 'moral evil' and accounts for it by examining the structure of individual morality, claiming that it is grounded in a freely chosen moral maxim.

With this, he subtly rethinks Augustine's notion of will to suggest that evil results from the wilful adoption of a moral maxim that is not guided by the moral law. Evil is, as a consequence, radical in the sense pointed to by its Latin etymological origin *radix*, meaning 'root' or 'base.' However, that evil is a consequence of an act of noumenal freedom means that an individual can always change his moral maxim and so stop being evil, although Kant recognises that, because it is a noumenal choice, an individual's reasons for doing so are beyond the scope of phenomenal knowledge: accounting for such a change would require a purely theoretical account of practical activity, which is precisely what is rejected by the noumenal/phenomenal distinction introduced by his critical philosophy.

Chapter 7 examines a long-neglected response to Kant: Schelling's 1809 essay *Philosophical Investigations into the Essence of Human Freedom*. Schelling is an important milestone in the history of evil because he argues that Kant was mistaken to reject metaphysical speculation – indeed, he argued that Kant's critical philosophy depended upon it – before developing a post-Kantian metaphysical explanation for evil. Whereas Kant was happy to accept that his critical philosophy fell into a number of antinomies, Schelling objects that this was because Kant failed to recognise that they were effects of a metaphysical whole termed the Absolute. Importantly, the Absolute, otherwise called God, is not an undifferentiated totality, but differentiated and self-differentiating: God creates Himself through an autopoietic action whereby His dark abyssal ground finds expression in the light of existent beings. This dark metaphysical abyss is the source of the possibility of evil in actual existence. Schelling terms it 'general evil' and claims that it is manifested in and through the 'particular evils' of individuals. With this, he rejects not only the Augustinian notion that evil entails the privation of being, to explain that evil has real positive being, but also Kant's claim – itself tied to the Augustinian affirmation of individual will – that evil is located in the noumenal choice of *individuals*. Instead, Schelling insists that evil has real being and is a possibility grounded in the structure of *existence*.

Schelling goes on to claim that this metaphysical schema, in which a dark abyss finds expression in the light of existent beings, is mirrored in the structure of the human psyche: a dark unconscious grounds reflective consciousness. Rather than a noumenal/phenomenal division, Schelling proposes an unconscious/conscious one: evil is understood to result when an individual unconsciously chooses to affirm the dark principle of abyssal chaos over the light of God. Whereas Kant holds that this choice could be reversed, Schelling rejects this possibility: once an individual has unconsciously chosen, he cannot subsequently alter his moral choice. Not only is evil located in the depths of existence, but, if chosen, it cannot be overcome.

This conclusion stands out in the history of philosophy: it not only criticises the Judaeo-Christian conception of evil, to develop another rooted in an alternative conception of God, but is the only account that does not offer the individual the possibility of overcoming evil. When this is combined with his insistence that evil exists as a latent possibility in the structure of reality, we see that Schelling's conception of evil is one of the darkest and most imposing ever thought.

History was not, however, kind to Schelling: his thought, including his account of evil, was almost immediately forgotten, eclipsed by his one-time room-mate Georg Hegel.[24] Hegel produced an interesting account of evil which, very crudely put, synthesises a secular version of Leibniz's theodicy with Kant's autonomous reason read through the lens of history. Rather than hold that the world as it is now is the best of all possible ones, Hegel concluded that a historical process was under way that held out the possibility of eventually realising a fully rational world.[25] The importance that Hegel attributed to historical alteration was crucial for subsequent thought, which would find it increasingly difficult to hold that the meaning of concepts was ahistoric. As such, the nature of 'evil' had to be rethought from a thoroughly historical perspective. The most radical proponent of this was Friedrich Nietzsche (Chapter 8).[26]

Nietzsche is an important figure in studies of evil because he does not accept that 'evil' has always existed or is defined by a universal, ahistoric meaning. 'Evil' is born of a particular worldview and semiotic system, with the consequence that its meaning depends upon changing, heterogeneous, power relations manifested through pre-personal, socio-historical interactions and relations. For Nietzsche, moral categories are grounded not in theological sources or autonomous reason, but in dynamic, naturalist, socio-historic power structures and processes.

Employing a genealogical methodology that distinguishes between 'master' and 'slave' forms of morality, Nietzsche shows how the former, defined by a good/bad distinction, initially reigned before being overthrown by the latter's good/evil opposition. Associating the latter schema with the Judaic-Christian tradition, he implicitly points out that any discussion of evil remains tied to that tradition. With this, he introduces two particular innovations to analyses of evil: first, he utilises an original methodology to return to the origins of the logic that underpins Western morality to argue that it results from the socio-historical situation of different groups. This allows him to tie the meaning of evil to concrete social relations manifested through different power relations. Second, he suggests that not only do moral concepts change meaning based on alterations to the power relations subtending them, but, far more radically, not all power relations need to employ the concept 'evil'. Contrary to what Christian theology tells us, 'evil' is not an objective, ahistoric moral category, but one born of a particular theological worldview and semiotic system that always remains tied to that theological origin.

Part III moves from the nineteenth to the twentieth century to show that Schelling's focus on subterranean unconscious processes in combination with the socio-historical methodology employed by Nietzsche continued to shape much thinking on evil. Rather than try to identify the nature of evil, what reality must be like to permit evil, or the historical processes that gave rise to the moral category 'evil', there was a gradual shift towards emphasising the social processes that bring individuals to commit evil and the semantic structures that give rise to the notion 'evil'.

Chapter 9 shows how the former is manifested through Hannah Arendt's analysis of the concept. While she initially relied upon a Kantian-inspired radical conception of evil, her experiences of the Holocaust brought her to abandon it for a banal one. To outline the main contours of Arendt's analyses of evil, I pay particular attention to the problems that she claims the Kantian notion of radical evil suffers from as a result of the rise of totalitarian regimes, before showing that the key features of banal evil are the existence of social-political regimes that foster a moral attitude in individuals whereby they (1) fail to examine an issue from the perspective of another and, linked to this, (2) lack the capacity for substantive thinking about moral ends. Arendt's importance for studies of evil emanates from her rejection of the foundational logic underpinning Kant's conception of radical evil and her claim that, while individual choice remains a crucial component of evil (which binds her to the Augustinian tradition), (banal) evil is fundamentally socio-political in nature.

The emphasis Arendt placed on the subterranean social structures and processes shaping thought was complemented by the rise of structuralism in the 1950s and its focus on unconscious, concealed, and implicit *linguistic structures* that, far from being ahistoric, are diachronically relational. That meaning is generated from relations meant that each aspect of the relation is as important as the other. What had previously been overlooked or downgraded to a secondary phenomenon was, all of a sudden, elevated to an equal footing with that which had previously dominated it. Initially, this found expression in the fields of anthropology and psychoanalysis: the former sought to understand cultures through the structural relations of their symbolic codes, while the latter's notion of the unconscious was particularly important in showing that these structures operate at a 'hidden', implicit level of human organisation.

Chapter 10 outlines Jacques Lacan's account of how meaning is generated from a pre-personal symbolic order, before, briefly, developing what a Lacanian theory of evil might entail by reading it through the symbolic–real relation. This explains how the meaning of evil is generated, demonstrates its instability, and complements Nietzsche's critique of the notion that 'evil' has a unitary, ahistoric meaning. However, whereas Nietzsche argues that this is because of the changing dynamic of historical group formations, Lacan claims that it is a result of the differential symbolic relations that give rise to meaning. This, in turn, has consequences for belief in God and the meaning of evil.

For Lacan, atheism does not entail a radical rupture with theology, but continues to unconsciously believe in God or an ordering principle that fulfils the same role as the signifier 'God' previously did, while 'evil' is understood to be the signifier that aims, but, due to the nature of the Lacanian real – which points to that which escapes symbolic meaning – always fails, to designate the non-signifiable real *within* the symbolic order. Explanations of evil are therefore palliatives designed to incorporate the unknowable real into the knowable symbolic register. Doing so sanitises the unknowable and makes the individual feel safe and secure in the face of 'it'. Responding to 'evil' requires a psychoanalytic reaction, not a philo-theosophical one, to understand why the individual has created that particular conception of evil, as a precursor to bringing the individual to better understand how he faces the real.

Lacan's thought was both influential and highly controversial. One of the most polemic critiques came from Cornelius Castoriadis (Chapter 11), who argues that because Lacan claims that meaning emanates from the closed binarity inherent in symbolic relations, he is unable to account for originality, upon which Lacan's creation of the three registers depends. Castoriadis charges then that Lacan's thought is both internally inconsistent and, by trapping thought within the confines of a closed, totalised system, unable to offer any radical political prescriptions to break repressive structures. By claiming that the imaginary entails the imposition of an illusionary order on a chaotic, differentiating world, Lacan, on Castoriadis's telling, associates the imaginary with repression and illusion, not creativity and expression.

In contrast, Castoriadis argues that the 'motor' of Lacan's system and, indeed, of meaning in general is the imaginary, which Castoriadis associates with radical, disjunctive creativity. Terming this the 'radical imaginary', and subsequently dividing it between individual and social aspects, he argues that it is only when the imaginary is given pre-eminence as the creative 'force' of existence that we can properly understand the nature of radical innovation and creativity and, in so doing, account for the originality inherent in Lacan's system.

Castoriadis does, however, agree with Lacan that thought cannot simply proceed on the assumption that a concept's meaning is clear or uncontested. If we are to understand what 'evil' means, we must understand how meaning is attributed to it. Castoriadis departs from Lacan in claiming that this occurs not through anonymous, differential, linguistic, symbolic relations, but through the anonymous, collective, social-historical imaginary of each society. Explaining how meaning is created allows us to determine the framework that generates conceptual meaning, which can then be used to outline whether a particular act can be properly described by that concept.

Castoriadis focuses on the first part of this tripartite schema (how meaning is created) and has very little to say on the subsequent parts. This is not due to a failing on his part, but results from the nature of his ontogenetic account of meaning: given that moral meaning is an effect of an anonymous social imaginary, it will be different for each society, with the consequence that we cannot treat it as if it had universal, ahistorical significance. By claiming that meaning is a consequence of the anonymous actions of the social collective, Castoriadis radicalises Arendt's claim regarding the importance that social and political structures have in shaping individual life.

The great problem with Castoriadis's position, however, is that it appears to make it extremely difficult if not impossible to hold socialised individuals responsible for 'their' actions. Strictly speaking, 'their' actions are not 'theirs;' they are effects of the social imaginary. Despite affirming the moral and political significance of individual autonomy, thereby tying himself to the Kantian and Augustinian traditions, Castoriadis's approach was criticised for being incapable of holding individuals responsible for their actions. It was, therefore, unable to resolve practical issues relating to how to deal with the perpetrators or victims of evil. To correct this, thinking on evil turned away from the question of how meaning is constructed, to examine the topic from the perspectives of the agents involved.

Part IV shows that late twentieth-century thought, manifested through John Kekes's *Facing Evil*[27] (published in 1990), and early twenty-first-century thinking, specifically Claudia Card's *The Atrocity Paradigm* (published in 2002) and *Confronting Evils* (published in 2010),[28] sought to resolve this dilemma by ignoring the question of how meaning is generated, to simply adopt an axiomatic definition of 'evil' to examine the harm caused by an agent's actions from the perspectives of those involved. This gave rise to what have become known as perpetrator-based and victim-based accounts of evil.

Chapter 12 outlines John Kekes's attempt to develop the former by distinguishing between the historically dominant 'choice-morality', which argues that an agent's actions alone are subject to moral judgement, and 'character-morality', which holds that an agent's act, developed through habits learnt from the encounter with others, reveals not just its moral worth but also the moral worth of the perpetrator's character. Thus, moral choices are grounded in individual habits, rather than autonomously chosen actions, and are therefore socially acquired.

While this breaks with the Augustinian claim that evil results from free will, Kekes quickly reaffirms it by claiming that individuals can break from environments that habitually condition evil actions if they so choose. With this, he reaffirms Arendt's argument that, while social norms condition individual action, they do not determine it. Individual moral action may be habitually learnt, but it is ultimately a consequence of individual, wilful choice; a position that, despite his best efforts, demonstrates his continued dependence on the Augustinian theological tradition.

Kekes uses a perpetrator's actions to understand his moral character and, in so doing, brings questions of moral psychology into analyses of evil. This does, however, raise the following question: if evil entails causing or suffering undeserved harm, should we not focus on the victims of that action? After all, Kekes can only make judgements about the moral worth of a perpetrator by first identifying a victim who has suffered undeserved harm. For this reason, Claudia Card (Chapter 13) rejects Kekes's perpetrator-based approach to suggest that we must never forget, and, indeed, can only ever understand evil by focusing on, its victims. In contrast to Kekes's insistence that evil entails undeserved harm, Card insists that evils are reasonably foreseeable, intolerable harms produced by inexcusable wrongs. From this starting point, she distinguishes evil from lesser wrongs, while also pointing out that there are degrees of evils. Emphasising this gradation allows her to define what counts as an evil while also expanding the examples that are called evil.

This is important because she does not want to limit 'evil' to the monstrous actions typically identified with 'evil', but claims that it also incorporates often-ignored evils such as rape, domestic or gender violence, and the torture of animals. In so doing, she combats three historical myths about evil: evil-doers are monstrous; there is a cosmic battle between good and evil; and there is a metaphysical force that controls individual actions. This not only rejects the Christian narrative on evil, but also questions the simplistic binary logic (good versus evil) that underpins it.

For Card, agents are not merely faced with a binary opposition of good and evil. Morality is far more complex than this logic implies. Conceptually speaking, good and evil are distinct, evil is distinguished from lesser wrongs, and all are defined by degrees, while Card maintains that, experientially, agents often find themselves in situations that require actions that are not clearly good or evil. She develops this through Primo Levi's notion of 'grey zones', which entail the creation of extremely stressful spaces or relationships wherein victims become perpetrators of evil against other victims. This brings her analysis into the socio-political realm, and so is reminiscent of Arendt's approach, while, by linking grey zones to diabolical evil, also distinguishing her position from Kant's rejection of the latter form of evil: there is, on Card's telling, an absolute, diabolical form of evil entailing evil done for its own sake. In positing this notion, she returns us to an absolute conception of evil that had long been downplayed by secular theories of evil. Indeed, by developing her notion of diabolical evil from the Biblical figure of Satan, her 'secular' theory of evil returns, however ephemerally, to the figure and conception of evil inherent in Christian thinking on the topic.

While this reveals that Card's thinking on evil is not as secular as she insists it is, the conclusion notes that it is simply the latest manifestation of a trend that has marked Western so-called 'secular' thinking on evil. From the continuing emphasis on a radicalised conception of Augustinian will (Arendt, Castoriadis, Kant, and Kekes), Schelling's rejection of Judaeo-Christian conceptions of God to develop a radical conception of evil rooted in a different conception of God, Nietzsche's claim that 'evil' is an inherently Judaeo-Christian concept, Kekes's and Card's use of the foundational logic grounding the Judaeo-Christian tradition, and Card's use of the figure of Satan and absolute evil, we see that despite its long history of conceptual innovation and its supposed increasing turn towards secularity, a trace of the theological narrative on evil, and, in particular the logic and figures underpinning the Christian account of it, continues to find expression in Western philosophical thinking on the topic.

## Notes

1. Plato, *Republic*, trans. G. M. A. Grube and C. D. C. Reeve, 508e–509a, in *Complete Works*, ed. John M. Cooper (Indianapolis: Hackett, 1997), pp. 971–1223.
2. Richard Bernstein, *Radical Evil: A Philosophical Investigation* (Cambridge: Polity, 2002); Susan Neiman, *Evil in Modern Thought: An Alternative History of Philosophy* (Princeton: Princeton University Press, 2002); Peter Dews, *The Idea of Evil* (Oxford: Blackwell, 2008).
3. Steve Bruce, *Secularisation: In Defence of an Unfashionable Theory* (Oxford: Oxford University Press, 2011), p. 1.
4. Ibid. p. 2.
5. Ibid. p. 5.
6. Ibid. p. 3.

7. To give one example, Bruce quotes a Mannheim Eurobarometer survey showing that the percentage of the population attending church once a week or more often changed dramatically between 1970 and 1999: in France from 23 to 5 per cent; in Belgium from 52 to 10 per cent; in Holland from 41 to 14 per cent; in Germany from 29 to 15 per cent; in Italy from 56 to 39 per cent; and in Ireland from 91 to 65 per cent (ibid. p. 10).
8. Ibid. p. 56.
9. Ibid. p. 23.
10. For a discussion of this, see Gregg Lambert, *Return Statements: The Return of Religion in Contemporary Philosophy* (Edinburgh: Edinburgh University Press, 2016).
11. See Michael Allen Gillespie, *The Theological Origins of Modernity* (Chicago: University of Chicago Press, 2008); Jason A. Josephson-Storm, *The Myth of Disenchantment: Magic, Modernity, and the Birth of the Human Sciences* (Chicago: University of Chicago Press, 2017).
12. Dominic Erdozain, *The Soul of Doubt: The Religious Roots of Unbelief from Luther to Marx* (Oxford: Oxford University Press, 2016).
13. Charles Taylor, *A Secular Age* (Cambridge, MA: Harvard University Press, 2007).
14. Clayton Crockett, *Radical Political Theology: Religion and Politics after Liberalism* (New York: Columbia University Press, 2011); Jeffrey W. Robbins, *Radical Democracy and Political Theology* (New York: Columbia University Press, 2011); Simon Critchley, *The Faith of the Faithless: Experiments in Political Theology* (London: Verso, 2012).
15. Hent de Vries, *Philosophy and the Turn to Religion* (Baltimore: Johns Hopkins University Press, 1999).
16. Bruce, *Secularisation*, p. 13.
17. For a discussion of the history of the concept of alienation, including its theological roots, see Gavin Rae, 'Alienation, Authenticity, and the Self', *History of the Human Sciences*, 23:4, 2010, pp. 21–36.
18. Two excellent studies of which are Henry Kamen, *The Spanish Inquisition: A Historical Revision*, 4th edn (New Haven: Yale University Press, 2014); and Joseph Perez, *Brève Histoire de L'Inquisition en Espagne* (Paris: Faynard, 2002).
19. René Descartes, *Meditations on First Philosophy*, trans. and ed. John Cottingham (Cambridge: Cambridge University Press, 1986).
20. Voltaire, *Candide* (Paris: Magnard, 2013).
21. Immanuel Kant, *Religion within the Boundaries of Mere Reason and Other Writings*, trans. and ed. Allen Wood and George di Giovanni (Cambridge: Cambridge University Press, 1998).
22. F. W. J. Schelling, *Philosophical Investigations into the Essence of Human Freedom*, trans. Jeff Love and Johannes Schmidt (Albany: State University of New York Press, 2006).
23. Friedrich Nietzsche, *On the Genealogy of Morals*, trans. Walter Kaufman and

R. J. Hollingdale, in *On the Genealogy of Morals and Ecce Homo*, ed. Walter Kaufman (New York: Vintage, 1989), pp. 15–198.

24. It was only with Martin Heidegger's 1936 lecture course on the 1809 freedom essay that Schelling started to once again be taken seriously philosophically. See Martin Heidegger, *Schelling's Treatise on the Essence of Human Freedom*, trans. Joan Stambaugh (Athens: Ohio University Press, 1985).

25. For far less crude explanations of Hegel's conception of evil, see Michael Theunissen, *Hegels Lehre vom absolutem Geist als theologisch-politischer Traktat* (Berlin: De Gruyter, 1970), pp. 266–74; and Timothy Brownlee, 'Hegel's Moral Concept of Evil', *Dialogues: Canadian Philosophical Review*, 52:1, 2013, pp. 81–108.

26. For discussions of the relationship between Hegel and Nietzsche, see Stephen Houlgate, *Hegel, Nietzsche and the Criticism of Metaphysics* (Cambridge: Cambridge University Press, 1986); and Will Dudley, *Hegel, Nietzsche, and Philosophy: Thinking Freedom* (Cambridge: Cambridge University Press, 2002).

27. John Kekes, *Facing Evil* (Princeton: Princeton University Press, 1990).

28. Claudia Card, *The Atrocity Paradigm: A Theory of Evil* (Oxford: Oxford University Press, 2002), and Claudia Card, *Confronting Evils: Terrorism, Torture, Genocide* (Cambridge: Cambridge University Press, 2010).

# PART I THEOLOGICAL FOUNDATIONS

# 1
# The Rise of the Problem of Evil

The problem of evil, as a *conceptual problem* – that is, as a problem to be dealt with through rational means – came to the fore with the rise of monotheism.[1] It is, therefore, intimately connected to the Judaeo-Christian tradition.[2] This is not to say that polytheistic systems did not have conceptions of evil, only that, conceptually speaking, polytheism can deal with the problem of evil relatively easily: a 'good' god can be simply opposed to an 'evil' one.

With monotheism, however, the problem of evil is far more complex because, as the source of all, God must be the source of both good and evil. This gives rise to the question of how God can be good and evil, an issue compounded once it is accepted that God is all-powerful and supremely good: If His omnipotence is privileged, it would appear that God is capable of simply annihilating the evil principle. If His goodness is privileged, then He is simply incapable of committing evil acts. Why then does evil continue to exist?

One way to resolve this would be to accept that evil has an alternative source to God, but this seems, at best, to call into question God's all-powerfulness, and, at worst, threatens polytheism. On the contrary, if God is all-powerful, all-knowing, and supremely good, how or why does He permit evil to exist? And where does it come from? These were some of the questions that occupied the inter-Testament years (350 BC to AD 300). During this time, tremendous debates took place regarding the nature of evil, its relationship to God, and the figure(s) associated with it.

Generally speaking, Judaic thought accounts for the existence of evil by clinging to a strict monotheism whereby God lies at the source of all. Because God is everything, He is light and dark, good and evil, this and that, and so on; He is, in other words, a complex of opposites. Due to the precarious historical situation of the Hebrewic[3] community and conceptual problems associated with thinking of God in terms of a complex of opposites, God became associated solely with good, while evil was located in an alternative source. With this, the strict monotheism of Judaism gradually gave way to an *implicit* dualism, manifested in the Christian division between God and Satan, whereby evil was expelled from God to find expression 'in' another, inferior being that exists in confrontational opposition to God. However, by appearing to call into question its monotheistic principles, this splitting has ensured that the questions of the nature and figure of evil have been particularly troubling issues for Christianity. Indeed, on one reading, the problem of evil is *the* problem of Christianity.

The subject of evil in the Judaeo-Christian tradition is then intimately bound up with God's relationship to another figure that comes to be called Satan.[4] Initially, evil was not associated with a figure who personified evil; it only comes to be so in the New Testament. This understanding had to be created, and was so over many centuries, in response to alterations in the meaning and place of this figure in relation to God, the relationship God was thought to have with 'evil', and, indeed, the metaphysical structure underpinning the Judaeo-Christian framework. The overview[5] provided in this chapter will not engage in the deep-seated theological debates of these traditions, nor will it argue for one conception over the other. It will simply aim to identify a number of the major structural alterations that took place as Judaic thinking gave rise to Christianity. By charting the different ways that the figure who will come to be known as Satan was transformed through the movement from the Old Testament to the New Testament, we will better understand how the problem of evil arose, which, in turn, will reveal how it was thought historically, and, indeed, the parameters through which those thinkers who defend the theological narrative of evil will develop their responses.

## Monotheism and the Problem of Evil

The notion of evil has its origins in ancient mythology, but the first conceptualisation of it, including the first *philosophical* engagement with the problem, had to await the rise of philosophy in Ancient Greece.[6] While mythology was a crucial aspect of Greek thinking, the Greeks were the first to recognise that the existence of evil was a question that needed to be asked conceptually. The problem that comes to occupy so much of subsequent thought was anticipated by Epicurus (341–270 BC), who famously summarised it in the following terms:

> God either wishes to take away evils, and is unable; or He is able, and is unwilling; or He is neither willing nor able, or He is both willing and able.

If He is willing and is unable, He is feeble, which is not in accordance with the character of God; if He is able and unwilling, He is envious, which is equally at variance with God; if He is neither willing nor able, He is both envious and feeble and, therefore, not God; if He is both willing and able, which alone is suitable to God, from what source then are evils? Or why does He not remove them?[7]

This formulation is remarkably clear and succinct. Unfortunately, Greek responses were not. There were, at least, two reasons for this: first, Greek thought was based on a polytheistic system that split the concept of evil across many figures that were either in conflict or existed harmoniously depending on the myth.[8] Second, while recognising that it was a significant problem, the Greeks held that, ultimately, evil could not be solved through human reason; it simply had to be accepted as being either inherent in the cosmos or a consequence of the will of the Gods. The Greeks recognised that evil was a problem and held that it was split between competing Gods, but gave up trying to rationally understand or explain why this is the case. Doing so would require knowing the will of the Gods, a futile endeavour grounded in hubris and likely to be punished by those same Gods. As a consequence, the Greeks rationalised the problem, but not the answer, which was still thought from myth. Rather than try to know the will of the Gods, the Greeks tended to focus on how to satisfy them. Justice, not evil, was the motivating concern. It is only with the movement from polytheism to monotheism that the problem of evil becomes explicit and occupies centre stage in philosophical (and theological) debate.

By bringing the question of evil to the fore and treating it as a serious philosophical question requiring rational answers, monotheism generated a host of questions not previously asked, including: what is evil? Where is evil located? Does God permit evil? If He does, why? And, if He does not, what does this mean for God's infinite power and glory? Responding to these questions required engagements with fundamental metaphysical questions, including: what role does God play in existence? Is God good? How can God's goodness be reconciled with the existence of evil? And what is God's relationship to evil?

Judaism is historically important to the development of the problem of evil because it first provided thinkers with the conceptual tools to engage with the issue. To understand the narrative role and development of the problem of evil within the Judaeo-Christian tradition, we need then to return to Judaic thinking and the way it conceives and conceptualises evil, the figure of evil, and this figure's role and place in relation to God.

The problem immediately encountered is that the figure that will later become known as Satan is virtually absent from the Old Testament and, when he does appear, he does not play the same role that Satan plays in the New Testament. For example, '[n]owhere in the Old Testament does Satan achieve the status of a dualistic opponent of God who restricts God to serving as the principle of the Good'.[9] This is not only because the Old and New Testaments have different conceptions of God and evil, but also because they view the relationship between the two differently. Whereas Christian thinking tended to perceive evil as being located in a figure external to and hell-bent on the destruction of the Kingdom of Heaven, the Judaic tradition associated evil with something akin to Christian conceptions of individual sin, itself associated with a wandering from the Covenant with God. This wandering could be because of individual choice or because the individual is influenced by a figure, called *the satan*, who exists in Heaven and is sent by God to test individual devotion to Him. In either case, *the individual*, not the satan or, as he will later be known, Satan, is held to be solely responsible for any wandering from the path of God.

To understand this, we need to say something about the metaphysical structure underpinning the Old Testament. Judaic monotheism is structured around a unitary cosmos, headed by the Kingdom of Heaven, wherein God resides surrounded by a hierarchical army of angels. The Judaic figure of evil – the satan – is 'one of God's obedient servants – a messenger, or *angel*, a word that translates the Hebrew term for messenger (*mal'āk*) into Greek (*angelos*)'.[10] The satan is fully conversant with God and, in many cases, a messenger of God. There is no separate realm divorced from God where the satan resides, nor is it the case that the satan is engaged in a battle with God. Rather, this figure fulfils a functionary role: he is God's servant doing God's work.

Supporting this is a particular conception of God. If, as Judaism claims, Yahweh, the god of Israel, is the one God – and, indeed, there is only one God – then that God, as the one God, must create all. While Yahweh is singular, the properties defining Yahweh are not and cannot be. Yahweh must be a complex of opposites, meaning that He must be 'both light and darkness, both good and evil'.[11] The key point here, one that distinguishes the Judaic notion of evil from the narrative of the later Christian notion, is that evil is 'part' of God; it is not something distinct from God, whether thought conceptually or existentially.

The institutionalisation of Abrahamic texts into a coherent religion was underpinned by the belief that when Abraham encountered God, God set forth a number of laws to be followed. God had entered into a Covenant, or agreement, with the Hebrews whereby He decreed certain laws and the followers were responsible for implementing these decrees. This was not a relationship of equals, but a hierarchical one, in which the human followed God's laws. This did not entail passive participation, but required active involvement as each individual had to take responsibility for himself and his actions. Each was, therefore, placed under an infinite responsibility to ensure that he lived up to the Covenant.

Because the Law covered social, moral, legal, and ritual aspects of life, it was both complex and holistic and so very easy to break. This, in turn, led to the development of conceptual distinctions to determine and delineate if, when, and how any violations took place. For this reason, a whole conceptual apparatus sprung up around violations of the Covenant. Such was the ease with which the Law could be broken that there were 'about thirty words in all to refer to this possibility'.[12] Three of the most important were *ḥṭ*, *pshʻ*, and *ʻawon*.[13]

*Ḥṭ* means to miss the mark, as in missing a target or falling short of an expectation. Within the boundaries of the Covenant, it was used when the inferior party failed to uphold their duty as described by the Covenant. Thought in terms of contract between humans, this entails one party not fulfilling the obligations it has agreed to. This is bad enough, but becomes exponentially worse when thought in terms of God so that one, for instance, breaches an agreement with God. It is important to note, however, that *ḥṭ* is only a possibility once the Covenant has been given. Prior to the Covenant, there is no Law and, as such, no way to break the Law. There cannot, therefore, be *ḥṭ*.

For this reason, 'evil' or sin marks out not an ontological condition of human beings, but a relationship between humans and God. As such, *ḥṭ* is closely associated with *pshʻ*, which, in its general sense, means 'the breaking of a relationship',[14] but can have a stronger sense of rebellious behaviour against the Covenant. The notion of rebelling against the Covenant becomes more prominent as the Judaic figure of *the satan* is transformed into the Christian figure of *Satan*: a being who is in open rebellion against God. Both *ḥṭ* and *pshʻ* are also intimately connected to the third word associated with evil, *ʻawon*, meaning 'crooked, twisted or wrong',[15] as in travelling down the wrong path away from God.

Crucially, Judaic thought insisted on a direct relationship between the individual and God and, for this reason, held that any departure from the Covenant was the responsibility of humans alone. Evil was thought in terms of an immediate relationship to God where the human failed in some way to adhere to the path set out by God. Even the interjections of the satan do not break this immediate relationship because the role of the satan is to oppose God *to do the work of God*. Evil arises if the individual is seduced by the satan and so chooses to abandon the Covenant with God. The satan does not have dominion over humans nor does he aim to seduce them for his own ends, but tests them to determine individual devotion to God.

This is significant because it means that the satan does not challenge God's authority to establish alternative truths, but is used by God to test the individual's faith in God; a challenge or opposition that is always aimed at the affirmation of God. Perhaps the most explicit manifestation of this is

> found in the book of Job (written about 400 BC), [where] the Satan [sic], or the Accuser, is one of the sons of God whose duty it is to test a person's faithfulness to God. Hence God gives the Satan [sic] permission to test Job to find out whether Job's dutifulness to God is simply a sham or whether it is sincere.[16]

For this reason, the Hebrews thought of the satan 'as an obstructor',[17] someone who played an accusatory role that tested (1) God by asking Him questions in the Heavenly court, a questioning that was, however, always deferential to God, or (2) humans as they tried to fulfil the Covenant with God.

This, however, led to a number of questions, including: if God is omnipotent and all-knowing and so knows an individual's commitment to the Covenant, why is the figure of the satan needed to test and determine this commitment? Does God's introduction of the figure of the satan mean that God is not the all-powerful, all-knowing deity worshipped? And why would an all-powerful, all-knowing God permit humanity to sin? Responses given to these questions led to substantial changes in early Hebrewic thinking, so that 'by the time we reach the New Testament, the adversary has become entirely separate from Yahweh, an independent threat for the faithful to beware'.[18]

## From a Strict Monotheism to an Implicit Metaphysical Dualism

There were historical and conceptual reasons for this alteration. Jewish thought did not develop in a vacuum, but was a movement conditioned by the society it was located in. Alterations in Hebrew thought must be seen in light of these social alterations and, in particular, the struggles over meanings, doctrines, and interpretations that result from any community's attempt to define itself.

The Hebrew community, like all communities, was, therefore, constituted by differences in opinion. The dominant group thought of itself as adhering to the true Covenant with God. It understood that it was representing God's message whereas the others were violating this Covenant and so were sinners. Sin (= evil) gradually became associated with those who had departed from the 'true' meaning of the Covenant. Designations of truth and evil became determined by power relations between social groups. Outsider groups had to be guarded against because they threatened the righteousness of those who did adhere to the Covenant. For this reason, 'stories of Satan and other fallen angels proliferated in these troubled times, especially within those radical groups that had turned against the rest of the Jewish community and, consequently, concluded that others had turned against them – or (as they put it) against God'.[19]

The strife that the Hebrew community (understood as a whole) experienced became manifested in its conceptual understanding: First, the dominant aspect of the Hebrew community (= good) found itself opposed to an outsider group that challenged and so threatened its doctrine. Through its departure from the Covenant (as understood by the dominant aspect of the Hebrew community), this outsider group became associated with sin (= evil). Second, the social splitting of the Hebrew community led to a conceptual splitting of God, who was divided between a 'good' aspect and a 'bad' aspect. Once this occurred, God was understood to be defined by the former alone, with the latter existing independently of Him. Third, Hebrew thought developed a 'combat myth'[20] whereby God (= authentic Hebrew community) was thought to be besieged and so in combat with evil (= outsiders). In combination, the conceptual schema of the Hebrews underwent a gradual, profound change. Rather than a unitary God defined by a complex of opposites, the oppositions that were 'in' God were split, with one side held to exist 'outside' of God. God was associated with the 'good' aspect while the 'bad' aspect was held to be external and opposed to Him. This is not a peaceful relationship, but a combative one where each side fights for supremacy.

Importantly, the monotheistic principles of Judaism meant that these changes did not result in a straightforward dualism. The evil principle was still held to be subordinate to God. How to account for this brought about the alterations in the understanding of the satan, including his role and relationship to God, that mark late Judaic thinking, the debates of the inter-Testament years, and latterly Christian thinking. As Jeffrey Alexander explains, the notion of an evil principle separate from God became even more widespread and powerful as Christianity developed, for the simple reason that the early Christian sects saw in it 'the possibility of attributing evil to forces outside their own cultural system. The Christian devil was a means of separating the "good religion" of Jesus from the evil (primarily Jewish) forces from which it had emerged.'[21]

As a consequence, John Sanford argues that 'what we find ... in the New Testament, is that there is not one point of view about evil, its origins, and its place in the Divine Economy, but two points of view'.[22] The first is a monistic view of evil that holds that it is only from the perspective of humans that evil appears as something negative. In an argument that will underpin Leibniz's theodicy, what appears to humans to be evil is, in actuality, part of God's overall plan. 'From this point of view it would seem as though God *allows* evil to operate, evidently because evil plays some kind of essential role in the Divine Economy.'[23] What appears to be evil is, in reality, a necessary aspect that adheres to and enhances God's divine plan.

The second view entails 'an outright Dualism in which Satan and evil play no part at all in the Divine Economy'.[24] God is synonymous with the good, Satan is synonymous with evil. Sanford argues that, despite Christianity's monotheism, it was this second view that became dominant, with the consequence that it 'has been more characteristic of the general attitude of the Church throughout the centuries than the first'.[25] It is for this reason that Christianity tends to hold that God is not responsible for evil: 'the instigator of evil [is] a malignant spirit whose power to offend [is] far greater than that of mere mortals'.[26]

To allow this to happen, a twinning had to occur 'in the divine nature, similar to the twinning in the God of Egypt or of Canaan. The one God split into two parts. One, the good aspect of the God, became "the Lord." The other, the evil aspect, became "the Devil".'[27] As a consequence, the early Christians were caught in a bind of their own making. 'At the same time [as they] continued to insist upon monotheism as the essential element of their religion, they moved unconsciously toward dualism.'[28] The figure of *the satan* was no longer thought to be the servant of God in Heaven, but became *Satan*, the personification of evil, who, like the radical Hebrew groups, was cast out of Heaven to exist in opposition to it.[29]

This movement towards dualism meant that, from the third century BC, evil became increasingly associated with a being distinct from God. In turn, this resulted in a number of alterations taking place in the conception of God, the human relationship to God, and the nature and place of evil in the cosmos. Evil was no longer thought to be part of God, but was divorced from Him. God was then no longer taken to be a complex of opposites, but a being thought in terms of pure goodness.

It will be remembered that, initially, evil was understood in terms of an immanent relationship between humans and God in which the former upheld the Covenant with the latter. Evil was synonymous with the human choosing to wander from God's path, whether this was because of his own autonomous choice or because he listened to the satan. In either case, however, the individual human was held responsible for his actions. Indeed, the actions of the satan are not those of a malicious independent being, but entail the word of God which is used to test an individual's devotion to Him.

This changed with the rise of Satan. Not only was Satan thought to be independent of God, he was understood to have his own agenda diametrically opposed to God. Rather than one God challenging humans through a third figure loyal to God, there are now two cosmic forces – God and Satan – competing for the human, who is capable of choosing either. Good arises when individuals work with God, evil results when individuals turn to Satan. Christian thinking comes, therefore, to understand that, if the individual follows God, this is due to an action of the individual and God; if the individual chooses evil, this is a consequence of individual choice and Satanic action.

By splitting evil from God in this way, Christians secured God's goodness. They did so, however, by appearing to sacrifice His omnipotence and, by extension, the monotheistic principles that Christianity was based on. After all, God, as pure goodness, now found Himself confronted by pure evil in the figure of Satan; a figure that He does not appear to be able to overcome even though His omnipotence should easily allow it. Overcoming evil while respecting the tenets of Christianity required that God be shown to be supremely good *and* omnipotent. These characteristics are difficult to combine. It is, for example, easy to account for evil by recognising that God is singular and all-powerful, but not good. We just have to accept that God can do anything, including evil actions. Alternatively, God can be thought to be good but not all-powerful by positing the existence of another being responsible for evil. This, however, undermines God's omnipotence. If God's goodness, omnipotence, and omniscience were to be reconciled, it required significant conceptual innovation and subtlety.

This took time, but eventually early Christian thinking resolved the dilemma by 'implicitly and unconsciously separat[ing] the evil side of the God from the good side, calling the good side the Lord and the evil side the Devil'.[30] As noted, this did not entail a straightforward dualism. The Devil was left in an

> anomalous position. On the one hand he was the author of evil, and his existence relieved the Lord of direct responsibility for many of the evils

of the world. On the other hand, he was not an independent principle but the creature and even the servant of the Lord. This anomaly led to an implicit tension between monism and dualism. The Devil, who was not prominent in the Old Testament, gained stature in the Apocryphal, Apocalyptic, and New Testament literatures. Far from being a mere accretion of peripheral superstitions, the Devil has his genesis in . . . God himself. He is a counterpart, a doublet of the good Lord. He is the shadow of God.[31]

The figure of the satan moved from being a loyal functionary of God who resides in God's court to an independent entity that not only exists outside of His court, but actively tries to undermine God for alternative (evil) ends. Satan's expulsion from God's court takes place through two means, depending on whether it refers to the rank of angels, known as the *bene ha-elohim*, or God's representative on Earth, known as the *mal'ak Yahweh*.

The *bene ha-elohim* were angels who were, initially, part of the Heavenly court. Some of them, however, sinned, which led to their exit from Heaven. How they descended depended on their crimes. If members of the *bene ha-elohim* experienced pride, and so, for example, no longer served God but themselves, they were 'cast down from heaven'.[32] If, however, they were lustful, they initially descended voluntarily towards the flesh they desired before being 'cast down into the pit as punishment for their sins'.[33] In either case, the *bene ha-elohim* fell from Heaven, a fall that, because it affected a split in the Heavenly court, was important for the development of evil as a separate cosmic force to God.

However, the decisive event in the creation of Satan was the conceptual alteration that the *mal'ak Yahweh* underwent. It is with this movement that the fundamental changes from the Hebrew conception of the satan to the Christian notion of Satan take place.

> The *mal'ak Yahweh* is the emissary or messenger of the God. Like the *bene ha-elohim*, the *mal'ak* is an aspect of the divine nature. But he differs from the *banim* in one important respect: they remain in heaven with the God, but the *mal'ak* roams the world in his service. The *mal'ak* is the voice of the God, the spirit of the God, the God himself.[34]

Due to the modifications that took place in early Hebrew thinking as a consequence of the split in the historical Hebrew community and the conceptual questions that resulted from its monotheism, the figure of the *mal'ak* gradually changed. Rather than being the voice of God, the *mal'ak* first 'obtain[ed] its independence from Yahweh',[35] before, second, 'its destructive aspect was emphasised',[36] leading to it 'finally ... becoming the personification of the shadow of the Lord, of the dark side of the divine nature'.[37] Only then did the *mal'ak* become 'the evil angel, Satan, the obstructor, the liar, the destroying spirit'.[38] It is at this point that *the satan* turns into *Satan*, an independent being defined by pure evil who is not only opposed to God, but also engaged in an adversarial battle with Him to overcome God's goodness and instantiate a reign of pure evil.

This conceptual alteration was substantial, but it seemed to pose two conceptions of God and two conceptions of evil: one from the Old Testament and one from the New. It was not, therefore, sufficient to simply develop a new cosmic narrative that sees God opposed to Satan. The monotheistic premises of the Judaeo-Christian tradition meant that the Old and New Testaments had to be reconciled. To do so, prior doctrine was gradually read in light of the conceptual apparatus of the New Testament. As such, Christian thought undertook a re-reading of the Old Testament to account for the horrors that were previously understood to be inflicted on humans by God to, instead, ascribe them to Satan. For this reason, we find that

> Chronicles [a late book of the Hebrew Bible] ... protects God by attributing to Satan what God did in [the earlier book] Samuel. In the same way, we learn from [the Book of] *Jubilees* that the less savoury acts attributed to Yahweh in the Torah – for example, the demand for the sacrifice of Isaac and the attempt to kill Moses – were in fact prompted by the prince of the hostile angels, whose name in *Jubilees* is usually 'Mastema'.[39]

The introduction of the name 'Mastema' is crucial to the development of the figure of Satan because, with it, the figure of evil is, for the first time, explicitly associated with hatred and enmity. The reason behind this is relatively simple: while 'Mastema' 'is etymologically linked to *śāṭān*'[40] and, as such, carries the adversarial or oppositional connotations that define the figure of the satan in the Old Testament, it is explicitly linked to 'enmity' itself.[41] Whereas the figure of the satan was one of God's angels who acted in God's service, the conceptual relationship that this figure has to God gradually changed until, with the Fall, there arose the figure of Satan, who is not only defined by hatred, but actively 'stands in open rebellion against God'.[42] A cosmic battle was understood to be under way between the forces of good and those of evil, with humans caught between them.

## The New Testament and the Problem of Evil

The notion and figure of evil are, therefore, fundamentally different in the New Testament and in the Old. Evil is no longer thought in terms of individual sin, nor is it simply tied to the God–human relationship. Evil is divorced from sin, thought of on its own terms as something far stronger, extensive, and dangerous, and is located in the figure of Satan, who is understood to be the personification of evil. In many respects, the New Testament is wholly concerned with the battle against Satan and the overcoming of evil. Although Satan 'seldom appears onstage in these gospel accounts, [he] nevertheless plays a central role in the divine drama [because the story told] would make little sense *without* Satan'.[43] After all,

> the function of the Devil in the New Testament is as counterprinciple to Christ. The central message of the New Testament is salvation: Christ saves us. What he saves us from is the evil power of the Devil. If the power of the Devil is dismissed, the Christ's saving mission becomes meaningless. The Devil occupies a central position in the New Testament as the chief enemy of the Lord.[44]

Without a figure of pure evil, it is not possible to develop a narrative that sees the son of God as being persecuted, let alone executed, by mere mortals who have been led astray by another figure. Similarly, the apocalyptic narrative makes little sense unless God, in his all-powerfulness, returns to overcome this alternative figure. When and how this return will take place are much debated in theological discussions, but the point is that the Christian narrative is developed from a subtly, but nevertheless significantly, different understanding of the cosmos from that found in Judaic thought. Rather than being the main players seeking to fulfil the Covenant with God, humans are bit-part players in the ongoing cosmic battle between good and evil, God and Satan.

A number of immediate consequences result from this: first, the battle for the souls of humans is based no longer on their actions alone, but on how successful the figure of evil is in corrupting them. Evil does not result from the individual simply failing to live up to the norms of the Covenant with God, but is thought in terms of an external source. Blame is placed not solely on individuals, but on the corrupting figure of evil. Second, the God of the New Testament is, in many respects, conceptually kinder. He is no longer a complex of opposites, but is associated with pure goodness. Third, there is an often unacknowledged, but very pertinent, splitting of the properties attributed to God. While there is only one God, evil does not emanate from God, nor is it God's responsibility; rather, evil is caused by another being, Satan, who somehow exists independently from God and is able to challenge God's supremacy. As a consequence, there is, fourth, a deep sense of metaphysical crisis underpinning the traditional Christian narrative wherein God is not alone in the cosmos, but is challenged by a usurper: the Prince of darkness, the personification of evil, the corruptor of souls, Satan. This split leads to, fifth, an uneasy tension between the ideas that God is, on the one hand, the omnipotent, all-knowing, supremely good foundation of existence, but yet, on the other hand, somehow not responsible for evil. As noted, Christianity responded by establishing an implicit dualism between an omnipotent, all-knowing God and an evil cosmic being responsible for evil, but this brought forth a number of conceptual problems and questions that would occupy it for much of its history.

## Concluding Remarks

Among the many questions that arose, arguably the most important relate to the source or genesis of this division, centred on the question: where does this evil being emanate from? Two options appear to present themselves: (1) evil comes from God, but is subsequently independent of and somehow subservient to God; or (2) a straightforward metaphysical dualism is established so that evil is, from the beginning, located in a figure other than God. The first option leads to questions such as: how and why did God create evil? How can evil be subservient to God and yet challenge God? And how can it be independent of God if God is omnipotent? The second option accounts for these, but contradicts the monotheistic principles that the Judaeo-Christian tradition affirms.[45] The question arose as to whether it was possible to find a third option, one that remained true to monotheistic principles, held that God is omnipotent and all-knowing, and separated evil from God to secure God's goodness.

Christian thinkers initially took up this challenge by turning to Scripture. They found, however, that it is full of contradictions. For example, 'several different interpretations of the fall of Satan and his fellow angels have at one time or another been put forward depending on whether it is viewed as (1) a moral lapse; (2) a loss of dignity; (3) a literal ejection from heaven; (4) a voluntary departure from heaven'.[46] There are also scriptural inconsistencies over the geography of the fall depending on whether it entails a fall '(1) from heaven to earth; (2) from heaven into the underworld; or (3) from earth (or air) into the underworld',[47] and, indeed, over the chronology of the fall depending on whether it was thought to occur '(1) at the beginning of the world before the fall of Adam; (2) from envy of Adam; (3) with the Watchers about the time of Noah; (4) at the advent of Christ; (5) at the Passion of Christ; (6) at the second coming of Christ; (7) a thousand years after the second coming'.[48]

In turn, this created significant differences in terms of when and how the oppositional relationship between God and Satan arose. For example, accounts in the New Testament differ in terms of whether

(1) At the beginning of the world there was war in heaven ... (2) The angels fell long after Adam ... (3) The Kingdom of God arrive[d] on earth with the advent of Christ ... (4) The Kingdom of Satan [was] weakened but not finally toppled by the coming of Christ [who] will come again [to destroy Satan] or cast [him] forever into hell ... (5) at the second coming, Christ will bind Satan for a thousand years ... at the end of [which] he will issue forth to harm [Satan] one final time [before] finally [destroying him].[49]

If Scripture could not solve the problem, Christian thinkers came to recognise that *they* would have to. To do so, three logical options presented themselves: (1) simply ignore the problem; (2) turn away from monotheism to a straightforward dualism; or (3) try to reconcile the objective existence of evil with God's omnipotent, omniscient, supreme goodness.

The first option had, to that point, been the dominant one, in so far as Hebrew thought came to implicitly depend upon a metaphysical dualism, with the tensions that this caused for its monotheistic foundations being largely ignored or, if treated, dealt with by simply reaffirming God's omnipotence. This, however, was no longer viable. Not only had the problem become explicit, but Christian thinkers,

such as Justin and Irenaeus, recognised that when Christianity claimed universality it had to compete intellectually with both rabbinic thought and Greek philosophy. Christians also faced the hostility of the Roman [S]tate and of the established Roman pagan religion (which was, however, already in deep decline).[50]

Initially, this led to the second option; that is, a turning away from monotheism to a straightforward dualism. It will be remembered that Christian thought *implicitly* made this movement when it thought of evil as being located in a cosmic figure distinct from God, despite its continued explicit adherence to a strict monotheism. The *implicit* reliance on a metaphysical dualism gradually became *explicit*. This culminated in the rise of Manichaeism in the third century AD, a system that offered a 'straightforward solution for the problem of evil [whereby] God is doing the best he can against evil, but finds himself facing an independent opponent as formidable as he'.[51] Despite, or possibly because of, its simplicity, Manichaeism offered the most extreme and successful challenge to Christianity.

Manichaeism did not, however, go unanswered and, indeed, in many respects, was the stimulus that brought Christian thinkers to develop a robust response to the problem of evil within monotheistic parameters. Rather than ignore the problem of evil or have recourse to a metaphysical dualism, Christian thinkers became increasingly creative in their attempts to reconcile the objective existence of evil with the central tenets of monotheism; that is, a singular God who is omnipotent, all-knowing, and supremely good.

Logically, four options were open: '(1) God is neither all-good nor all-powerful (an option usually excluded on the grounds that no one would call this God); (2) God is all-good but not all-powerful; (3) God is all-powerful but not all-good; (4) God is both all-good and all-powerful'.[52] The last option was adopted by Judaeo-Christian thinkers, but, as previously mentioned, is particularly difficult to defend because it requires the reconciliation of the all-goodness and all-powerfulness of God with the existence of evil, something that seems to call into question both. After all

> if God is all powerful, He has it in His power to prevent the existence of Satan (and evil human beings like him) from the outset. Evil people, and evil spirits, Satan chief amongst them perhaps, exist only because He permits them to. If God is creator and Satan really does exist, then God is responsible for Satan's creation also. By tradition, of course, Satan is not created as an evil spirit; on the contrary, he is a fallen angel. But even this does not appear to let God off the hook. If He is omniscient then He could foretell Satan's future conduct, and must accordingly have permitted it.[53]

This issue only grew in significance as a result of the social alterations taking place in the third to fifth centuries. The most notable, the decline and fall of the Roman Empire, was particularly problematic because the Empire had recently (AD 380) converted to Christianity. This led some to question how the Roman Empire, supposedly under God's protection by virtue of representing Him on Earth, could fall. It appeared that there existed another cosmic force in contradistinction to God, one that seemed to be winning.

The threat posed by these historical and conceptual challenges meant that Christian thinkers became increasingly frantic in their efforts to develop conceptual resources to explain both. The most influential of these thinkers was Augustine of Hippo (354–430), who proposed a theologically inspired account of evil that was hugely influential for the development of Christianity, for theological attempts to reconcile an all-powerful God with the existence of evil generally, and, indeed, for subsequent non-theological attempts to understand evil.

## Notes

1. For a discussion of the rise of monotheism, see Thomas Römer, *L'Invention de Dieu* (Paris: Éditions du Seuil, 2014).
2. The Judaeo-Christian tradition is also, obviously, intimately linked to Islam and so we would, ideally, also explore the conceptions of evil at play in Islam; a topic that has received relatively little attention. However, because Western *philosophical* thinking on the topic develops from the Judaeo-Christian trajectory, this chapter focuses on the way 'evil' is thought in these traditions, paying particular attention to the alterations that occur as Christianity arises from Judaism. For a discussion of evil in Islam, see Adnan Aslam, 'The Fall and Overcoming of Evil and Suffering in Islam', in *The Origin and the Overcoming of Evil and Suffering in the World Religions*, ed. Peter Koslowski (Dordrecht: Kluwer, 2001), pp. 24–47.
3. Throughout, the term 'Hebrewic' will refer to the general community from which Jewish and latterly Christian thinking emerged. It is not meant to indicate that there was ever a strict homogeneity to the Hebrewic community, but simply provides a narrative tool to outline the alterations in thinking that led to the Jewish and Christian conceptions of evil.
4. Satan has, of course, gone by many names throughout history, including the Devil, Lucifer, Mephistopheles, Mastema, Azazel, Sammael, Semyaza, and Belial, to name but a few of the more dominant ones. These names delineate not so much different beings as different nomenclatures for the same principle. As Jeffrey Burton Russell explains, 'the victory of "Satan" over "Azazel" or "Belial" is less the victory of one kind of *being* over another than the victory of one *name* over the others. Satan, Azazel, Belial, and Mastema were none of them in their origins a principle of evil, but in the Apocalyptic literature they converge in that direction. What is important is the development of the *concept* of the principle of evil, with which the name of Satan was linked more closely than any other' (*The Devil: Perceptions of Evil from Antiquity to Primitive Christianity* [Ithaca: Cornell University Press, 1977], p. 189).
5. This chapter is predominantly based on material from Neil Forsyth, *The Old Enemy: Satan and the Combat Myth* (Princeton: Princeton University Press,

1987); Elaine Pagels, *The Origin of Satan* (London: Penguin, 1995); Russell, *The Devil*; Jeffrey Burton Russell, *Satan: The Early Christian Tradition* (Ithaca: Cornell University Press, 1981); Donald Taylor, 'Theological Thoughts about Evil', in *The Anthropology of Evil*, ed. David Parkin (Oxford: Blackwell, 1985), pp. 26–41.
6. Russell, *The Devil*, p. 122. Although it does not much discuss evil, the classic account of Greek religion is Walter Burkert's *Griechische Religion der archaischen und klassischen Epoche* (Stuttgart: W. Kohlhammer, 1977).
7. Cited in Neil Forsyth, 'The Origin of "Evil": Classical or Judeo-Christian?', *Perspectives on Evil and Human Wickedness*, 1:1, January, 2002, pp. 17–52 (p. 20).
8. For example, Atë was associated with evil and misfortune, Eris was responsible for discord and strife, and the Keres were destructive or malevolent female spirits of the dead.
9. Hans Schwarz, *Evil: A Historical and Theoretical Perspective*, trans. Mark W. Worthing (Minneapolis: Fortress Press, 1995), pp. 61–2.
10. Pagels, *The Origin of Satan*, p. 39.
11. Russell, *The Devil*, pp. 177–8.
12. Taylor, 'Theological Thoughts about Evil', p. 28.
13. Ibid. p. 28.
14. Ibid. p. 29.
15. Ibid. p. 29.
16. Ibid. p. 34.
17. Ibid. p. 34.
18. Forsyth, *The Combat Myth*, p. 122.
19. Pagels, *The Origin of Satan*, p. 49.
20. Forsyth, *The Combat Myth*, pp. 298–9.
21. Jeffrey C. Alexander, 'Toward a Sociology of Evil: Getting beyond Modernist Common Sense about the Alternative to "the Good,"' p. 159, in *Rethinking Evil: Contemporary Perspectives*, ed. Maria Pia Lara (Berkeley: University of California Press, 2001), pp. 153–72.
22. John Sanford, *Evil: The Shadow Side of Reality* (New York: Crossroads, 1981), p. 43.
23. Ibid. p. 39.
24. Ibid. p. 43.
25. Ibid. p. 43.
26. Russell, *The Devil*, p. 183.
27. Ibid. p. 183.
28. Ibid. p. 183.
29. For a more detailed discussion on how these occurrences contributed to the development of the Jesus movement and, by extension, the relationship between Judaism – manifested in Judaic apocalyptic literature – and Christianity, see Forsyth, 'The Origin of "Evil"', pp. 29–32.
30. Russell, *The Devil*, p. 251.

31. Ibid. p. 251.
32. Ibid. p. 197.
33. Ibid. p. 197.
34. Ibid. pp. 197–8. *Banim* literally means 'sons', which, in the context of this quotation, refers to the 'sons of heaven' or, more generally, 'heavenly angels', as opposed to the *mal'ak*, who is an angel that roams the Earth in the service of God.
35. Ibid. p. 203.
36. Ibid. p. 203.
37. Ibid. p. 203.
38. Ibid. p. 203.
39. Ibid. p. 182. The Book of Jubilees, also known as the Lesser Genesis, is a work of Jewish origins written around the second century BC that records an account of the Biblical history of the world from the creation to Moses. Its theological status, especially within Christianity, is controversial: the Ethiopic Church accepts the book as Scripture, while the Roman, Orthodox, and Protestant churches reject it. For a discussion of its content and status, see James C. Vanderkam, *Book of Jubilees* (London: Bloomsbury, 2001).
40. Ibid. p. 188.
41. Ibid. p. 188.
42. Pagels, *The Origin of Satan*, p. xvii.
43. Ibid. p. 12.
44. Russell, *The Devil*, pp. 229–30.
45. Russell, *Satan*, p. 25.
46. Russell, *The Devil*, p. 241.
47. Ibid. p. 241.
48. Ibid. pp. 241–2.
49. Ibid. pp. 242–3.
50. Russell, *Satan*, p. 51.
51. William E. Mann, 'Augustine on Evil and Original Sin', p. 40, in *The Cambridge Companion to Augustine*, ed. Eleonore Stump and Norman Kretzmann (Cambridge: Cambridge University Press, 2001), pp. 40–8.
52. Russell, *Satan*, p. 17.
53. Gordon Graham, *Evil and Christian Ethics* (Cambridge: Cambridge University Press, 2001), pp. 198–9.

# 2

# Augustine, Free Will, and Evil

In his *Confessions*, Augustine writes that the sole purpose of his intellectual efforts was to identify 'the origin of evil'.[1] As we saw in the previous chapter, Judaeo-Christian efforts to respond to the problem of evil led from an initial (Judaic) monotheism to the implicit dualism of Christianity and, finally, with Manichaeism, to an explicit dualism. Augustine was initially attracted to this dualism, before converting to Christianity and devoting himself to resolving its problem of evil.

Attempts to resolve the problem of evil within a monotheistic metaphysics tended to try to dissolve it by emphasising God's supreme goodness, omniscience, or power. Augustine's conceptual innovation was to think of the problem of evil not from the perspective of God *per se*, but from the perspective of humans in a world created by God. To do so, he focuses on the role that the *will* plays in human morality. William Maker explains that this is different from Platonic and early Christian thinking on the subject, which thought of evil in terms of immutable, impersonal, cosmic forces. In contrast, Augustine recognises that

> tying human wrongdoing to the impersonal entrapment of the soul in the body or regarding evil as a cosmic force – however superficially satisfying these approaches may be – [trivialises] the complex character of evil. For by locating evil outside of the 'true self' they ignore the personal dimension of its presence in human affairs and deny individual responsibility for it.[2]

By examining the problem of evil from the perspective of human will, Augustine introduces a morality of responsibility. On the one hand, this is burdensome as it makes humans responsible for the evil in the world. But, on the other hand, it also offers significant solace because it seems to mean that human action can overcome evil. Augustine's position is more complex than this because of the role that grace plays in the good–evil relationship,[3] but his basic point is that individuals must take responsibility for their moral choices and can only do so if they 'have' free will.

The problem immediately encountered when attempting to outline Augustine's thought, however, is that his analysis is not presented in a coherent and organised fashion. It is found in a number of partial fragments in different texts, written decades apart. For this reason, Jean-Luc Marion complains that Augustine's thinking on the topic is both 'unavoidable and inaccessible'.[4] While this lack of systematisation causes significant exegetical problems, I tackle them by focusing on Augustine's discussions of the topic in *On the Free Choice of the Will*,[5] *Confessions*, and *The City of God against the Pagans*[6] to respond to three questions: (1) what metaphysical assumptions does Augustine base his analysis of evil on? (2) What does Augustine hold evil to consist of? (3) If human will comes from God, could God not have created a world without evil?

## Metaphysical Foundations

As noted in Chapter 1, the Judaeo-Christian tradition started as a strict monotheism before gradually morphing into an implicit metaphysical dualism, which became explicit with Manichaeism. Manichaeism could easily deal with the problem of evil because its dualist metaphysics allowed a good and a bad god to face one another. Augustine, however, defended a strict monotheism. He also rejected the Manichaean notion that evil entails a substance. To do so, he depended upon an understanding of God that perceives Him to be foundational, but, when creating, doing so *ex nihilo*.

That God creates 'all things from nothing'[7] is important for two reasons: first, because God creates from nothing, there is nothing prior to God's will,[8] meaning that He is the foundation of all. Second, and linked to this, it allows Augustine to distinguish between being and nothing. By claiming that the former, through an act of God, emanates from the latter, Augustine not only makes being dependent on God's action, thereby again confirming His foundational role in existence, but also lays the foundation for his subsequent claim that being is good, whereas nothing, as the absence of good, is evil. This allows Augustine to claim that evil, as the absence of being, cannot have emanated from God, who is responsible for being.

The fundamental problem that Augustine faces at this point is that while he has *stated* that God is the foundation of being, which is created *ex nihilo*, he has not *argued for* and so supported this conclusion. Christian thinkers will develop a number of increasingly complex arguments to prove the existence of God, but, in *On the Free Choice of the Will*, Augustine provides two. First, he claims that it is clear that 'since He gave ... reason the ability to think about Him so accurately and religiously',[9] God must exist. The argumentation is severely underdeveloped but Augustine is pointing to the idea that our capacity to clearly think of God is proof that God exists. Second, Augustine provides a more formal and extended proof for God's existence by thinking of God's existence from the interaction of the mind/body and unchangeable/changeable distinctions.

Starting with the mind/body distinction, Augustine distinguishes reason from the bodily senses, claiming that the former distinguishes humans from animals and non-organic entities. While human reason stands at the pinnacle of finite beings, Augustine inquires as to whether 'we are able to find something that ... not only exists but also is more excellent than our reason;'[10] the implication being that this would be an attribute of God. Augustine returns to the reason/senses distinction to claim that, while each individual has different bodily senses, each of which is experienced differently, the data gained from the bodily senses is interpreted by something called 'the internal sense'.[11] The internal sense co-ordinates the activities of the different bodily senses, with reason being that which provides knowledge of the internal sense.[12]

Having shown that reason stands above the internal sense, which is above the bodily senses, Augustine inquires into the possibility that there might be something higher than reason.[13] To clarify what this means, he distinguishes between things that are unchangeable and those that change. The eternal nature of the former is linked to God. Thus, 'if reason sees something eternal and unchangeable through itself, without recourse to any bodily organ ... [r]eason must then admit itself to be inferior, and the eternal and unchangeable being [that it sees] to be its God'.[14]

Augustine turns to the senses to explain that each sense is unique and provides a distinctive experience to every individual. For example, it is not possible to know what it is for another person to hear. The same holds for the internal sense. However, while each sense provides each individual with a different experience, Augustine claims that there is 'something' common to all experiences; namely, being. Augustine then asks whether the same commonality holds of reason. His interlocutor, Evodius, suggests that there are many things that all reasoning beings hold in common, but mentions one in particular: number.[15]

Two options present themselves at this point: (1) numbers are imprinted on the mind from an external source, meaning that they come from the senses, or (2) numbers exist independently of the senses. Augustine argues for the latter, claiming that numbers emanate not from the senses but 'from how many times [a number] includes *one*'.[16] Thus 'if it includes *one* twice it is called "two" and if three times "three"'.[17] The notion of *one* 'cannot be sensed with the bodily senses',[18] which are only capable of ascertaining the many. Even if we perceive what appears to be one object, that object actually has different components (width, height, texture, and so on) that reveal it to be a composition of many. Importantly, the many that the bodily senses perceive are actually composed of multiple singular aspects.

Augustine is pointing to an atomistic understanding of objects: the body perceives multiple objects, but these objects are amalgamations of multiple, singular objects.[19] By identifying that the logical structure underpinning numerical schemas proceeds by a fixed law, Augustine concludes that the example of number points towards truths that are 'pure and unchangeable'.[20] He claims that the same logic applies to wisdom. While there are different applications of wisdom, 'the light of wisdom itself . . . is one and common to all wise people'.[21]

Augustine links this to Scripture to claim that because the truth is unchangeable it is superior to our minds, which, due to their finiteness, are changeable.[22] Since truth is superior to our rational minds by virtue of being unchangeable, it must belong to something superior to reason. Furthermore, because what is eternal makes us happy, turning towards the eternal is the supreme good.[23] The next and final step is to identify the eternal laws underpinning truth with God's existence, so that God is that which is foundational and eternal.

Having established that God exists and creates being *ex nihilo*, Augustine links both to morality to claim that being, as a creation of God, is good. Thus, by virtue of existing, each thing is better than nothing. By connecting ontology and ethics in this way, Augustine creates a hierarchy whereby those beings with more being are better than those with less. Because God is the supreme being, He has more being than all others. Indeed, He must also be the transcendent foundation for other beings.

With regard to human being, Augustine claims that this generates two conclusions: first, human beings, by virtue of being, are better and hence more moral than non-beings. But, at the same time, and second, this ontological superiority must be complemented by a mode of being that actively wills the good. It is not sufficient that human being simply exists and through its existence is good. Being good requires that human being comport itself to being (= the good = God) in a certain manner. When it does, 'the will adheres to the common and unchangeable good [and] achieves the great and fundamental goods of a human being'.[24]

Having identified that good is associated with being, which is created *ex nihilo* by God, Augustine turns to the question of evil. Evil is not a substance, but is derived from the individual's relationship to the good. It will be remembered from Chapter 1 that one of the key aspects of the Judaic conception of sin was the notion of `awon, meaning 'crooked, twisted or wrong',[25] as in travelling down the wrong path away from God. Augustine implicitly adopts this to hold that evil entails any action whereby the will turns away from God.

There is, however, some ambiguity in his account. In the earlier *On the Free Choice of the Will*, Augustine states that 'the movement of "turning away" pertains [to] sin, since it is a defective movement, and every defect is from nothing'.[26] On this understanding, evil entails a turning away from God that emanates not from God, but from nothing. Indeed, by claiming that the turn towards evil is also a turn towards nothing, Augustine seems to undercut the need for an analysis of evil. If evil is nothing, it cannot have a being of its own and so cannot exist. This calls into question the reality of evil.

Presumably, this is why in the later *Confessions*, Augustine no longer thinks in terms of the binary opposition between good-being/evil-nothing. Rather, 'the movement of the will away from you [God] ... is a movement towards that which has *less* being'.[27] This can entail a turning 'away from the unchangeable and common good',[28] whereby the will 'wants to be its own power'.[29] Alternatively, it can turn towards something external, such as 'when it is eager to know the personal affairs of other people, or anything that is not its business'.[30] Further still, the will sins when it turns towards 'something lower',[31] specifically when it turns away from the truth as revealed through the mind and 'takes delight in bodily pleasures'.[32]

The confusion between the two texts is clarified in *The City of God against the Pagans*, where Augustine explains that 'to defect from that which supremely is, to that which has a less perfect degree of being: this is what it is to begin to have an evil will',[33] and 'to be sure, man did not fall away from his nature so completely as to lose all being. When he turned towards himself, however, his being became less complete than when he clung to Him Who exists supremely.'[34] Evil does not then result from attaining a lower form of being; it entails the turning away from the good and the descent to a lesser form of being.[35] As Augustine puts it:

defections of the will are not towards evil things, but are themselves evil: that is, they are not defections towards things which are evil by nature and in themselves; rather, it is the defection of the will itself which is evil, because [it is] against the order of nature. It is a turning away from that which has supreme being and towards that which has less.[36]

However, no sooner has Augustine clarified this than he claims that 'evil has no nature of its own. Rather, it is the absence of good which has received the name "evil"',[37] which again appears to conceive of evil as a state defined by the absence of good.

Despite the confusion regarding its culmination, it is clear that evil is only a possibility from the good (= being). There is no evil being opposed to a good being. Rather, evil is an effect of a particular relationship to the good that always starts from the good. As an action, it must be performed by a being, meaning that evil is always parasitical on being and hence the good. Augustine is walking a fine line that aims to take evil seriously while also denying it the status of being. His strategy is to claim that evil is real by virtue of being an action undertaken by human will, but, somewhat paradoxically, the reality or essence of evil is absence, meaning that evil entails 'a defect'[38] of being and so a turning away from God.

However, given that Augustine's cosmology is based on a chain of being headed by a supreme being which gradually falls away to lesser types of being, it might be thought that the lesser types of being are, in some way, defective and thus evil. Augustine gets round this in two ways: first, he claims that the natural inequalities in being belong to the natural order and so do not count as evils. If each entity is defined by different quantities of being, this simply means that those beings are different. If differences in being were a sufficient condition of evil, evil would be defined by the being of those entities and so would be conceived as a being and hence substance. Evil is not a substance, however, but an action.

Second, to understand the 'absence' of evil, we have to distinguish between *negation* and *privation*. Whereas negation refers to the differences and hence natural inequalities that exist between beings, privation entails a lack of a part of the being that is inherent in its natural being. For example, that a human does not have wings but a bird does means that, in relation to a bird, a human suffers from the *negation* of wings. This is not an evil because it is not in the nature of a human to possess wings, whereas if a bird lacked wings, this would be a *privation* because the bird would lack something that is part of its essence. In relation to humans, Augustine makes this point through the example of feet, explaining that 'if you saw someone without feet, you would admit that a great good is lacking in his body's wholeness'.[39] Such a person would then suffer a privation.

Augustine claims, however, that while privation is the first condition of evil, it is not the only one. If it were, evil would be synonymous with a degraded form of being. Evil is not a being, but arises from an action that a being, in this case human being, undertakes with regards to its natural being.[40] To understand this, we have to follow a particular logic. First, we must remember that human being is a form of being, which means that it emanates from God. Second, human will emanates from God, who is supremely good. Third, being is defined by the good, meaning that human being as a form of being is intimately connected to the good. Fourth, evil is defined by a turning away from the good, which means that, fifth, humans must first be orientated to the good to subsequently choose to turn away from it. Augustine concludes that, while it must be affirmed, the human has a natural propensity to the good that is subsequently either affirmed or denied. Because of its natural propensity to the good, any turning away from this propensity, and hence away from the good, is a turning away from its nature and thus, on Augustine's understanding, an evil.[41]

Importantly, neither inanimate objects nor animals can commit evil, because the former have no spontaneity and, thus, no possibility of making a moral choice, while the latter 'can behave only according to their natures, and their natures are good because God made them'.[42] Furthermore, while God is omnipotent, He is not capable of doing evil. Only humans have the ontological characteristic, namely free will, that allows them to choose to turn from the goodness of God-given being to nothing. This is, as Joseph Torchia points out, the key

> ontological difference between God and creatures: if God is distinct from what He creates (and God is immutable and external), then creatures are bound up with mutability and a gravitation toward non-being. In this respect, creatures exist in so far as they were created, but tend toward non-being to the extent that they differ from God.[43]

Because they are, in a sense, caught between being and nothing, humans have the choice to turn to either option. The former leads to the good, the latter to evil. Evil arises then not simply from a privation of its natural being, but from a particular choice made with regard to the good.

## Evil and Free Will

To properly understand Augustine's explanation of evil, including what he is and is not trying to account for, we must recognise that he distinguishes between whether someone has 'done evil (*malum culpae*)'[44] or 'suffered something evil (*malum poenae*)'.[45] This distinction will come to be known as the distinction between moral evil and natural evil.

Whereas moral evil entails something that an individual does to another, natural evil implies an evil that the individual receives from 'the elements of the universe itself'.[46] While humans are responsible for moral evil, they are not responsible for natural evils. This is the preserve of God. His actions are not, however, due to malice, but because 'He hands out punishments to evildoers.'[47] Natural evil emanates from God and is divine punishment for the moral evils committed by humans. However, since natural evils depend upon and so are justified by moral evils, Augustine claims that the latter 'are to be regarded either as the only evils or as the greatest evils'.[48]

Analysing the nature and status of moral evils requires not only an investigation into what they entail, but also an account of how and why they are possible within a world created by a supremely good, all-knowing, omnipotent God. In response to the first problem, Augustine reaffirms the metaphysical premise that being is synonymous with the good. Given that God is supremely good and creates *ex nihilo*, that which He creates is also held to be good; although there are differences in degrees of being, meaning that there are natural inequalities in the beings created.

Humans, however, are not simply created with being; they also have the possibility of moral choice. This requires free will, for only this allows humans to voluntarily choose to affirm or reject the good. In turn, this ensures that they are morally responsible for their actions, which, in turn, necessitates and justifies the natural evils experienced. If humans did not have the capacity to do otherwise than their nature dictated, it would be unjust to punish them for something they have no control over. Thus, divine justice and hence natural evil require that humans have free will.

Given that humans have the option of affirming or turning away from the good, the question arises as to why either option would be chosen. Augustine's response is that it emanates from the human's status as a being, which it will be remembered is synonymous with the good. Augustine claims, however, that it is not sufficient for humans to simply be good, they must also actively affirm the good. This is because he links goodness to happiness, which results when the free will *morally* affirms its natural *ontological* propensity to the good.[49] Presumably, although Augustine never makes this point, there is also some sort of desire to be happy inherent in human being.

Evil, in contrast, is constituted by the free will turning away from its ontological propensity to the good, which, given the intimate connection between the good, being, and God, also entails a turning away from God.

There are three ways in which this can happen: first, evil arises when the free will privileges its bodily desires over its rational judgement.[50] Second, Augustine links the choice of good or evil to the perception of and attachment to different things. The person who has a proper relationship to things is not defined by them. His healthy distance from them allows him to remain 'completely above them, possessing and governing them when there is need'.[51] Indeed, he is 'ready to lose them, and more ready not to have them'.[52] While things may be used, there is a self-sufficiency associated with the good that means that the will dominates the thing. In contrast,

> the person who uses them in an evil manner holds fast to them with love and is tangled up with them. That is to say, he is controlled by things that he ought to control and, in setting them up as goods for himself that need to be put in order and treated properly, he holds himself back from the [true] good.[53]

This complements Augustine's insistence that affirming bodily desires is synonymous with evil. Rather than look to the city of God, evil results from turning away from the divine realm to affirm the corporeal.

The third way in which the individual can turn away from the good is a consequence of Augustine's affirmation of the perceived eternal, unchanging aspect of things over their changing appearance. By claiming that 'the eternal law commands us to turn our love aside from temporal things and to turn it, purified, towards eternal things',[54] Augustine understands good to be the affirmation of the eternal, unchanging moment of things, specifically God, and evil to entail the turning away from this to the affirmation of

> temporal things and whatever is perceived through the body (the least valuable part of a human being), which can never be fixed, as though they were great and wonderful, having neglected eternal things, which the mind enjoys through itself and perceives through itself and which it cannot lose while loving them.[55]

Augustine recognises that desire plays a necessary role in human existence, but insists that 'normal' desire is defined by the 'right' amount of bodily satisfaction. In contrast, evil is 'wanton will'[56] that 'will[s] to have more than is enough',[57] where 'enough' means 'as much as is required for a nature of a given kind to preserve itself'.[58] By recognising that humans have natural bodily needs which need to be met, but claiming that morality cannot be dominated by those bodily needs, Augustine shows that morality depends upon natural being but cannot be determined by it. Connecting natural needs to evil and ontology (= being) to the good brings him to conclude that morality requires that the human will control its natural desires and affirm its ontological propensity to the good.

However, if the human is defined by a natural propensity to affirm the good, it may be questioned how it is possible that the will can turn away from this to the non-being or lesser being of evil. Augustine takes up this issue in *On the Free Choice of the Will*. He admits that he does not know why some choose this path. Indeed, he claims that this question is not a legitimate one because 'to seek the causes of [the] defections [that constitute evil actions] is like wishing to see darkness or hear silence'.[59] Rather than a failure in his thinking, Augustine's inability to adequately respond is a consequence of his understanding that evil entails a lack of being.[60] After all, 'what is nothing cannot be known'.[61] Confirming this in *The City of God against the Pagans*, Augustine explains that the cause of evil is 'not efficient, but deficient, because the evil will itself is not an effect of something, but a defect'.[62] Only beings have causes and because evil is the absence of being, it cannot be caused by anything else. Given the lack associated with evil, the search for its cause is a futile one.

While it is not possible to know why some turn towards evil and others choose the good, Augustine reaffirms his claim that 'nothing makes the mind a devotee of desire but its own will and free choice'.[63] That which makes the will exercise itself is nothing other than 'will itself',[64] and 'anyone who wills to live rightly and honourably, if he wills himself to will this instead of transient goods, acquires so great a possession with such ease that having what he willed is nothing other for him than willing it'.[65] Conversely, evil results when the will chooses to turn away from the good to affirm its bodily desires and transient state, and becomes dominated by external objects.[66]

Augustine develops this somewhat when he realises that it does not accord with Christian Scripture. By claiming that there is no efficient cause of evil, he seems to downplay the role that the New Testament gives to Satan in this respect. For this reason, Augustine supplements his account by claiming that the will is always faced with a choice whether to affirm the good or turn away from it towards evil. This choice is presented to it from external sources: from God in relation to the good and from Satan in relation to evil. Thus, 'whoever wills surely wills *something*. But he cannot will unless this "something" is either suggested externally through the bodily senses or enters into the mind in hidden ways.'[67] The latter, of course, is understood to have occurred with 'the Devil's suggestion to . . . Adam'.[68]

## Free Will and God's Omnipotence

Augustine's free-will defence[69] raises three questions: (1) if human will comes from God, could God not have created it in such a way that it could not choose evil? (2) How does freedom of the will relate to God's omnipotence? And (3) why would human will choose evil over its natural propensity to the good?

Augustine does not respond directly to these questions because he thinks that they are underpinned by a more important issue: the relationship between God's foreknowledge and human free will. The problem motivating his account is as follows: if God is omnipotent, all-knowing, and supremely good, He must have foreknowledge of whether an individual will choose evil and so can presumably take steps to prevent him from doing so. Yet evil continues to exist, which seems to point to the conclusion that either God is not all-knowing, or He is all-knowing but does not step in to prevent evil. Both seem to violate the central tenets of monotheism: the former because it seems to undermine the notion that God is all-knowing and omnipotent, the latter because it seems to undermine His supreme goodness. Augustine's response to this dilemma is as problematic as it is innovative.

The first thing to note is that, for Augustine, this question only arises for those who 'do not raise it in a religious way'.[70] It is necessary to engage with the question with a particular religious sentiment already in place, one that assumes the supremacy of God. There is, therefore, no suggestion in Augustine's analysis that God does not exist. This seems to leave two options: first, that divine necessity rules over everything, meaning that there is no free will;[71] or, second, that, while divine necessity rules over everything, it is 'weak or unjust or evil'.[72] The first option denies human free will and so is unacceptable to Augustine, while the second option denies God's supreme goodness and so is also rejected.

Rather than hold that God's omnipotence is opposed to human free will, Augustine offers a compatibilist understanding whereby God foreknows all, but evil results from human free will. To do so, he distinguishes between God's *foreknowledge* and *action* to claim that, whereas God knows all (including what the good entails, and what each individual is capable of doing and, crucially, will do), He does not cause human action. Human will is the cause of human action. Because it is free, the will can only be grounded in itself.

Augustine also claims that God's foreknowledge means that He already knows what will happen and has factored this into His creation. Thus, He 'foresee[s] what He is going to do with regard to the just and the irreligious'.[73] But if God foresees what is going to happen and, indeed, what He will do to punish those who transgress, why does He not stop an individual from committing evil in the first place? Does this not mean that, in some sense, God wants and so wills these acts to happen?

Augustine claims not. Creation is based not on God's *knowledge*, but on His *will*. Furthermore, responsibility requires action. Because God does not necessarily will what He knows, in this case that a transgression will occur, He cannot be held responsible for something that He knows will happen but does not will. This therefore requires that God create the world, have foreknowledge of all that will happen, but be absent from any continuous involvement in it. The obvious objection is that this undermines God's omnipotence because, while He creates and sustains the world, He does not determine its contents, nor is He responsible for all that occurs.

For Augustine, however, God's omnipotence is thought in terms of knowledge, not action. That God *knows* all but does not cause all *action* is precisely why human will is free. For this reason, Augustine explains that 'although God foreknows our future wills, it does *not* follow from this that we do not will something by our will'.[74] God is the foundation of the world, but not of all actions within the world. Similarly, God has foreknowledge of everything, but human will is free and so must make a choice regarding whether to affirm or deny the good. God's foreknowledge means that He knows what will happen, but this foreknowledge does not impact on the individual's decision.[75] The conclusion reached is that 'God, although He does not force anyone into sinning, nevertheless foresees those who are going to sin by their own will.'[76] Nothing occurs without God's knowledge, but not everything occurs because of His knowledge.

## Concluding Remarks

Of course, the question arises as to why 'a God equipped with justice and foreknowledge [does] not redress what he does not force to happen'.[77] In other words, why does a supremely good God not design the universe in such a way that the human will cannot turn away from Him to evil? Augustine explains that this question is implicitly premised on the claim that the human world should be exactly like the divine one, before concluding that this is not so: 'you should not be envious at all, I think, that something lesser was made . . . (and it was the Earth), since you have not been cheated out of something else'.[78] It seems that Augustine simply thinks that there should be a natural distinction between the perfection of Heaven and the imperfection of Earth.

Later thinkers, in particular Leibniz, will spend much time offering arguments to support this conclusion, but, for Augustine, it seems obvious not only that the human world was, of necessity, created in an inferior way to Heaven – it is pure folly to 'think of anything in Creation that has escaped the Maker of Creation'[79] – but also that this implies no failure on God's part. After all, 'God made all natures, not only those who would abide in virtue and justice but also those who would sin – not in order that they sin, but in order that they adorn the universe, whether they willed to sin or not to sin.'[80] That God created individuals that He knew would sin was not, as it will be for Leibniz, because their existence was necessary to create the best of all possible worlds. It was simply because God wanted to 'adorn the universe'[81] with the possibility of evil regardless of whether it was exercised or not. It is not clear, however, why this would be the case.

One response would be to reiterate that it is only if God admits the possibility of evil that free will is possible, which, in turn, allows individuals to show God that they freely follow Him and so are morally good.[82] Of course, it could be objected that God's foreknowledge would ensure He knows this, but it will be remembered that, for Augustine, this is not sufficient. Humans must *show* that they are morally good by freely choosing the good, which requires that the human world be created imperfectly because only this permits the possibility that humans can and will choose to turn away from the good. It also has the added advantage of explaining the necessary existence of natural evils.[83] Not only do they punish moral evils, but, as Augustine explains, they 'are permitted to exist in order to demonstrate ... the justice and perfect foresight of the Creator'.[84]

Augustine does not develop this further, but three points stand out from it: first and most extraordinarily of all, it means that God *purposefully* admits the existence of evil to demonstrate that He can continue to reign despite the existence of opposing forces. It also points to the notion that *things* can be evil, which, given that things are a form of being, indicates that evil can take substantial form and does not simply entail an action. Finally, it ensures that Augustine accepts that God permits evil to exist, with the consequence that there is a sense in which Augustine is admitting that the existence of evil emanates from God.

Issues arise from all three points: the first depends on the notion that God must, in some sense, prove His power to Himself. It is not clear why this is the case or how it fits with His perfect foreknowledge. The second contradicts Augustine's earlier claim that evil implies an action, not a form of being. And the third points to a theodicy that Augustine does not fully develop. Recognising this, he nevertheless defends it by claiming that it accords with Scripture and 'whatever we are told about any creatures, whether past or future, should be believed on divine authority'.[85]

It is here that we most explicitly see that Augustine's account of evil is grounded in a particular metaphysical narrative wherein Christian doctrine establishes the parameters of the problem to be investigated and, ultimately, is to be deferred to when seeking answers to it. This is not to say that Augustine simply parrots Christian Scripture. As I have argued throughout this chapter, there is significant conceptual innovation in his account of evil, itself dependent on a sophisticated, if, at times, underdeveloped metaphysics.

## Notes

1. Augustine, *Confessions*, trans. Henry Chadwick (London: Penguin, 2008), Book VII, sec. VII.
2. William Maker, 'Augustine on Evil: The Dilemma for the Philosophers', *International Journal for Philosophy of Religion*, 15:3, 1984, pp. 149–60 (pp. 151–2).
3. For a discussion of this, see Phillip Cary, *Inner Grace: Augustine in the Traditions of Plato and Paul* (Oxford: Oxford University Press, 2008).
4. Jean-Luc Marion, *In the Self's Place: The Approach of Saint Augustine*, trans. Jeffrey L. Kosky (Stanford: Stanford University Press, 2012), p. 1.
5. Augustine, *On the Free Choice of the Will, On Grace and Free Choice, and Other Writings*, ed. and trans. Peter King (Cambridge: Cambridge University Press, 2010).
6. Augustine, *The City of God against the Pagans*, ed. and trans. R. W. Dyson (Cambridge: Cambridge University Press, 1998).
7. Augustine, *On the Free Choice of the Will*, 1.02.5.12.
8. Augustine, *Confessions*, Book XI, sec. X.
9. Augustine, *On the Free Choice of the Will*, 2.6.14.55.
10. Ibid. 2.6.14.54.
11. Ibid. 2.3.9.29.
12. Ibid. 2.3.9.29; 2.3.9.35.
13. Ibid. 2.6.14.54.
14. Ibid. 2.6.14.56.
15. Ibid. 2.7.15.61.
16. Ibid. 2.8.22.84.
17. Ibid. 2.8.22.84.
18. Ibid. 2.8.22.85.
19. Ibid. 2.8.22.87.
20. Ibid. 2.8.24.93.
21. Ibid. 2.9.27.108.
22. Ibid. 2.11.30.124.
23. Ibid. 2.13.35.140–2.13.35.141.
24. Ibid. 2.19.53.199.

25. Donald Taylor, 'Theological Thoughts about Evil', p. 29, in *The Anthropology of Evil*, ed. David Parkin (Oxford: Blackwell, 1985), pp. 26–41.
26. Augustine, *On the Free Choice of the Will*, 2.20.54.204.
27. Augustine, *Confessions*, Book XII, sec. XI (emphasis added).
28. Augustine, *On the Free Choice of the Will*, 2.19.53.199.
29. Ibid. 2.19.53.199.
30. Ibid. 2.19.53.199.
31. Ibid. 2.19.53.199.
32. Ibid. 2.19.53.200.
33. Augustine, *The City of God against the Pagans*, p. 507.
34. Ibid. p. 601.
35. For an extended discussion of this, see J. Patout Burns, 'Augustine on the Origin and Progress of Evil', *The Journal of Religious Ethics*, 16:1, Spring, 1988, pp. 9–27.
36. Augustine, *The City of God against the Pagans*, p. 508.
37. Ibid. p. 461.
38. Ibid. p. 507.
39. Augustine, *On the Free Choice of the Will*, 2.18.48.183.
40. Ibid. 3.1.2.10.
41. In *On the Free Choice of the Will*, Augustine explains that 'vice ... is evil simply because it is opposed to the nature of the thing of which it is the vice' (3.14.41.142). This is repeated in the later *The City of God against the Pagans*, where he explains that those who are called God's enemies do evil 'because it corrupts the good of their nature' (p. 501).
42. G. R. Evans, *Augustine on Evil* (Cambridge: Cambridge University Press, 1982), p. 95.
43. Joseph Torchia, 'Creation, Finitude, and the Mutable Will: Augustine on the Origin of Moral Evil', *Irish Theological Quarterly*, 71, 2006, pp. 47–66 (p. 55).
44. Augustine, *On the Free Choice of the Will*, 1.1.1.1.
45. Ibid. 1.1.1.1.
46. Augustine, *The City of God against the Pagans*, p. 144.
47. Augustine, *On the Free Choice of the Will*, 1.1.1.1–1.1.1.2.
48. Augustine, *The City of God against the Pagans*, p. 144.
49. Augustine, *On the Free Choice of the Will*, 1.13.28.95.
50. Ibid. 1.3.8.20.
51. Ibid. 1.15.33.113.
52. Ibid. 1.15.33.113.
53. Ibid. 1.15.33.113.
54. Ibid. 1.15.32.108.
55. Ibid. 1.16.34.115.
56. Ibid. 3.17.48.166.
57. Ibid. 3.17.48.165.
58. Ibid. 3.17.48.165–3.17.48.165.166.
59. Augustine, *The City of God against the Pagans*, pp. 507–8.

60. For an interesting discussion of this, see Carlos Steel, 'Does Evil have a Cause? Augustine's Perplexity and Thomas's Answer', *The Review of Metaphysics*, 48:2, 1994, pp. 251–73.
61. Augustine, *On the Free Choice of the Will*, 2.20.54.202.
62. Augustine, *The City of God against the Pagans*, p. 507.
63. Augustine, *On the Free Choice of the Will*, 1.11.21.76.
64. Ibid. 1.12.26.86.
65. Ibid. 1.13.29.97.
66. Ibid. 3.17.48.164.
67. Ibid. 3.25.75.259.
68. Ibid. 3.25.75.259.
69. For a contemporary discussion and formulation of this argument, see Alvin Platinga, *God, Freedom, and Evil*, (Cambridge: William B. Eerdmans, 1974), pp. 29–34.
70. Augustine, *On the Free Choice of the Will*, 3.2.5.16.
71. Ibid. 3.2.5.17.
72. Ibid. 3.2.5.18.
73. Ibid. 3.3.6.23.
74. Ibid. 3.3.7.28.
75. 'Power is not taken away from me due to His foreknowledge' (ibid. 3.3.8.35).
76. Ibid. 3.4.10.39.
77. Ibid. 3.4.11.40.
78. Ibid. 3.5.13.46.
79. Ibid. 3.5.13.49.
80. Ibid. 3.11.32.113.
81. Ibid. 3.11.32.113.
82. Ibid. 2.1.3.7.
83. Ibid. 2.1.3.5-2.1.3.7.
84. Augustine, *The City of God against the Pagans*, p. 605.
85. Augustine, *On the Free Choice of the Will*, 3.21.60.204.

# 3
# Aquinas, Privation, and Original Sin

Augustine's response to the problem of the origin of evil was immensely influential and, in many respects, became the standard one for Christian theology. But his account was sufficiently underdeveloped to allow, and to an extent demand, revision. This was supported by the continued institutionalisation of Christianity and, indeed, the ongoing Christianisation of Europe.

John Marenbom points out that having gained widespread, institutional support through its adoption by the Roman Empire, Christianity gradually spread throughout medieval Europe in three stages. First, 'there was the acceptance of Catholic Christianity by the barbarians who, starting with the Visigoths in 376, followed by the Ostrogoths, Vandals, Burgundians, and Franks, had entered the Roman Empire and started to settle and establish kingdoms there'.[1] Marenbom claims that this stage was completed by the end of the sixth century. At this point, the second stage, from the fifth to the ninth centuries, had begun and entailed 'the evangelisation . . . of areas which had never been Romanised or where Christianity had disappeared – Ireland, Britain, Saxony, Frisia, Bavaria, and Denmark'.[2] In turn, this was complemented by the third stage, in which 'the Christianisation of outlying northern and eastern areas, a process full of reversals . . . was officially completed only in 1386 when Lithuania . . . adopted the Catholic Church'.[3]

The Christianisation of Europe occurred, therefore, over a period of eight hundred plus years, during which time the doctrine supporting it altered to take into consideration and, to a degree, accommodate the discrepancies inherent in the various cultures engaged with and the religious forms encountered. Not surprisingly, this led to significant discussion about different aspects of Christian doctrine, including the nature and meaning of evil.

The development of the Christian tradition was not, however, simply an 'internal' matter. With the rise of Islam in the Near East in the seventh century and its spread thereafter, Christian doctrine encountered a new religion that not only challenged its truths, but claimed to go beyond them. From a Christian perspective, this was a direct threat posed by pagans who rejected salvation through Christ. The paradox of Christianity's relation to Islam was that as it sought to distance itself from the nascent, and increasingly successful, religion, the engagement needed to secure this distancing greatly influenced its own development.

While a simplification, there is much to the notion that Christian and Islamic thinking developed from a privileging of different Greek sources: Christian thinking looking to a greater extent to Plato and Islamic thinkers looking to Aristotle.[4] This led Islamic thinking to a greater focus on logic, argumentation, and natural science, none of which were

> available to Western Europe until the twelfth century, when Christians, Jews and Arabs began to exchange and translate texts in Spain. By the beginning of the thirteenth century, a flood of Aristotelian scholarship came to the West and constituted a rival way of doing philosophy to the more traditional Neoplatonic approach.[5]

Through their interaction with Islamic thinkers and their readings of Aristotle, Christian thinkers gradually came to depend to a far greater extent on the natural realm and strict logical deduction.

These developments were accompanied by a particular alteration to the institutionalisation of knowledge within the Christian world. Whereas up to the thirteenth century, the focal point of knowledge was the monasteries, with study being individual and defined by an informal relationship to a considered authority, the rise of a new institution called 'the university' moved knowledge out of the monasteries, formalised the procedures necessary for knowledge, and, through the methodologies employed therein, transformed how knowledge was gained, understood, and analysed.

Jan Aertsen explains that the laws establishing universities typically identified a common text, considered to be definitively authoritative, to be studied by all. This rigidity meant that students worked on the same text and arguments and so developed not only detailed knowledge about them, but also 'a sophisticated hermeneutics [wherein] . . . much attention was devoted to items such as the multiple senses of words and "the properties of terms" – the effect of a word's syntactic context on its semantic function'.[6] Rather than broad discussions using undefined concepts, much greater emphasis was placed on the various meanings of the terms and the structural relationships between the diverse number of possibilities, with the consequence that arguments developed around the different possible *textually based* conclusions that could be drawn about the text's fundamental meaning.

These socio-historico-epistemological alterations find their clearest and fullest expression in the thought of Thomas Aquinas (1225?–74). Not only was Aquinas's thinking central to the debates taking place in the new universities, but, in contrast to his Christian contemporaries who continued to focus on Neoplatonic sources, Aquinas drew inspiration from Aristotle[7] and Islamic sources[8] to reconsider core issues within Christian doctrine. His analysis of evil is the most important development in the history of evil after Augustine. Engaging with it will show how Christian thinking on evil evolved from its early manifestations to the Middle Ages, when its position of dominance was secured.

However, when we turn to Aquinas's thinking, we encounter a problem that all commentators on his work highlight: the sheer volume of his writings. To overcome this, while also doing justice to his thinking, this chapter will focus primarily on his *On Evil*,[9] while using other texts, notably the *Summa Theologiae*,[10] to back up or develop an underdeveloped point in the first text. *On Evil* is, however, a long text and so the discussion will focus on three questions: (1) how does Aquinas conceptualise the relationship between good and evil? (2) What does he understand by the notion of Original Sin? And (3) what role does the body play in Aquinas's conception of evil? The responses given to these questions reveal that, while Aquinas was influenced by Augustine, he departs from his predecessor in a number of subtle but important ways, particularly regarding the relationship between good and evil, and the conceptualisation of the body, including its relationship to evil.

## The Nature of Good

To transition from Augustine's analysis of evil to Aquinas's is to move from a suggestive account of evil to a more developed, conceptually nuanced, and holistic one. Broadly speaking, Aquinas agrees with the metaphysical framework underpinning Augustine's analysis. This is perhaps understandable given that both work from a specifically Christian metaphysics, which holds God to be omnipotent, all-knowing, and supremely good.

Aquinas departs from Augustine in terms of the question motivating his analysis of evil.[11] Whereas Augustine tries to account for the *origins* of evil, Aquinas is not so much concerned with this issue (although he does tackle it) as with trying to account for the existence of evil within a monotheistic framework based on Church dogma. This alteration resulted from the fact that Augustine and Aquinas were writing at different historical periods and thus had different opponents and purposes. In Augustine's time, Christianity was still trying to establish itself and so had to contend with alternative metaphysical schemas. Augustine was therefore more preoccupied with establishing the primacy of Christian doctrine by reasserting a monotheistic metaphysics against the polytheism of the pagans and Manichaeans. When we reach Aquinas, Christianity has become established, at least in Western Europe, as the dominant religion and metaphysical schema upon which knowledge is based. Aquinas's main aim was not then to provide anything conceptually new to defend the primacy of Christian dogma against external alternatives, but to settle doctrinal disputes *within* the Church.

In relation to the question of evil, Aquinas identifies a variety of possible explanations before defending his own definitive doctrinal interpretation. Specifically, he holds that evil cannot be understood other than through its relationship to good, which in Christian metaphysics is identical to being and emanates from and is synonymous with God. When discussing evil's relationship to the good, Aquinas is really discussing evil's relationship to God, thereby bringing us back to the question of how evil can exist within a universe created by an all-powerful, omniscient, supremely good being.

Aquinas holds that the good is defined by universality, understood as the extent to which a thing acts as the cause of another thing. Using a governmental analogy, he explains that whereas 'the administrator of a city strives for a particular good that is the welfare of the city . . . the king, who is superior to the city administrator, strives for the universal good, namely, the security of the whole kingdom'.[12] Aquinas rejects an endless regress to this movement, claiming that it must lead to a 'first cause that is the universal cause of being'.[13] Given the connection between being and the good, there must also 'be a universal good to which we trace back all goods'.[14] With this, he links the good to a supreme universal being who is the first cause of all.

By relating the good to the universal and the latter to God, Aquinas concludes that God must be understood as that which is most universal and desirable: the supreme good. To explain what this means, he identifies three senses of the good. First, good refers to 'the very perfection of a thing',[15] in the sense that the thing fulfils its function. Thus, 'vision [is] the eyes' good and virtue the good of human beings'.[16] Second, good refers to 'the thing that has its proper function',[17] meaning that it does what it is supposed to naturally do. Third, good refers to a 'subject that has potentiality for perfection',[18] meaning that a thing is good because it can potentially become perfect in relation to how its natural being permits. For example, 'we call good, the soul that has potentiality for virtue, and eyes that have potentiality for accurate vision'.[19] Aquinas links good to perfection and perfection to the nature of the being in question to conclude that some beings are more perfect than others.

To determine this, we need to distinguish between the absolute and proper senses of 'perfection'. The former refers to the good absolutely, good in-itself, meaning that it 'has the greatest extension'.[20] In contrast, the proper sense of good refers to 'particular goods [which] have their proper perfection. For example, we call human beings good when they have the perfection proper to human beings, and eyes good when they have the perfection proper to eyes.'[21] Not all beings are absolutely good, nor does each have the same amount of goodness. Rather, the differences in the being of each entity mean that each thing is composed of a different amount of being and thus goodness.

This is important for three reasons: first, by distinguishing between good in an absolute and a proper sense Aquinas identifies a standard from which evil can be determined. Second, he follows Augustine in explaining that evil results not simply from a being having less perfection than another, but because it lacks the perfection proper to its particular being. For this reason, Jacques Maritain explains that 'evil is neither an essence nor a nature nor a form nor an act of being – evil is an absence of being; it is not mere negation, but a *privation*: the privation of the good that should be in a thing'.[22] What is evil for one species will be different from that for another. As such, there is a relativist strand within Aquinas's thinking on evil. Third, holding that God is essentially good and claiming that good and perfection are synonymous allows Aquinas to conclude that God is essentially perfect.

Whereas Augustine sought to prove God's perfection through number, specifically the unitary nature of one, Aquinas rejects this, claiming that '"one" does not include the idea of perfection, but only of indivision, which belongs to everything according to its own essence'.[23] For Aquinas, the perfection of a thing is determined by the extent to which that thing combines three moments: first, the constitution of its own being, that is, the extent to which it is perfect, meaning universal and good; second, the extent of the things added to it to ensure it operates perfectly, where fewer entails more perfection; third, the extent to which it desires an end other than itself, meaning whether it affirms the universal or not. Finite beings can have different combinations of all three, but only God fulfils all: absolute perfection belongs to Him alone; He *is* existence, meaning that whatever belongs to Him does so essentially, not accidentally; and, finally, He is not and cannot be directed to another end because He is the foundation of all.[24]

By identifying the nature of good, including its relationship to universality and perfection, and showing why God is the supremely good, universal, and perfect being, Aquinas has established the preliminaries for his account of evil.

## The Being of Evil

It is important to note that the word that Aquinas uses for evil (*malum*) is a particularly expansive one, meaning 'all that is repugnant to right reason'.[25] In many respects, his understanding of evil is closer to what we usually now associate with bad. Acknowledging that the expansiveness of the concept leads to certain ambiguities brings him to distinguish between different senses of evil. Thus, we find that *evil* in the most general sense of wrongdoing entails 'the privation of form or right order or due measure in anything';[26] *sin* refers to 'acts lacking due order or form or measure',[27] meaning that it happens when the natural order is disturbed; and *moral wrong* is a derivative of sin that occurs when the act 'is voluntary . . . and within the person's power'.[28] Thus, evil refers to any privation of the natural order; sin refers to a disorder in nature, so that, for example, 'limping itself [is] a sin';[29] and moral wrongdoing entails a more specific version of this whereby a particular action purposefully and wilfully lacks its correct form.

By claiming that sin and moral wrongdoing are derivations of the privation inherent in evil, Aquinas reveals that his conception of evil is associated with any deviation from the good inherent in the natural order of each particular being.[30] Because it is the foundation of sin and moral wrongdoing, he focuses on the possibility, meaning, and existence of the privation of being inherent in evil.

Doing so brings Aquinas to distinguish between evil-as-such, which is the epitome of evil, and evil in the sense of a property of a subject. The latter results from the former, in so far as we depend upon the essence of evil to describe a particular entity as evil.[31] Importantly, Aquinas claims that rational creatures (i.e. humans) have a special relationship to evil. While non-rational creatures can only do as nature intends and have no comprehension of the good, rational creatures comprehend the good and desire to do good. For rational creatures, therefore, it is necessary to distinguish the evil of moral wrong (*malum culpae*), also called moral evil in the tradition, from the evil of punishment (*malum poenea*), known historically as natural evil. The former entails a *voluntary* deviation from the good while the latter entails *non-voluntary* suffering resulting from a voluntary deviation from the good.[32] Thus, the evil of moral wrong lies at the foundation of the evil of punishment, while the latter 'is inflicted to restrain and rectify the wickedness of moral wrong'.³³ Because of its foundational role, Aquinas concludes that moral wrong 'has more of the character of evil than punishment has'.³⁴

This conclusion is supported by four further arguments: first, moral wrong is an active movement, whereas receiving punishment is passive. As an active movement, moral wrongdoing requires a prior readiness to commit an act of evil, meaning that the will that does it is already open to the possibility of evil. The moral wrongdoer has a closer affinity to evil-as-such than the individual who passively and non-voluntarily suffers punishment.³⁵ Second, while moral wrongdoing and punishment both separate the human from God, the moral wrongdoer does so in a way that is 'contrary to the union of charity whereby [an individual] will[s] the good of God himself as he is in himself'.³⁶ Moral wrongdoing entails the individual voluntarily turning away from the charity that marks the defining essential characteristic of God. Punishment, in contrast, merely prevents individuals from enjoying the relationship with God. The voluntary turning away from God constitutive of moral wrongdoing is, therefore, 'worse than the separation involved in punishment'.³⁷ Third, because it emanates from God, who is supremely good, the evil of punishment is always associated with the good because it reaffirms the good against the wrong of evil.³⁸ And fourth, because God is supremely good, the punishment inflicted to correct moral wrongdoing is always the least amount necessary to do so. There is, in other words, a control and purpose to punishment that are lacking from the disorder of moral wrongdoing.³⁹ By tentatively suggesting that evil-as-punishment is divinely inspired and orientated towards the good, Aquinas points to the possibility that a form of evil exists in the world out of divine necessity. With this, he sets the scene for later theodicies which claim that all forms of evil are divinely ordained and constitutive of the divine plan.

## Evil in the Good

Aquinas continues the Augustinian tradition by insisting that evil entails the absence of good. Because the good is synonymous with being and evil is the contrary of the good, evil cannot 'signif[y] being, or any form of nature. [Rather,] by the name of evil is signified the absence of good.'⁴⁰ This can be understood to mean that evil signifies the negation or privation of good.

In the *Summa Theologiae*, Aquinas explains that while evil implies the absence of good, 'not every absence of good is evil'.⁴¹ Absence in the sense of negativity is not evil because, if it were, 'it would follow that what does not exist is evil, and also that everything would be evil, through not having the good belonging to something else; for instance, a man would be evil who had not the swiftness of the roe, or the strength of a lion'.[42] If negation were a sufficient condition of evil then every being, simply by virtue of being finite, would, in some sense, lack something and so be evil. Because every species of being is defined by a different kind of perfection, this difference alone is insufficient for evil to occur.

To understand what evil is for each species requires that we understand what good is for each species: 'We need to understand in different ways the good proper to animals and the good proper to human beings and the good of horses and the good of oxen and we need to say the same about the contrary evils.'[43] Herbert McCabe explains that, for Aquinas, 'a thing is good if it achieves the perfection that is possible and proper for it, and evil if it fails in this achievement'.[44]

Aquinas's account of evil combines, therefore, universal and relative aspects: universally speaking, evil arises from a privation of the good, but what a privation of the good entails is relative to the natural being of each kind of being. As such, 'we should understand that only the deficiency of a good that nature has designed for something to possess, not every sort of deficiency, has the character of evil. And so there is no deficiency in the inability of human beings to fly, and hence neither moral wrong nor punishment.'[45] Similarly, 'not having eyes is not evil for a stone'.[46]

This is linked to an issue that caused Augustine some trouble: whether the movement away from the good is one towards nothing or whether it entails a movement to a lesser form of good (= being) than that which naturally defines the being. Augustine vacillates on this issue, at times, especially in his earlier formulations, appearing to claim the former, at other times the latter. Ultimately, Aquinas accepts both options, in so far as he identifies two distinct types of privation: privation in the sense of a lesser form of being and privation in the sense of the annihilation of being.

Regarding the first sense, Aquinas claims that the turning away from the good entails a movement to a *lesser form of being*, explaining that 'sin is "nothing" in the way in which human beings in sinning become nothing, not indeed in such a way that they become nothing itself, but that they, as sinners, are deprived of a good, and the privation of itself is a nonbeing in the subject'.[47] Aquinas also claims that 'although evil always lessens good ... it never wholly consumes it; and thus, while good ever remains, nothing can be wholly and perfectly bad'.[48] While a being exists, the relationship between being and good means that the good must also exist. As such, pure evil is not possible for an existing being.

Regarding the second sense of privation, Aquinas introduces the notion of 'pure privation',[49] which is linked to 'darkness, which leaves no light, and death, which leaves nothing of life'.[50] Pure privation entails a form of privation that does not simply lessen the perfection of being, but *annihilates* it.

Both forms of privation are, however, defined from and so are parasitic on the good. For this reason, Aquinas rejects the notion that evil is opposed to the good to claim that evil is *contrary* to good.[51] This is a very subtle difference, but it is an important one. If evil is opposed to the good, Aquinas holds that evil is understood to be, in some sense, separated from the good. This, however, risks establishing a metaphysical duality between the two that would undermine God's omnipotence. Evil as the contrary of good, however, is perceived to overcome this problem because the notion holds that evil is always defined relationally from the good. While evil is different from the good, it is never separated from the good. Rather, 'there is evil in good',[52] although 'as a privation and not as an entity'.[53] This does not mean that the good is a hollowed-out whole with evil existing within it. Evil is an absence 'in' good resulting from a privation of the natural being of an entity.[54] Evil is, in many respects, a failing of the good.

Furthermore, whereas good is unitary, in so far as a being either does or does not have the perfection naturally defining it, evil admits of degrees. The greater the privation of the good, the greater the evil, until, at its most extreme, it entails absolute evil and the annihilation of the good constitutive of pure privation. As such, the good–evil relationship is one of (1) rupture between good and evil – it is this that permits a notion of 'absolute' evil divorced from all good, and (2) continuum within evil based on the extent of the privation of the natural good inherent in each being. This logical structure brings Aquinas to explain that 'it is plain that fault has more evil in it than pain'[55] because the former is opposed 'to the fulfilment of the divine will'[56] whereas 'the evil of pain takes away the creature's good'.[57] Importantly, the extent of the privation is not defined from evil-as-such, which would posit evil as something opposed to the good. It depends on the extent to which it entails a turning away from the good naturally adhering to each being.

There are, however, at least, three problems with this understanding: first, it depends upon each entity being defined by a natural state of being. There is, in other words, no becoming at the essential, ontological level. Each entity is defined in an essential way and if a part of that essential form is missing, the being is said to be evil. This essentialist ontology will increasingly be challenged.

Second, if pure evil is only a possibility for a being that has no being, it is difficult to see both how it exists and why it is a problem. After all, how can pure evil exist if it is possible only for a being that lacks all being? As neither an act nor a state of being, it appears that evil-as-such is not an existential possibility for actual, existing beings, but a descriptive term that (presumably only) delineates the moral status of those no longer living.

This brings us to the third issue with Aquinas's formulation: it is so broad that any action that goes against the natural state of being of each entity is considered evil. Suffering amputation of a human arm, for example, is defined as an evil, rather than simply being a misfortune or, perhaps, even a necessary event. Indeed, the duality inherent in Aquinas's understanding of privation leads to a fundamental ambiguity regarding death. For a finite being, death must, by definition, be a part of its natural being. Because it is part of its natural being, death cannot entail a privation of being and so cannot entail an evil. But Aquinas's notion of pure privation claims exactly that: death, as the pure absence of life, entails the absolute absence of the good and so is synonymous with the pure privation of evil-as-such. While this may be thought to entail a contradiction, it does confirm Aquinas's claim that evil exists 'in' the good and, as such, is always related to the being synonymous with the good.

The issue that arises at this stage is whether it is possible to characterise 'evil in such a way that it is not a positive reality in itself, while still being real'.[58] One of the problems that arose from Augustine's claim that evil entails a lack of being is that it seems to undermine the seriousness of evil. If evil is not a 'thing', why should we take it seriously? Does it actually do anything? How can we talk of that which has no being?

Aquinas's response depends on a subtle, and often ignored, distinction, between substance and existence: evil exists, but not as a substance.[59] To account for this, Aquinas introduces the notion of *conceptual* being, which, while never defined, appears to correspond to a non-substantial, yet existent, phenomenon. We find then that 'evil is a conceptual being and not a real [i.e. substantial] being, since evil is something in the intellect and not an entity'.[60] By positing evil as a conceptual, rather than substantial, being, Aquinas means to describe how evil comes into existence without having a definitive or substantial form. As a conceptual being, evil is 'real' and so must be taken seriously. But it is not 'real' in the sense of being a substance.

## The Causes of Evil

Because the good is the ground of evil, it might be thought that it directly causes evil. To explain why, Aquinas distinguishes between intrinsic and accidental causes, with the former describing an essential link to that which emanates from them and the latter entailing an indirect or unintended causal relation, before concluding that the good can cause evil accidentally but not intrinsically.

This is supported by five arguments: first, intrinsic causation presupposes a relationship between beings and, as such, cannot apply to evil, which lacks substantial being. Second, 'effects that have an intrinsic cause are effects that their cause aims to bring about'.[61] Evil is never intentionally brought about and so does not qualify for an intrinsic cause. Rather, evil is caused accidentally by a misunderstanding of the good. For example, 'it seems good to the adulterer that he enjoy sense pleasure, and he commits adultery for that reason'.[62] However, Christian dogma rejects the notion that the good is synonymous with sensory pleasure, with the consequence that the evil of adultery results not from the good *per se* but from a misunderstanding (i.e. that bodily pleasure is good) of the good. Third, Aquinas holds that every intrinsic effect 'resembles its cause in some way',[63] which can only occur because causation is bound to substantial being. The problem is that evil has conceptual, not substantial, being and so cannot resemble something else. Fourth, Aquinas explains 'that every intrinsic cause has a sure and fixed ordination to its effect'.[64] There is, in other words, a strict order between cause and effect. But evil has no ordination; 'it' 'results when ordination is neglected'.[65] As such, evil cannot have an intrinsic cause. Nevertheless, Aquinas does admit that evil exists in something as a privation and so must have a cause 'in some way'.[66] The difficulty is that, as a privation of good, evil is not a necessary part of the order of being and, as such, the cause of it cannot be the same as the causality of being. To overcome this, Aquinas claims that 'evil has a cause, but only by accident'.[67] Accidental causation emanates from that which exists intrinsically. For example, it may be the case that an action that intends the good accidentally causes some other privation that counts as an evil when trying to bring about this good. Aquinas concludes that only the good is linked to intrinsic causality. Fifth, 'intrinsic causes produce things like themselves'.[68] Just as good can only have the good as its intrinsic effect, being can only have being as its intrinsic effect. Evil as both contrary to the good and the privation of being cannot, therefore, be caused by the good (= being). Aquinas's conclusion is that, because the good is the intrinsic cause of things, but evil is not part of the intrinsic order, evil is caused by the good, but only accidentally.

There are two ways in which this occurs, depending on whether the good that causes evil is deficient or accidental. Aquinas claims that the former can be understood through the relationship between semen and the production of what he calls 'monsters'.[69] Whereas semen, as the procreator of being, is normally good, Aquinas claims that it is possible for semen to undergo 'a source of mutation, which induces a quality contrary to the quality required for the right disposition of the semen'.[70] He concludes that this mutation is a privation of the semen, which, far from being an evil as his theory of evil would seem to warrant, is a deficient good. As such, the 'monster'[71] that results is caused not by evil but by a good that is, in some way, deficient. In contrast, good accidentally causes evil when its actions aim at the good, but, in the fulfilment of that good, an evil arises. Aquinas gives the example of fire, which intends to 'induce the form of fire in matter',[72] but, in so doing, 'necessarily involves the destruction of water'.[73] In trying to fulfil its intrinsic cause, fire accidentally causes the evil that is the destruction of water. As such, good accidentally causes evil.

So far Aquinas has discussed the ways that the good can cause evil. At this point, he turns to the question of whether the good is responsible for moral wrong. To do so, he notes, following Augustine, that moral wrong is only possible for rational creatures that have free will. Whereas the evil that results from the everyday interactions of natural beings is unintentional and beyond the control of those beings, the free will of rational beings means that each is free to affirm or reject the impressions it receives from natural being. Hence, ultimately, 'man is master of his actions',[74] although Aquinas also accepts that moral decisions are decisions about natural being. They are, therefore, dependent on and, to a degree, influenced by external factors; namely, circumstances, the Devil, and God.

Aquinas explains that circumstances impact on sin in numerous ways. For example, they may 'alter the species of sin [and/or] make sins more serious'.[75] Furthermore, circumstances define whether an act is to be considered morally significant. Aquinas gives the example of picking up straw from the ground to show contempt to another or the giving of alms within specific situations 'to gain human praise'.[76] More importantly, he recognises that 'the act to which a circumstance is added may be generically evil, and the circumstance adds a species of malice to the act (as when a person steals a sacred object)'.[77]

Aquinas's point is that in-themselves certain acts are not morally right or wrong; it is only when their circumstances are taken into consideration that their moral worth becomes apparent. This occurs because the circumstance introduces something into the act that contributes to or contradicts reason. The former means the act becomes a good one, the latter that it becomes a sin. For example,

> taking a great amount of something describes nothing contrary to reason. But taking a great amount of someone else's property describes something

more contrary to reason than taking a small amount, and so the circumstance of quantity makes the sin of theft more serious inasmuch as quantity determines the extent of the circumstance that specifies the sin.[78]

This is not to say that Aquinas rejects the notion that some things are absolutely morally wrong. He is merely pointing out that taking into consideration the context within which an act is committed is key to determining whether *some* acts are morally wrong, and, indeed, can contribute to the determination of how much moral wrong an act entails. However, while Aquinas recognises that circumstances are important to understanding evil, they are a second order phenomenon dependent upon an evil act. This act requires that the will choose to undertake a morally wrong act; an action that Aquinas explains through a cosmic struggle between God and the Devil.

In accordance with Christian dogma, Aquinas understands that God is omnipotent, all-knowing, and supremely good; He is the foundation of being from which all things emanate. Because evil entails a privation of being, 'it' does not emanate from God, who also cannot do evil because evil entails a turning away from Him. If God were to try to turn away from Himself, it would require an action on His part, which would reaffirm God and, by extension, the good.[79]

However, whereas God cannot do evil, it may be thought that He can cause evil. Returning to the distinction between efficient and accidental causes, which are now named first and second order causes, Aquinas explains that, while God is the efficient first cause of existence in the sense that He creates the world, He is not necessarily the accidental secondary cause of all that exists. The idea is somewhat complicated, but, very simply, Aquinas is distinguishing those actions and things that God directly causes (first order efficient causation) from those that result indirectly (second order accidental causation) from His actions. Aquinas holds that God does not directly cause evil because He is good and cannot be held to be responsible for evils that result from second order accidental causes, in so far as He did not directly will them.[80]

This conclusion seems, however, to be in tension with God's omnipotence, which requires that God be responsible for everything that occurs in the world. Augustine gets round this problem by implicitly relying on a modified deism whereby God creates the world, but does not subsequently adhere to every action in it. Aquinas, on the contrary, explicitly holds that God permeates His creation at all moments and so looks to an alternative explanation based on an analysis of causation. Specifically, he claims that God is expressed through each thing differently according to the particular being of each species. Thus, 'the movement from the first mover is not received in all moveable things in only one way but received in each kind of moveable thing in its own way'.[81] For example, God causes inanimate things to move differently from animate things. Aquinas also holds that each thing reacts to God in different ways, with this reaction being independent of God. Thus, if each thing is predisposed to God, 'the aim of the first mover results. But if something is not properly disposed or fit to receive the causal movement of the first mover, imperfect action results.'[82] This deficiency is, however, due not to God, but to the thing moved not being predisposed to God.

Furthermore, Aquinas points out that the exercise of free will must, by definition, be distinct from God and so accepts the Augustinian point that there are lacunae in God's actions in the world. As such, God 'can incline the will to whatever he should will',[83] but cannot cause sin. While it may be thought that this calls into question God's omnipotence, Aquinas understands omnipotence in a particular manner: although God is everywhere at once, He is not the efficient cause of all. Human free will means that there are some things that must remain beyond His power. Moral evil is, therefore, a consequence of human, not divine, will, and must be corrected through (the evil of) divine punishment. With this, Aquinas accepts that God causes evil as punishment, which, despite its name, is, in fact, ultimately a good, but rejects the notion that God causes moral evil, which is a consequence of human free will.

Importantly, while the individual may choose to simply turn away from God, Aquinas notes that he may also do so because of the actions of the Devil, who spreads 'wicked desires'[84] and uses 'vapors and fluids'[85] to trick individuals away from God. Like God, however, the Devil is not the efficient cause of evil, but merely manipulates the environment to incite the human will to do evil.

On Aquinas's telling, therefore, moral evil results from a complex interaction of different factors, including the goodness of God, the temptations of the Devil, circumstances, and free will. Ultimately, however, the responsibility for committing moral evil lies with the individual's free will. Thus, while 'sense pleasure moves the will to adultery and influences it to delight in such pleasure contrary to the ordination of reason and God's law',[86] the will that acquiesces is one that has chosen to proceed 'without using the rule of reason or God's law'.[87] There is, in other words, no natural necessity why the sensory pleasures should be followed. The immoral act requires the external stimulus gained from sensory experience *and* an act of free will to realise it. By accepting that the socio-natural circumstances of the human shape its wilful decision, Aquinas argues that evil is linked to factors other than the will, to an extent not found in Augustine. With this, Aquinas brings the natural world into analyses of evil.

## The Natural Body and Original Sin

Whereas Augustine privileges the unchangeable soul against the changeable body, there is no extended discussion of this in his writings. Aquinas develops this relationship in much greater detail. Even if the general conclusion matches that of his predecessor, namely that evil is associated with a privileging of sensual pleasure over God, the arguments used to support it are subtly different. This is clearly seen in Aquinas's conception of the role that the material body plays in defining human being.

Aquinas understands Augustine to claim that the soul was created prior to the body, but holds that, in fact, this 'is quite impossible [because] if the soul is united to the body as its form, and is naturally a part of human nature ... it is clear that God made the first things in their perfect natural state, as their species required'.[88] For Aquinas, the human being is composed of an incorporeal soul *and* material flesh and bones. It is not possible to have one without the other.[89] This entwinement is, however, simply asserted without being explained.

By thinking of the soul–body relationship in terms of entwinement, Aquinas recognises that corporeality is a key component of human being and is also crucial to the manifestation of the soul.[90] Because the soul lives on after the body dies, the soul subsists; but it only exists in 'substantial form'[91] when entwined with a body. There are two aspects to this: first, the soul is that which actualises the form of the body. And, second, the soul is the motive power that moves the body.[92] These two moments are entwined so that the soul and body generate the human together.[93]

This is a substantial innovation with regard to thinking of the soul–body relationship that, by extension, alters the analysis of evil. If the soul and body are distinct and evil results from the actions of the former as this is manifested through the will, the body becomes largely irrelevant to further discussion or, as it was for Augustine, the source of evil that has to be denied. If, however, the soul and body are entwined, the body gains in importance. It is not simply the case that the soul is good and the body evil; a subtler understanding of both aspects and their relationship is called for.

Aquinas tries to achieve this by *explicitly* calling greater attention to the body's form, distinguishing between various ways in which the body's needs and desires can influence moral judgement, and, in so doing, demonstrating that the soul *and* the body must be engaged with to understand the nature of evil. It is not, in other words, simply the case that, through its physical desires, the body is the source of evil. Human being, as a composition of soul and body, has, by nature, physical desires that must be satiated for it to exist. Not all physical desires are, therefore, contrary to the good; some, fulfilled in the correct manner, are actually necessary for the good.

David Kelsey explains that because Aquinas holds that the human body is a creation of God that initially exists in a state of perfection as defined by human being, he offers a 'sacramental' view of the body that sees it as being, in the quoted words of Benedict Ashley, a 'mirror of the Creator'.[94] This is a logical consequence of Aquinas's claim that being is good, emanates from God, and is defined by differing degrees of perfection. As a creation of God, the human body is, indeed, a good. But we must recognise that this celebratory aspect in Aquinas is also accompanied by a profound wariness about the human being and nature in general.

While he does not criticise and reject the body in the way that Augustine does, Aquinas remains suspicious about the natural body, as evidenced by his claim that it is created by God 'from the slime of the earth'.[95] This entails both a description of the unformed mass that was, according to Christian doctrine, sculpted by God into the determinate forms we know, and a moral judgement about the worth of nature. As such, Aquinas *recognises* that nature must be contended with in analyses of human existence, but does not fully *celebrate* this. This also applies to his understanding of evil.

The link between the human body and evil is seen from two sources: first, Aquinas's claim that each body has its own determinate nature. This, it will be remembered, is important to his account of privation, which results not from lack *per se*, but from a lack of that which naturally belongs to the species.[96] What counts as a privation, and hence evil, differs for each kind of being. It is also seen from his analysis of the way in which Original Sin is transmitted between the generations. Original Sin is integral to Christian orthodoxy and explains how sin not only enters the human condition, but also continues to adhere to it. In discussing it, and indeed making it a central part of his thinking on evil, Aquinas demonstrates the extent to which his account of evil is constrained and conditioned by Christian doctrine. Indeed, he even holds that the doctrine of Original Sin is needed to justify salvation by, and hence belief in, Christ.[97]

To account for Original Sin, Aquinas explains that the human is both an individual being and a member of a species and so combines singularity with universality.[98] The doctrine of Original Sin refers to the universal aspect which subsequently impacts on and determines the being of the individual. Aquinas claims that, initially, 'God had bestowed a supernatural gift, namely, original justice, on the first human being at his creation.'[99] Original justice, on Aquinas's telling, means that 'human being's reason was subject to God, and his lower powers subject to his reason, and his body to his soul'.[100] Divinely inspired order ruled at both the universal and individual levels of human existence. Human flesh in this natural condition was good and only became corrupted after the first human sinned.[101] There was a time when evil was not part of the human condition. For Adam, evil was not, initially, possible.[102] No human, other than Christ, has ever lived in that state of sinless perfection since.[103] However, when the first human sinned by his free choice, he 'lost the gift in the same habitual condition in which he received it, namely, for himself and all his descendants'.[104]

Aquinas notes that the first sin was composed of two different, but related, elements: a formal element, which entailed the 'turning away from the immutable good',[105] and a material element, which entailed a 'turning toward a transient good',[106] namely concupiscence, which is understood to be '[O]riginal [S]in materially'.[107] Aquinas's comments on concupiscence are, however, ambiguous.

Having identified that it is synonymous with Original Sin, he elsewhere claims that 'concupiscence is not a greater evil than moral wrong',[108] and that 'pleasure and everything else in human affairs should be measured and regulated by the rule of reason and God's law'.[109] Concupiscence has, therefore, a troubled place in Aquinas's account. On the one hand, it is the material manifestation of Original Sin and so is directly linked to evil, which would appear to mean that it should be rejected. But, on the other hand, Aquinas recognises that it entails a lesser form of evil than moral wrong and, as long as it is satisfied in accordance with ordered reason and God's law, is accepted as necessary to the perpetuation of human being.

By claiming that Original Sin is transmitted through sexual intercourse, Aquinas explains that the privation of Original Sin is passed through the flesh. This depends on his insistence that the body and soul are naturally entwined. Because the human being has a universal and individual aspect manifested through the entwinement of its soul and body, Aquinas understands that whatever happens to the soul at the universal level is infused into the structure of the body. The evil attached to the human soul by the Fall from original justice is, then, passed along through procreation. Importantly, the 'privation is due to the flesh propagated by Adam both regarding the material substance of the flesh and regarding the seminal source of the flesh'.[110] While Aquinas is aware that there are different moral forms of sex, with ordered, marital sex, in which the passions do not overcome each individual, privileged over lust-driven, non-marital sex, he claims that sex has a unique relation to evil because it is the means through which the privation of Original Sin is transmitted. Original Sin as the transcendental condition of an evil act is, therefore, transmitted via natural means: the body.

## Concluding Remarks

This does, however, seem to generate a problem in so far as Aquinas appears to be caught in a bind between the non-corporeality of Original Sin and his insistence that it is passed on. For it to be passed on, it must, in some sense, have substantial being. This, however, would mean that Original Sin would have the characteristic of being, which is explicitly rejected by Aquinas.

Aquinas appears to be aware of this issue and explains that 'the corruption in the flesh is indeed actually physical, although moral in its orientation and power'.[111] This is underpinned by the notion that morality entails an ahistoric, non-material essence that is transmitted through semen. We find, therefore, that 'the sin of our first parent deprived his flesh of the power to be capable of ejecting semen that would propagate original justice in others'.[112] All semen since then has been marked by a deficiency that prevents original justice from being attained. This returns us to our original question: how can Original Sin entail the absence of being, but be passed on via the substantial being of semen?

Aquinas's solution is innovative. Having distinguished between substantial and conceptual being, he identifies the existence of a third form of being, termed *virtual* being, to explain that 'the corruption of [O]riginal [S]in is virtually, not actually, in the semen in the same way that human nature is virtually in the semen'.[113] Original Sin is not a thing and so cannot be pointed to or witnessed in semen. It is a virtual presence that adheres to semen and is passed along through sexual intercourse. The extent to which this virtual possibility is actualised depends, however, on the will of each individual.

With this, Aquinas's general response to the problem of evil continues Augustine's free-will defence, although he does introduce significant conceptual nuances and innovations to the metaphysical understanding underpinning it. As we will see in coming chapters, however, these metaphysical underpinnings were increasingly challenged as we move beyond the Middle Ages, with this having dramatic implications for thinking on evil.

# Notes

1. John Marenbom, *Pagans and Philosophers: The Problem of Paganism from Augustine to Leibniz* (Princeton: Princeton University Press, 2015), p. 67.
2. Ibid. p. 67.
3. Ibid. p. 67.
4. See, for example, F. E. Peters, *Aristotle and the Arabs: The Aristotelian Tradition in Islam* (New York: New York University Press, 1968).
5. Paul O'Grady, *Aquinas's Philosophy of Religion* (Basingstoke: Palgrave Macmillan, 2014), p. 31.
6. Jan A. Aertsen, 'Aquinas's Philosophy in its Historical Setting', p. 15, in *The Cambridge Companion to Aquinas*, ed. Norman Kretzmann and Eleonore Stump (Cambridge: Cambridge University Press, 1993), pp. 12–38.
7. On Aquinas's relationship to Aristotle see the collection of essays published in Gilles Emery and Matthew Levering (eds), *Aristotle in Aquinas's Theology* (Cambridge: Cambridge University Press, 2015). For a detailed study of Aquinas and Aristotle on the good, see Mary M. Keys, *Aquinas, Aristotle, and the Promise of the Common Good* (Cambridge: Cambridge University Press, 2008).
8. For a discussion of Aquinas's relationship to Islamic (Avicenna) and Jewish (Maimonides) thinkers, see David B. Burrell, 'Aquinas and Islamic and Jewish Thinkers', in *The Cambridge Companion to Aquinas*, ed. Norman Kretzmann and Eleonore Stump (Cambridge: Cambridge University Press, 1993), pp. 60–84.
9. Thomas Aquinas, *On Evil*, trans. Richard Regan (Oxford: Oxford University Press, 2003).
10. Thomas Aquinas, *Summa Theologiae*, trans. Fathers of the English Dominican Province (Einsiedeln: Benziger Bros, 1947).
11. Aquinas discusses the metaphysics of God in the *Summa Theologiae*, PI, Q2–26. For a general summary of Aquinas's metaphysics, with particular reference to his notions of being, essence, and causality, see Brian Davies, *Thomas Aquinas on God and Evil* (Oxford: Oxford University Press, 2011), pp. 19–28.
12. Aquinas, *On Evil*, Q1, A1.
13. Ibid. Q1, A1.
14. Ibid. Q1, A1.
15. Ibid. Q1, A2.
16. Ibid. Q1, A2.
17. Ibid. Q1, A2.
18. Ibid. Q1, A2.
19. Ibid. Q1, A2.
20. Ibid. Q1, A2.
21. Ibid. Q1, A2.
22. Jacques Maritain, *St. Thomas and the Problem of Evil*, trans. Gordon Andison (Milwaukee: Marquette University Press, 1942), p. 1.

23. Aquinas, *Summa Theologiae*, PI, Q6, A3, RO1.
24. Ibid. PI, Q6, A3.
25. Ibid. PI–II, Q18, A9, RO2.
26. Aquinas, *On Evil*, Q2, A2.
27. Ibid. Q2, A2.
28. Ibid. Q2, A2.
29. Ibid. Q2, A2.
30. For a discussion of the relationship between privation in Aquinas and the Christian tradition more generally, see Patrick Lee, 'The Goodness of Creation, Evil, and Christian Teaching', *The Thomist*, 64, 2000, pp. 239–69.
31. Aquinas, *On Evil*, Q1, A1.
32. Ibid. Q1, A4.
33. Ibid. Q1, A5, RO7.
34. Ibid. Q1, A5.
35. Ibid. Q1, A1.
36. Ibid. Q1, A1, RO3.
37. Ibid. Q1, A1, RO3.
38. Ibid. Q1, A1.
39. Ibid. Q1, A1.
40. Aquinas, *Summa Theologiae*, PI, Q48, A1.
41. Ibid. PI, Q48, A3.
42. Ibid. PI, Q48, A3.
43. Aquinas, *On Evil*, Q2, A4.
44. Herbert McCabe, *God and Evil in the Theology of St Thomas Aquinas*, ed. Brian Davies (London: Continuum, 2010), p. 87.
45. Aquinas, *On Evil*, Q1, A4, RO10.
46. Ibid. Q11, A5, RO1.
47. Ibid. Q2, A1, RO4.
48. Aquinas, *Summa Theologiae*, PI, Q49, A3.
49. Aquinas, *On Evil*, Q2, A9.
50. Ibid. Q2, A9.
51. Ibid. Q11, A4, RO3.
52. Ibid. Q1, A2.
53. Ibid. Q1, A1, RO20.
54. Aquinas, *Summa Theologiae*, PI, Q48, A5, RO1.
55. Ibid. PI, Q48, A6.
56. Ibid. PI, Q48, A6.
57. Ibid. PI, Q48, A6.
58. O'Grady, *Aquinas's Philosophy of Religion*, p. 124.
59. Aquinas, *On Evil*, Q1, A1, RO19.
60. Ibid. Q1, A1, RO20.
61. Ibid. Q1, A3.
62. Ibid. Q1, A3.

63. Ibid. Q1, A3.
64. Ibid. Q1, A3.
65. Ibid. Q1, A3.
66. Ibid. Q1, A3.
67. Ibid. Q1, A3.
68. Ibid. Q1, A3.
69. Ibid. Q1, A3.
70. Ibid. Q1, A3.
71. Ibid. Q1, A3.
72. Ibid. Q1, A3.
73. Ibid. Q1, A3.
74. Aquinas, *Summa Theologiae*, PI–II, Q21, A3, RO2.
75. Aquinas, *On Evil*, Q2, A7.
76. Ibid. Q2, A7.
77. Ibid. Q2, A7.
78. Ibid. Q2, A7.
79. Ibid. Q3, A1.
80. Ibid. Q3, A2.
81. Ibid. Q3, A2.
82. Ibid. Q3, A2.
83. Ibid. Q3, A3.
84. Ibid. Q3, A3, RO2.
85. Ibid. Q3, A5.
86. Ibid. Q1, A3.
87. Ibid. Q1, A3.
88. Aquinas, *Summa Theologiae*, PI, Q90, A4.
89. Ibid. P1, Q75, A4; P1, Q76, A7. For an interesting discussion of Aquinas's conception of human being, see Jason T. Eberl, 'Aquinas on the Nature of Human Being', *The Review of Metaphysics*, 58:2, 2004, pp. 333–65.
90. Aquinas, *Summa Theologiae*, PI, Q76, A1.
91. Ibid. PI, Q76, A6.
92. Ibid. PI, Q76, A6.
93. Ibid. PI, Q91, A4, RO3.
94. David Kelsey, 'Aquinas and Barth on the Human Body', *The Thomist*, 50:4, 1986, pp. 643–89 (p. 643).
95. Aquinas, *Summa Theologiae*, PI, Q91, A1.
96. Ibid. PI, Q75, A2.
97. Aquinas, *On Evil*, Q4, A6.
98. Ibid. Q4, A1.
99. Ibid. Q4, A1.
100. Ibid. Q4, A1.
101. Ibid. Q4, A1, RO6.
102. Ibid. Q7, A7.

103. Ibid. Q4, A7, RO6.
104. Ibid. Q4, A1.
105. Ibid. Q4, A2.
106. Ibid. Q4, A2.
107. Ibid. Q4, A4, RO2.
108. Ibid. Q1, A5, RO20.
109. Ibid. Q1, A3.
110. Ibid. Q4, A1.
111. Ibid. Q4, A1, RO9.
112. Ibid. Q4, A1, RO6.
113. Ibid. Q4, A1, RO12.

# 4

# Descartes and the Evil of Error

From the High Middle Ages (eleventh to thirteenth centuries), through the Late Middle Ages (fourteenth to sixteenth centuries), to the period characterised as Modern in philosophy (sixteenth to eighteenth centuries),[1] a number of crucial epistemic alterations took place that fundamentally transformed, amongst other things, how God and the individual and, by extension, evil were conceptualised. These developments contributed to an increasing theological and political interest in the question of evil.

Specifically, the question of evil came to the fore as a consequence of the increasing entrenchment of the Roman Catholic Church. To cement its dominance, it waged war against alternatives, which were cast in the role of evil threats. The most famous consequence of this was the Spanish Inquisition. This *political* war on sections of the population deemed to be evil was supported by substantial *theological* interest in the question of Satan and demons that gave rise to what later became known as demonology and Satanism.[2] This obsession with the metaphysical figures of Satan and demons was, somewhat paradoxically, accompanied by a growing interest in the natural world, which needed to be explained empirically rather than through recourse to metaphysical theological speculation.[3] The theistic and naturalist explanations existed in an uneasy tension, at first continuing to give primacy to the former before gradually moving to privilege the latter. This tension did, however, give rise to an important intellectual development regarding the position of the human.

Again, the historical trajectory is complex, but gradually the realisation arose that if any demonstration of God's existence is premised on human knowledge about God, the focus should be on the mediating aspect – the human – through which God is reached. However, because human being is limited, any conclusion arrived at can, potentially, be wrong. Resolving this issue required a fundamental alteration in the underlying epistemic framework. Rather than simply believe in God's existence and subsequently engage in rational discussion about His attributes, modes, substance, and so on, thinking became far more sceptical and this-worldly. It was no longer considered sufficient to simply base truths on faith. Truth-claims had to be rationally and empirically verifiable. Only this lent them credibility. This led to a greater focus on sceptical questioning of, as opposed to simple blind obedience to, authority, past truths, and/or faith.

It was also accompanied and re-enforced by the rise of what Charles Taylor calls 'inwardness',[4] whereby the 'inner' aspects of human being, such as emotions, attitudes, and reflexivity, were discovered and emphasised. Instead of a passive being existing in a cosmos created by an all-powerful God, the human was understood to be an individuated being, something distinct from its surroundings, autonomous, and in control of itself and its life. This had implications for ethics. With Augustine, as with Aquinas, there was recognition of the inner life of humanity, but this was guided by God, who was understood to exist 'externally' to individuals. The individual had to choose to follow His external moral law. Renaissance humanism and modern scepticism altered this.[5] Rather than focus on individual subjectivity directed by external moral sources, much greater moral responsibility was placed on the shoulders of individuals; a responsibility that re-enforced the turn to naturalism, epistemological scepticism, and subjectivity.[6]

These historical modifications find their most cogent and radical expression in the thought of René Descartes. His *Meditations on First Philosophy*,[7] first published in 1641, insist that we need to question all foundations to ground knowledge in the realm of certainty, not mere faith. Truth requires 'a mind ... completely free from preconceived opinions and which can easily detach itself from involvement with the senses'.[8] Thinking must be presuppositionless, meaning that it must be based on what can be rationally defended, rather than on what is assumed, conventional, or determined by faith.

Descartes is important because, by explicitly starting from a sceptical standpoint, he takes seriously the possibility that God may not be the ground of all existence. It is only once this foundation has been proven that the question of evil can be engaged with. He confronts these issues across his *oeuvre*, but the most famous and important treatments are found in the *Meditations*, specifically the first four meditations, which outline the problem motivating his analysis (First Meditation), the methodology to be employed (Second Meditation), a first proof for God's existence (Third Meditation), and a questioning of how error is possible in a world created by an all-powerful, good deity (Fourth Meditation).

While Descartes explicitly rejects the notion that his discussion of error is linked to evil, claiming that 'I do not deal at all with sin, i.e. the error which is committed in pursuing good and evil, but only with the error that occurs in distinguishing truth from falsehood',[9] his analysis of error can be used to understand how evil arises in a world created by an all-powerful, supremely good being.[10] Gary Hatfield justifies this connection by explaining that the Fourth Meditation

> considers a problem analogous to the theological problem of evil. If God is perfectly good and can do anything, why is there evil in the world? If God is no deceiver and can do anything, why doesn't he make us so that we never fall into error at all? Yet there is evil, and we do fall into error.[11]

Whereas Descartes insists that the problem of error is epistemological, not moral, Hatfield explains that it is an epistemological problem with moral significance. Although Descartes claims that they must be separated, both Augustine and Aquinas held that error lies at the root of evil, whether this is moral evil thought in terms of individual action or natural evil thought in terms of natural events. Indeed, as noted in Chapter 1, three of the most important Judaic words associated with evil ($ḥṭ$, $psh'$, and $`awon$) entail a sense of turning away from God to follow an alternative path. There is, in other words, a long lineage in the Judaeo-Christian tradition that identifies error with a turning away from God, and this turning away from God to be at the root of evil. Descartes continues (in) this tradition.

## Meditations on First Philosophy

Descartes's *Meditations* start with the explicit aim of providing 'demonstrative proofs'[12] of the existence of God and the soul. Because knowledge based on faith is only convincing 'for us who are believers',[13] it fails to offer the stable ground and hence certainty that the existence of God would appear to warrant. Rather than be content with shoring up the 'knowledge' of believers, Descartes tacitly implies that if knowledge is to be certain, it must be clear to all. It is not sufficient to premise the existence of God on faith or authority, nor is it sufficient to start from belief in God to subsequently rationally engage with the qualities and properties of God.[14] Rather than starting from a foundational God, his innovation is to offer the possibility that God may not exist, as a precursor to showing, through the use of reason alone, that He must exist.

In so doing, Descartes rejects the notion that faith and reason, theology and philosophy, Jerusalem and Athens, are opposed to one another. Indeed, he points out that the Faculty of Theology at Paris, the most prestigious Theological Faculty at the time and to whom the Meditations are dedicated, holds that God's existence is capable of being rationally discussed, and 'all other theologians assert that the existence of God is capable of proof by natural reason'.[15] God must be capable of rational deduction given his omnipotence, meaning that it is valid to use reason to inquire into God's existence. In turn, the clarity of deductive reasoning is the only way in which non-believers can be convinced of God's existence.[16]

The purpose of Descartes's Meditations is not to prove the existence of God per se, but to inquire into the foundations of knowledge to determine if human cognition can know anything with certainty. Its starting point must be presuppositionless.[17] Only this will permit the inquiry to reach the conclusion necessitated by deductive logic, rather than the one sought by the presupposed foundation.

From this, Descartes concludes that philosophical thinking should be modelled on mathematics, specifically geometry. After all, 'in geometry everyone has been taught to accept that as a rule no proposition is put forward in a book without there being a conclusive demonstration available'.[18] 'In philosophy, by contrast, the belief is that everything can be argued either way; so few people pursue the truth, while the great majority build up their reputation for ingenuity by boldly attacking whatever is most sound.'[19]

Descartes recognises that despite Socrates' efforts, philosophy tends to be associated with sophistry, based on the need to win an argument regardless of its truth-content. Geometry is, for Descartes, different in that it is based on the truth-content alone as this is determined by deductive propositions. Philosophy must, then, be revolutionised to not only focus on the truth, but also adopt the fundamental lesson of geometry: each truth-claim must be explained by deductive propositions. Only this will provide 'proofs [that] are of such a kind that they leave no room for the possibility that the human mind will ever discover better ones'.[20] This will reveal what human cognition can be certain of and, by extension, demonstrate the foundations of knowledge.

## Presuppositionless Thinking

The First Meditation concerns the problem to be tackled and the method to be used. Having recognised that he believed in a number of falsehoods, Descartes claims 'that it was necessary ... to demolish everything completely and start again right from the foundations if I wanted to establish anything at all in the sciences that was stable and likely to last'.[21] Rather than accept certain truths based on faith, convention, or authority, *all* that he previously believed must be set aside so that questioning and thinking can be done anew. Only this will reveal what can genuinely be considered truthful.

To do so, Descartes claims that 'it will not be necessary . . . to show that all my opinions are false'.[22] Because these opinions are based on a few general principles, it will be sufficient to go straight to those foundational principles to see if they stand reason's test. If they do, the opinions that emanate from them may also be considered true.

Questioning his presuppositions brings Descartes to the relationship between the senses and truth. While common sense tells us that the senses can be trusted, Descartes points out that 'from time to time I have found that the senses deceive, and it is prudent never to trust completely those who have deceived us even once'.[23] Similarly he explains that 'there are many other beliefs about which doubt is quite impossible, even though they are derived from the senses'.[24] Descartes seems to have in mind immediate first-person experiences, such as that I am here in this particular room, dressed a particular way, writing this sentence. This experience seems so obvious that it would be madness to deny it. But we must, at least, suspend it to ensure that our inquiry is presuppositionless.

While Descartes claims that we cannot appeal to madness to call into question the knowledge gained from the senses, he does question how it is that we know that we are present at any moment and that this experience is a real one. Could it not be that the action I am engaged in is that of a dream? After all, 'my eyes are certainly wide awake when I look at this piece of paper; I shake my head and it is not asleep; as I stretch out and feel my hand I do so deliberately, and I know what I am doing'.[25] The distinctness of these actions simply would not, so Descartes initially countenances, be available if I were dreaming. As he comes to realise, however, there is no guarantee that the experience I am having now, even if it is so clear and distinct that I apparently cannot doubt it, is one in which I am awake. Indeed, as Descartes thinks about it, he explains that 'I see plainly that there are never any sure signs by means of which being awake can be distinguished from being asleep.'[26] Just because I think that I am awake does not, in fact, mean that I am.

Descartes explains how it may be that I am being tricked into something that is not true by offering us a dramatic and controversial possibility: existence is not created by 'God, who is supremely good and the source of truth, but rather some malicious demon of the utmost power and cunning [who has employed all his energies in order to deceive me'.[27] As a consequence, it is possible that my mathematical truths – although the point stands for more general ones – are created by a malicious demon who tricks us into thinking about nature in a particular, false way. Either this means that God is, in reality, evil, or there are two beings competing for dominance, with any deviation from the truth being the consequence of the actions of the malicious one.

Given that both options violate Descartes's presuppositionlessness, he claims that, at this stage, he cannot draw a conclusion, but must inquire into this question. Because he thinks that there must be a foundation for the truth, but has not yet shown that this foundation is associated with the good, he claims that he must accept and work with the hypothesis that his reality is created by a deceptive supreme being.

While this supports his argument that we should not simply trust our senses, it also establishes a conclusion – reality is created by a malicious demon – that he can and will subsequently question with the aim of proving God's existence, goodness, and omnipotence. However, by setting up his inquiry in this way, he recognises the need to (1) prove that a singular being grounds existence, (2) show that this singular being is not malicious but supremely good, and (3) demonstrate that this supremely good singular being is not responsible for the existence of the deception of error and, by extension, evil. The Third Meditation deals with (1), while the Fourth Meditation deals with (2) and (3).

## Establishing a Foundational Certainty

Having established the method of radical doubt in the First Meditation to question his received truths and existence, the Second Meditation asks whether anything can survive this radical doubt. Descartes realises that the answer is found within the question. To employ the method of doubt requires a thought, which in turn requires a being that thinks. There is, in other words, a logical movement from doubting to thinking to being that holds even if 'there is a deceiver of supreme power and cunning who is deliberately and constantly deceiving me'.[28] With this, Descartes has a first, immutable truth: I think and so I know I exist. Of course, he admits that 'I do not yet have a sufficient understanding of what this "I" is',[29] but out of the method of doubt has arisen one truth that is logically immutable: I think, therefore I am. The conclusion drawn is that he is 'in the strict sense only a thinking that thinks . . . a thinking thing'.[30]

Having identified that the method of doubt leads to the certainty that

I exist, which, in turn, gives rise to the conclusion that my essence is a thinking thing, the Third Meditation questions whether this solipsistic conclusion can be overcome. Descartes engages with whether he can be sure that anything external to him exists. This entails an investigation into the origins or foundations of the external world, which, ultimately, brings him to offer a proof of God's existence.

With this, Descartes seeks to disprove the malicious demon argument posited in the First Meditation by (1) engaging with whether there is in fact a foundational being to existence and, hence, knowledge, and, if it is found that there is, (2) determining whether it is good or evil. However, given that the inquiry cannot presuppose anything, Descartes cannot simply offer a logical proof for the existence of an external world that emanates from God; he has to show that the existence of an all-powerful God logically follows from the thinking I that was revealed in the previous Meditation.

Given that the Second Meditation revealed him to be a thinking thing, Descartes, in the Third Meditation, examines the nature of thinking itself to distinguish between *images of things*, which conform to pure ideas, and *thoughts*, where the image is accompanied by an additional reflective judgement or emotive volition.[31] Pure ideas cannot be false because, by definition, they do not refer to anything and so cannot be said to represent anything for better or worse. The same reasoning underpins the claim that emotive volitions cannot be associated with truth or falsity. They are, in other words, expressive rather than representational and so can never be associated with the judgement necessary for truth-claims. As a consequence, 'the only remaining thoughts where I must be on guard against making a mistake are judgements'.[32]

The main problem that arises when judging is determining whether 'the ideas which are in me resemble, or conform to, things located outside of me'.[33] While it may appear that Descartes is criticising the correspondence or representational model of truth, wherein it is thought that a truth-claim is valid if it accurately corresponds to or represents something outside of it, he is simply pointing out that, *at this stage* in the Meditations, it is unwarranted to focus on judgement because it has not been established that there is anything external to human cognition. To rely on the correspondence theory of truth would be to make an unwarranted metaphysical assumption. We must focus rather on the ideas that lie at the foundation of emotive volition and reflective judgement.

When we do, we find that ideas are either innate, adventitious – meaning they are external in origin – or imaginary. Given that he wants to inquire into the existence of the external world, Descartes gives preference to adventitious ideas. To do so, he appeals to nature, in the form of a natural light or impulse, and to experience to conclude that these ideas emanate from something else.[34] Descartes recognises, however, that the problems with this conclusion are that it has not been established that there is a natural light; his natural impulses have frequently pushed him 'in the wrong direction when it was a question of choosing the good',[35] thereby revealing that they cannot be trusted; and he has not established that these things have a source external to him.[36] Even if this were established, 'it would not follow that [his ideas] must resemble those things'.[37] There may, for example, be a great disparity between the idea of the thing and that which it represents.

Because this calls into question the seemingly obvious idea that there is an external world, Descartes looks for another means to proceed. He claims that ideas are distinguished by virtue of what they represent. He explains that 'undoubtedly, the ideas which represent substances to me amount to something more and, so to speak, contain within themselves more objective reality than the ideas which merely represent modes or accidents'.[38] As such, 'the idea that gives me my understanding of a supreme God, eternal, infinite, immutable, omniscient, omnipotent and creator of all things that exist apart from him, certainly has in it more objective reality than the ideas that represent finite substances'.[39]

These are complex passages that need to be unpacked by explaining the substance–attributes and formal–objective reality axes. Substance refers to the basic material that defines an individual thing. There are two types of substance for Descartes: finite substances which are partially independent, and an infinite substance defined by independence. Attributes define the individual parts of an individual substance. Put differently, substance refers to what the whole of an entity is composed of, whereas attributes describe the various parts of the substantive whole. A hierarchy is established where infinite substance is fully independent, finite substance is somewhat independent, and attributes are wholly dependent on a substance for their existence.

Formal reality is not mentioned in the passages above but is crucial to understanding objective reality. Simply put, it describes the degree of substantial independence a thing has. Frederick Broadie claims that the basic point of this distinction is to explain that 'within a logical system the formulae which do not depend upon another formulae within the system may be regarded as more fundamental to the system than those that do so depend'.[40] As such, 'whatever we can think about independently of what cannot be thought about independently of it, has more being, or, as [Descartes] says (also following a long tradition) a greater degree of reality than it'.[41] This implies that there is a hierarchy to beings based on the degree of independence (= formal reality) each has. God has the most formal reality, in so far as God is fully independent in His being, whereas humans, as a finite substance, have less formal reality, but more than the formal reality of attributes, which are always dependent on a substance. Because Descartes conflates perfection with formal reality, this hierarchy means that the more formal reality a being has, the more perfect it is.

Objective reality describes the degree of representational content an idea has. Because it represents a thing with formal reality, an idea's objective reality corresponds to the formal reality, or substantial independence, of the thing being represented.[42] For example, an idea of a horse has more objective reality than an idea of a leg because a horse is a finite substance and so has more formal reality than a leg, which is an attribute. In turn, the idea of God, as an idea of an infinite substance, must have more objective and hence formal reality than the idea of a finite substance such as a human being.

The principle driving this hierarchy is Descartes's assertion that 'it is manifest by the natural light that there must be at least as much reality in the efficient and total cause as in the effect of that cause'.[43] Two options result from this: either an effect comes from a being with the same amount of reality as it or it must have come from something with a greater amount of reality than it. An attribute, for example, can emanate from another attribute or it can emanate from a substance. Likewise a finite substance can emanate from another finite substance or an infinite substance.

While these two options present themselves, Descartes is clear that

> although one idea may perhaps originate from another, there cannot be an infinite regress here; eventually one must reach a primary idea, the cause of which will be like an archetype which contains formally [and in fact] all the reality [or perfection] which is present only objectively [or representatively] in the idea.[44]

The infinite regress, whereby a finite substance comes from another finite substance, which comes from another and so on, must, at some point, be grounded by recognising that the finite substance is an effect of a substance with more formal reality than it. In other words, to explain the ontogenesis of a finite substance requires a foundational infinite substance. This holds for both actual things and ideational things: the idea of a leg (an attribute) must have come from an idea of a finite/infinite body (substance). Similarly, an actual leg (an attribute) must have come from a finite physical substance, which, in turn, must have been caused by an infinite substance.

Importantly, 'in order for a given idea to contain such and such objective reality, it must surely derive it from some cause which contains at least as much formal reality as there is objective reality in the idea'.[45] As a representation, the objective reality of an idea must represent something, which as a thing must have a degree of formal reality. The objective reality of a human being is an idea of a finite substance, meaning that it has more objective and hence formal reality than the idea of a leg, which is an attribute. Not only are there differences in the degree of formal and objective reality of things/ideas, but ideas derive their objective reality from the amount of formal reality inherent in the thing being represented. There is, in other words, a hierarchy between formal and objective reality, with the former grounding the latter. Determining the amount of objective reality an idea has will reveal not only its existence, but also the amount of formal reality and hence the type of formal existence it has. This may not seem like much, but it means that

> if the objective reality of any of my ideas turns out to be so great that I am sure that the same reality does not reside in me, either formally or eminently, and hence that I cannot be its cause, it will necessarily follow that I am not alone in the world, but that some other thing which is the cause of this idea also exists.[46]

Given that Descartes recognises that he is a finite substance, it follows that he could create another finite substance and attribute. However, because he is finite, this would only prove the existence of finite substance. If, however, he can think of an infinite substance, which he, as a finite substance, would not be able to create, it *would* point to an infinite being and, hence, a being that, he, as a finite substance, would not be able to create. This would, in other words, mean that there was another being external to him, which would also point to the existence of an external world.

The only idea that Descartes finds that conforms to this is the idea of God, by which he means 'a substance that is infinite, [eternal, immutable,] independent, supremely intelligent, supremely powerful, and which created both myself and everything else (if anything else there be) that exists'.[47] With this, Descartes concedes that it does not seem possible that he, a finite substance, could have created such a substance. The only way that the idea of an infinite substance could be found in a finite substance would be if 'this idea proceeded from some substance which really was infinite'.[48]

Given that the formal reality principle states that an idea, in this case God, must 'derive ... from some cause which contains at least as much formal reality as there is objective reality in the idea',[49] we find that the idea of God, as the idea of an infinite substance, must have come from a being with the formal reality of an infinite substance. As a consequence, 'it must be concluded that the mere fact that I exist and have within me an idea of a most powerful being, that is, God, provides a very clear proof that God indeed exists'.[50] The final steps in the argument are to recognise that this infinite being (1) must be singular, and (2) cannot be a deceiver because deception implies an imperfection, or lack, which, if possessed, would contradict the perfection that an infinite being must be.[51] Given that there can be only one infinite substance, the fundamental tenet of monotheism is affirmed and confirmed.

## The Evil of Error

This, however, returns Descartes to the problem that continues to haunt monotheism: if there is one supremely powerful and good God, where does the evil of error emanate from? This brings back the problem of the evil demon outlined in the First Meditation. Descartes's response covers the contents of the Third and Fourth Meditations: the Third Meditation demonstrates that there is a supreme being that causes all, while the Fourth Meditation engages with whether this supreme being is good or evil. The Fourth Meditation is therefore particularly important for our purposes because it is here that Descartes specifically talks of the problem of error.

Descartes starts by claiming that the preceding analysis has shown that 'it is impossible that God should ever deceive me. For in every case of trickery or deception some imperfection is to be found.'[52] Far from being an indication of 'cleverness or power',[53] deception is related to morality in the form of 'malice or weakness';[54] characteristics that cannot belong to God, who, as the Third Meditation demonstrated, is supremely powerful. Beyond this, Descartes also claims that he knows by experience that he possesses a faculty of judgement given by God. By holding that God does not wish to deceive him, Descartes concludes that God 'surely did not give me the kind of faculty which would ever enable me to go wrong while using it correctly'.[55] The question that arises, however, is how is it possible for us to err if God creates the faculty of judgement that cannot do so?

Descartes responds with three clarifications: first, error is a privation of something rather than a thing itself and so cannot, strictly speaking, originate from God. Second, error results from human finitude, which is necessarily required by God's existence. Third, human error emanates from the relationship between the faculties of the human mind. From this, he aims to show that error is possible in a world created by an all-powerful, supremely good God, while also ensuring that God is blameless for any error that occurs.

To do so, Descartes examines the human's relationship to God. Recognising that humans have an understanding of (1) God as supremely perfect and omnipotent and (2) the idea of nothingness, Descartes concludes that humans are 'something intermediate between God and nothingness, or between supreme being and non-being'.[56] Because the supreme being is perfect, nothing that emanates from Him can be imperfect. As such, perfection adheres to human being. But, at the same time, 'in so far as I participate in nothingness or non-being, that is, in so far as I am not myself the supreme being and am lacking in countless respects, it is no wonder that I make mistakes'.[57] Because the human is linked to the imperfection of nothingness, it can also commit errors. Since error is an imperfection, it cannot emanate from God and, as such, does not have substantial form. Rather, error entails 'a defect'.[58]

The argumentation process is severely underdeveloped, but Descartes has in mind the notion that error entails a turning away from the potential to be perfect and thus describes a privation of the good. Error results not from the application of a faculty created by God, but from the misapplication of the faculty of judgement that emanates from God. It is not a defect *per se*, but rather arises from the *defective use* of the faculties that God did create. Error does not then result from God, although it is a consequence of the structures that God created.

At this point, it may be questioned why, if this is the case, God did not simply make us perfect, or, at least, create us in a way that does not err. After all, 'the more skilled the craftsman the more perfect the work produced by him; if this is so, how can anything produced by the supreme creator of all things not be complete and perfect in all respects?'[59] How could and why did God create something that entailed a lack? Why did the supremely good and perfect being not make His creation in a way that prevented the defective use of judgement? By not doing so, despite it being within God's supreme power, it appears that God is either not all-powerful or not supremely good.

Descartes offers an explanation that builds on the lessons learned from the Third Meditation to suggest that, upon reflection, 'it is no cause for surprise if I do not understand the reasons for some of God's actions'.[60] First, humans cannot know the rationale for God's actions because God is absolutely free. Whereas human cognition is determined by God, His infinite power is only constrained by itself. Therefore, 'it is impossible to imagine that anything is thought of in the divine intellect as good or true, or worthy of belief or action or omission, prior to the decision of the divine will to make it so'.[61] The meaning of God's action is beyond human cognition because our understanding of God's actions is determined by God's will. We can never transcend God's will to understand its purpose.

However, as Michael Latzer points out, 'if God is not bound by the logically possible, if there are literally no limits to what his omnipotent power can accomplish, then no possible theodicy will be effective'.[62] After all, 'the omnipotent God who decides what is itself logically possible could easily have brought it about that the most perfect world is one containing no evil at all. That he did not choose this course casts doubt on God's moral character, and the problem of theodicy menaces all over again.'[63] In other words, affirming God's power brings forth the question as to why God has not created and does not create a world that lacks evil. Descartes does not respond to this issue, but the next chapter will show that Leibniz gets round this problem by claiming, contra Descartes, that it is God's *understanding*, not His *will*, that creates existent beings. Because God understands the good, He always wills the good. There is necessity to God's will which emanates from His understanding. This, however, will cause its own problems.

Second, we can never understand the reasons for God's actions because of the hierarchy of beings established in the Third Meditation. Remembering that God's creation must conform to the formal reality principle, which states that each being must 'derive ... from some cause which contains at least as much formal reality as there is objective reality in the idea',[64] we find that God *must* create beings that are less perfect than Him. While the formal reality clause insists that there must be *at least as much* formal reality in the cause as in the effect, which might seem to offer the possibility that God could create another being with the same formal reality as Him, this would mean that there would be, at least, two supremely perfect and all-powerful beings; an impossibility given the way in which Descartes, following the monotheistic tradition, understands God to be a unitary and infinite substance.[65] It seems that the nature of God as an infinitely perfect being necessitates that He create based on the premises of the formal reality principle, meaning that there is a logical necessity to His creation that is out-with God's control: God cannot create another supreme being; He must create an inferior one.

Descartes would, of course, argue that God's will lies at the foundation of the formal reality principle, meaning that it is only because God wills its truth that it is true. The resolution of this paradox brings us back to the classic argument, famously outlined in Plato's *Euthyphro*, regarding whether something is good because God wills it or whether it is willed by God because it is good.[66] In other words, does God create all and in so doing make it right, a summation that may entail an arbitrariness that would undermine universalism, or are God's creations the result of a prior foundation, a position that undermines God's omnipotence? Descartes privileges the first option: the truth of the formal reality principle emanates from God's will; a decision that, because of our necessary imperfection, is beyond our understanding.

Descartes goes on to account for why we have been made imperfectly and so can err in a world created by a God who is capable of creating us so that we never do so. He claims that whenever we examine whether God's creation is perfect we tend to focus on the part and fail to recognise the way it fits into the whole. This is not a failing of application, meaning that it does not simply result because we are not paying attention to the issue at hand and/or reason improperly. It is a consequence of the finitude of human cognition, which is simply incapable of examining the whole to see how the pieces fit perfectly together. The assumption lying behind Descartes's point is that, while we tend to expect that a perfect whole is comprised of perfect parts, it may be that perfection of the whole is dependent upon imperfect parts. Rather than look at only one thing, we have to examine how it relates to the larger universal picture. After all, 'what . . . perhaps rightly appear[s] [to be] very imperfect if it exist[s] on its own is quite perfect when its function as a part of the universe is considered'.[67]

While the necessary finiteness of human cognition means that we can never know, Descartes is pointing to the possibility that human error is a necessary part of God's overall plan that, of necessity, exceeds our finitude understanding. For this reason, Frederick Broadie argues that the question dealt with in the Fourth Meditation relates, strictly speaking, not to the relationship between God's essence as supremely good and hence truthful being and the empirical fact that we err, but, rather, to a deeper problem 'in which it is not the empirical fact of human error, but the apparent necessity of it, that has to be squared with God's truthfulness'.[68] By pointing to the possibility that human error is necessary because of the perfection inherent in God's unknowable plan, Descartes points to a theodicy that, as we will see in the next chapter, Leibniz develops to suggest that the all-powerful, supremely good God must create the best of all possible worlds. By doing so, Leibniz disagrees with Descartes's claim that the ontological gap between the finitude of human cognition and the infinity of God means that we can never know the purposes of God: He must create the best world possible.

## Concluding Remarks

Having shown how error might be part of God's cosmic plan despite not emanating from Him, Descartes concludes by explaining how error arises from God's creation; that is, from the *human* use of the faculties of cognition created by God. Descartes argues that human cognition is made up of different parts; specifically, 'the faculty of knowledge which is in me, and ... the faculty of choice or freedom of the will'.[69] If properly employed, the intellect simply provides material for possible judgements, which, because the faculty of judgement comes from God, must be error free. The finiteness of human being means, however, that the faculty of judgement is necessarily limited (we cannot, for example, know God's purpose), but this is not something that God can be blamed for. The logic underpinning the formal reality principle demands that God create us to be finite and, hence, imperfect.

At the same time as the faculty of judgement is capable of functioning perfectly, if in a limited way, human cognition is also composed of will, which 'is not restricted in any way'.[70] Descartes claims that, even if the faculties of judgement, memory, and imagination are necessarily limited,

> it is only the will, or freedom of choice, which I experience within me to be so great that the idea of any greater faculty is beyond my grasp; so much so that it is above all in virtue of the will that I understand myself to bear in some way the image and likeness of God.[71]

Although the application of the will is more extensive in God's case, its intensive quality is the same in humans because 'the will simply consists in our ability to do or not do something (that is, to affirm or deny, to pursue or avoid)'.[72] The will is simply that through which, when the intellect proposes something, we are moved to act or reject it. Because the act of will comes from us, it is not subject to external imposition and so is always free. Descartes even claims that this freedom escapes God's omnipotence because 'neither divine grace nor natural knowledge ever diminishes freedom; on the contrary, they increase and strengthen it'.[73] In a similar vein to Augustine and Aquinas, Descartes concludes that, because error results from an act of free will, it cannot emanate from or be the responsibility of God.[74]

Importantly, freedom of the will does not entail arbitrary choice, which Descartes links to 'a defect in knowledge'.[75] Freedom is related to the true and good, themselves determined by God's will, meaning that if we know the true and good, we never have 'to deliberate about the right judgement or choice'.[76] If I know what is right and true, no deliberation is necessary; the will simply has to act on that knowledge. As a consequence, the will, like the faculty of judgement, is not the cause of error.

Indeed, in the earlier *Discourse on Method*, Descartes recognises that everyone tends to think of themselves as having good judgement and draws the conclusion that this 'provides evidence that the power of judging well and of distinguishing the true from the false (which is, properly speaking, what people call "good sense" or "reason") is naturally equal in all men'.[77] This is not to say that all apply it equally. Good judgement is not innate in some and lacking in others, but entails a specific mode of application of the faculty of judgement in relation to the other faculties, especially the will.[78]

The Fourth Meditation develops this argument by explaining that error results when the will, which it will be remembered is infinite, extends itself beyond what the faculty of judgement, which is finite, can clearly and distinctly perceive. Because 'every clear and distinct perception is undoubtedly something, and hence cannot come from nothing, [it] must necessarily have God for its author'[79] and so, by implication, be true. While the faculty of judgement, properly used, clearly and distinctly perceives what is true, the infinite will, unbound by the constraints of the finite faculty of judgement, can seek to exceed what can be clearly and distinctly perceived. When it does this, the will is no longer guided by what is clear and distinct, but is simply left to make a choice. While it may choose the right option, it does so not out of knowledge, but by sheer luck. It can also choose the wrong option, resulting in error.

This is not only irrational, but also, for Descartes, morally wrong.[80] His point is that the infinite will must be guided by and so constrained by the finite faculty of judgement so that only that which is clearly and distinctly perceived is acted upon. If the will is not guided by the clear and distinct perception of the finite faculty of judgement, the will is said to suffer the privation of judgement, which leads to the arbitrary action that 'constitutes the essence of error'.[81] The solution is to ensure that 'I restrain my will so that it extends to what the intellect clearly and distinctly reveals, and no further',[82] for, if I do this, 'it is quite impossible for me to go wrong'.[83] The evil of error arises when human cognition bases itself on the infinite will, rather than on the finiteness of human judgement.

By highlighting the intimate connection between evil and error, Descartes demonstrates the important link between epistemology and morality. Furthermore, his claim that human cognition must limit itself to ensure that it does not fall into error will subsequently feed into Kant's claim that reason should be limited to phenomenal experience. However, perhaps Descartes's most important contribution is that he tries to reconcile two positions:

one that explains evil in terms of individual actions that exculpate God from any responsibility for error or evil, and the other that affirms a theodicy that remains true to the notion that all that happens emanates from God, the supreme, omnipotent, all-knowing being. Whether to account for the existence of evil in individualistic or teleological terms dominates subsequent, post-Cartesian thinking. Initially, the latter prevailed through Leibniz's affirmation of theodicy, before Kant responded by claiming that evil is a consequence of an individual's autonomous, rational moral choice.

## Notes

1. These dates are not meant to be exact; there is, of course, significant overlap between these periods. They do, however, orientate the reader to the timeframe being discussed and to the alterations that take place during it.
2. For a discussion of the former see Alain Boureau, *Satan hérétique: Naissance de la démonologie dans l'Occident Médiéval, 1280–1330* (Paris: Éditions Odile Jacob, 2004); and of the latter, Ruben van Luijk, *Children of Lucifer: The Origins of Modern Religious Satanism* (Oxford: Oxford University Press, 2016).
3. See Stephen Gaukroger, *The Emergence of a Scientific Culture: Science and the Shaping of Modernity 1210–1685* (Oxford: Oxford University Press, 2009).
4. Charles Taylor, *Sources of the Self: The Making of the Modern Identity* (Cambridge: Cambridge University Press, 1989), p. 131.
5. For an interesting recent discussion of Renaissance humanism, see Patrick Baker, *Italian Renaissance Humanism in the Mirror* (Cambridge: Cambridge University Press, 2015).
6. Taylor, *Sources of the Self*, p. 143.
7. René Descartes, *Meditations on First Philosophy*, trans. and ed. John Cottingham (Cambridge: Cambridge University Press, 1986).
8. Ibid. p. 5.
9. Ibid. p. 11.
10. This connection is also proposed by Zbigniew Janowski, *Cartesian Theodicy: Descartes' Quest for Certitude* (Dordrecht: Kluwer, 2000), p. 27. For a wider discussion of Descartes's moral thought, see John Marshall, *Descartes's Moral Thought* (Ithaca: Cornell University Press, 1998).
11. Gary Hatfield, *Descartes and the Meditations* (Abingdon: Routledge, 2003), p. 186.
12. Descartes, *Meditations on First Philosophy*, p. 3.
13. Ibid. p. 3.
14. Ibid. p. 3.
15. Ibid. p. 3.
16. Ibid. p. 4.
17. Ibid. p. 5.

18. Ibid. p. 5.
19. Ibid. p. 5.
20. Ibid. p. 4.
21. Ibid. p. 12.
22. Ibid. p. 12.
23. Ibid. p. 12.
24. Ibid. pp. 12–13.
25. Ibid. p. 13.
26. Ibid. p. 13.
27. Ibid. p. 15.
28. Ibid. p. 17.
29. Ibid. p. 17.
30. Ibid. p. 18.
31. Ibid. pp. 25–6.
32. Ibid. p. 26.
33. Ibid. p. 26.
34. Ibid. p. 26.
35. Ibid. p. 27.
36. Ibid. p. 27.
37. Ibid. p. 27.
38. Ibid. p. 28.
39. Ibid. p. 28.
40. Frederick Broadie, *An Approach to Descartes' Meditations* (London: Athlone Press, 1970), pp. 61–2.
41. Ibid. p. 62.
42. 'For just as the objective mode of being belongs to ideas by their very nature, so the formal mode of being belongs to the causes of ideas – or at least the first and most important ones – by *their* very nature' (Descartes, *Meditations on First Philosophy*, p. 29).
43. Ibid. p. 28.
44. Ibid. p. 29.
45. Ibid. pp. 28–9.
46. Ibid. p. 29.
47. Ibid. p. 31.
48. Ibid. p. 31.
49. Ibid. p. 28.
50. Ibid. p. 35.
51. Ibid. p. 35.
52. Ibid. p. 37.
53. Ibid. p. 37.
54. Ibid. p. 37.
55. Ibid. pp. 37–8.
56. Ibid. p. 38.

57. Ibid. p. 38.
58. Ibid. p. 38.
59. Ibid. p. 39.
60. Ibid. pp. 38–9.
61. Ibid. p. 93.
62. Michael Latzer. 'Descartes's Theodicy of Error', p. 46, in *The Problem of Evil in Early Modern Philosophy*, ed. Elmar J. Kremer and Michael J. Latzer (Toronto: University of Toronto Press, 2001), pp. 35–48.
63. Ibid. p. 47.
64. Descartes, *Meditations on First Philosophy*, p. 28.
65. This argument does not apply to the example of finite substances because it is in the nature of finitude to be limited and so multiple. For example, all organic finite substances are capable of producing other finite substances in the form of children. God, despite being all-powerful, cannot create another God as this would require the creation of another infinite substance, which, by virtue of being multiple, would violate the limitlessness or, put differently, the unity that defines infinity and hence God.
66. Plato, *Euthyphro*, trans. G. M. A. Grube, 10d–11b, in *Complete Works*, ed. John M. Cooper (Indianapolis: Hackett, 1997), pp. 1–16.
67. Descartes, *Meditations on First Philosophy*, p. 39.
68. Broadie, *An Approach to Descartes' Meditations*, p. 101.
69. Descartes, *Meditations on First Philosophy*, p. 39.
70. Ibid. p. 39.
71. Ibid. p. 40.
72. Ibid. p. 40.
73. Ibid. p. 40.
74. For an extended discussion of free will in the Fourth Meditation, see Cecelia Wee, 'The Fourth Meditation: Descartes and Libertarian Freedom', in *The Cambridge Companion to Descartes' Meditations*, ed. David Cunning (Cambridge: Cambridge University Press, 2014), pp. 186–203.
75. Descartes, *Meditations on First Philosophy*, p. 40.
76. Ibid. p. 40.
77. René Descartes, *Discourse on the Method*, trans. R. Stoothoff, p. 111, in *The Philosophical Writings of Descartes*, vol. 1 (Cambridge: Cambridge University Press, 1985), pp. 111–51.
78. Ibid. p. 111.
79. Descartes, *Meditations on First Philosophy*, p. 43.
80. Thomas M. Lennon, 'The Fourth Meditation: Descartes' Theodicy *Avant la Lettre*', p. 169, in *The Cambridge Companion to Descartes'* Meditations, ed. David Cunning (Cambridge: Cambridge University Press, 2014), pp. 168–85.
81. Descartes, *Meditations on First Philosophy*, p. 41.
82. Ibid. p. 43.
83. Ibid. p. 43.

# 5
# Leibniz and Theodicy: Evil as the Good

Leibniz devoted much attention to the problem of evil. Indeed, it is the motivation for the only book he published in his lifetime – *Theodicy: Essays on the Goodness of God, the Freedom of Man, and the Origin of Evil* (published in 1710).[1] In their introduction to a recent edited collection on this book, Larry Jorgensen and Samuel Newlands point out that 'although Leibniz's reputation remains closely tied to his project in the *Theodicy*, the work has received scant attention by scholars in the past century'.[2] This is somewhat strange given that in the eighteenth and nineteenth centuries it was widely read and, in no small part, helped to establish Leibniz's reputation.[3] In the twentieth century, however, the *Theodicy* was rejected as other parts of his system, specifically his accounts of logic and mathematics, were extolled.

The *Theodicy* is a wide-ranging book, dealing with topics including contemporary (for Leibniz) debates in theology, predestination, the nature of substances, and the mind/soul/body problem. Its main aim, however, is to explain and account for the existence of evil in a world created by an omnipotent, all-knowing, and supremely good deity. Building on Descartes's insight that the evil of error may be necessary to secure God's overall plan,[4] Leibniz combines the Greek *theo* (= God) with *dikē* (= justice) to argue that the existence of evil is based on a notion of God's justice.

Donald Rutherford points out that Leibniz sees two benefits to this: first, 'in understanding God's justice, we acquire confidence in the rightness of all his actions'.[5] This insulates us from 'the disturbing effects of worldly evil'[6] while also ensuring that, if we are disturbed by evil, 'we have the means of recovering our tranquillity through reflection on the nature of divine justice'.[7] Second, theodicy is crucial to the attainment of happiness because, by comprehending the justice of God's actions, 'we acquire our fullest knowledge of the unity of divine perfections of power, knowledge, and goodness',[8] which, in combination with our love of God is, for Leibniz, 'the source of true happiness'.[9]

Leibniz bases his analysis on a particular metaphysical understanding underpinned by a calculus of maximisation, wherein God's infinite perfection, power, and supreme goodness mean that He calculates, from all the possible worlds, the best one. We will develop this as we proceed, but the overall conclusion drawn is that 'despite the evil contained in the actual world, God's justice is vindicated because permitting that evil was a necessary condition for securing the good of . . . the best possible world'.[10]

The importance of Leibniz's thinking on evil is three-fold: *historically*, his analysis is a crucial development in attempts to account for evil within a monotheistic framework. While the Augustinian-Aquinian tradition explains evil from the perspective of a human will divorced from God, Leibniz emphasises that human will is intimately connected to God. In doing so, he offers a corrective to their 'individually focused' accounts that brings us (back) to a universal orientation; one that places God at the core of our thinking.

Leibniz's theodicy also has *scholarly* importance, in so far as recent Leibnizian scholarship has returned to the *Theodicy* to argue that this long-neglected book actually comprises 'an essential part of Leibniz's philosophy'.[11] Examining the veracity of this claim is beyond the scope of this chapter, but it does point to the key role that Leibniz's analysis of the problem of evil plays in his thinking, a role that warrants further scrutiny.

*Conceptually*, Leibniz introduces a number of innovations into the understanding of evil. By distinguishing between metaphysical, physical, and moral evils, while also introducing a distinction between God's antecedent and consequent will, he explains why God necessarily permits the existence of evil, but yet is not responsible for it. The aim of these conceptual innovations is to develop an account of evil that roots it in and sees it contributing to the greater good of the cosmic order. From this, Leibniz develops a *perspectival* view of evil, wherein an action is perceived to be evil from the finite perspective of humans, when, in fact, from God's infinite perspective, it is not only necessary, but one that contributes to the greater good.

## Metaphysical Assumptions

Leibniz outlines the questions motivating his analysis in the following manner: 'How [has] a sole Principle, all-good, all-wise and all-powerful . . . been able to admit evil, and especially to permit sin, and how . . . could [it] resolve to make the wicked often happy and the good unhappy?'[12] He grounds his response in the principle of sufficient reason, which he takes to mean that 'nothing exists or comes about unless a reason can be given, at least by an omniscient being, why it exists rather than doesn't, or why it is this way rather than otherwise. In a word, *a reason can be given for everything.*'[13] This does not mean that human cognition can comprehend this reason; only that nothing happens without a reason. It is combined with the metaphysical premise that the principle of sufficient reason does not create an infinite regress, but is grounded in one source: God. When seeking to explain the existence of evil, we have to remember the ontological limitations of human beings; limitations not present in God, who is the first principle from which all else emanates.[14] In many respects, bringing us to recognise and think from this ontological gap is Leibniz's overall aim. Understanding it, and, by extension, Leibniz's solution to the problem of evil, requires an understanding of what is meant by God.

In the *Discourse on Metaphysics*, Leibniz explains that 'the conception of God which is the most common and the most full of meaning is expressed well enough in the words: God is an absolutely perfect being'.[15] Perfection is linked to power and knowledge, which, in God, know no limit. 'It follows that God who possesses supreme and infinite wisdom acts in the most perfect manner not only metaphysically, but also from the moral standpoint.'[16]

Whereas Descartes aimed to prove the existence of God in the Third, Fourth, and Fifth Meditations, Leibniz simply affirms a characterisation of God to develop an analysis from it. Furthermore, while Descartes claimed that existence is dependent on God's will, which, being infinite, cannot be constrained, Leibniz holds that such a view destroys, 'without realising it, all the love of God and all his glory; for why praise him for what he has done, if he would be equally praiseworthy in doing the contrary?'[17] Tying God to His will would mean that justice was something arbitrary: God could justifiably 'condemn the innocent without [this action] violating his justice',[18] which would make God into 'the most wicked spirit, the Prince of evil, the evil principle of the Manichaeans'.[19] Indeed, if Descartes is correct and God arbitrarily decides based on His will, Leibniz wonders 'what means would there be of distinguishing the true God from the false God of Zoroaster if all things depended upon the caprice of an arbitrary power and there were neither rule nor consideration for anything whatever?'[20] While Descartes aimed to prove and defend the God of monotheistic Christianity, Leibniz charges that his privileging of God's will actually led us away from Him.

Leibniz's corrective is to claim that God's omnipotence lies, not in His will, but in His understanding: 'the will of God is not the reason why *God wills something* (for what leads someone to will is never his willing to will but rather his believing that the thing merits it); the reason *why God wills something* is rather the nature of things themselves contained in ideas themselves of these things'.[21] Each thing is defined by an essence that 'contain[s] the very possibility of entities, which God does not bring about, as he does existence, since these very possibilities – or ideas of things – coincide rather with God himself'.[22] God creates all, but does so based on the idea of the thing itself rather than from His arbitrary will.[23]

For this reason

> the power of God is always subordinated to his wisdom. His absolute independence and freedom do not imply he could decide and act without considering any law or rule. God always acts according to wisdom, goodness, and justice, never in an arbitrary manner, even if we are unable to understand all the reasons of his Providence.[24]

God's infinite wisdom means that He is capable of ascertaining the good, while His perfection ensures that He always acts in accordance with the good. As a consequence, reason lies at the foundation of God's will as His actions are always the consequence of His understanding of the good. God always wills the good, not because it emanates from His will, but because God understands the good and acts in accordance with this understanding. Rather than privilege His omnipotence, Leibniz values God's goodness; it is this that lies at 'the basis of the love which we owe to God in all things'.[25]

Nevertheless, God cannot create a perfect world. To understand why, we need to distinguish between God's antecedent and consequential will. The *antecedent will* 'is detached and considers each good separately in the capacity of a good'.[26] God 'tends to all good, as good, *ad perfectionem simpliciter simplicem* [and is] earnestly disposed to sanctify and to save all men, to exclude sin, and to prevent damnation'.[27] Taken on its own, this means God always aims for the absolute good. In contrast, the *consequent will* relates to action which can be brought about from 'the conflict of all the antecedent wills'.[28] The consequent will cannot always realise the good because this would make the world perfect, which would violate the singularity of God's infinite perfection. There is a necessary discrepancy between God's antecedent will, which wills the pure good, and His consequent will, which must calculate the best possible world that can be created. If something exists, it must have been created by an infinite, all-powerful, all-good God, and, as a consequence, must exist in that manner because it is necessary for the existence of the best possible world.

This allows Leibniz to introduce a conceptual innovation with regard to evil. While we have already noted that Augustine and Aquinas distinguish between moral evil (*malum culpae*) and natural evil (*malum poenae*), Leibniz adds a third: metaphysical evil. This sense of evil describes the different degrees of being constitutive of the beings created by God and is, therefore, closely related to Augustine's and Aquinas's conceptions of negation. Whereas they hold that this is not a form of evil, Leibniz claims that it is. Thus, *metaphysical evil* is necessary for God's creation; *moral evil* is defined by an unnecessary turning away from God that must be corrected, but also entails a necessary aspect of God's plan and so is permitted without being willed by God; and *physical evil* is willed by God to correct moral evil and always supposes the least amount necessary to ensure the existence of the best of all possible worlds.

God acts then in accordance with the 'principle of the best'[29] to perceive and contemplate all the options possible, as a precursor to creating the best that can be created. To do so, He creates in accordance with certain principles, namely 'those most simple and uniform: for he chooses rules that least restrict one another. They are also the most *productive* in proportion to the *simplicity of ways and means*.'[30] To do so, God undertakes a calculus of maximisation that configures existence so that the beings created are the most perfect that could be created and all pieces fit together in the best way, where 'best way' (1) entails the most efficient and simplest production that leads to (2) the greatest possible 'richness and abundance'[31] of life.

Leibniz concludes that 'in whatever manner God might have created the world, it would always have been regular and in a certain order. God, however, has chosen the most perfect, that is to say the one which is at the same time the simplest in hypotheses and the richest in phenomena.'[32] Nothing happens without God willing it, meaning that if an event occurred, it did so because God permitted it to happen. Leibniz supports this with the example of Judas, explaining that

> the necessity of the future sin of Judas existed before Judas existed. Therefore, it did not arise from Judas's will. God foresaw that Judas would sin. Therefore, it was certain, infallible, inevitable, and necessary that Judas would sin before Judas existed. Judas was not in the divine intellect, but the idea of a Judas who would sin was ... Then when Judas deliberated whether he would betray Christ or not, it was already necessary for Judas to choose betrayal, otherwise Scripture would be false.[33]

Leibniz's point is that God creates having identified all possible permutations of the being to be created and, having deliberated, creates a being who must act in accordance with the necessity inherent in God's choice. This does not mean that we simply sit back and wait for God's plan to unfold – a position that Leibniz calls 'lazy reason'[34] – but requires that we 'act conformably to the presumptive will of God as far as we are able to judge it, trying with all our might to contribute to the general welfare'.[35] He never explains, however, how we are able to know the presumptive will of God. If we cannot do so, the question arises as to what gives us the confidence to act in accordance with our understanding of God's will and, indeed, from where does this understanding emanate.

Leibniz seems to be pushing us to just commit to a course of action, although it could also be that he is merely drawing out the conclusions of our finite understanding: we must act, but do not know what our actions hold for the future and so, in a sense, must simply have faith that our chosen actions are correct. Nevertheless, he offers a palliative solution in this scenario by claiming that the correctness of the choice made will be revealed in due course. As long as we intend to act in the interests of the general welfare, any action that deviates from God's plan will be forgiven.[36] It may, however, be wondered how we can (1) know what the general welfare entails, given our finite understanding, and (2) do other than God permits if God only permits that which is part of His plan as this accords with the best of all possible worlds. In any case, Leibniz seems to think that everything will work out for the best because God has foreseen all possibilities and already incorporated our action into the best of all possible worlds, or will correct our mistake through physical evil, or will use it for the greater good and so ensure that the best possible world always exists. That the world is not perfect does, however, bring forth the question of the nature of evil.

## Conceptual Innovations

As noted, Western thinking about evil had up to this point long distinguished between 'natural' and 'moral' evil, wherein the former refers to events that do not emanate from human will and the latter to events that occur from human will. Earthquakes, for example, are an example of *natural evil* because they create suffering that is not willed by humans. Murder, on the other hand, is a *moral evil* because it is an act that breaks a moral law and originates from human will. Traditionally, the focus tended to be on moral evil because its genesis in human willing meant that something could be done to thwart it, and/or natural evil was thought to be a punishment for it. So, the natural evil of earthquakes was understood to be divine punishment for the moral sins of individuals/communities. Leibniz, however, introduces a tripartite understanding composed of metaphysical, physical, and moral evil: '*metaphysical evil* consists in simple imperfection, *physical evil* in suffering, and *moral evil* in sin'.[37]

For Leibniz, moral evil (= sin) results from the breaking of moral law. The question that arises is why God has created a world in which sin is possible. This seems to make God responsible for the moral evil that occurs.[38] Leibniz thinks that God *permits* moral evil without being responsible for it, because moral evil (1) is a privation that emanates, not from God, but from individual will; (2) must be permitted by God as it contributes to the overall good; and (3) must be allowed by God to ensure that individuals can be held responsible for their moral decisions. The last is linked to Leibniz's conception of physical evil, which entails suffering aimed at punishing the breaking of the moral law. Physical evil is a consequence of moral evil, both of which result from the necessity of metaphysical evil.[39]

According to Maria Rosa Antognazza, it has often been assumed that 'Leibniz['s] "physical evil" corresponds to the category of natural evil strangely absent from [his] typology, as if "physical" had been used as a synonym of "natural"'.[40] To explain this, she notes that whereas 'natural' evil was traditionally linked to suffering resulting from a natural event caused by God, Leibniz's notion of 'physical' evil entails punishment for human transgression of the moral law. The conflation of both has occurred because, for Leibniz, physical evil is synonymous with suffering, what Augustine and Aquinas called *malum poenae* (otherwise known as natural evils), with moral evil being synonymous with sin, which Augustine and Aquinas called *malum culpae* (often called moral evils). All agree that physical and natural evil are consequences of individual moral sin, but Leibniz examines both from the perspective of the cosmic order to claim that the creation of the best possible world *necessarily* creates metaphysical evils that permit the possibility of sin which requires rectification through the punishment of physical evil. To understand Leibniz's conception of physical evil we need, then, look not to moral evil, but to metaphysical evil.

Leibniz disagrees with Augustine's claim that evil is fundamentally a consequence of moral sin.[41] There is a more originary sense of evil that is grounded in the structure of the universe created by God and which relates to the '*original imperfection in the creature* before sin',[42] meaning that it exists prior to the Christian doctrine of Original Sin. Without the ontological imperfections of metaphysical evil, it would not be possible for moral evil to occur. Because Leibniz recognises the need for ontological imperfections in God's creation, he rejects Augustine's claim that all are guilty because of the Original Sin committed in the Garden of Eden. This (1) unjustly condemns all humans who follow from Eve because of her actions, (2) fails to recognise that just punishment must be based on the actions of the individual, and (3) needs to be explained by a prior notion of evil.[43]

Leibniz claims that it is because Augustine has no equivalent to metaphysical evil that, while he (and presumably Aquinas) could explain how (moral) evil arose from human will, he was not capable of explaining why a just, good, and all-powerful God permitted and continues to permit the 'prevalence of evil'[44] found in the universe. To overcome this issue, Leibniz appears to implicitly depend upon Descartes's cosmological argument for God's existence in the Third Meditation: while the formal reality principle – 'everything must come from something with at least as much formal reality as that which causes it'[45] – appears to offer the possibility that God could create another infinite substance, He must, in actuality, create finite substances that have less reality than Him, because the creation of an infinite substance would ensure the existence of two infinite substances, which would violate the unitary nature of infinity. As such, God creates everything, but with less reality or, in Leibniz's terms, perfection than His perfect infinity.

Leibniz departs from Descartes by claiming that God creates based on His knowledge rather than on His will. God does not then create arbitrarily, but, if He decides to create, does so in conformity with certain conditions, which are determined by the idea (= essence) of the thing being created. For example, God did not need to create humans, but having decided to do so, 'He had of necessity to make man a rational animal [because] the essence of man lay in the properties of being animal and rational.'[46] While God creates in accordance with the essence of each thing, what He creates must be inferior to His infinite perfection. Given the principle of the best, God weighs up all the possible imperfect worlds that can be created to ensure that the one created is the most perfect imperfect world possible. As a consequence,

> God wills the whole, which is the best, but by willing the all-things-considered best leaves open the possibility that some created being will choose to act immorally. If God intervened to limit or prevent evil in the world, the result would be a world-sequence that is less than the best-of-all-possible worlds.[47]

This necessary imperfection is, for Leibniz, a form of evil; indeed, it is the fundamental form of evil. Augustine and Aquinas reject this, explaining that natural imperfection is not a sufficient condition of evil. For them, there must be a privation of a state that ought to be. For Leibniz, in contrast, not all forms of evil have to entail a privation. The imperfection of the different beings created entails metaphysical evil. However, if all beings are by nature evil by virtue of not being God, how are they to prevent evil or, indeed, limit it? How can a limited being impact on God's creation in the manner necessary to minimise it?

Michael Latzer tries to surmount this issue by limiting the meaning of metaphysical evil. On his reading, metaphysical evil is an imperfection, but 'to extend the concept of metaphysical evil to cover even the original imperfection or limitation of creatures is a construction which both goes beyond anything which Leibniz himself says, and disregards his explicit adherence to Augustine's position'.[48] Latzer's conclusion is drawn from an argument that sees Leibniz as being wholeheartedly tied to the Augustinian tradition, which, it will be remembered, distinguishes between negation and privation, with the former entailing a simple lack and the latter entailing a lack of something that the being, in its being, should have. Latzer claims that Leibniz relies on Augustine's free-will argument, according to which moral evil arises from a privation that results from individuals failing to live up to their moral duty to God. As a consequence, Latzer explains that Leibniz follows Augustine in understanding evil to be a privation, not a negation.

As we will see shortly, Leibniz does make this claim about evil, but Latzer's innovation is to argue that it does not apply to all forms of evil identified; it only applies to moral evil. As such, metaphysical evil is an imperfection, in the sense of negation of God's perfection, but not a privation because humans should never be considered infinite.[49] The imperfection of metaphysical evil is then merely a condition of possibility for the privation of moral evil.[50] While the terminology is different, Leibniz is, on Latzer's account, simply extending the Augustinian tradition without introducing anything new to the conceptual matrix used by this tradition to understand evil.[51]

However, while Latzer's analysis is interesting and thought-provoking, it is problematic on three counts. First, by playing up Leibniz's fidelity to Augustine, it seems, as he admits, to downplay the innovative aspects of Leibniz's account. This not only side-steps those moments where Leibniz explicitly rejects Augustine's thinking,[52] but also gives rise to the question of why we should bother studying what Leibniz has to say on the matter. The response may be that, on this topic, we should not, but I think that would be a mistake: Leibniz's analysis is both historically and conceptually relevant.

Second, while Latzer wants to downplay the significance of metaphysical evil to affirm the privation of moral evil, the simple fact is that Leibniz introduces metaphysical evil as a sense of 'evil'. This alone should make us wary of discarding it; or, put conversely, should be sufficient for us to take it seriously as a sense or form of evil. Latzer gets round this problem by claiming that metaphysical evil is defined by negation and so is not a proper sense of evil, which is only ever defined by privation. But it is precisely this point that Leibniz rejects: 'negation' – the simple differences between created beings – is a form of evil. This is what distinguishes Leibniz from Augustine and Aquinas.

Showing why Leibniz defends this position brings forth the third problem in Latzer's analysis: its anthropocentrism. Latzer holds that metaphysical evil is a negation rather than a privation and so is not a form of evil despite its designation as such, because he examines the problem from the perspective of the human. Because the human must be imperfect, the human perceives its imperfection to be a simple negation and so not evil.

However, the central message of Leibniz's *Theodicy* is that, rather than account for things from the perspective of finite human existence, we must remember that our actions gain meaning from the perspective of the whole. So, when examined from the perspective of humans, the lack inherent in finite being is not a privation, but a negation, and, as such, does not entail a form of evil. But, when looked at from God's infinite perfection, the simple imperfection of metaphysical evil *is* a privation because it entails a lack that, given God's perfection, should not be. Because it entails privation from the perspective of God, metaphysical evil refers to the relationship between God and His creation *from the perspective of God* and is introduced because it portrays a form of evil different from moral and physical evils.

This demonstrates how the different senses of Leibnizian evil fit together: metaphysical evil is evil because, from God's perspective, every being created by Him entails a privation of His infinite perfection, while moral evil arises when humans turn away from God's moral law, and thereby suffer a further privation in their relation to Him. Physical evil entails suffering justly incurred from God (1) as a penalty for moral evil, (2) to prevent greater evils or obtain greater good, (3) to amend bad behaviour, and (4) to make us savour the good.[53] In each form, evil must be understood by relating it back to the whole; that is, back to God's infinite perfection.

## God and the Problem of Moral Evil

Having outlined the metaphysical structure that informs Leibniz's thinking on evil and detailed his tripartite understanding of the concept, including the foundational role that metaphysical evil plays in his analysis, we are brought to the problem of moral evil. While metaphysical evil exists because God must, out of necessity, create imperfect, finite being, it appears that God could prevent the existence of *moral evil*. This brings forth two questions: why does Leibniz think that moral evil is permitted, without being caused, by God? And why does God not prevent moral evil from occurring?

In response to the first question, Leibniz claims that God creates under certain conditions. As noted, God antecedently wills the good, in that He always wills the absolute good, but, because of the maximisation calculus inherent in creation, consequentially wills the best, meaning that He cannot create an absolutely good world. For this reason, a degree of metaphysical evil must exist in the world. To the objection that God's omnipotence means that He 'could have avoided all these evils',[54] Leibniz explains that this could only occur if the natural differences of metaphysical evil were avoided and all beings were created equally and, presumably, perfect. This would, however, violate God's infinity. Furthermore, because He did not do this, as evidenced by the existence of evil, it follows that God could not do it. There was, in other words, a constraint on God's will, meaning that any evil encountered is permitted by God without being caused by Him.[55]

At this point, it may be objected that Leibniz is trying to have it both ways: God is omnipotent but does not cause moral evil, and even if He permits moral evil to happen, does not cause it, despite being the cause of all. This is compounded by Leibniz's claim that God 'condemns only those whose will is evil',[56] which, by virtue of human will emanating from God, seems to imply that God made them evil. Leibniz responds that, although the necessary existence of metaphysical evil permits the possible existence of moral evil, evil moral acts are dependent on the will of finite beings. God permits the *existence* of an evil will for the greater good,[57] which, given God's omnipotence, seems to make Him, at least, partially responsible for the actions of that which He creates. Leibniz rejects this, however, by claiming that God is responsible for the existence of the *possibility* of moral evil but not the *actions* that are morally evil. To understand why, we need to turn to what Leibniz understands moral evil to entail.

In his early *Confessio Philosophi* writings, Leibniz dismisses the notion that evil entails a privation, claiming that it is 'a manifest illusion ... a leftover from the visionary philosophy of the past; it is a subterfuge with which a reasonable person will never be satisfied',[58] but in the later *Theodicy* he reverses this conclusion and accepts that evil is a privation.[59] As a consequence, moral evil entails a privation, not a negation, meaning that it involves a lack of something that should be as this is determined by the essence of the thing. For example, a lack of sight would be an evil for a bear, but not for a rock.[60]

Moral evil is made possible by and so is marked by the privation inherent in metaphysical evil: it is only because beings are (necessarily) created imperfectly (= metaphysical evil) that moral evil is possible. Importantly, moral evil occurs, for Leibniz, not because God wills it, but because an individual fails to live in accordance with the maximum amount of good his ontological capacity permits. By failing to do so, the individual fails to will the good (= God) as he should do, thereby giving rise to a moral privation. By turning away from the good, he sins (= moral evil).

To explain why the individual is capable of moral evil, Leibniz turns to the structure of the will. Even if the will 'tends towards the good in general',[61] the individual can choose to forgo this natural tendency. Furthermore, 'when one is limited to the pleasures of the senses, or to other pleasures to the detriment of greater good, as of health, of virtue, of union with God, of felicity, it is in this privation of a further aspiration that the defect consists'.[62] By turning away from the general good towards particular pleasures, not only does the will turn away from and so develop a privative relation to God, but such action also 'tends towards new privations'.[63] A will that has chosen evil has a tendency to continue to do more evil.

It is at this moment that Leibniz's notion of physical evil comes into play. When the will chooses to depart from the good to enact the privation of moral evil, the suffering of physical evil is a penalty for such action, although Leibniz also claims it stops greater sin.[64] The problem, however, is that the amount of suffering an individual receives is not always in accordance with the moral evil committed.[65] To account for this, Leibniz makes two points: first, the individual can take comfort that the next life will compensate for the physical suffering endured in this life,[66] and, second, God has factored in the individual's moral evil when calculating whether this is the best of all possible worlds. The moral evil and hence physical suffering incurred as a consequence are, therefore, necessary for the greater good.[67] Those suffering physical evil should be soothed by this and seek to exalt the good in their lives over their suffering.[68]

While this establishes that human choice lies at the foundation of the turn towards evil, it may be argued that God is responsible for this given that He creates human beings in this manner or, as the source of all, because He could have done otherwise if He so chose. Leibniz responds that both interpretations fail to understand the nature of privation, which he holds to be a lack and so not a thing in the sense of a substance. Because God is perfection, lack cannot be part of His essence, meaning that He cannot create 'it'. The privation of evil emanates not from God, but from the human will turning away from its natural tendency towards the good. Leibniz does not explain how this turning takes place, or what motivates it, but he assures us that any turning to moral evil is (1) configured into God's plan and (2) necessary for the creation of this world, which is the best of all possible worlds.

This brings us to the sense in which Leibniz thinks God creates; that is, whether God creates existence and subsequently leaves it to run its course devoid of His support, or whether God creates and maintains existence in each moment. If the former were the case, Leibniz could argue that God necessarily creates beings who can commit moral evil, but leaves it up to their free will to determine whether they do or not. Leibniz, however, takes a different route: God not only creates existence to ensure it is the best of all possible worlds, but 'penetrates at one and the same time all the possible connections'.[69] God 'co-operate[s] in all the actions of creatures'.[70] However, Leibniz reminds us that while God creates each being continually, meaning that He, at least, permits the moral evil that arises when an individual turns away from the good, it is human will that is responsible for moral evil.

With this, Leibniz tries to reconcile two apparently different positions: God (1) continuously creates everything and every action in existence, but yet (2) is not responsible for all that exists or happens in that world. While we may wonder whether and how this is possible, Robert Sleigh points out that Leibniz continued to struggle with this problem, which resulted in many 'changes in attitude on his part concerning how best to handle it',[71] before falling back on what we might call his fundamental claim: our finite imperfection means that, no matter how hard we try, we are unable to understand the structure of the universe. All that we can do is affirm the general good and take comfort in knowing that this is the best of all possible worlds.

## Concluding Remarks

Leibniz's analysis both synthesises and extends previous theological accounts of evil, but there are a number of troubling aspects to it. By arguing that evil is a necessary component of the good, Leibniz does not, in reality, improve our understanding of evil, but collapses 'it' into the good to claim that we only hold that something is evil because our finiteness prevents us from seeing how it contributes to the overall good. For this reason, Isabel Cabrera points out that Leibniz's 'solution' to the problem of evil leaves us

> just as we were: without understanding and without being able to help thinking that the suffering we undergo, and for which we as a species are

not responsible, is a senseless evil that appears entirely gratuitous. We are told that we cannot blame God for this; but we are not told why not. This response offers no explanation; it merely points out a limit, and tells us that the problem has no solution.[72]

This highlights a strange disjunction in Leibniz's theory, which, on the one hand, questions and so takes seriously the existence of evil, but, on the other hand, assures us that evil is an absence that is actually a good in that it is necessary for the realisation of the best possible world. By arguing that evil is, in reality, a good, Leibniz seems to be unintentionally committed to a certain quietism, whereby we do nothing because everything that happens has already been preordained based on God's calculations and, thus, choice. Leibniz explicitly rejects this in his critique of 'lazy reason',[73] but it is difficult to see why we should will anything if all that occurs, including punishment and moral evil, has already been incorporated into God's plan. By extension, Leibniz's argument also seems to sanction some sort of divine necessity to moral evil. Again, Leibniz rejects this, but if all moral evil has been calculated into God's plan for the best possible world, it is difficult to see how Leibniz can consistently hold that moral evil is an anomaly that is not willed by God who accompanies and sustains each act. Indeed, admitting that moral evil is permitted by God seems to entail that it has some sort of minimal, divine necessity attached to it. This is not necessarily Leibniz's explicit position, but, despite his efforts to the contrary, his analysis implicitly points in that direction.

It does so because his argument is premised on a particular Christian metaphysics,[74] which requires that we accept his claim that there is a God, that He has the characteristics that Leibniz describes, and that we are able to understand God's purpose; that is, that He, of necessity, must will the good and always act to affirm the good. In turn, this requires that we not only accept that God has created the best world possible, but also accept that all actions, no matter how perverse they seem to us, occur to ensure the existence of the best possible world. Whatever our willingness to accept these conditions, his contemporaries found them to be a tough ask.[75] Leibniz's account was soon rejected not only because of its content, but because, unbeknownst to him, the dominance of the theological framework he based his analysis on was coming to an end. Indeed, Leibniz's account contributed to and, to an extent, hastened its demise.

For example, Renée Jeffery points out that experience seemed to cast doubt on the idea that actions, no matter how much suffering they produced, could emanate from a benevolent God and contributed to the greater good.

It seemed perverse to claim, for example, that the Lisbon earthquake of 1755 occurred because God needed it to punish the citizens of Lisbon, who were not exactly renowned for their lack of moral piety or for their moral sins.[76] This 'brought into question Leibniz's monist account of evil that maintained that despite the existence of evil, this was the best of all possible worlds. Evidence of the suffering inflicted by the earthquake seemed to suggest that this was not the case.'[77]

The Lisbon earthquake was a pivotal event for Western culture, shaking not just its physical ground but also its conceptual ground.[78] It ultimately led to a questioning of the 'firm connection between sin and suffering that had dominated accounts of evil since well before the works of Augustine'.[79] While it was still held that individual moral transgression could and should be punished, the Lisbon earthquake called into question the idea that individuals should be held to be responsible for suffering caused by natural events. This brought about a renewed questioning of the meaning of human suffering in the world, one that ultimately rejected the cosmology upon which Leibniz's account is based.

Leibniz's theodicy was also heavily criticised for its apparent lack of sensitivity towards the victims of evil. While, on one reading, it appears to be highly sensitive to the victims of natural events in that it maintains that their suffering contributes to the greater good, from another perspective it seems to rather callously downplay that suffering. After all, if individuals die for a greater cause, there is no need to mourn them or seek to redress the perceived injustice. At its most extreme, there *seems* to be an inbuilt, implicit movement towards the glorification of martyrdom, wherein individual sacrifice is not in vain, but actually necessary for the greater good.

Finally, in 1791, Immanuel Kant published the important short essay 'On the Miscarriage of all Philosophical Trials in Theodicy'[80] in which he argued that the great problem with theodicies is that they are based on faith, not reason, and so are not capable of demonstrating their two fundamental claims: first, that there is a divine plan to existence and, second, that it is possible for human cognition to understand what God's plan is. Kant does not mention Leibniz, but it is clear that his critique is aimed at him. In particular, Kant highlights a tension that runs throughout Leibniz's theodicy: it is not obvious how Leibniz can coherently claim that evil is a necessary component of God's plan as this is evidenced by the creation of this (best possible) world *and* hold that human understanding is, by necessity, limited and, as such, unable to ascertain either the purpose of God's will or the understanding upon which God's will is based. If human understanding cannot know the purpose behind God's will, Leibniz cannot logically claim that this is the best possible world. In other words, Leibniz's conclusion appears to rest on premises that he has explicitly rejected.

It could be objected that Leibniz insists on a distinction between understanding and comprehending God's plan, so that human cognition can understand that there is a plan without necessarily comprehending what that plan entails, but this seems to require that humans be able to traverse, however ephemerally, the ontological gap that Leibniz continually insists separates the human from the divine. It could also be claimed that God's goodness necessitates that He act in the manner described by Leibniz. We do not then need access to God's will directly, but are able to reason our way to a conclusion based on His perfect essence. This, however, still requires that we know that God is perfect and follows reason, which brings us back to the original charge: human cognition does not have access to the divine. For this reason, Kant took seriously Leibniz's claim regarding the limits of human cognition to develop an analysis of evil from *within* those limits. As we will see in the next chapter, Kant's is an account based not on unknowable metaphysical pretensions, but on autonomous and rational individual choice.

## Notes

1. G. W. Leibniz, *Theodicy: Essays on the Goodness of God, the Freedom of Man, and the Origin of Evil*, trans. E. M. Huggard (Chicago: Open Court, 1985). The main other discussions are found in G. W. Leibniz, *Confessio Philosophi: Papers Concerning the Problem of Evil, 1671–1678*, trans. Robert C. Sleigh Jr. (New Haven: Yale University Press, 2005); and G. W. Leibniz, *Discourse on Metaphysics, Correspondence with Arnauld, and Monadology*, trans. George R. Montgomery (Chicago: Open Court, 1950).
2. Larry M. Jorgensen and Samuel Newlands, 'Introduction', p. 1, in *New Essays on Leibniz's Theodicy*, ed. Larry M. Jorgensen and Samuel Newlands (Oxford: Oxford University Press, 2014), pp. 1–12.
3. For an interesting account of the reception of Leibniz's theory of evil in the eighteenth century, especially in relation to Malebranche and Arnauld, see Steven Nadler, *The Best of All Possible Worlds: A Story of Philosophers, God, and Evil in the Age of Reason* (Princeton: Princeton University Press, 2010).
4. Descartes outlines this in the Fourth Meditation of his *Meditations on First Philosophy*, trans. and ed. John Cottingham (Cambridge: Cambridge University Press, 1986).
5. Donald Rutherford, 'Leibniz and the Stoics: The Consolations of Theodicy', pp. 138–9, in *The Problem of Evil in Early Modern Philosophy*, ed. Elmar J. Kremer and Michael J. Latzer (Toronto: University of Toronto Press, 2001), pp. 138–64.
6. Ibid. p. 139.
7. Ibid. p. 139.

8. Ibid. p. 139.
9. Ibid. p. 139.
10. Michael J. Murray, 'Vindicatio Dei: Evil as a Result of God's Free Choice of the Best', p. 153, in *New Essays on Leibniz's Theodicy*, ed. Larry M. Jorgensen and Samuel Newlands (Oxford: Oxford University Press, 2014), pp. 153–71.
11. Donald Rutherford, *Leibniz and the Rational Order of Nature* (Cambridge: Cambridge University Press, 1995), p. 1.
12. Leibniz, *Theodicy*, Preliminary Dissertation, §43.
13. Leibniz, *Confessio Philosophi*, p. 123.
14. Leibniz, *Theodicy*, §7.
15. Leibniz, *Discourse on Metaphysics*, §1.
16. Ibid. §1.
17. Ibid. §2.
18. Leibniz, *Theodicy*, Preliminary Dissertation, §37.
19. Ibid. Preliminary Dissertation, §37.
20. Ibid. Preliminary Dissertation, §37.
21. Leibniz, *Confessio Philosophi*, p. 49.
22. Ibid. p. 3.
23. Leibniz, *Discourse on Metaphysics*, §2.
24. Paul Rateau, 'The Theoretical Foundations of the Leibnizian Theodicy and its Apologetic Aim', pp. 94–5, in *New Essays on Leibniz's Theodicy*, ed. Larry M. Jorgensen and Samuel Newlands (Oxford: Oxford University Press, 2014), pp. 92–111.
25. Leibniz, *Discourse on Metaphysics*, §4.
26. Leibniz, *Theodicy*, §22.
27. Ibid. §22.
28. Ibid. §22.
29. Ibid. Preface, p. 68.
30. Ibid. §208.
31. Leibniz, *Discourse on Metaphysics*, §5.
32. Ibid. §6.
33. Leibniz, *Confessio Philosophi*, p. 117.
34. Leibniz, *Discourse on Metaphysics*, §4.
35. Ibid. §4.
36. Ibid. §4.
37. Leibniz, *Theodicy*, §21.
38. This is known in the literature as the problem of divine concurrence. Space constraints prevent me from dealing with it, but, for an interesting discussion, see Jill Graper Hernandez, 'Moral Evil and Leibniz's Form/Matter Defence of Divine Omnipotence', *Sophia*, 49:1, 2010, pp. 1–13.
39. Leibniz, *Theodicy*, §21.
40. Maria Rosa Antognazza, 'Metaphysical Evil Revisited', p. 122, in *New Essays*

on *Leibniz's Theodicy*, ed. Larry M. Jorgensen and Samuel Newlands (Oxford: Oxford University Press, 2014), pp. 112–34.
41. For an extended discussion of the differences between Leibniz's and Augustine's conceptions of Original Sin, see Elmer J. Kremer, 'Leibniz and the "Disciples of Saint Augustine" on the Fate of Infants who Die Unbaptized', in *The Problem of Evil in Early Modern Philosophy*, ed. Elmar J. Kremer and Michael J. Latzer (Toronto: University of Toronto Press, 2001), pp. 119–37.
42. Leibniz, *Theodicy*, §20.
43. Ibid. Preface, p. 60.
44. Ibid. §19.
45. Descartes, *Meditations on First Philosophy*, p. 28.
46. Leibniz, *Theodicy*, §183.
47. Hernandez, 'Moral Evil and Leibniz's Form/Matter Defence of Divine Omnipotence', p. 9.
48. Michael Latzer, 'The Nature of Evil: Leibniz and his Medieval Background', *The Modern Schoolman*, 71:1, 1993, pp. 59–69 (p. 65).
49. For an extended discussion of this, see Michael Latzer, 'Leibniz's Conception of Metaphysical Evil', *Journal of the History of Ideas*, 55:1, January, 1994, pp. 1–15.
50. Ibid. p. 63.
51. Ibid. p. 59.
52. For example, see Leibniz, *Theodicy*, Preface, p. 70; and §284.
53. Ibid. §23.
54. Ibid. Preface, p. 61.
55. Ibid. Preface, p. 61.
56. Ibid. Preface, p. 62.
57. Ibid. §100, 127.
58. Leibniz, *Confessio Philosophi*, p. 111.
59. Samuel Newlands adds a caveat to this by arguing that, while Leibniz moves from an explicit rejection of privation theory to an explicit acceptance of it, the *content* of the privation theory that Leibniz latterly accepts is not equivalent to that which he earlier rejects. More specifically, Newlands's argument is that Leibniz comes to adopt a privation theory that is different in content, but not name, from the privation theories constitutive of medieval scholasticism that he earlier rejected (Samuel Newlands, 'Leibniz on Privations, Limitations, and the Metaphysics of Evil', *Journal of the History of Philosophy*, 52:2, April, 2014, pp. 281–308).
60. Leibniz also links privation to evil and error, stating that 'evil is therefore like darkness, and not only ignorance but also error and malice consist formally in a certain kind of privation' (Leibniz, *Theodicy*, §32). In other words, privation has epistemological and moral consequences.
61. Ibid. §33.
62. Ibid. §33.
63. Ibid. §33.

64. Ibid. §23.
65. Ibid. Preliminary Dissertation, §43.
66. Ibid. §17.
67. Ibid. §19.
68. Ibid. §15.
69. Ibid. §23.
70. Ibid. Preface, p. 30.
71. Robert C. Sleigh Jr., 'Remarks on Leibniz's Treatment of the Problem of Evil', p. 167, in *The Problem of Evil in Early Modern Philosophy*, ed. Elmar J. Kremer and Michael J. Latzer (Toronto: University of Toronto Press, 2001), pp. 165–79.
72. Isabel Cabrera, 'Is God Evil?', p. 21, in *Rethinking Evil: Contemporary Perspectives*, ed. Maria Pia Lara (Berkeley: University of California Press, 2001), pp. 17–26.
73. Leibniz, *Discourse on Metaphysics*, §4.
74. On this connection, Michael Latzer claims that there is an 'unmistakeable Christocentrism [to] his theodicy', which demonstrates the extent to which Leibniz's thinking 'is fully at home in the Western Christian tradition of theodicy' ('Leibniz's Conception of Metaphysical Evil', p. 15).
75. Voltaire, *Candide* (Paris: Magnard, 2013).
76. A similar argument might be put forward in the twenty-first century regarding the Holocaust: it seems perverse to claim that the Holocaust was part of God's plan and/or necessary for the greater good.
77. Renée Jeffery, *Evil and International Relations: Human Suffering in an Age of Terror* (Basingstoke: Palgrave Macmillan, 2008), p. 75.
78. The impact of the Lisbon earthquake on conceptual thought is nicely summarised by Susan Neiman, who explains that 'for Voltaire, Lisbon proved that law was impossible and philosophy vain. Rousseau found another occasion to quarrel with him over it, but the earthquake was not confined to the best minds in Europe. Popular reaction ranged from sermons to eyewitness reports to very bad poetry. Only in Prussia, it seems, were the consequences said to be less than earth-shaking. Frederick the Great thought it was overdoing things to cancel carnival preparations months after the disaster' (Susan Neiman, 'What's the Problem with Evil?', pp. 27–8, in *Rethinking Evil: Contemporary Perspectives*, ed. Maria Pia Lara [Berkeley: University of California Press, 2001], pp. 27–45).
79. Jeffery, *Evil and International Relations*, p. 75.
80. Immanuel Kant, 'On the Miscarriage of all Philosophical Trials in Theodicy', in *Religion within the Boundaries of Mere Reason and Other Writings*, trans. and ed. Allen Wood and George di Giovanni (Cambridge: Cambridge University Press, 1998), pp. 17–30.

# PART II  FROM AUTONOMOUS REASON TO HISTORY

# 6

# Kant on Radical Evil

'Kant's teaching', so wrote Arthur Schopenhauer, 'produces a fundamental change in every mind that has grasped it. This change is so great that it may be regarded as an intellectual rebirth.'[1] It is difficult to disagree with this description. The rebirth brought forth by Kant was not simply individual, but extended to the cultural and conceptual levels of Western thinking. While we have seen that thinkers within the Christian tradition uncritically accepted the notion that there was a definitive divine truth capable of being revealed by human cognition, Kant's innovation, one he likened in the *Critique of Pure Reason*[2] to that of Copernicus, was to introduce a critical philosophy that radically questioned the assumptions upon which previous thinking was based.

The importance to subsequent philosophy of this methodological alteration cannot be overstated. By examining the categories of cognition, Kant transformed the standard against which philosophical thought would subsequently be judged. Three different, but related, aspects stand out: first, Kant combined empirical realist and transcendental idealist positions to claim that while 'there is no doubt whatever that all our cognition begins with experience',[3] sensory experience passes through transcendental structures of cognition. These structures do not reveal objective reality as it is, but represent it through the lens of the universal structures of cognition. What human cognition takes to be the truth is, therefore, different from what truly is.

Second, Kant introduced the famous noumenal/phenomenal distinction, wherein the former refers to things-in-themselves and delineates what things truly are, and the latter refers to things as they appear to human cognition. Kant concluded that human cognition is incapable of passing beyond the phenomenal realm to the noumenal and, as such, is unable to know anything in-itself. This does not, however, mean that Kant falls into nihilism.

He claimed that, because the pure use of reason can lead cognition to unprovable metaphysical speculations about the unknowable thing-in-itself, human cognition must limit itself to the phenomenal, experiential realm.

Tying human cognition to the phenomenal realm led Kant away from the theocentric model of evil to an anthropocentric one. Rather than look to God to explain the nature of evil, the question must be asked and answered within the boundaries of the phenomenal experiences and possibilities of human understanding. This, third, instantiates a fundamentally different understanding of evil. Referring back to the noumenal/phenomenal distinction, Kant explains that, while human cognition is limited to the phenomenal realm, the human also has a noumenal aspect. While the phenomenal realm is composed of and determined by natural laws, the noumenal aspect is defined by freedom. Because the noumenal realm defines the 'essence' of human being, freedom entails the defining feature of human cognition, and because human cognition is that through which truth is affirmed, 'the concept of freedom ... constitutes the *keystone* of the whole structure of a system of pure reason, even of speculative reason'.[4] It is for this reason that Henry Allison concludes that 'Kant's critical philosophy is a philosophy of freedom.'[5]

Importantly, however, 'freedom' does not entail the capacity to arbitrarily choose, but is construed in terms of autonomy which, for Kant, is 'the capacity to act and think in accordance with principles whose validity we establish for ourselves through insight'.[6] The juxtaposition between the natural laws of the phenomenal realm and the freedom inherent in the noumenal realm brings Kant to the question of morality. After all, the human being is not simply determined by natural laws, but is also endowed with the capacity to choose its actions. The questions that arise include: how can the individual act in a phenomenal world conditioned by natural laws? And how should he act to be moral?

The *Critique of Practical Reason* provides an account of *practical reason*,[7] meaning practical activity guided by subjectively determined objective moral rules established by pure reason, to show that moral action is guided by a supreme maxim which, if adopted, affirms individual freedom. This is linked to the noumenal/phenomenal distinction, which, it will be remembered, claims that each particular thing entails a truth-in-itself, albeit one that, because it exists outside the boundaries of the transcendental structures of the phenomenal world, is inaccessible to human knowledge. There is, in other words, a truth to each particular thing, which means, in relation to the practical reason of morality, that there is one conception of the good manifested in a particular moral law.

Importantly, however, the will must choose to adopt this truth as its universal moral law. Only this will ensure that the moral law does not impinge on and so violate human freedom. This is compounded by Kant's claim that it is not sufficient for cognition to know the moral law; cognition must adopt it for the correct reasons, namely because it has internalised the moral law and identifies it as good in-itself.[8]

Kant recognises, however, that there are, at least, two ways in which cognition can relate to the objective moral imperative. An imperative commands *hypothetically* if 'the practical necessity of a possible action [is] a means to achieving something else that one wills (or that it is at least possible for one to will)'.[9] In other words, an imperative is hypothetical if cognition relates to it for the sake of something else, namely its own desires or ends. A *categorical* imperative, on the other hand, 'is that which represent[s] an action as objectively necessary of itself, without reference to another end'.[10] It is, in other words, good in and of itself and, as such, is necessary for 'a will in itself conforming to reason'.[11] Whereas a hypothetical imperative sees the action as means to another end, a categorical imperative sees the action as an end in itself.

Kant famously claims that this requires that cognition adopt, as its guiding principle, the maxim: '*I ought never to act except in such a way that I could also will that my maxim should become a universal law.*'[12] Whenever we act, we will act in a way that we wish all would act in accordance with. Practically, the human being should be treated '*never merely as means but always at the same time as ends in themselves*'.[13] The problem, however, is that human freedom and the limitations of human cognition ensure that cognition can never know, for sure, whether it is adopting the moral law for the correct moral reasons. After all, in Kant's famous phrase, 'the depths of the human heart are unfathomable'.[14] There is then always an ambiguity to the individual's self-designation of his moral worth and, as such, always a question mark over the moral worth of an action.[15]

Kant recognises that the adoption of the categorical imperative also has social consequences, in so far as its universal adoption would instantiate a 'kingdom of ends'[16] wherein every individual would will the same thing. This would, on Kant's terms, abolish violence, conflict, and suffering caused by the actions of others because he thinks that no rational individual would or could will that these become universal. Doing so would violate the universalist principle upon which the categorical imperative and hence individual moral action depend.

Importantly, whereas Kant claims that the categorical imperative should direct human action, it is up to each individual to affirm it. Each individual is, therefore, a sovereign who imposes rules on himself.[17] The problem, of course, is that the kingdom of ends depends upon each individual affirming the categorical imperative, an unlikely occurrence, and nature creating the conditions that permit each to do so, something that is beyond each individual's control.[18] This does not, however, mean that we should not try to achieve it. While the kingdom of ends is, as Kant admits, 'only an ideal',[19] it is one that he aims to motivate us towards.

With this, Kant affirms human cognition to an extent not previously seen, defines human morality based on the adoption of a subjectively determined universal maxim, makes human reason, not God, the ground of cognition, and, in so doing, usurps any privileging of theology. His moral framework is, therefore, fundamentally different from the Judaeo-Christian one that sees human freedom as being an operational act within a predetermined moral matrix delineated by God that is, to varying degrees, dependent upon God. For Kant, on the contrary, the moral law is not prescribed by an external source, but must be realised by human cognition limiting its activities to the phenomenal world as these are delineated by *a priori* rational reflection.

Kant's moral system is, then, one in which God has been displaced and replaced by reason. Two issues arise from this: first, if morality is dependent upon the human will choosing to adopt a maxim that it takes to be universal, what ensures that it will do so? And second, what happens if it does not? It is here that the question of evil rears its head.

The *Groundwork of the Metaphysics of Morals* and the *Critique of Practical Reason* do mention evil, but only in passing as they try to establish that there is a 'supreme principle of morality'[20] to subsequently delineate what this entails. There is an optimism to these texts, in so far as they seem to conclude that our morally bad world can be made better. Kant counterbalances this in the essay 'Of the Radical Evil in Human Nature', which first appeared in 1792 in the *Berlinische Monattsschrift* before being republished the next year as the first part of *Religion within the Boundaries of Mere Reason*. By undertaking an extended analysis of the possibility that cognition may not choose to adopt the categorical imperative as its moral maxim, he balances his previous optimistic tone, offers a new understanding of evil, and, with his notion of radical evil, introduces a conceptual innovation in our understanding of evil.

## The Structure of Individual Morality

While the Judaeo-Christian tradition distinguishes between moral, natural, and metaphysical evils, Kant reduces evil to a moral phenomenon based on free choice. He explains that morality entails two aspects, 'a conception of the human being as one who is free, but who also, just because of that, binds himself through his reason to unconditional laws'.[21] Morality 'in no way needs religion'[22] because it is self-sufficient, grounded in 'the universal lawfulness of [its] maxims'.[23] If the chosen maxim accords with the universal law, individual morality is good; if not, it is evil. The choice of maxim occurs through an act of will.

Kant adopts Augustine's affirmation of the relationship between will and evil, but refines it substantially by distinguishing between *Wille*, defined both as the faculty of volition generally speaking and as the choice of legislating rational norm specifically, and *Willkür*, entailing the power of choice. If the will was reduced to the faculty of volition (*Wille*), each choice would express the rational norm, which, for Kant, means the categorical imperative. There would not, in other words, be the possibility that the *Wille* could depart from the good to commit evil acts.[24] With the *Wille/Willkür* distinction, Kant holds that the will, broadly construed, is a two-stage process that both 'legislates norms through practical reasoning (*Wille*) and makes executive decisions to adopt maxims in the light of those norms (*Willkür*)'.[25] Human cognition is both free to determine the legislating moral norm adopted and responsible for its implementation. From this perspective, evil must be thought from the human perspective (rather than that of God) and, more specifically, an individual's moral choice.

Kant explains that 'we call a human being evil ... not because he performs actions that are evil (contrary to law), but because these are so constituted that they allow the inference of evil maxims in him'.[26] Gordon Michalson explains that 'a maxim is the guiding principle that I could state to myself were I to reflect upon the overall policy determining a given act ... A maxim is thus a subjective determining ground of the will, and its relation to the objective demands of the moral law determines the maxim's morality.'[27] This maxim 'can only be a single one [that] applies to the entire use of freedom universally'.[28] It can, therefore, either affirm the categorical imperative and so be good or fail to do so and so be evil.[29] The problem, of course, is that 'we cannot observe maxims'[30] and so 'the judgement that an agent is an evil human being cannot reliably be based on experience'.[31] It must, instead, 'be possible to infer *a priori* from a number of consciously evil actions, or even from a single one, an underlying evil maxim and, from this, the presence in the subject of a common ground, itself a maxim, of all particularly moral evil maxims'.[32]

The moral maxim chosen by the individual does not simply define his *moral* being. Kant goes beyond this to claim that it constitutes his nature.[33]

He warns, however, that nature is not meant in the sense of some determinism opposed to freedom. 'By "the nature of human being" we only understand ... the subjective ground – wherever it may lie – of the exercise of the human being's freedom in general (under objective moral laws) antecedent to every deed that falls within the scope of the senses.'[34] This subjective ground is never given to the individual, but is 'always ... a deed of freedom'.[35] If it were not, 'the ... abuse of the human being's power of choice with respect to the moral law could not be imputed to him, nor could the good or evil in him be called "moral"'.[36]

That the choice of moral maxim is a free one does not, however, mean that we can determine the ground motivating the choice. In a famous footnote, Kant explains that because 'any such maxim must have its ground as well ... no *determining ground* of the free power of choice ought to, or can, be adduced'.[37] 'We are endlessly referred back in the series of subjective determining grounds, without ever being able to come to the first ground.'[38]

Kant is here relying on the noumenal/phenomenal distinction. Freedom, rooted in the noumenal, always remains beyond the legitimate scrutiny of (phenomenal) human understanding. It is illegitimate to come to conclusions about anything that may have to do with the noumenal or, indeed, to even ask about what the noumenal means, entails, or sanctions. For this reason, he reminds us that

> whenever we say ... 'The human being is by nature good' or 'He is by nature evil', this only means that he holds within himself a first ground (to us inscrutable) for the adoption of good or evil (unlawful) means, and that he holds this ground *qua* human, universally – in such a way, therefore, that by his maxims he expresses at the same time the character of his species.[39]

Because it conditions an individual's moral being, the choice of maxim determines his phenomenal and hence natural being.

Whereas Kant claims that an individual's moral maxim is revealed through his action, it should be noted that, strictly speaking, this is not so. Rather than a causal relation, the moral maxim '*is posited* as the ground antecedent to every use of freedom given in experience'.[40] It is, therefore, 'present in the human being at the moment of birth – not that birth itself is its cause'.[41] This is a very difficult idea to think as it postulates the existence of a free individual choice prior to the advent of the individual's natural being. It does, however, emanate from Kant's noumenal/phenomenal distinction:

the individual's noumenal freedom chooses the moral maxim that will define his phenomenal being.

While noting that there is a tendency to seek a middle ground so that the individual is 'good in some parts and evil in others',[42] Kant rejects this by explaining that 'it is of great consequence to ethics in general ... to preclude, so far as possible, anything morally intermediate, either in actions (*adiaphora*) or in human characters; for with any such ambiguity all maxims run the risk of losing their determinations and stability'.[43] This rigorist position is underpinned by

> the morally important observation that freedom of the power of choice has the characteristic, entirely peculiar to it, that it cannot be determined to action through any incentive *except so far as the human being has incorporated it into his maxim* (has made it into a universal rule for himself, according to which he wills to conduct himself).[44]

Individuals act on the basis of their moral maxims because they have incorporated that maxim as their own. Their action is, therefore, not something that is tacked on to their being; it expresses their moral disposition (*Gesinnung*). To be moral, the individual must adhere to the moral law precisely because he recognises that this law is moral. The absence of ulterior motives and the recognition that the moral law is good in-itself means that whoever makes the moral law his maxim is '*morally* good'.[45] If, on the contrary, the individual does not adopt the moral law as his maxim, Kant claims that this is because he has previously adopted an evil moral maxim and is motivated by 'an incentive'[46] that is contrary to the moral law. He is, as a consequence, 'an evil human being'.[47]

Kant's point is to show that because an individual's action is a consequence of a single moral maxim, it is never indifferent, meaning neither good nor bad, nor can the individual

> be morally good in some parts, and at the same time evil in others. For if he is good in one part, he has incorporated the moral law into his maxim. And were he, therefore, to be evil in some other part, since the moral law of compliance with duty in general is a single one and universal, the maxim relating to it would be universal yet particular at the same time: which is contradictory.[48]

Later thinking will take seriously the notion that the individual is a complicated, paradoxical moral being, but Kant rejects this: the individual's moral maxim 'can only be a single one, and it applies to the entire use of freedom universally'.[49] With this, he reiterates his warning that 'there cannot be any further cognition of the subjective ground of the cause of this adoption (although we cannot avoid asking about it), for otherwise we would have to adduce still another maxim into which the disposition would have to be incorporated, and this maxim must in turn have a ground'.[50]

While it is tempting to question why an individual would choose a particular moral maxim, Kant warns that the structure of an individual's moral disposition (*Gesinnung*) prevents this. We can say much about how the individual's cultural background, upbringing, social circumstances, and so on influence the decision, but we are unable to give an ultimate answer as to why some choose a good moral maxim and others an evil one. This would require that we give a *theoretical* account of human freedom, which is precisely what Kant's critical philosophy denies as possible. Richard Bernstein points out, however, that 'from a practical point of view, we can (and must) postulate freedom, and assert that moral agents have the capacity to choose freely good or evil maxims'.[51] Even if we cannot explain it, we have to hold that individuals are morally free and, hence, responsible for their moral choices and character.

## The Predisposition (*Anlage*) and Propensity (*Hang*) of Human Being

If Kant's analysis merely held that individuals can choose between following the moral law or not, the innovation of his account would simply lie in showing that moral reason was autonomous. He goes beyond this by claiming that the individual's moral options reveal truths about human being *as a species*, specifically that it is constituted by a (non-determining) predisposition (*Anlage*) to the good and a propensity (*Hang*) to evil.[52] By predisposition (*Anlage*) to the good, Kant does not mean that the human being is good *per se*, but that 'it has been created for good'.[53] His point is that within the make-up of human being lies the *possibility* that the individual will choose a moral maxim that affirms the moral law.[54]

While noting that the choice of moral law must be made because it is taken to be an end in-itself, Kant claims that individuals affirm it because of three (non-determining) *incentives*: animality, rationality, and moral personality.[55] The animal aspect is orientated in relation to '*mechanical* self-love',[56] meaning 'a love for which reason is not required'.[57] This includes self-preservation, propagation of the species, and 'community with other human beings'.[58] The adoption of a good moral maxim facilitates all of these. The second motivation for affirming the moral law is due to an 'inbuilt' desire to compare ourselves with others, with this comparison requiring a form of reason.[59] It is only by comparing oneself to another that we can be happy or unhappy. The third form, personality, describes 'the susceptibility to respect ... the moral law *as of itself a sufficient incentive to the power of choice*'.[60] It reveals the extent to which the moral law acts as its own motivation. These incentives are not determinate or conscious; they are the inspiration for making the choice of moral maxim. Taken as a whole they are compatible with the moral law and 'demand compliance with it'.[61]

Kant recognises, however, that humanity is not just marked by a predisposition (*Anlage*) to the good. Working back from evil actions, he postulates that humanity also has a propensity to evil (*Hang zum Bösen*). He explains that 'by *propensity* (*propensio*) I understand the subjective ground of the possibility of an inclination (habitual desire, *concupiscentia*), in so far as this possibility is contingent for humanity in general'.[62] This is refined in a footnote where he explains that '*propensity* is actually only the *predisposition* to desire an enjoyment which, when the subject has experienced it, arouses *inclination* to it'.[63] This seems to conflate propensity with predisposition, but Kant clarifies that a propensity 'is distinguished from a predisposition in that a propensity can ... be innate yet *may* be represented as not being such: it can rather be thought of (if it is good) as *acquired*, or (if evil) as *brought* by the human being *upon* himself'.[64]

This, however, raises a further problem in that Kant seems to posit the possibility that a propensity can be good – 'it [a propensity] can be thought of (if it is good) as acquired'[65] and 'the will's capacity or incapacity arising from this natural propensity to adopt or not adopt the moral law in its maxims can be called *the good or evil heart*'[66] – before going on to claim that 'we are only talking of a propensity to genuine evil, i.e. moral evil'.[67] It is not clear why Kant makes this move, or what a propensity to the good entails, or even whether it is coherent given the predisposition (*Anlage*) to the good. One option would be to claim that the positing of a propensity to the good is simply another way of describing the predisposition (*Anlage*) to the good. This, however, depends on taking seriously the intimate connection between propensity (*Hang*) and predisposition (*Anlage*) in the statement that '*propensity* is actually only the *predisposition* to desire an enjoyment'.[68] But if this is the case, it is not clear why Kant needs to introduce the distinction between predisposition (*Anlage*) to the good and propensity (*Hang*) to evil in the first place.

Kant's account of propensity does not stop with the claim that propensity describes 'the subjective ground of the possibility of an inclination (habitual desire, *concupiscentia*), in so far as this possibility is contingent for humanity in general'.[69] He also explains that it entails 'a subjective determining ground of the power of choice *that precedes* every deed, and hence is itself not yet a deed'.[70] The problem is that it is not exactly clear that these two definitions of propensity are compatible. The first claims that a propensity is the subjective ground of an inclination that is contingent for all humanity, while the second claims that it describes the subjective determining ground of every individual's free choice.

Understanding the relation between these descriptions requires that we follow Kant in distinguishing between different forms of propensity. For Kant, 'a propensity is either physical, i.e. it pertains to a human's power of choice as natural being; or moral, i.e. it pertains to a human's power of choice as moral being'.[71] A physical propensity refers to the first definition above ('the subjective ground of the possibility ...'), while a moral propensity refers to the second ('a subjective determining ground of the power of choice ...'). In both cases, however, the propensity does not *determine* the choice made. The propensity is 'only attach[ed] to the moral faculty of choice',[72] although Kant reminds us that 'nothing is ... morally (i.e. imputably) evil but that which is our own deed'.[73]

Kant is here suggesting that human being *as a species* is defined by natural, physical possibilities manifested differently in each specific individual. The individual is not responsible for those physical propensities, but he is morally responsible for what he chooses to do with them, a choice permitted because of his *Willkür*. After all, 'the alcoholic who has a physical propensity to alcohol is not responsible for that physical propensity, but only for the use they make of it'.[74] The propensity to evil is, then, that which supports or grounds the individual's decision to choose a moral maxim that departs from the moral law. It 'is not identical to choosing evil, but it is the condition that implies that one *will* choose evil'.[75]

The individual can only choose evil, however, if it is a possibility inherent in human being as such. For this reason, Kant explains that 'the propensity to evil is here established (as regards actions) in the human being, even the best; and so it also must be if it is to be proved that the propensity to evil among human beings is universal, or, which here amounts to the same thing, that it is woven into human nature'.[76] That evil is woven into the fabric of human being is a marked departure from previous thought on the topic.

The problem, however, is that Kant has not yet actually shown this. It is for this reason that he explains that '*if* it is legitimate to assume that this propensity belongs to the human being universally (and hence to the character of the species), the propensity will be called a *natural* propensity of the human being to evil'.⁷⁷ This is exacerbated by Kant's claim that he does not actually need to provide a formal proof for this: 'we can spare ourselves the formal proof that there must be such a corrupt propensity rooted in human being, in view of the multitude of woeful examples that the experience of human *deeds* parades before us'.⁷⁸ With this, he lists a number of empirical examples, from anthropological studies of the ritual murders of the Tofoa in New Zealand and the Navigator Islands, to the 'never-ending cruelty ... in the wide wastes of northwestern America from which, indeed, no human being derives the least benefit',⁷⁹ before turning his sights to 'civilised state[s]'⁸⁰ to show the litany of moral wrongs that occur there. The implication is that the widespread existence of moral wrongs across such diverse geographical spaces and socio-political formations indicates the existence of some propensity to evil within human nature.

However, he subsequently warns that

> even though the existence of this propensity to evil in human nature can be established through experiential demonstrations of the actual resistance in time of the human power of choice against the [moral] law, these demonstrations still do not teach us the real nature of that propensity or the ground of this resistance.⁸¹

This is because the choice of moral maxim has to do with 'the power of free choice (the concept of which is not empirical)'⁸² with regard 'to the moral law (of which the conceptual is equally purely intellectual)',⁸³ with the consequence that the moral maxim 'must be cognised *a priori* from the concept of evil, so far as the latter is possible according to the laws of freedom (of obligation and imputability)'.⁸⁴ Much recent scholarship has tried to understand what Kant is pointing to here and, indeed, what it means for his attempt to demonstrate that human being is constituted by a propensity to evil. The key question is whether it is legitimate for Kant to posit a natural human propensity to evil from the widespread empirical evidence or whether he needs to provide an *a priori* proof for its existence independent of the empirical evidence.⁸⁵

At this stage, however, it might be helpful to bring together the different strands of Kant's analysis. When we do, we find that human being is defined by a non-determining predisposition (*Anlage*) to the good and a non-determining propensity (*Hang*) to evil. Each particular human being must choose, through his *Willkür*, which to affirm as his moral maxim and, hence, the subjective ground of his moral disposition or character (*Gesinnung*). Those that choose to affirm their predisposition to the good choose a moral maxim in conformity with the moral law and so are morally good; those that affirm the propensity to evil choose a moral maxim that departs from the moral law and so are morally evil.

Kant does, however, recognise that there are gradations of evil that emanate from the way in which the individual turns away from the moral law:

> *First*, it is the general weakness of the human heart in complying with the adopted maxims, or the *frailty* of human nature; *second*, the propensity to adulterate moral incentives with immoral ones (even when it is done with good intention, and under maxims of the good), i.e. *impurity*; *third*, the propensity to adopt evil maxims, i.e. the *depravity* of human nature, or of the human heart.[86]

These exist in a descending order of seriousness. The first, for example, points to the possibility that the individual may choose a good moral maxim, but in its application not always follow it. The second points out that the individual may choose a good moral maxim and *intend* to follow it, but 'has not, as ... should be [the case], adopted the law *alone* as its *sufficient* incentive'.[87] He, therefore, 'often (and perhaps always) needs still other incentives besides it in order to determine the power of choice for what duty requires'.[88]

The first two forms seem to imply that the individual can choose the moral law as its moral maxim, but subsequently not live up to its exalted status. The moral law is affirmed, but the individual does not always act from the right moral incentive. Kant explains that this can occur because 'an evil heart can co-exist with a will which in the abstract is good'.[89] It is not, however, clear that Kant's rigorism permits this moral ambiguity. If the choice of moral maxim conditions an individual's subsequent moral action, how can the individual who has chosen the moral law as its maxim subsequently act contrarily to it? Kant never responds specifically to this question, although presumably it has to do with the fundamental role that freedom plays in morality.

Depravity is the third and most serious form of evil because it entails 'the *corruption* (*corruptio*) of the human heart'[90] and the subordination of the moral law to other, non-moral ends. This does not entail something as simple as intending to affirm the good but misunderstanding what is required. It points to a far more serious form of 'diabolical evil',[91] wherein the individual understands that what he is doing is evil and continues to affirm it. In other words, he does evil for evil's sake. However, while a logical possibility, diabolical evil is not, for Kant, a practical one.

Importantly, Kant explains that the incentive motivating the adoption of an evil moral maxim 'reverses the ethical order as regards the incentives of a *free* power of choice'.[92] This is repeated later in the essay: 'the human being (even the best) is evil only because he reverses the moral order of his incentives in incorporating them into his maxims'.[93] Kant's point is that, while the individual's choice of moral maxim is premised on numerous incentives, two dominate: self-love and the duty of the moral law. To be morally good, the incentive that stimulates action must be the latter because it is understood that the moral law is good 'in-itself'. In contrast, evil arises when the former is privileged and actions are committed out of moral self-love.

This is different from the '*mechanical* self-love'[94] that emanates from the animal aspect of human being and describes those actions that humans naturally desire, such as self-preservation, propagation of the species, and to live in community with others. These accord with the moral law. In contrast, when acting from *moral* self-love, the individual

> makes the incentives of self-love and their inclinations the condition of compliance with the moral law – whereas it is this latter that, as *the supreme condition* of the satisfaction of the former, should have been incorporated into the universal maxim of the power of choice as the sole incentive.[95]

Whereas affirming moral self-love over the moral law, or, more subtly, asserting the moral law for reasons of self-love, ensures that individual action may still be moral (i.e. in conformity with the demands of autonomous reason) and, indeed, 'legally good',[96] because it is done for non-moral reasons, such action will always be *morally* wrong.

Kant is not, then, claiming that the morally evil individual is simply asocial. A morally evil individual is still able to function in society because he can still act in accordance with social laws. However, 'while [his] empirical character is ... good [his] intelligible character [is] evil'.[97] Kant is simply pointing out that the worth of an action is not defined by its consequences or whether it follows social laws. It is defined by the incentive that motivates the moral action. Individuals can, therefore, appear to be moral, when, in actuality, they are not.

## The Origin of Evil in Human Nature

Recognising that his account of evil operates at the levels of the individual *and* the species, Kant clarifies that 'the statement, "The human being is *evil*," cannot mean anything else than that [the individual] is conscious of the moral law and yet has incorporated into his maxim the (occasional) deviation from it'.[98] The statement that '"He is evil *by nature*" simply means that being evil applies to him considered in his species'.[99] This does not indicate that it can be inferred from 'the concept of his species',[100] only that 'through experience . . . we may presuppose evil as subjectively necessary in every human being, even the best'.[101] At both the individual and the species level, Kant is using the term 'natural' in the sense of a determining, sensuous nature. Moral evil cannot be explained in this way because sensuous nature 'contains too little to provide a ground for moral evil in human being, for, to the extent that it eliminates the incentives originating in freedom, it makes of the human, a purely *animal* being'.[102] As a moral concept, evil must be explained through freedom and not through sensuous nature.

However, despite rejecting the notion that the propensity to evil is something natural, Kant claims that 'if a propensity to [evil] does lie in human nature, then there is in the human being a natural propensity to evil; and this propensity is itself evil, since it must ultimately be sought in a free power of choice'.[103] This is, initially, somewhat confusing, but it becomes clearer when we remember that the propensity to evil exists at both the level of the human species and that of the individual human. Assuming that a propensity to evil exists at the level of the human species, we can say that there is a natural propensity to evil 'within' human being considered as a species. This simply means that the possibility of turning away from the moral law is part of human being. While this possibility is inherent in the human species, it does not determine an individual's moral choice. Each individual human has the option to choose a moral maxim that affirms or denies the moral law. This choice is, of course, a noumenal one and so exists prior to the advent of the individual *in time*.[104] As a noumenal choice, it subsequently appears at the 'start' of the individual's phenomenal being and so appears as part of the individual's 'nature'.

'Nature' must, however, be understood in the sense of the subjective ground of moral character, not in the sense of an individual's sensuous, bodily nature. Because the propensity (*Hang*) to evil exists as a non-determining possibility of *human being*, it can and must be affirmed by each individual through the choice of a moral maxim contrary to the moral law. Since the noumenal choice of moral maxim creates the subjective ground of the individual's future morality, Kant claims that this choice determines the *nature* of an individual's moral character (*Gesinnung*). It is, however, 'natural' not in the sense of being biologically determining, but in the sense of the autonomously chosen foundation of the individual's *moral character*.

It is for this reason that Kant claims that there is 'a *radical* innate *evil* in human nature (not any the less brought upon us by ourselves)'.[105] It is *radical* in the Latin etymological sense of the term (*radix*), meaning root or base; *innate*, in that the choice of moral maxim is undertaken prior to the phenomenal appearance of the individual and so appears at the 'start' of the individual's phenomenal being; and in *human nature*, in so far as Kant holds that evil is a possibility of the human species.

With this, Kant departs radically from the Christian account of Original Sin. Rather than hold 'that a prior innate propensity to transgression is presupposed in us but not in the first human being, in whom rather innocence is presupposed with respect to time',[106] he claims that there never was a moment of phenomenal innocence. The nature of human being is marked by 'a prior innate depravity'.[107] This is not, of course, determinate for the individual. It simply means that the possibility of evil marks human being.

## Concluding Remarks

That the individual makes himself morally is the fundamental argument of Kant's moral theory. It requires that the individual be free to choose his own moral existence. By grounding the choice of moral evil in individual will, Kant remains tied to the Augustinian conception of moral subjectivity even as he rejects Augustine's metaphysics and conception of evil. Because 'the human being must make or have made *himself* into whatever he is or should become in a moral sense',[108] Kant warns that the individual always has the possibility of altering the maxim he adheres to. The problem is that it is not clear 'how it is possible that a naturally evil human being should make himself into a good human being'.[109]

This is compounded by a remark Kant makes in the 1793 essay 'On the Common Saying: "This may be True in Theory, but it does not Apply in Practice"' that evil 'destroys itself' whereas 'good ... continues to maintain itself once it has been established'.[110] He does not expand on this, so it is not clear why or how evil destroys itself or how this is possible if a moral maxim depends on an individual's choice. One way to resolve it would be for Kant to once more fall back on his insistence that the choice and ultimate meaning of evil are noumenal ones that are, by definition, beyond our phenomenal knowledge.[111]

This does, however, bring forth the question of why an individual would choose to alter his moral maxim. Again, the explanation is underdeveloped, but one reason postulated is derived from Kant's claim that, if the individual chooses to adopt an evil moral maxim, 'the command that we *ought* to become better human beings still resounds unabated in our souls'.[112] We must, then, 'presuppose in all this that there is still a germ of goodness left in its entire purity, a germ that cannot be extirpated or corrupted'.[113]

It is not clear how this fits with Kant's moral rigorism, which demands that the choice of moral maxim be singular, but it presumably requires a distinction between the moral choice of the individual and the conditions constitutive of the human being as a species. Remembering that the individual must choose whether to affirm the predisposition to the good or the propensity to evil inherent in human being as a species, we discover that, even if the *individual* chooses evil, the good still adheres to him given his membership of the human species. In other words, the individual's choice affirms one of the options presented by his membership of the human species but does not obliterate the other option. A good maxim can always be replaced by an evil one and vice versa.

For evil to be overcome requires that an individual recover 'the *purity* of the law, as the supreme ground of all our maxims, according to which the law itself is to be incorporated into the power of choice, not merely bound to other incentives, nor indeed subordinated to them (to inclinations) as conditions, but rather in its full purity, as the self-*sufficient* incentive of that power'.[114] This is not, however, a gradual alteration. Because the ground of an individual's moral action is a single principle, changing his moral disposition requires that the single principle be altered. For this reason, 'it must be effected through a *revolution* in the disposition of the human being (a transition to the maxim of holiness of disposition)'.[115] Through this revolution 'a "new man"'[116] is born.

As Kant recognises, the problem is that 'if a human being is corrupt in the very ground of his maxims, how can he possibly bring about this revolution by his own forces and become a good human being on his own?'[117] That his moral maxim is grounded in freedom means that the individual must, in theory, be able to simply alter his chosen moral maxim, meaning that he can move from an evil to a good one. However, because the moral maxim chosen determines subsequent values and choices, the choice of evil seems to prevent the individual from being able to countenance, let alone choose, an alternative. After all, 'this could only happen through good maxims – something that cannot take place if the subjective supreme ground of all maxims is presupposed to be corrupted'.[118] An evil maxim is radical precisely because 'it corrupts the ground of all maxims'.[119]

As noted, explaining how this is possible would require a *theoretical* analysis of freedom, which is precisely what is rejected by Kant's critical philosophy. Practically speaking, however, Kant recommends that the 'predisposition to the good is cultivated in no better way than by just adducing the *example* of good people (as regards their conformity to law)'.[120] It is never spelt out, but the thinking seems to be that their example will wear off on others. How or why this occurs is never engaged with. Its success presumably depends upon the individual learning the 'correct' lessons from the experience of moral individuals.

The problem, however, is that the individual cannot be assured of the success of any alteration to his moral maxim because 'the depths of his own heart (the subjective first ground of his maxims) are to him inscrutable'.[121] Nonetheless, we 'must be able to *hope* that, by the exertion of *his own* power, he will attain to the road that leads in that direction, as indicated to him by a fundamentally improved disposition'.[122] Kant cannot say any more on the topic for the simple reason that the choice of moral maxim is a *practical* action, not a theoretical endeavour. We cannot *know* why or how one individual chooses a moral maxim over another or, indeed, is able to change it. Explaining this would impose logical necessity on our will (*Willkür*) and so undermine its freedom. We can only *experience* the choice and the conversion. That Kant cannot explain the choice of individual moral maxim or the conversion process from one to the other is not, however, a failure; it is a direct consequence of his critical philosophy, one that emphasises that freedom lies at the foundation of our moral choices and *must* lie there if we are to be morally responsible.

## Notes

1. Arthur Schopenhauer, *The World as Will and Representation*, 2 vols, trans. E. F. J. Payne (New York: Dover, 1966), vol. 1, p. xxiii.
2. Immanuel Kant, *Critique of Pure Reason*, trans. and ed. Paul Guyer and Allen Wood (Cambridge: Cambridge University Press, 1998), B.xvi.
3. Ibid. B1.
4. Immanuel Kant, *Critique of Practical Reason*, trans. Mary Gregor (Cambridge: Cambridge University Press, 1997), 5:3.
5. Henry E. Allison, *Kant's Theory of Freedom* (Cambridge: Cambridge University Press, 1990), p. 1.
6. Peter Dews, *The Idea of Evil* (Oxford: Blackwell, 2008), p. 18.
7. Kant, *Critique of Practical Reason*, 5:3.
8. Immanuel Kant, *Groundwork of the Metaphysics of Morals*, trans. Mary Gregor (Cambridge: Cambridge University Press, 1998), 4:413.
9. Ibid. 4:414.
10. Ibid. 4:414.
11. Ibid. 4:414.
12. Ibid. 4:402.

13. Ibid. 4:433.
14. Immanuel Kant, *The Metaphysics of Morals*, trans. and ed. Mary Gregor (Cambridge: Cambridge University Press, 1996), 6:447. See also Kant, *Groundwork of the Metaphysics of Morals*, 4:407; and Immanuel Kant, *Religion within the Boundaries of Mere Reason and Other Writings*, trans. and ed. Allen Wood and George di Giovanni (Cambridge: Cambridge University Press, 1998), 6:51, 71, 87–8.
15. For an interesting discussion of this issue, see Owen Ware, 'The Duty of Self-Knowledge', *Philosophy and Phenomenological Review*, 79:3, November, 2009, pp. 671–98.
16. Kant, *Groundwork of the Metaphysics of Morals*, 4:433.
17. Ibid. 4:438.
18. Ibid. 4:438.
19. Ibid. 4:433.
20. Ibid. 4:392.
21. Kant, *Religion within the Boundaries of Mere Reason*, 6:3.
22. Ibid. 6:3.
23. Ibid. 6:3.
24. For a good summary of the need for the *Wille/Willkür* distinction, see Joshua Glasgow, 'Kant's Conception of Humanity', *Journal of the History of Philosophy*, 45:2, 2007, pp. 291–308 (p. 293).
25. Paul Formosa, 'Kant on the Radical Evil of Human Nature', *The Philosophical Forum*, 38:3, 2007, pp. 221–45 (p. 221).
26. Kant, *Religion within the Boundaries of Mere Reason*, 6:20.
27. Gordon Michalson, *Fallen Freedom: Kant on Radical Evil and Moral Regeneration* (Cambridge: Cambridge University Press, 1990), pp. 32–3.
28. Kant, *Religion within the Boundaries of Mere Reason*, 6:25.
29. Ibid. 6:24.
30. Ibid. 6:20.
31. Ibid. 6: 20.
32. Ibid. 6:20.
33. Ibid. 6:21.
34. Ibid. 6:21.
35. Ibid. 6:21.
36. Ibid. 6:21.
37. Ibid. 6:21fn.
38. Ibid. 6:21fn.
39. Ibid. 6:21.
40. Ibid. 6:22, emphasis added.
41. Ibid. 6:22.
42. Ibid. 6:22.
43. Ibid. 6:22. Given that we will return to her thought, it is worth noting that Claudia Card criticises Kant's rigorism in her 'Kant's Moral Excluded Middle',

in *Kant's Anatomy of Evil*, ed. Sharon Anderson-Gold and Pablo Muchnik (Cambridge: Cambridge University Press, 2014), pp. 74–92.
44. Kant, *Religion within the Boundaries of Mere Reason*, 6:23–4.
45. Ibid. 6:24.
46. Ibid. 6:24.
47. Ibid. 6:24.
48. Ibid. 6:24–5.
49. Ibid. 6: 25.
50. Ibid. 6:25.
51. Richard Bernstein, *Radical Evil: A Philosophical Interrogation* (Cambridge: Polity, 2002), p. 25.
52. A large literature has grown that tries to explain what exactly Kant means by these concepts and how they fit together. For example, Henry E. Allison, 'On the Very Idea of a Propensity to Evil', *The Journal of Value Inquiry*, 36, 2002, pp. 337–48; Stephen R. Grimm, 'Kant's Argument for Radical Evil', *European Journal of Philosophy*, 10:2, 2002, pp. 160–77; Patrick R. Frieson, 'Character and Evil in Kant's Moral Anthropology', *Journal of the History of Philosophy*, 44:4, 2006, pp. 623–34; Formosa, 'Kant on the Radical Evil of Human Nature'; and Samuel Duncan, '"There is none Righteous": Kant on the *Hang zum Bösen* and the Universal Evil in History', *The Southern Journal of Philosophy*, 49:2, 2011, pp. 137–63.
53. Kant, *Religion within the Boundaries of Mere Reason*, 6:44.
54. For more on this, see Samuel Loncar, 'Converting the Kantian Self: Radical Evil, Agency, and Conversion in Kant's *Religion within the Boundaries of Mere Reason*', *Kant-Studien*, 104:3, 2013, pp. 346–66 (p. 357).
55. Kant, *Religion within the Boundaries of Mere Reason*, 6:26.
56. Ibid. 6:26.
57. Ibid. 6:26.
58. Ibid. 6:26.
59. Ibid. 6:27.
60. Ibid. 6:27.
61. Ibid. 6:28.
62. Ibid. 6:29.
63. Ibid. 6:29fn.
64. Ibid. 6:29.
65. Ibid. 6:29.
66. Ibid. 6:29.
67. Ibid. 6:29.
68. Ibid. 6:29fn.
69. Ibid. 6:29.
70. Ibid. 6:31.
71. Ibid. 6:31.
72. Ibid. 6:31.

73. Ibid. 6:31.
74. Formosa, 'Kant on the Radical Evil of Human Nature', p. 224.
75. Patrick R. Frieson, *Freedom and Anthropology in Kant's Moral Philosophy* (Cambridge: Cambridge University Press, 2003), pp. 109–10. On this point, see also Sharon Anderson-Gold, 'Kant's Rejection of Devilishness: The Limits of Human Volition', *Idealistic Studies*, 14:1, 1984, pp. 35–48 (p. 46).
76. Kant, *Religion within the Boundaries of Mere Reason*, 6:30.
77. Ibid. 6:29, emphasis added.
78. Ibid. 6:32–3.
79. Ibid. 6:33.
80. Ibid. 6:33.
81. Ibid. 6:35.
82. Ibid. 6:35.
83. Ibid. 6:35.
84. Ibid. 6:35.
85. The former option is defended in Allen Wood, *Kant's Ethical Thought* (Cambridge: Cambridge University Press, 1999), p. 287, the latter in Henry E. Allison, 'Ethics, Evil, and Anthropology in Kant: Remarks on Allen Wood's *Kant's Ethical Thought*', *Ethics*, 111, 2001, pp. 594–613 (pp. 606–7).
86. Kant, *Religion within the Boundaries of Mere Reason*, 6:29.
87. Ibid. 6:30.
88. Ibid. 6:30.
89. Ibid. 6:37.
90. Ibid. 6:30.
91. Ibid. 6:37.
92. Ibid. 6:30.
93. Ibid. 6:36.
94. Ibid. 6:26.
95. Ibid. 6:36.
96. Ibid. 6:30.
97. Ibid. 6:37.
98. Ibid. 6:32.
99. Ibid. 6:30.
100. Ibid. 6:32.
101. Ibid. 6:32.
102. Ibid. 6:35.
103. Ibid. 6:37.
104. 'We must not however seek an origin in time of a moral character for which we are to be held accountable, however unavoidable this might be if we want to *explain* the contingent existence of this character' (ibid. 6:43).
105. Ibid. 6:32.
106. Ibid. 6:42.
107. Ibid. 6:42.

108. Ibid. 6:44.
109. Ibid. 6:44–5.
110. Immanuel Kant, 'On the Common Saying: "This may be True in Theory, but it does not Apply in Practice,"' p. 91, in *Political Writings*, ed. Hans Reiss, trans. H. B. Nisbet (Cambridge: Cambridge University Press, 1991), pp. 61–92.
111. Kant, *Religion within the Boundaries of Mere Reason*, 6:45.
112. Ibid. 6:45.
113. Ibid. 6:45.
114. Ibid. 6:46.
115. Ibid. 6:47.
116. Ibid. 6:47.
117. Ibid. 6:47.
118. Ibid. 6:37.
119. Ibid. 6:37.
120. Ibid. 6:48.
121. Ibid. 6:51.
122. Ibid. 6:51.

# 7
# Schelling and the Metaphysics of Evil

The power and implications of Kant's critical philosophy were immediately recognised, with its influence pervading intellectual life. This is not, however, to say that it was universally and uncritically accepted. Despite its depth and rigour, many felt uncomfortable with various aspects of Kant's thinking. Kant's claim that he 'had to deny knowledge in order to make room for faith'[1] made those who were religiously orientated uneasy about the implications of the noumenal/phenomenal distinction. Faith was the bedrock of Christianity, but was, as we have seen in previous chapters, accompanied by a long-standing attempt to understand God, His actions, and the universe He created. For Kant to reject such an endeavour not only challenged the dominant epistemological framework of Western Europe, but also struck at the very heart of Christian intellectual life.

In contrast, those who were willing to follow Kant's critical perspective quickly noticed that there were a number of problems with it. First, although Kant insisted that knowledge must be limited to the phenomenal realm, meaning that we cannot know anything positive about the contents of the noumenal realm, he claimed that the positing of the existence of the noumenal realm was necessary to explain and account for the phenomenal one. In other words, Kant distinguished between the form and content of the noumenal realm. He accepted that human cognition had to *posit* the noumenal realm to explain the phenomenal one, but was careful to claim that human cognition could not *know* anything of the content of the former. However, in making the latter claim, it appeared that Kant relied upon knowledge of the noumenon; namely, that 'it' is so structured that we cannot know anything about it. Kant's positing of the noumenon therefore violated the central tenet of his critical philosophy.

Second, Kant's acceptance of antinomies of reason, such as theoretical and practical reason and freedom and necessity, were attacked. Whereas

Kant held that these arose from and, indeed, reaffirmed the noumenal/phenomenal distinction, others were not so sure, instead claiming that these seemed to point to an incompleteness that needed to be explained.

Third, it was suggested that Kant's analyses of morality and, in particular, evil resulted in what Terry Pinkard calls a 'paradox'.[2] Kant famously argued that we are practically self-determining, with this occurring through our autonomous choice of moral maxim. Pinkard points out, however, that 'if the will imposes such a "law" on itself, then it must do so for a reason (or else be lawless)'.[3] A lawless will, however, cannot be regarded as a free will because freedom, for Kant, is synonymous with morality, and hence law, not arbitrary action. As a consequence, 'the will must impose this law on itself for a reason'.[4] But, if it does so, it 'cannot itself be self-imposed (since it is required to impose any other reasons)'.[5] In other words, the choice of a moral law cannot be arbitrary but must depend on and be legitimated by a founding reason, which in turn must be justified by a reason and so on. 'The "paradox" is that we seem to be both required not to have an antecedent reason for the legislation of any basic maxim and to have such a reason.'[6] The Kantian solution seemed to run into and, indeed, depend upon a vicious circularity.

It appeared, therefore, that Kant's position, for all its originality, scholarly endeavour, and rigour, was both internally contradictory and foundationally problematic in that it was unable to explain the ground of moral choice (*Willkür*); that is, what brings some to affirm the universal law and others to turn away from it. Whereas Kant contented himself with the notion that this choice is a question that cannot be legitimately posed within the boundaries of human cognition, others argued that this was because he either drew the wrong conclusions from his arguments or formulated the problem incorrectly.[7]

Johann Gottlieb Fichte, for example, claimed that the problems in Kant's account could be resolved by intensifying Kant's affirmation of the autonomous I.[8] Frederick Beiser notes that there are two dominant understandings of what this entails: one that sees Fichte as offering a form of absolute idealism that 'affirms the existence of an absolute ego that posits itself as all reality',[9] and another, termed subjective idealism, that 'limits all knowledge down to the presentations of the *finite* subject and confers only a regulative status upon the absolute ego'.[10] There is no space to debate the finer points of this interpretative disagreement, but both positions agree that, whereas Kant posits this autonomy as the foundational point of morality, but locates it in the unknowable noumenal realm, Fichte accepts the principle of the autonomous I but rejects the Kantian noumenal.[11] In the case of the absolute idealist position, the noumenon is replaced by an absolute ego, and in the case of the subjective idealist position, the noumenon is displaced by a regulative ideal posited by the finite subject. In either scenario, 'the subjective, the I, alone remain[s]'.[12]

In turn, the one-sidedness of Fichte's approach was rejected by Friedrich Schelling, who argued that the problem addressed by Kant and Fichte had to be radically reconfigured. Specifically, Schelling charged that Kant settled on several antinomies that, on Schelling's telling, pointed to the existence of a prior unity. As such, the question must be orientated around this 'prior' whole. While Fichte claimed that this prior unity is the autonomous ego, Schelling points out that Fichte's notion of an I that becomes from the non-I depends upon the prior existence of the latter.[13] As a consequence, Schelling concludes, contra Fichte, that the 'I cannot possibly produce the world'.[14] The human ego is not the whole of nature, but an effect of the whole that is nature. The fundamental question, then, is not the nature of the I, but the existence and nature of the world that grounds the I. Questioning this ground brought Schelling to conceive of it as a tumultuous, unconscious abyss that generates being and individual decisions. In his famous 1809 treatise *Philosophical Investigations into the Essence of Human Freedom*,[15] he uses this abyssal ground to analyse the possibility and nature of evil.

## The Problem of Previous Explanations of Evil

Schelling follows Kant and Fichte in maintaining the central importance of freedom. Evil is a possibility for each individual because each is fundamentally free.[16] Freedom is not, however, simply located at the individual level. It describes the fundamental structure of existence. In turn, evil is a possibility woven into the 'fabric' of existence in general.

To outline what this means, Schelling distinguishes his understanding of evil from previous ones, starting with the Platonic. According to Schelling, Platonism is rooted in a strict metaphysical duality between a privileged ideal world reachable through pure reason and a secondary, degraded, natural world. Platonic thought does not, then, 'oppose heaven with hell, as is fitting, but with the earth'.[17] By conceiving of evil as the absence of pure reason and, hence, the good, it collapses 'evil' into the secondary natural realm.[18] If, however, '*all* natural beings are ... evil by virtue of being ... the natural world just is evil [and] no analysis of evil is required because natural beings cannot be described in any other way. As a consequence, the concept is superfluous.'[19] Schelling rejects this and, in so doing, rejects the conflation of evil with natural being: 'a determination of nature ... cannot be objectively evil'.[20] The natural and the moral are distinct conceptual categories. Evil belongs to morality and so must be explained by the freedom that defines it.

Schelling next engages with theological debates relating to whether monotheistic and polytheistic traditions can adequately understand the concept. Regarding the former, he asks whether a positive conception of evil is compatible with the notion of a supreme being thought in terms of omnipotence and supreme goodness.[21] He concludes that this formulation leads to the following antinomy:

> either real evil is admitted and, hence, it is inevitable that evil be posited within infinite substance or the primal will itself, whereby the concept of a most perfect being is utterly destroyed, or the reality of evil must in some way be denied, whereby, however, at the same time the real concept of freedom [which requires a choice of good or evil] vanishes.[22]

In other words, either God, understood as the most perfect being, or freedom must be abandoned. Both possibilities are rejected by Schelling.

He does, however, recognise that the problem may lie in how the two concepts are related to one another. Rather than conceiving of God as the being that continuously supports human action, Schelling considers whether the situation changes if we assume 'the most distant connection between God and beings in the world'.[23] This would respect the monotheistic tradition's insistence that God was the creator of the world while allowing the beings created sufficient autonomy from Him.

No sooner has Schelling proposed this, however, than he identifies two problems with it: first, 'if God were to withhold his omnipotence for a moment, man would cease to be'.[24] In other words, if God is the ground of human being, this ground can never be removed without, at the same time, annihilating that which it supports, including human being. Second, if God maintains only a tenuous connection between Himself and human action, there is still a connection, which means, according to Schelling, that 'God appears undeniably to share responsibility for evil in so far as permitting an entirely dependent being to do evil is surely not much better than to cause it to do so'.[25] Responding to this problem brought the Augustinian-Aquinian tradition to conclude that 'the reality of evil must be denied in one way or the other'.[26] For Schelling, this is unacceptable. Evil has real being. It is this that is innovative and original about his analysis.

Schelling goes on to distinguish his position from the Christian tradition by rejecting the notion that evil is the consequence of Original Sin or came about due to a Fall from a prior state of perfection. While this may establish *that* an evil principle comes to exist in a world created by an all-powerful, supremely good deity, it does not explain *how* this is possible. Claiming that an individual turned against God does not explain how this was possible *if* God is supremely good, all-powerful, and omniscient. For the same reason, 'we ... cannot presuppose something like a created spirit which, having fallen itself, tempted man to fall, for the question here is exactly how evil arose in creatures'.[27]

Schelling initially responds by proposing the idea that evil results from individual alienation from God. He claims that there are three ways to think this. First, the estrangement could entail 'an involuntary estrangement on the part of things but not on the part of God'.[28] However, in this case, the things affected are cast out by God, meaning that 'God is the originator of this condition'.[29] He would then be the originator of evil. Second, it could entail an involuntary act on both sides caused 'by an overflow [*Überfluß*] of being';[30] a position rejected by Schelling as 'an utterly untenable idea'.[31] Third, the estrangement from God could be a consequence of a voluntary action of non-divine things where they tear themselves away from God. The problem, however, is that this requires that there be a propensity in things that brings them to tear themselves away from God and so do evil. Not only would this propensity have to be installed in beings, which, based on Christian doctrine, means it emanates from God, but simply focusing on the voluntary act of estranging oneself from God does not explain where the motivation for that act came from. It provides 'no explanation of [evil's] origin'.[32]

Similar reasoning lies behind Schelling's rejection of the notion that the good–evil relationship be thought quantitatively along a continuum wherein 'evil ... is [a] lower degree of perfection'.[33] A continuum may allow us to distinguish between different forms of evil, but it does not explain the origins of 'evil' *per se*, especially if it is held that the universe was created by an all-powerful, supremely good God.[34] One possible response, of course, would be to move from a monotheistic metaphysics to a dualistic one to explain that the possibility of freedom is a consequence of the actions of another cosmic being independent of God. Schelling rejects this, however, claiming that metaphysical dualism can only ever entail 'a system of ... self-destruction and [the] despair of reason'.[35]

Having shown that Platonism and the Christian narrative about Original Sin and the Fall fail to properly account for evil,[36] Schelling turns to modern conceptions manifested in the thinking of Leibniz and Kant. Schelling's problem with Leibniz can be boiled down to his rejection of the necessity inherent in the latter's theodicy. By claiming that God's action are governed by His understanding, which is always perfect, Leibniz proposes a metaphysics of necessity whereby God's and, by extension, human actions emanate from the laws of reason. Schelling argues that Leibniz explains natural occurrences through divine affirmation of certain universal laws, with the consequence that his thinking 'is ruled far too much by the spirit of abstraction'.[37] When Leibniz tries to prove the existence of these universal laws, 'something must always be presupposed which is not entirely geometrically necessary'[38] and is, as such, contrary to the determinism Leibniz insists on. Schelling concludes that Leibniz's affirmation of natural laws to explain divine and, by extension, individual action 'is nothing else than th[e] reduction of natural laws to mind, spirit and will'.[39]

If Leibniz's thinking on evil is too mechanical and determined, Kant's is too general, abstract, and formal;[40] an assessment that brings Schelling to conclude that Kant's theory of freedom provides us with no guidance once 'we wish to enter into what is more exact and decisive'.[41] Schelling also notes that Kant's comments on the choice of moral law fall into two problems: first, he identifies the Kantian paradox described earlier wherein the Kantian subject is caught between, on the one hand, being a self-legislating moral being and, on the other hand, needing to base his actions on a reason for them to be moral. If the former alone were the case, the choice of moral law would be arbitrary. But if the latter were true, the moral law adopted would be given to the individual, with the consequence that he would not be self-legislating.[42] Schelling argues that Kant compounds this problem by failing to explain what motivates some individuals to choose a moral maxim based on the universal law and others to abandon the moral law.[43] As a consequence, Schelling claims that Kant is simply unable to tell us anything substantial about the issue.

Second, Schelling rejects the anthropocentrism inherent in Kant's theory of freedom and, by extension, his notion of evil. While noting that Kant 'first distinguished things-in-themselves from appearances only negatively through their independence from time and later treat[ed] independence from time and freedom as correlate concepts in the metaphysical discussions of his *Critique of Practical Reason*',[44] Schelling finds it 'odd'[45] that Kant did not go further to recognise that the notion of the noumenal world applied not just to human cognition but 'also to things'.[46] If he had done so, Kant would have acknowledged that freedom is not simply the defining condition of human subjectivity; it is the defining feature of all nature. Realising this would, on Schelling's estimation, 'have raised [Kant] to a higher standpoint of reflection and above the negativity that is the character of his theoretical philosophy'.[47] Freedom must not then be thought of as belonging to one being in the world, but in terms of the fabric of the world itself. This requires a fundamentally different approach to metaphysics.

## Metaphysics as Differentiating Identity

There is some disagreement over what exactly Schelling is trying to do with his metaphysical analysis. Dale Snow[48] argues that Schelling takes the human experience of evil as primary and develops his metaphysical analysis to explain the sort of God needed to coexist with our knowledge of evil. Michelle Kosch,[49] in contrast, insists that the question occupying Schelling's thinking is not God, but freedom, meaning that he is trying to work out what conception of freedom is needed for the choice between good and evil to be possible. While both identify the transcendental nature of Schelling's thinking, in so far as both recognise that he is trying to explain what the world must be like for evil to exist, Snow and Kosch are too one-sided in their presentations, both forgetting that, for Schelling, God and freedom are intimately connected. As such, Schelling's metaphysics is premised on two different, but ultimately overlapping, questions: what does God have to be like in order for good and evil to be possibilities for human being? And how must human freedom be to allow the choice between good and evil?

To respond, Schelling returns to Kant to point out that his thinking falls into a number of antinomies, namely those between the noumenon and phenomenon, practical and theoretical reason, and freedom and necessity. Whereas Kant held that this is due to and, indeed, reaffirms the noumenal/phenomenal distinction, Schelling disagrees, instead claiming that they affirm and depend upon unity, which he calls the absolute. Andrew Bowie points out that Schelling's insistence on the importance of the absolute is premised on the notion 'that the determination of something is the determination of what it is not'.[50] For something to exist implies that it is not something else. As a consequence, 'each object is part of a chain of ob-jects (*Gegen-stände*), which "stand against" each other. Objects, then, are not absolutely real because they only become themselves by not being other objects.'[51] However, this begs the question and so 'demands an account of what makes these interrelated moments intelligible as objects, which cannot therefore itself be an object'.[52] If it were, it would be defined in relation to another object and so not be that which transcends and binds the objects relationally. The notion of the 'absolute' is used to define this overarching whole because it implies 'something' that 'cannot be understood in terms of its relation to something else'.[53] Of course, it could be objected that the God of traditional monotheism also appears to have this role as the ultimate non-objective being who transcends the relationship between beings and makes possible their relationship. Indeed, Schelling makes this move and calls the absolute: 'God'.

We do, however, need to engage with what exactly Schelling means by God and the relationship between this first principle and the beings that emanate from it. Schelling defends a form of pantheism, derived in part from Spinoza's thought, but which breaks with Spinoza, who is perceived to be too deterministic in his understanding of the ways in which beings emanate from God. On Schelling's telling, Spinoza creates a duality between God and the beings that emanate from Him, with the act of creation from the former to the latter proceeding mechanically. There is then a 'lifelessness to his system'[54] which is unable to examine the organic dynamism of creation. In contrast, Schelling maintains that God should not to be conceived as a homogeneous bloc facing off against His creations: 'God is not a god of the dead but of the living.'[55] Indeed, God is life itself and so must be thought dynamically and in terms of material existence. Rather than an abstraction, God is, for Schelling, the most concrete 'thing' there is.

Schelling develops this by outlining what it means to say that God is living. There are two aspects to this: first, the development of the notion that God bears a differentiating identity; second, an account of the way(s) in which God is His own ground, which will pave the way for the later discussion of the ontogenesis of existent beings and, in turn, re-enforce the notion that God is a differentiating identity. Whereas Schelling recognises that the God of the Christian tradition is split into different moments, he holds that there is a sense in which the being that is split simply exists as it is. There is no sense of becoming to the Christian conception of God, mainly because time is generally considered to be that which emanates from God, rather than being that which defines Him. Schelling, however, holds that God and time are one to suggest that He alters, changes, and, in a very specific, non-teleological sense, develops.

To outline this, Schelling notes that God is not a static, monolithic thing from which everything emanates, but is that which expresses itself and unfolds through a specific process of self-differentiation. Schelling agrees therefore that 'there is in this system one principle for everything',[56] and, in so doing, affirms a monotheistic understanding, but immediately qualifies this by claiming that it should never be forgotten 'that the one being divides itself in two sorts of being'.[57] It is from this division that life is generated. As a consequence, there is 'one being [Ein Wesen] for all oppositions, an absolute identity of light and darkness, good and evil'.[58]

Kant's antinomies were a consequence of his staying at the level of oppositions and not moving 'beyond' them to question the differentiating/ed ground from which they emanate. Understanding the truth requires, according to Schelling, that thought 'seek that which lies outside of, and beyond, all opposition'.[59] The possibility of making this move is what most clearly distinguishes Schelling's metaphysics from Kant's.

Importantly, God's 'living unity of forces'[60] is not a unity of opposition, which, for Schelling, is too mechanistic, simply positing one principle against another and ignoring the extent to which each aspect, and, indeed, the relationship between the aspects, intermingles and intertwines to create a dynamic, entwined whole. God is not opposed to beings, but 'is nothing else than their very not-Being [Nichtsein] and ... for this reason, also has no predicate, except as the very lacking of a predicate, without it being on that account a nothingness or non-thing'.[61] God exists and exists through the beings that emanate from Him and has, therefore, real concrete being.

God's being is one of non-presence, meaning that He never appears and so cannot enter into a relationship, let alone one of opposition. After all, if God did exist in opposition to that which emanates from Him, this would establish a relational bond between the two that would undermine God's absolute status. God is not then defined by opposition to existent beings. He is a living unity of forces defined by 'indifference'[62] to the opposition He grounds. This is important because 'indifference is its own being separate from all opposition, a being against which all oppositions ruin themselves'.[63] Indifference is that which is defined non-relationally and so does not fall into the trap of forming an opposition between God and beings.

Schelling is developing a metaphysics of difference, whereby God, as the ground of existent beings, is differentiated and differentiating and the beings that emanate from Him are differentiated.[64] He recognises, however, that the God–beings relationship cannot be conceptualised through opposition or difference, whose relationality would undermine God's absolute status. Securing God's absolute status is achieved, according to Schelling, by thinking of God's relationship to the beings created from Him in terms of *indifference*. God's relationship to existent beings is not then an equal one, nor is it relational; it starts from God and is, in a sense, unilinear in so far as He is expressed through beings who are defined from Him, but to whom He is indifferent.

## God as Ground and the Ground of God

God's differentiating identity is not an identity composed of a collection of different properties, but a continuous process of becoming from the interaction between two hierarchically split realms. This split is deemed necessary to explore and account for the ground of God's existence. In other words, Schelling does not simply place God as the ground of existent beings, but claims that explaining the being of God, and so securing His foundational role, requires that the ground of God's existence be explained. The problem, of course, is, as Schelling recognises, that, because God is the foundation of existence, He cannot be grounded in anything else. How, then, to ground God's existence without usurping His foundational role?

Schelling responds by distinguishing between God and the ineffable ground of His existence. Crucially, 'since nothing is prior to, or outside of [außer], God, he must have the ground of his existence in himself'.[65] This ground is not static or abstract, but 'real [reell] and actual [wirklich]',[66] meaning that it is concrete; a position that Schelling arrives at because he conceives of this ground not in terms of a transcendent realm, but as 'nature',[67] 'which, although belonging to [God], is yet also different from Him'.[68] God is not split between two distinct domains, but is split 'within' Himself, meaning that 'in God there is an independent ground of reality'[69] that 'precedes him in existence'.[70] This independent ground is, as Patrick Roney explains, 'the selfless, dark, unruly (regellos) One that yearns to give birth to itself and thus to bring its ground into existence as a self that stands in the open'.[71]

Importantly, the self that emerges

> is not the determination of some pre-existing essence, for only in relation to the existent self does the ground truly become a ground. God becomes, and becomes something other than what was originally there – an individual self whose forms of individuation proceed through definite stages, beginning with nature and reaching its highest and purest self-revealing in Man, who, as distinct from God, possesses the Word of the *Logos* that reveals him most clearly.[72]

God's existence and the ground of that existence exist in dialectical entwinement: God's ground 'precedes' Him despite God being 'the *prius* [that is before] the ground in so far as the ground, even as such, could not exist if God did not exist *actu*'.[73] To resolve the apparent paradox, Schelling explains that God relates to His ground not temporally, but non-temporally, in so far as His being is split between two entwined moments, each of which depends on, but is distinct from, the other: the ground of His being depends on His actual being, which only *is* because it is grounded in the former.[74]

The ground of God's existence does not, however, constitute another being, but is defined by darkness.[75] This darkness is not an imposition on

God, but the condition of His existent being. Indeed, to ensure that we do not think of the ground of God in terms of another being, Schelling describes this ground as being 'before all ground',[76] with the consequence that it should be thought of as 'the non-ground'.[77] Reaffirming the earlier point that God's self-differentiation grounds opposition, David Farrell-Krell points out that God's non-ground 'precedes both opposition and identity, binary sets and units, dualism and monism'.[78] It is that which grounds these.

Schelling's basic point is that the ground of God cannot be thought in terms of a fixed ground or an entity that presents itself, but must be thought of as an aspect of being that remains hidden from view. This is compounded by his claim that this non-ground is dynamic, in the sense that it immediately and continuously 'divides [itself] into two equally eternal beginnings, not that it can be both *at once*, but that it is in each *in the same way*, thus in each the whole, or its own being'.[79] God is then immediately split between His ground, thought of as non-ground, and His identity as this is manifested through existent beings emanating from and grounded in this non-ground.[80]

To explore the relationship between the dual aspects of God, Schelling rejects the idea that God is the foundational light from where existent beings emanate and to which they can always return, by claiming that God's light originates from the dark ground of His existence. God *is* a duality of darkness and light, with the former grounding the latter. Through His creative act, God brings light and 'order to the disorderly offspring of chaos'[81] that is His non-ground. As such, 'the first period of creation is . . . the birth of light',[82] whereby 'the seed kernel must be sunk into the earth and die in darkness so that the more beautiful shape of light may lift and unfold itself in the radiance of the sun'.[83] God's creative act brings forth light from the dark ground. In so doing, it 'delivers [*erlöst*] the life hidden in the ground from non-Being and lifts it from potentiality [*Potenz*] into actuality [*zum Aktus*]'.[84]

Importantly, God's creative act does not create anything distinct from God *per se*; rather, 'the procession [*Folge*] of things from God is a self-revelation of God'.[85] God unfolds Himself through His creative act, meaning that the being created is both distinct from God and expressive of Him.[86] Through this unfolding, God comes to see 'himself in an exact image of himself'[87] and so learns what He is. In turn, the natural beings created from this act of unfolding are, as manifestations of God, defined by His duality and so are constituted by an existent 'objective' being emanating from and driven by a dark underside, manifested in a 'pure craving or desire, that is, blind will'.[88]

While each existent being is a natural expression of God, Schelling claims that there is one being, the human being, who is particularly important to the self-revelation of God. This is because 'in man there is the whole power of the dark principle and at the same time the whole strength of the light'.[89] Humans are a unique combination of the chaotic force of the dark abyss with the light of reason. Their link to the latter guarantees that they are able to reflect on nature and so reveal God to Himself in ways that other natural beings cannot.

Indeed, Schelling suggests that, because the human is both an independent being and one tied to God, it is imbued by a unique spirit manifested in a sense of selfhood that allows it to choose its existence. There are two consequences of this: first, the individual is defined by both a universal will orientated towards God and a particular will based on his own self-interests.[90] He must choose which he will follow. This is possible because, second, the human being's intimate relationship to God means that it partakes in the freedom synonymous with God. This distinguishes the human from non-human entities, who are simply natural beings.

The movement from the ground of God to His existence as this is manifested in particular existent beings is a movement from dark chaos to ordered light. However, light and dark do not exist in binary opposition. The tension between the two is fluid and creative, determining the structure, form, and content of the divine and the beings that emanate from the divine. Through God's unfolding in nature, His dark, chaotic ground is transformed into order, which is understood as unity, and a world capable of being understood.[91] As Jason Wirth explains, the emergence of the light is very much an act of the dark, in so far as 'the dark substitutes itself or betrays itself through contraction so that it can appear at all'.[92] The dark is simply too powerful to present itself and so, to do so, must contract into the order of light. The notion that something is simply too powerful to be present is somewhat paradoxical, but it hints at certain Christian notions that the power of God is too great to appear in the world as it is in-itself. The best we get, if we get anything at all, is a pale imitation.

We have to remember, however, that the light does not *imitate* but *expresses* the dark in contracted form. For this reason, the emergence of light does not abolish the dark ground. The dark ground remains because without it the light cannot exist. As Schelling explains,

> after the eternal act of self-revelation, everything in the world is, as we see it now, rule, order, and form; but anarchy still lies in the ground, as if it could break through once again, and nowhere does it appear as if order and form were what is original but rather as if initial anarchy had been brought to order.[93]

The darkness continues to ground existence as an 'invisible remainder'[94] that cannot be removed.

To develop this, Schelling introduces the analogy of the relationship between gravity and light, noting that 'gravity precedes light as its ever dark ground, which itself is not *actua* [actual], and flees into the night as the light (that which exists) dawns'.[95] The emergence of light does not, however, annihilate gravity, which continues to attach itself to light. Gravity is not 'the pure essence nor the actual being of absolute identity',[96] but something akin to 'a particular potency'.[97] There is an intimate entwinement between gravity and light wherein light emanates from gravity's darkness, which continues to adhere to that which it generates. Similarly, the darkness of God's ground generates the light of His existence, but continues to struggle against the re-emergence of the former: 'the ground reacts against this unity and asserts the initial duality'.[98] The ascendency of light does not then defeat its dark ground; if anything, it provokes the dark ground to rise again, thereby reaffirming the struggle between the two. It is this conflict that generates life and, as we will see, individual freedom.

Bringing light and hence existent beings from the dark is, however, always accompanied by the certainty that this success will fail as the dark, manifested most clearly in death, eventually overcomes the existent being and drags it back to the dark abyss. While there is, as a consequence, a 'sadness [that] clings to all finite life',[99] this is mitigated by the existence of 'a final purpose of creation',[100] which separates light from dark, fully realises the former in actuality, and 'cast[s] out [the latter] eternally into non-being'.[101] The light of existent beings is, somewhat paradoxically, always expulsed from the eruptions continuously taking place in the tumultuous chaos of the dark abyssal ground.[102] This expulsion does not mean that God's creations come to exist in opposition to Him. Because He *is* nature, they continue to exist 'in' Him as existent natural beings.[103]

## Evil as Positive Being

Schelling now moves from the cosmic to the individual level to explain what the former means for the later and explicitly engage with the problem of evil. In a similar vein to his metaphysics, Schelling's conception of evil breaks decisively from previous thought. Evil cannot be thought in quantitative terms, as something distinct from God or, importantly, as a privation, which Schelling holds to be 'in complete conflict with the actual nature of evil'.[104] By denying evil being, privation accounts prevent individuals from ever choosing it and so annihilate the condition upon which freedom depends.[105]

Contra the Augustinian-Aquinian tradition, Schelling claims that evil has a positive being of its own[106] in distinction from the good.[107] To outline it, he notes that there is 'the lifeless concept of the positive according to which only privation can oppose it'.[108] This underpins the Augustinian-Aquinian privation account of evil, but fails to appreciate that there is another form structured around 'an intermediate concept that forms a real opposition to [the positive] and [which] stands far removed from the concept of the merely negated'.[109]

The meaning attributed to this intermediary concept depends upon how we understand 'the relation of the whole to the individual'.[110] Defining the positive as 'the whole or the unity'[111] leads Schelling to claim that that 'which opposes unity is [a] severing of the whole, disharmony, ataxia of forces'.[112] Evil is not distinct from the good, but entails a disordering of the harmonious whole that defines the good. Importantly, 'the same elements are in the severed whole that were in the cohesive whole'.[113] The opposite of positive being (= good) is not necessarily the negative understood as absolute non-being, but *dishevelled* positive being. Schelling holds that this is the structure of evil and the relationship it has to positive being. This is a particularly innovative and bold conceptual move that brings forth the notion that evil is a real, existing phenomenon on its own terms; it is not simply the lack of something else.

Schelling goes further, however, by seeking to explain how and from where evil enters the world. This takes him beyond the Kantian approach that denies that this is a legitimate question for human cognition. Schelling also departs from the Christian tradition that has long struggled to explain the existence of evil within a world created by an all-powerful, omniscient, supremely good being, typically responding by claiming that it emanates from human freedom or perception. Schelling, in contrast, looks to his metaphysical analysis to maintain that the reason that evil exists in the world is because of the dark abyssal ground of existence.

Evil, for Schelling, must emanate from somewhere if it is to have real being. Given that real existent beings arise from the dark abyss, evil, as an existent being, is also grounded there. This dark realm is not good or evil *per se*, but, rather, the source of both. As Schelling explains, 'it cannot . . . be said that evil comes from the ground or that the will of the ground is the originator of evil. For evil can always only arise in the innermost will of our own heart and is never accomplished without our own act.'[114] From the abyssal ground, the human must choose whether to affirm good or evil; a choice granted to it because the human (1) has a unique relationship to God that allows it to share the freedom of the latter, and (2) must be able to choose good or evil, otherwise 'man would not be distinguishable from God',[115] who is the light and thus incapable of evil. For this reason, 'evil at first remains latent in the ground',[116] only to be brought to existence through individual choice.

That evil is latent 'in' the ground of existence means that there is a *general* evil ... which, though it never becomes real ... continually strives toward that end'[117] by becoming manifested in the *particular evils* committed by individual existent beings.[118] We will turn to the nature of particular evil in the next section, but general evil exists because God is the ground of His own existent being. God's light cannot exist without His dark abyssal ground and, by extension, the possibility of evil. If evil were to be abolished, this 'would abolish the condition of [God's] existence'.[119]

Schelling's point is two-fold: first, God is not opposed to evil, but actually depends on the existence of evil. Second, the existence of evil is always latent in any conception of the good. Good and evil 'are the same thing only seen from different sides, or evil is in itself, that is, considered in the root of its identity, the good, just as the good, to the contrary, considered in its turning from itself [*Entzweiung*] or non-identity, is evil'.[120]

Schelling does not then collapse good into evil or vice versa; rather he claims that good and evil are relational so that the existence of one *implicitly* depends upon the existence of the other. The choice of the good does not abolish evil. Evil remains latent in the good not only because the identity of the good is defined from evil, but also because the ground of the good is the dark abyss, in which (the possibility of) evil lies latent. Richard Bernstein is, therefore, correct to conclude that, as a consequence, 'Schelling portrays a much more ominous sense of the power of evil – a power that is never completely mastered and can always break out with ever-renewed vigor.'[121] Good is always tied to evil and, as such, can always (re)turn to evil.

With this, Schelling departs from Kant in two different, but ultimately related, ways: first, while Kant claims that the individual has an original predisposition (*Anlage*) to the good that must be affirmed through the choice of moral maxim,[122] Schelling rejects the notion that the good has primacy in human reality. Because existent beings are grounded in the dark, abyssal ground, individual existence is orientated in relation to evil:

> if ... evil already has been aroused in the first creation, and through the ground being-active-for-itself was developed finally into a general principle, then a natural propensity (*Hang*) of man to do evil seems to be explicable on that basis because the disorder of forces engaged by awakening of self-will in creatures already communicates itself to them at birth.[123]

Second, whereas Kant maintains that evil is possible because a propensity (*Hang*) to evil defines human being as a species, Schelling introduces the notion of general evil to maintain that evil is a latent possibility tied to the abyssal ground of existence itself. It is not enough to assert that evil arises from an individual (noumenal) decision. The possibility of that decision must be explained and only is, on Schelling's account, if reality is structured from and around a metaphysical duality constituted by a visible existent being that is underpinned by, grounded in, and emanates from dark, unseen, and, psychologically speaking, unconscious forces that generate possibilities to be actualised in reality by (unconscious) individual choice.

## The Human Reality of Evil

Having discussed the possibility and nature of evil, Schelling moves to the human reality of evil. As previously noted, while good and evil are defined relationally, this relationality is dependent on and originates from a prior genetic moment. Schelling claims that evil occurs when the human adopts a particular orientation towards God. Holding that the human is separated from but always related subordinately to God,[124] he insists that recognising and affirming this relation creates a harmony that is 'true freedom'.[125] However, because the individual is free, he can turn against this natural order so that 'instead of making his selfhood into the basis, the instrument [of the general will of God, he strives] to elevate [his particular will] into the ruling and total will and, conversely, to make the spiritual within himself into a means'.[126] This leads not to the annihilation of the universal will by the particular, but to the creation of an *imbalance* between the two whereby the particular will attempts to affirm its priority over that which it depends upon: the universal will. While there is still unity between the universal and particular wills, it is 'a false unity'[127] because of its disharmony.

Schelling claims that this imbalance between God and the individual, or the universal and particular wills, is also manifested '*within*' each individual. This is possible because God's dark/light dichotomy finds expression in the individual through the unconscious/conscious one. Good results when the light–conscious aspect is dominant over the dark–unconscious one. Evil arises when the dark–unconscious aspect gains ascendency.

Importantly, because the individual emanates from God, Richard Bernstein explains that Schelling affirms

> what has always seemed unacceptable for Christian theodicies. God 'is' the origin of the reality of evil. But he is the origin in a very special sense.

It is the ground of God's being, the potentially independent principle of darkness, that *becomes* the origin of evil in human beings.[128]

The meaning of the dark ground is, therefore, different for God and the individual. In the former, the dark ground is God, ensuring that He is at one with it. As a consequence, the dark ground does not have moral significance for God. In contrast, because the individual emanates from this dark ground and, in so doing, departs from God, the question of whether his existence accords with the light of God arises. For this reason, the individual's actions do have moral value: the way he comports himself to God and God's dark ground brings forth the possibility and hence question of evil. As Bernstein concludes, this ensures that 'what is not *intrinsically* evil in God becomes the source of evil in human beings'.[129]

By claiming that evil arises when the individual does not properly structure the dark/light forces 'within' him and/or has an improper relationship to God, Schelling asserts that evil arises from a disharmony in a similar way to how disease arises from the disharmony of bodily forces. This analogy is underpinned by a conception of disease that sees it occurring when 'the irritable principle, which is supposed to rule as the innermost bond of forces in the quiet depths, activates [*aktuiert*] itself'.[130] For this reason, Dale Snow explains that 'disease is the paradigm case of an entity inappropriately subsuming everything to itself at the expense of the whole of which it is a part'.[131] Disease is not, then, opposed to health, a lack of health, or the addition of another element or force to the make-up of the entity; it is an internal disruption to the configuration of forces constitutive of health.[132] This imbalance creates effects which are experienced as 'very real to feeling',[133] which is why disease has real being and is not considered to be the absence of being. Returning to health requires the re-establishment of the correct relationship between the forces that compose an entity.

Evil results from a similar imbalance, but differs from disease in being related to an individual's spiritual, rather than natural, being. Whereas disease occurs when the natural body is dominated by its dark desires, evil occurs when the individual is spiritually dominated by them. When this happens the 'selfish or dark principle'[134] rules and turns the individual against the light of God. From this, the individual tries to make himself the foundation of all reality rather than recognising that he is subordinate to God.

By noting that the turn to evil is a consequence of an individual's 'own act',[135] Schelling continues the Augustinian tradition's insistence that autonomous willing plays a key role in bringing forth evil. His innovation is to question where this autonomy lies within the individual. Rather than occurring at the level of reflection, Schelling explains that the

> general propensity to evil as an act of freedom which, in accordance with its origin, is utterly unconscious and even irresistible points to an act and, thus, to a life before this life, except that it is not to be thought just as prior in time since that which is intelligible is altogether outside of time.[136]

Because the unconscious choice is the condition of natural, temporal being, it precedes the individual's natural, temporal form. But, as the ground of natural being, the unconscious choice finds expression through its natural being.

To develop this, Schelling explains that the unconscious choice is *logically* prior to its temporal manifestation; it 'does not temporally precede life but goes through time (unhampered by it) as an act which is eternal by nature'.[137] As an unconscious choice, it is a decision that we are unaware of having made, although it is one that determines our natural being. According to S. J. McGrath, this is because the primordial act

> is my beginning, and my beginning is never available to me. I did not experience it consciously, for there was no I to experience it, nor can I revisit it in consciousness. The beginning is the past that was never present. I cannot experience my birth, for my birth makes all my experiencing possible. The person becomes who he is in an unconscious decision for good or for evil. In a non-temporal, eternally past, unconscious but free act, the person chooses the character that undergirds his temporal existence. He can only experience his free decision in time as something irretrievably past, that is, as necessity.[138]

Schelling is aware that this idea may appear to be 'incomprehensible',[139] but holds that it is correct because 'there is indeed in each man a feeling in accord with it as if he had been what he is already from all eternity'.[140] His point is that we unconsciously chose the type of life that we will live and realise this decision through nature in the form of our temporal, individual, reflective being. Individuals are born evil, but are born this way out of a 'prior', unconscious, individual choice. This is why the individual who commits evil actions finds it so easy to do so. Rather than struggle against himself, he 'performs his actions in accordance with rather than against his will'.[141]

The conclusion drawn is that 'the passions in themselves do not constitute evil, nor do we have to struggle just with flesh and blood but with an evil in and outside of us that is spirit. Only this evil, contracted through our own act but from birth, can on that account [daher] be called radical evil.'[142] For Schelling, the individual unconsciously chose his being prior to his actual, temporal existence; is, therefore, absolutely responsible for his being; and so must live with the consequences of that unconscious, pre-temporal choice.

## Concluding Remarks

Schelling's analysis of evil constitutes a remarkably original attempt to rethink its metaphysical ground that departs radically from previous conceptions of evil in terms of the metaphysics it relies upon, the understanding of evil offered, and, crucially, the consequences it has for individuals. Its departure from the classic Judaeo-Christian conception of God is not, however, a rejection of all forms of theology. Schelling rejects one theological tradition to adopt another based on a radically reconceptualised conception of God. Two problems stand out from this.

The first relates to what is perhaps the most innovative aspect of his analysis: the introduction of the unconscious to explain the origin of evil. One of the purposes of this conceptual innovation is to correct a problem that Schelling identifies within Kant's conception of evil. While Kant posited the notion of radical evil as the choice of moral maxim that precedes, but yet gives meaning to, individual action, Schelling maintains that Kant does not offer a coherent account of the origins of an individual's moral maxim because he first provides an incorrect, transcendental account based on the noumenal realm, before being 'led in his later investigations, merely by faithful observation of the phenomenon of moral judgement, to the recognition of, as he expressed it, a subjective ground of human actions preceding every act apparent to the senses but that itself must be nonetheless an *actus* of freedom'.[143]

Kant's problem, according to Schelling, is that while his later thinking recognises a subjective ground underpinning moral choice, he was unable to develop the conceptual tools, based on the notion of the unconscious, to formally outline what this means.[144] Instead, Kant grounds the choice of individual moral maxim in a noumenal decision that determines the individual's reflective actions, but he insists that we cannot say anything about the noumenal realm, with the consequence that we cannot, ultimately, explain the origins of evil. Schelling, in contrast, not only asserts that it is possible to question the noumenal, but claims that we must do so if the problem of evil is to be resolved.

This is a consequence of Kant's and Schelling's different approaches to metaphysics, namely about whether human cognition can legitimately question the absolute. Rather than locate individual moral choice in an unknowable noumenal realm, Schelling situates it in the dark unconscious recesses of human cognition, itself a manifestation of the metaphysical structure of reality. The problem with his formulation, however, is that while it assures us that moral choice is made unconsciously, not noumenally, and so explains *how* moral choice is made, it still does not explain *why* some individuals unconsciously choose evil and others do not. On this point, Kant and Schelling are distinguished by a terminological, not conclusive shift: Schelling continues the Kantian line that evil is radical and, ultimately, unknowable. For this reason, his conceptual innovation fails to do what it sets out to do: explain the lacuna in Kant's noumenal analysis and so account for why some choose evil whereas others do not.

Schelling's continuation of the Kantian line does, however, entail a radicalisation of Kant's thought through his claim that evil is locked in the depths of reality and his insistence that the individual's moral choice is determinative and inescapable. Whereas Kant is never able to explain how it is possible to do so, he does claim that an individual can change his moral maxim.[145] The individual who has chosen an evil moral maxim can save himself by altering it to affirm the universal law. Schelling offers no such concession. There is no possibility of redemption for the individual who chooses evil. Individuals are predestined for good or evil.

However, rather than being because of divine ordination, this is a consequence of their pre-temporal, unconscious, individual choice. Because it is the radical ground of his individual being, an individual's conscious 'action does not *become*, just as he himself does not *become* as a moral being, but rather it is eternal by nature'.[146] Once made unconsciously and so outside of time, this decision determines the individual's temporal choices and being. Lest we be in any doubt as to the hold that this choice has over the individual, Schelling informs us that 'not even the gates of hell themselves would be capable of overpowering his basic disposition [*Gesinnung*]'.[147]

On the one hand, this demonstrates the importance of the moral decision, but, on the other hand, it seems to downplay the diachronic nature of moral judgement. While Schelling's account is strong at explaining the unconscious nature of our moral choices, in failing to permit an alteration to those moral choices it locks us within an ethical framework that seems to betray the freedom upon which his notion of the unconscious depends. It is perhaps not surprising that subsequent thought departed from this conclusion by emphasising that change is a fundamental aspect of our moral codes. This was not simply because individuals could change their moral choices, but, far more radically, was because moral categories themselves came to be understood as being historical in nature.

## Notes

1. Immanuel Kant, *Critique of Pure Reason*, trans. and ed. Paul Guyer and Allen Wood (Cambridge: Cambridge University Press, 1998), B.xxx.
2. Terry Pinkard, *German Philosophy 1760–1860: The Legacy of Idealism* (Cambridge: Cambridge University Press, 2002), pp. 59, 226.
3. Ibid. p. 226.
4. Ibid. p. 226.
5. Ibid. p. 226.
6. Ibid. p. 226.
7. For a succinct overview of no fewer than five lines of critique developed against Kant's metaphysics, see Karl Ameriks, *Kant and the Historicist Turn: Philosophy as Critical Interpretation* (Oxford: Oxford University Press, 2006), pp. 154–60.
8. The Kantian heritage of this move is clearly seen when we remember Schelling's claim that the real historical importance of Kant lies in 'the fact that he *directed philosophy towards the subjective*'. See F. W. J. Schelling, *On the History of Modern Philosophy*, trans. Andrew Bowie (Cambridge: Cambridge University Press, 1994), p. 106.
9. Frederick C. Beiser, *German Idealism: The Struggle against Subjectivity 1781–1801* (Cambridge, MA: Harvard University Press, 2002), p. 217.
10. Ibid. p. 217.
11. For an excellent analysis of Fichte's theory of subjectivity, see Frederick Neuhouser, *Fichte's Theory of Subjectivity* (Cambridge: Cambridge University Press, 1990).
12. Schelling, *On the History of Modern Philosophy*, p. 106.
13. Ibid. p. 109.
14. Ibid. p. 109.
15. F. W. J. Schelling, *Philosophical Investigations into the Essence of Human Freedom*, trans. Jeff Love and Johannes Schmidt (Albany: State University of New York Press, 2006). Schelling first discusses evil in the 1804 essay *Philosophy and Religion*, trans. Klaus Ottman (Putnam: Spring, 2010) before returning to it in his *Philosophie der Offenbarung, 1841–42*, ed. M. Frank (Frankfurt am Main: Suhrkamp, 1977). The 1809 essay is, however, his most extensive treatment of the topic.
16. Ibid. p. 23.

17. Ibid. p. 39.
18. Ibid. p. 39.
19. Ibid. p. 39.
20. Ibid. p. 39.
21. Ibid. p. 23.
22. Ibid. p. 23.
23. Ibid. p. 23.
24. Ibid. p. 12.
25. Ibid. p. 23.
26. Ibid. p. 23.
27. Ibid. p. 42.
28. Ibid. p. 25.
29. Ibid. p. 25.
30. Ibid. p. 25.
31. Ibid. p. 25.
32. Ibid. p. 25.
33. Ibid. p. 24.
34. Ibid. p. 24.
35. Ibid. p. 24.
36. Schelling's relationship to Christianity in the 1809 essay is more nuanced than the summary account portrayed throughout this chapter indicates. While he is highly critical of the Platonic metaphysics underpinning Christian thinking and the privation thesis of evil emanating from the Augustinian and later Aquinian traditions, his engagement with them is important to the development of his own positive conception of evil. This positive conception of evil is also influenced by other strands of Christian thinking, notably Bruno's and Boehme's. Schelling's interest in the former is explicitly manifest in his 1802 essay *Bruno, or On the Natural and Divine Principle of Things* (trans. Michael G. Vater [Albany: State University of New York Press, 1984]), while his relationship to Boehme has long been noted. The classic study is Robert Brown, *The Later Philosophy of Schelling: The Influence of Boehme on the Works of 1809–1815* (Plainsboro: Associated University Press, 1977). Beyond these figures, Eric Guerrier, in his *Le problème du Mal dans une métaphysique de l'alchimie: Une filiation insolite entre Luther, Böhme et Schelling* (Paris: Éditions L'Harmattan, 2013), argues that Luther was also an important influence.
37. Schelling, *Essence of Human Freedom*, p. 60.
38. Ibid. p. 60.
39. Ibid. p. 60.
40. Ibid. p. 23.
41. Ibid. p. 22.
42. Ibid. pp. 49–50.
43. Ibid. p. 50.
44. Ibid. p. 22.

45. Ibid. p. 22.
46. Ibid. p. 22.
47. Ibid. p. 22.
48. Dale Snow, *Schelling and the End of Idealism* (Albany: State University of New York Press, 1996), p. 150.
49. Michelle Kosch, *Freedom and Reason in Kant, Schelling, and Kierkegaard* (Oxford: Oxford University Press, 2006), p. 87.
50. Andrew Bowie, *Schelling and Modern European Philosophy* (Abingdon: Routledge, 1993), p. 20.
51. Ibid. p. 50.
52. Ibid. p. 50.
53. Ibid. p. 50.
54. Schelling, *Essence of Human Freedom*, p. 20.
55. Ibid. p. 18.
56. Ibid. p. 70.
57. Ibid. p. 71.
58. Ibid. p. 68.
59. Ibid. p. 77.
60. Ibid. p. 59.
61. Ibid. p. 69.
62. Ibid. p. 68.
63. Ibid. p. 69.
64. In many respects, Schelling develops a metaphysics of difference that is remarkably similar to the differential ontology that Deleuze relies upon. There are important differences between them, but both agree that the ground of existents is differentiated and self-differentiating, that actual beings are differentiated, and that beings continue to differentiate based on a folding structure whereby the actual is 'overcome' by the 'prior' realm of reality; in Schelling's case, the dark–light movement and, in Deleuze's case, the virtual–actual movement. For an interesting comparative analysis of the two, see Christopher Groves, 'Ecstasy of Reason, Crisis of Reason: Schelling and Absolute Difference', *Pli*, 8, 1999, pp. 25–45. For a more detailed analysis of Deleuze's differential ontology, see my *Ontology in Heidegger and Deleuze* (Basingstoke: Palgrave Macmillan, 2014).
65. Schelling, *Essence of Human Freedom*, p. 27.
66. Ibid. p. 27.
67. Ibid. p. 27.
68. Ibid. p. 42.
69. Ibid. p. 59.
70. Ibid. p. 28.
71. Patrick Roney, 'Evil and the Experience of Freedom: Nancy on Schelling and Freedom', *Research in Phenomenology*, 39:3, 2009, pp. 374–400 (p. 388).
72. Ibid. p. 388.

73. Schelling, *Essence of Human Freedom*, p. 28.
74. Ibid. p. 28.
75. Ibid. p. 62.
76. Ibid. p. 69.
77. Ibid. p. 70.
78. David Farrell-Krell, 'The Crisis of Reason in the Nineteenth Century: Schelling's Treatise on Human Freedom (1809)', p. 26, in *The Collegium Phaenomenologicum: The First Ten Years*, ed. John Sallis, Giuseppina Moneta, and Jacques Taminiaux (Dordrecht: Springer, 1988), pp. 13–32.
79. Schelling, *Essence of Human Freedom*, p. 70.
80. Ibid. p. 71.
81. Ibid. p. 65.
82. Ibid. p. 66.
83. Ibid. p. 29.
84. Ibid. p. 66.
85. Ibid. p. 18.
86. Ibid. p. 31.
87. Ibid. p. 30.
88. Ibid. p. 32.
89. Ibid. p. 32.
90. Ibid. p. 32.
91. Ibid. p. 30.
92. Jason Wirth, *The Conspiracy of Life: Meditations on Schelling and His Time* (Albany: State University of New York Press, 2003), p. 160.
93. Schelling, *Essence of Human Freedom*, p. 29.
94. Ibid. p. 29.
95. Ibid. p. 27.
96. Ibid. p. 27.
97. Ibid. p. 28.
98. Ibid. p. 67.
99. Ibid. p. 62.
100. Ibid. p. 67.
101. Ibid. p. 67.
102. Ibid. p. 47.
103. Ibid. p. 67.
104. Ibid. p. 36.
105. Ibid. p. 23.
106. Ibid. p. 23.
107. Ibid. p. 38.
108. Ibid. p. 38.
109. Ibid. p. 38.
110. Ibid. p. 38.
111. Ibid. p. 38.

112. Ibid. p. 38.
113. Ibid. p. 38.
114. Ibid. p. 63.
115. Ibid. p. 41.
116. Ibid. p. 44.
117. Ibid. p. 47.
118. Ibid. p. 47.
119. Ibid. p. 66.
120. Ibid. pp. 63–4.
121. Richard Bernstein, *Radical Evil: A Philosophical Investigation* (Cambridge: Polity, 2002), p. 90.
122. Immanuel Kant, *Religion within the Boundaries of Mere Reason and Other Writings*, trans. and ed. Allen Wood and George di Giovanni (Cambridge: Cambridge University Press, 1998), 6:43–4.
123. Schelling, *Essence of Human Freedom*, p. 47.
124. Ibid. p. 33.
125. Ibid. p. 56.
126. Ibid. p. 54.
127. Ibid. p. 38.
128. Bernstein, *Radical Evil*, p. 89.
129. Ibid. p. 89.
130. Schelling, *Essence of Human Freedom*, p. 34.
131. Snow, *Schelling and the End of Idealism*, p. 166.
132. For an interesting discussion of the notion of disease in Schelling's account, see Martin Wallen, 'Schelling's Dialogue of Health in *Philosophical Inquiries into the Nature of Human Freedom*', *Studies in Romanticism*, 33:2, 1994, pp. 201–21.
133. Schelling, *Essence of Human Freedom*, p. 35.
134. Ibid. p. 40.
135. Ibid. p. 53.
136. Ibid. p. 52.
137. Ibid. p. 51.
138. S. J. McGrath, 'Schelling on the Unconscious', *Research in Phenomenology*, 40:1, 2010, pp. 72–91 (p. 88).
139. Schelling, *Essence of Human Freedom*, p. 51.
140. Ibid. p. 51.
141. Ibid. p. 51.
142. Ibid. p. 53.
143. Ibid. p. 53.
144. Ibid. p. 50.
145. Kant, *Religion within the Boundaries of Mere Reason*, 6:45.
146. Schelling, *Essence of Human Freedom*, p. 53.
147. Ibid. p. 51.

# 8

# Nietzsche and the Genealogy of Evil

While questions remain over the success and, indeed, the coherence of Schelling's account, what is most innovative about it, especially as it relates to subsequent thinking on evil, is the notion that reality is structured from a dark, hidden abyss. The idea that there is an obscure underbelly to the world of appearance contributed to a cultural transformation that gradually moved focus from the realm of autonomous reason to the dynamic, ineffable processes and structures subtending reason. Throughout the nineteenth century, this theme found expression in Schopenhauer's metaphysics of will,[1] Hegel's insistence on the 'cunning of reason',[2] and Marx's emphasis on the importance of economic structures to social life.[3] Each is different, but they all express the general idea that the world as it presents itself is an immanent effect of a shadow world of autopoietic forces and structures.

As the nineteenth century proceeded, there was also a gradual movement away from relying upon speculative thought to understand an issue to the study of actual phenomenal beings. This gave rise to and was re-enforced by the growing influence of scientific rationality, which insisted that empirical study of natural phenomena would reveal the truth of its objects. A key lesson learned from empirical observation was that change was a fundamental part of nature.[4] If thought emanated from nature, it had to reflect and express the fundamental changes it witnessed.

Ancient thought had of course recognised that phenomena change, but, ever since Parmenides, it had tended to either ignore or downplay it by privileging a static, universal foundation. The temptation to *explicitly* ground temporality in a fixed, ahistoric point of reference was increasingly resisted. The turn to historical and naturalist explanations brought about a gradual decline in explanations based on a transcendence model, where the truth of the object is understood to exist outside of this world, to an immanentist one, where the object is understood in terms of the natural world.[5]

This reorientation challenged the most basic assumptions of Western thinking, including understandings of evil. It opened up the possibility that the meaning of moral concepts, including evil, may change. The nature of this change, including what exactly changes, increasingly came to occupy thinking on the topic.[6]

Friedrich Nietzsche was among the first to explicitly and consistently employ a historical methodology to the study of moral concepts. At thirteen years of age, he developed an interest in the topic,[7] but quickly found inadequate what others had to say. As he explains in *Daybreak*, 'the subject reflected on least adequately has been good and evil: it was too dangerous a subject'.[8] Nietzsche aimed to rectify that. By calling into question the nature of the moral categories historically used and the source of those categories, he radically challenged Western narratives about history, morality, and foundations.

For Nietzsche, moral categories are grounded not in theological sources or autonomous reason, but in dynamic, naturalist, socio-historic power structures and processes. Claiming that traditional morality is a symptom of the weak, he aimed to uncover the origins of this morality to release more affirmative values that would allow 'the strong' to flourish. Only a fundamentally different way of thinking about existence and its relationship to ourselves would permit this and become a source of free, creative energy.

Good and evil are then themes that recur continuously in his thought, even finding expression in the title of one of his most famous books: *Beyond Good and Evil*.[9] It is, however, in the three essays of *On the Genealogy of Morals* that he undertakes his most sustained analysis of the distinction. The first of these explores 'the birth of Christianity out of the spirit of *ressentiment*',[10] the second engages with the 'psychology of *conscience*',[11] and the third analyses the nature and origin of the aesthetic ideal.

I will focus on the first essay because it is where Nietzsche develops most fully his insistence that the good/evil binary opposition is rooted in specific socio-historical processes. It also shows that 'evil' originates from the Judaeo-Christian semiotic system, thereby tying any conception of evil to that theological heritage. There are, at least, three aspects to his argument: first, Nietzsche endeavours to explain how this conceptual relation arose from specific social relations. Second, he aims to show that the transformation in moral understanding that took place was due to naturalist, rather than metaphysical or theological, phenomena. And third, the previous two critical points provide the foundation for the re-evaluation of all values he aims to instantiate.

Focusing on the first two aspects will reveal that the significance of the moral categories 'good' and 'evil', including their relationship, stems from a particular socio-historical power relation. The importance of this lies, so notes Keith Ansell-Pearson, in demonstrating 'that morality is something that has a history (it is something that has evolved and changed) [meaning] that there are different *types* of morality'.[12] 'Evil' as a moral category is not an objective, ahistoric concept, but is born of a particular worldview and semiotic system, a genesis that demonstrates its intimate dependence on subtending networks of theological meaning of which we are often unaware.

## Morals, History, and Genealogy

Nietzsche explains that his purpose in On the Genealogy of Morals is to engage with 'the *origin* of our moral prejudices'.[13] It is not clear, however, what Nietzsche means by 'moral prejudice', an issue that fits into a wider one within his works relating to his heterogeneous use of the term 'morality'. As one commentator explains,

> on some occasions [Nietzsche] is thinking of what commonly passes . . . as 'morality'; on others, of certain philosophical variants and developments of this sort of 'morality'; on others, of a variety of historical forms of 'morality'; on others, of 'morality' in a broader sense, relating to the conditions of social existence, or more broadly still, to the 'conditions of life' of creatures like ourselves; and on yet others, of what 'morality' might be in the case of human beings capable of attaining a higher form of humanity than that which is the general rule.[14]

Besides the question of what Nietzsche means by 'morality' and hence 'moral prejudice' lies the question of what he means by 'origin'. Moral argumentation has traditionally proceeded based on normative assertions or taken-for-granted epistemological and moral foundations. Nietzsche maintains that he will not engage in such 'hypothesis-mongering'.[15] He will, rather, explore the origin of our moral values by offering a critique of them, which will, by extension, question '*the value of these values*'.[16]

Therefore, instead of offering speculative reasons as to the origins of good and evil or grounding moral concepts in an ahistoric mythic origin,[17] Nietzsche argues for a more concrete approach based on the rejuvenation of a '*historical spirit*'[18] and the return to 'what is documented, what can actually be confirmed and has actually existed, in short, the entire long hieroglyphic record . . . of the moral past of mankind'.[19]

Robert Guay warns, however, that Nietzsche's 'use of irony is so pervasive that it cannot be relied upon to report Nietzsche's views, even at the moment of writing, on a historical sequence of events or the causal sources of the phenomena that Nietzsche identifies'.[20] While this does not necessarily undermine their *philosophical* veracity, Guay deduces that the conclusions that Nietzsche derives from his genealogy are based on a rhetorical rather than historical methodology.

Indeed, by pointing out that there appears to be a problem with the scholarship underpinning Nietzsche's position, Brian Leiter takes up and extends this line of criticism. After all, 'almost *nothing* is documented and almost no confirming evidence (other than some etymological evidence) is cited in the text of the *Genealogy*'.[21] Leiter helpfully explains, however, that this is not surprising given that the subtitle of the book indicates that it is a polemic, not a scholarly treatise, and that its purpose 'is to force people to think the unthinkable',[22] a task that Nietzsche clearly considers to be both necessary and increasingly difficult, given that '*the slave revolt in morality* . . . has a history of two thousand years behind it and which we no longer see because it . . . has been victorious'.[23] Shaking these foundations and bringing us to think differently would presumably be stifled by the demands of normal academic discourse.

A further problem relates to the nature of Nietzsche's genealogical methodology: he tends to use the terms 'genealogy' and 'history' interchangeably. This raises questions relating to the character of genealogy, including what makes it different from a historical analysis, its purpose, for whom it works, and, indeed, how it is intended to achieve its ends.[24] In response, four broad positions have been developed in the literature.

The first, expressed by Maudemarie Clarke, collapses genealogy and historical analysis into one another to claim that 'genealogy is simply a natural history'.[25] The second, manifested in the thinking of Eric Blondel, distinguishes the two by claiming that, while historical analysis links the present to the past through a particular narrative, genealogy is far more complex and multi-dimensional in that it aims to 'render problematic the "ideals" of our culture as they are revealed in our morals, science, religion, and philosophy and in the political assumptions that have been dominant for more than twenty centuries'.[26] Genealogy, on this understanding, looks at the psychological, physiological, and semiotic occurrences and structures that gave rise to moral values.

A third option, proposed by Michel Foucault, combines and develops aspects of the previous positions by focusing on the relationship between genealogy and origins. Foucault agrees with Clarke's claim that genealogy and history are not absolutely distinct, but departs from her conclusion by distinguishing between different senses of 'history'. His conclusion is that genealogy is linked to and dependent on one sense of history, all the while being distinct from another sense.

This relies on a distinction between what I will call 'genealogical history' and 'metaphysical history'. The two are based on different epistemological assumptions about history. *Metaphysical history* bases itself on a particular metaphysics and understands history through this lens. Specifically, it 'attempt[s] to capture the exact essence of things, their purest possibilities, and their carefully protected identities [which] assumes the existence of immobile forms that precede the external world of accident and succession'.[27] On this understanding, there is a clear, meticulously delineated, static, singular foundation that grounds the historical analysis, with interpretations of events being read through the lens of that foundation. An example would be analyses based on a particular reading of the origin myth of Christianity wherein, despite substantial evidence to the contrary, God is understood to have created the universe around six thousand years ago. This is not based on a historical record, but entails the creation of one from a prior, implicitly adopted, metaphysical framework.

On Foucault's telling, Nietzsche rejects this approach because of the ahistoric metaphysics grounding it and the essence/appearance duality that emanates from it. For this reason, *genealogical* approaches to history aim to identify the origin of an event, but 'find that there is "something altogether different" behind things: not a timeless and essential secret, but the secret that they have no essence or that their essence was fabricated in a piecemeal fashion from alien forms'.[28] Genealogy discovers that 'at the historical beginning of things is not the inviolable identity of their origin; it is the dissension of other things. It is disparity.'[29] Thus, when Foucault claims that genealogy 'opposes itself to the search for "origins"',[30] he means that it is opposed to the sense of origins inherent in metaphysical history, not to the dynamic, diffused sense that grounds genealogical history. Because of its grounding in a fixed, timeless essence, metaphysical history continues to glorify the past, in the sense that it venerates the origin the present came from. In contrast, genealogy looks to uncover its origins *for the future* by 'disturb[ing] what was previously considered immobile'.[31] By doing so, genealogy breaks up previous understandings and, by demonstrating 'the hazardous play of dominations'[32] inherent in them, reveals the heterogeneity of what was previously considered homogeneous.[33] This, in turn, offers the possibility of new categories of thought, new forms of understandings, different interpretations, and a re-evaluation of what has previously been considered valuable.

Foucault also argues that the 'spirit' in which genealogical and metaphysical histories undertake their tasks is very different. This is not simply due to a subjective decision, but results from the way that the investigator perceives his assignment and understands the structure of reality. Whereas metaphysical histories understand themselves to be proceeding in a linear, 'serious' manner towards a timeless, objective truth, genealogies recognise the heterogeneity of events, the sources of those events, and, indeed, the way in which the origins of an event are not delineated by clear-cut, black-and-white dichotomies, but entail shades of 'grey'[34] that seek to explore and bring to light the heterogeneity of things. This feeds into the multi-dimensional focus inherent in Blondel's line of thinking about genealogy that questions the 'meaning' of 'origins', the psychology 'behind' the two approaches, and also the way in which meaning and semiotics define realities.[35] For this reason, Foucault explains that 'genealogy is history in the form of a concerted carnival'.[36]

David Owen[37] offers a fourth understanding of 'genealogy' that extends Foucault's approach by identifying the philosophical positions from which Nietzsche develops his analysis of morality. Specifically, Owen claims that Nietzsche's genealogical method is grounded in the rejection of the essence/appearance metaphysical dichotomy that maintains that the true meaning of a thing lies in a reality that is essential but does not present itself. As Nietzsche explains, he 'ceased to look for the origin of evil *behind* the world',[38] whether this was by appealing to Christianity's transcendent God or to Kant's noumenal/phenomenal distinction, to, instead, focus on the actions and activities documented historically. This is underpinned by the notion that what something really entails is revealed through the way it presents itself in the world and that this changes historically. Owen also explains that Nietzsche depends upon a naturalist account of human subjectivity or agency that holds that human conscious activity is structured around and from a continuous striving. This striving aims not for the accumulation of external things, but for experiencing itself as a self-governing agent. The more an agent experiences itself as self-governing, the more ontologically and morally 'true' is that experience. For Nietzsche, different historical manifestations of moral reason disclose different attempts on the part of the subjects involved to experience themselves as self-governing agents. Nietzsche's genealogical approach allows us then to not only identify the normative claims inherent in different moral perspectives, but also evaluate them based on the extent to which they fulfil the ontological desire to be self-ruling; that is, whether the moral systems in place facilitate or stifle this. There is, as a consequence, an objective, absolute standard governing Nietzsche's critique of traditional forms of morality; namely whether and to what extent a moral system permits the individual to strive for self-governance. What this entails is different for each agent based on his specific ontological capacities for self-creation.

## Master Morality: The Good and the Bad

Nietzsche's use of the genealogical method brings him to explore the way(s) in which the idea of 'the good' arose and gained meaning. He rejects the notion that the 'good' was originally associated with utility or altruism, or that its meaning emanated from those to whom an act was done.[39] Nietzsche is thinking of the possibility that 'good' became associated with an altruistic act done to someone who subsequently designated that act as good because it was useful to them. This gets the order of signification backwards. It is not the recipient of the deed that determines its value, but the doer of the deed.

This was based on and re-enforced by a particularly powerful and explicit social division between the powerful noble and 'all the low-minded, common and plebeian',[40] which, in turn, depended upon a certain '*pathos of distance*',[41] defined as a 'protracted and domineering fundamental total feeling on the part of the higher ruling order in relation to a lower order'.[42] This allowed the nobles to 'create values and to coin names for values',[43] which, subsequently, re-enforced their initial sense of superiority over the 'lower' classes. It is this sense of superiority that lies at 'the origin of the antithesis "good" and "bad"'.[44]

Two aspects stand out from this: first, moral categories and values are the consequence not of transcendent values or *a priori* norms, but of socio-historical power relations. These take place at the level of social collectives, although these collectives are also heterogeneously composed of different individuals, social relations, and power struggles. Second, the initial moral categories that resulted from the pathos of distance between the social classes were not 'good' and 'evil', but 'good' and 'bad'. The 'good' was not initially opposed to 'evil', but had to become so. With this, Nietzsche emphasises that moral categories have to come into existence, as must the structural relations between them. Putting these two points together, Nietzsche anticipates Simona Forti's insistence that 'we have to investigate [evil] in its historical and contingent immanence: to realign it, that is, on the plane of human relations that are *always also power relations*'.[45] The notion of power relied upon here does not conform to a binary opposition in which power is either prohibitive or affirmative. Power relations are always simultaneously prohibitive and affirmative, in so far as to prohibit something is, at the same time, to, at least, implicitly affirm an alternative. Power relations are, therefore, always dynamic and give rise to the affirmation and prohibition of certain values, norms, and behaviours.

The good, then, was initially conceived and defined by the nobles, who received their position of authority because of their social position, itself a consequence of their individual ontological characteristics or, in Nietzsche's terminology, will-to-power. Appealing to the will-to-power demonstrates the extent to which Nietzsche's genealogical methodology is premised on his own metaphysics, where

> life itself is *essentially* a process of appropriation, injuring, overpowering the alien and the weaker, and at least, the very least, exploiting ... 'Exploitation' does not belong to a corrupted or imperfect, primitive society: it belongs to the *essence* of being alive as a fundamental organic function; it is a result of genuine will to power, which is just the will to life.[46]

Life, in its various forms, arises because of an implicit, subterranean play of forces, each of which struggles for superiority over others. The success of this endeavour generates the life-forms of existence. That one form rules over others is the consequence of that life-form having 'greater' will-to-power than those surrounding it. This is not a one-off occurrence, but a continuous process of domination and reaction. It is this pulsation that generates the becoming of life.

According to Nietzsche's genealogy, the nobles were dominant because they expressed a 'greater' will-to-power than those below them. Social status is, then, an effect of each individual's will-to-power. In turn, that social status, backed up by their greater will-to-power, allowed the nobles to determine what was considered good or bad, desirable or undesirable for society.

Nietzsche supports this by appealing to the etymology of the concept 'good' in various languages, all of which lead, so he claims,

> back to the *same conceptual transformation* – that everywhere 'noble', 'aristocratic' in the social sense, is the basic concept from which 'good' in the sense of 'with aristocratic soul', 'noble', 'with a soul of a high order', 'with a privileged soul' necessarily developed: a development which always runs parallel with that other in which 'common', 'plebeian', 'low' are finally transformed into the concept 'bad'.[47]

The common theme running through the various original meanings of 'good' is that it is always tied to an aristocratic sensibility: 'when dominating people determine the concept of "good," it is the elevated, proud states of soul that are perceived as distinctive and as determining rank order. The noble person separates himself off from creatures in which the opposite of such elevated, proud states is expressed: he despises them.'[48]

The noble's self-sufficiency and comfort in-himself means that 'he determines value, he does not need anyone's approval, he judges that "what is harmful to me is harmful in itself," he knows that he is the one who gives honour to things in the first place, he *creates values*'.[49] The noble man 'conceives the basic concept "good" in advance and spontaneously out of himself and only then creates for himself an idea of "bad"'.[50] There is a competitive autonomy to the noble spirit, one that continuously seeks to test itself. This competitive spirit exists as a latent 'hidden core that needs to erupt from time to time'.[51] Nietzsche famously writes that the noble spirit is like the 'blond beast'[52] that freely roams throughout nature doing what he wants and making the world his. This is a characteristic of all the great noble cultures: Roman, Arabian, Germanic, Japanese, Homeric, Scandinavian.[53]

From the nobles' autonomous action, the moral distinction arose between the nobles who determined the meaning of 'good' from themselves and those despised by them, the bad, those 'people who were cowardly, apprehensive, and petty, people who thought narrowly in terms of utility',[54] 'distrustful people with their uneasy glances ... grovelers ... dog-like types of people who let themselves be mistreated ... begging flatterers and, above all ... liars'.[55]

In *Human, All too Human*, Nietzsche recognises, however, that the noble is not just defined by a sense of individual comportment. The noble also has a particular *social spirit*. While the noble defines his values for himself, he does not affirm his status as a lone wolf, but continues to be bound to and, indeed, takes pride in belonging to 'the "good," a community that has a communal feeling ... entwined ... by their feeling of requital'.[56] For this reason, 'the noble person helps the unfortunate too, although not (or hardly ever) out of pity, but rather more out of an impulse generated by an overabundance of power'.[57] In contrast, those considered 'bad' belong 'to the "bad," to a mass of abject, powerless men who have no communal feeling'.[58] As a consequence, 'the good men are a caste; the bad men are a multitude, like particles of dust'.[59]

Good and bad men are, therefore, defined by opposing paradoxes: the former act autonomously to define their own values, all the while taking pride in the status of their community. The latter seek out communal values that are defined against the former, all the while looking to maintain their individual social status. The point is that the 'good' forge a communal spirit that safeguards their autonomy, whereas the 'bad' are unable and, indeed, unwilling to do so, instead clinging to homogeneous moral values to ensure social stability.

This brings up the question of why only a few achieved the exalted status of 'good'. Nietzsche recognises that 'in the majority of cases'[60] it happened because some 'designate[d] themselves simply by their superiority in power (as "the powerful," "the masters," "the commanders") or by the most clearly visible signs of this superiority, for example, as "the rich," "the possessors"'.[61] He also admits, however, that this explanation is not sufficient because it leads to the question of why some were able to achieve the social status or individual wealth that would allow them to create and define moral values.

Nietzsche's considered response is that it is because they possessed 'a *typical character trait*'[62] that permitted them to become synonymous with '"the truthful"'.[63] He backs this up by pointing out that for Greek nobility, for example, the word 'esthlos' 'signifies one who *is*, who possesses reality, who is actual, who is true; then, with a subjective turn, the true as the truthful'.[64] The noble becomes equivalent not just to telling the truth, but to the truth itself, which is not true of the '*lying* common man'.[65] In contrast, the Latin *malus* is associated with the dark-haired and coloured man as opposed to the blond, Aryan one, while 'Gaelic... offers us a precisely similar case – *fin* (for example in the name *Fin-Gal*), the distinguishing word for nobility, finally for the good, noble, pure, originally meant the blond-headed, in contradistinction to the dark, black-haired aboriginal inhabitants'.[66]

Initially, 'good' was associated with and defined by a particular social caste, itself defined through and from particular characteristics. It is for this reason that Thomas Brobjer explains that 'the fundamental aspect of Nietzsche's moral judgement and thinking is his concern and emphasis of personality and character. *Not principles, but personality and character are the determining criteria of value* according to his morality.'[67] Moral categories are not the consequence of free will or free choice, but emanate from and are associated with certain characteristics that are taken to be 'good'.

This is true to a point, but it does not go far enough in explaining why Nietzsche thinks that some characters were able to propel their 'owners' to social positions that allowed them to determine values. For Nietzsche, individual characteristics are themselves expressions of an individual's will-to-power or, put more formally, ontological constitution. Some are so ontologically constituted that they express 'more' will-to-power, meaning that they are able to overcome alternative viewpoints and positions to impose themselves onto the world. Moral values are not based on free choice, but express each individual's will-to-power as this is manifested through an individual's character (itself not freely chosen). Some individuals were then destined for positions of social status from which they could define the value and meaning of moral concepts, whereas others could not advance socially no matter how hard they tried.[68]

## The Role of the Priests

Having established the noble origins of the 'good' and shown that the 'good' was originally distinguished from the 'bad', Nietzsche turns to how it came to be that the opposite of the 'good' morphed from 'bad' to 'evil'. He explains that the alteration occurred when the priestly caste came to exist in opposition to the nobles. There is, however, an ambiguity in Nietzsche's account, in so far as it is not clear (1) where the priestly caste initially fits into the master/slave dichotomy – that is, whether it is part of the former or latter or, indeed, a third alternative; and, linked to this, (2) whether the priests effect a movement from the noble morality to the slave one or whether they introduce a third type of morality that gradually morphs into the dominant slave morality.

Nevertheless, Nietzsche claims that the actions of the priests separated the meaning of moral categories from individual actions and status to define it in terms of a transcendent essence. Good no longer designated the noble caste, but something 'in-itself' that transcends the noble class. Nietzsche is critical of this. Meaning does not reside in a transcendent, essential realm: 'there is no "being" behind doing, effecting, becoming; "the doer" is merely a fiction added to the deed – the deed is everything'.[69] Meaning is created from the act of attributing meaning, with this act being a consequence of the immanent unfolding of the possibilities that emanate from each individual's (or, more strictly, the human manifestation of the will-to-power's) ontological constitution.

As noted, for Nietzsche, each individual is a conglomeration of plays of forces that find expression through actual entities, each of which is defined by different 'quantum[s] of force'.[70] Each individual life is, therefore, defined by differences in what can be achieved by virtue of being constituted by a different quantum of force. Nonetheless, each strives to exert itself to the fullest extent that its ontology will permit. Meaning emanates from each individual's attempt to impose itself on and through the world. This does not imply that all are equally valid because only some meanings and values stimulate and release these quantum forces in ways that generate growth.

The historical movement towards transcendent conceptions of moral concepts was, for Nietzsche, accompanied and re-enforced by a movement towards purity so that things, including moral values, were thought in terms of a pure/impure binary opposition: a 'pure' good confronted a 'pure' evil.[71] Nietzsche suspects that the new appraisal of purity, while supposedly rooted in universal, *a priori* principles, was actually rooted in mundane reasons wherein 'the "pure one" is from the beginning merely a man who washes himself, who forbids himself certain foods that produce skin ailments, who does not sleep with the dirty women of the lower strata, who has an aversion to blood'.[72]

However, priestly morality quickly found itself in a bind, in so far as it soon discovered that its privileged 'pure' transcendent (moral) understanding was not always capable of dealing with the impurity and untidiness of concrete material conditions. To overcome this, the material world had to be made to conform to the purity of the transcendent one, which could only be achieved through periodic fits of anger against the material world aimed at 'removing' its impurity. This, for Nietzsche, is what lies at the base of the priest's ascetic ideal.[73]

The transcendent/concrete division introduced by the priests did, however, introduce depth to human existence, in so far as the former was understood to define the latter. This was also manifested in the understanding of the individual, who came to be thought of as an amalgamation of an external appearance and an inner hidden essence. Whereas the nobles were strong enough to be themselves, the introduction of depth into human existence meant that everything was not necessarily as it seemed. '[E]verything bec[a]me more dangerous'[74] as 'arrogance, revenge, acuteness, profligacy, love, lust to rule, virtue [and] disease'[75] arose. While he is highly critical of this movement, Nietzsche does point out that it is here 'that man first becomes an *interesting animal* [in so far as it is] only here [that] the human soul in a higher sense acquire[d] *depth* and bec[a]me *evil*'.[76] The priestly caste's split from the knightly aristocracy was, therefore, responsible for a fundamental alteration in the moral categories used, the way meaning was attributed to moral categories, and the relationship between them.

## The Defeat of Rome and the Rise of Judaea

According to Nietzsche, the split between the priestly caste and the knightly aristocratic one can be traced back to a particular moment: the rise of Judaism. This challenged the fundamental structures and values of previous moralities and, in so doing, ushered in their re-evaluation. For Nietzsche, this revolution had dramatic effects. Indeed, he calls it 'an act of the *most spiritual revenge*'.[77] All that had previously been valued was not only rejected, but also denigrated. Thus, it was the Jews who, with awe-inspiring consistency, dared to invert the aristocratic value-equation (good = noble = powerful = beautiful = happy = beloved of God) and to hang on to this inversion with their teeth, the teeth of the most abysmal hatred (the hatred of impotence), saying 'the wretched alone are the good; the poor, impotent, lowly alone are the good; the suffering, deprived, sick, ugly alone are pious, alone are blessed by God, blessedness is for them alone – and you, the powerful and noble, are on the contrary the evil, the cruel, the lustful, the insatiable, the godless of all eternity; and you shall be in all eternity the unblessed accursed, and damned!'[78]

Nietzsche calls this alteration *'the slave revolt in morality'*.[79] It was orientated in opposition to the values of Rome, which 'were the strong and noble'.[80] In contrast 'the Jews were the priestly nation of *ressentiment par excellence*'.[81] The 'essence' of *ressentiment* is, however, notoriously difficult to capture. Robert Solomon explains that, generally speaking, it 'suggests a feeling, a sensitivity ... [a] vulnerability, and implies a reaction to an offense (real or imagined, local or global), which includes (mostly imaginary) schemes of revenge'.[82] This captures the spirit of the notion, but, perhaps, Simon May's tripartite division is more analytically helpful:

> first, [*ressentiment*'s] object of hatred is universal in scope, embracing, at the limit, all of existence; second, it thoroughly falsifies that object in order to render the latter inescapably blameworthy – which, at the limit, means that it falsifies the whole character of existence; and, third, since such universal resentment is impossible to satisfy, its revenge must be, at least in part, imaginary.[83]

If we combine Solomon's and May's schemas, we find that the rise of the priestly class resulted from a process wherein its members gradually became more and more sensitive towards a perceived sleight conducted by the knightly class. This led the priests to construct a particularly monstrous conception of their enemy, which gradually morphed into an overwhelming hatred. As a consequence, 'when the eye of *ressentiment* look[ed] at the nobles, it [did] not see the tightly wound skein of power, wealth, courage, truthfulness, and the like that the nobles themselves have perceived; it [saw] instead only cruelty, tyranny, lustfulness, insatiability, and godlessness'.[84]

When put into historical terms, the priestly Jews resented their Roman masters, a sensation that gradually intensified until it exploded to challenge the social and moral structures of Rome.[85] A struggle between competing moral systems arose symbolised by the phrase '"Rome against Judea, Judea against Rome"'.[86] Such has been the importance of this struggle that Nietzsche explains that 'there has hitherto been no greater event than *this* struggle, *this* question, *this* deadly contradiction'.[87] As to which side won, Nietzsche points out that 'there can be no doubt: consider to whom one bows down in Rome itself today'.[88] Given that the Christian Catholic Pope resides in Rome, the only conclusion possible is that 'Rome has been defeated beyond all doubt.'[89]

There is, then, for Nietzsche, a constitutive link between the slave's revaluation of values and the content of subsequent Christian morality.[90] As he explains in *The Anti-Christ*, 'Christianity can be understood only by referring to the soil out of which it grew – it is *not* a counter-movement against the Jewish instinct, it is actually its logical consequence, one further conclusion of its fear-inspiring logic.'[91] By downplaying the differences between Judaism and Christianity, Nietzsche seems to be calling into question my insistence in Chapter 1 that evil is a specifically Christian problem.

This difference is only apparent. It will be remembered that I claimed that it is with the rise of Judaic monotheism that the metaphysical structures that generated the problem of evil were introduced. Judaic thinking was not, however, particularly concerned about the problem of evil. It was only with the rise of Christianity from Judaism that the problem of evil became a theological and philosophical one that attracted widespread attention. Genealogically speaking, Nietzsche is correct to insist that the problem of evil can be traced back to the rise of Judaism, but it only became an *explicit* problem once Judaism morphed into Christianity.

Crucially, he maintains that this heritage continues to implicitly underpin our supposedly secular sensibilities. After all, even the Christian Reformation and French Revolution, so often taken to entail breaks with the Christian past, are, on Nietzsche's telling, symptoms of Judaea's dominance over Rome. In fact, they cemented this dominance by, in the case of the Reformation, restoring the Catholic Church to its position of power, and, in the case of the French Revolution, removing 'the last bastion of political noblesse in Europe'.[92] We may not recognise our slave roots, but this is only because of the extent of the victory.[93]

## Slave Morality, *Ressentiment*, and the Rise of Evil

Importantly, Nietzsche claims that the slave revolt occurred when the slave's *ressentiment* became creative and gave birth to new values.[94] This required that the slaves develop a sense of *ressentiment* at the social status and individual capabilities of the nobles. Because the slaves, by virtue of their social status and individual capabilities, were unable to express their *ressentiment* against the nobles, they sublimated it against themselves and, in so doing, developed a particular ascetic ideal. This first entailed a personal ethic of austerity aimed at downplaying the sensuality of life, before it developed into an ethic based on

> qualities that serve to alleviate existence for suffering people . . . pity, the obliging, helpful hand, the warm heart, patience, industriousness, humility, and friendliness receive full honours here – since these are the most useful qualities and practically the only way of holding up under the pressure of existence.[95]

While this changed the content of 'the good', the man of *ressentiment* also inverted the privileged status that the noble gave to 'the good'. As previously noted, noble morality grew and expressed itself spontaneously and autonomously. It did not define itself against an opposite but sought 'its opposites only . . . to affirm itself more gratefully and triumphantly'.[96] Importantly, the nobility's 'negative concept "low", "common", "bad", [was] only a subsequently-invented pale, contrasting image in relation to its positive basic concept – filled with life and passion through and through – "we noble ones, we good, beautiful, happy ones!"'[97] The noble '"well-born *felt* themselves to be "happy"; they did not have to establish their happiness artificially by examining their enemies, or to persuade themselves, *deceive* themselves, that they were happy (as all men of *ressentiment* are in the habit of doing)'.[98] The noble also understood that his happiness was tied to his activity. He needed to test himself to determine what he was capable of doing. His activity was dynamic and entailed a process of self-discovery through doing rather than through comparison to a predetermined, abstract moral schema. For this reason, 'the noble man lives in trust and openness with himself'[99] and, while *ressentiment* can appear in him, if it does, it 'consummates and exhausts itself in an immediate reaction, and therefore does not *poison*'.[100]

This is the complete opposite of the man of *ressentiment*, who 'from the outset says No to what is "outside", what is "different", what is "not itself"; and *this* No is its creative deed'.[101] Whereas the noble affirms independently of its opposite, the slave defines himself from the negation of his other. There is a dependency built in to the slave's act of creative affirmation. Rather than the sheer affirmation of the noble morality, slave morality creates by first reacting to 'external stimuli'.[102] For Nietzsche, 'this *need* to direct one's view outward instead of back to oneself – is of the essence of *ressentiment*'.¹⁰³ The man of *ressentiment* defines himself through the other and so is unable to know himself as he is. He 'is neither upright nor naïve nor honest and straightforward with himself. His soul *squints*, his spirit loves hiding places, secret paths and back doors, everything covert entices him as *his* world, *his* security, *his* refreshment.'¹⁰⁴

Whereas the master saw in his enemy a chance to affirm himself, with the consequence that the enemy was considered to be an undesirable but necessary obstacle, the man of *ressentiment*'s loathing and hatred of his enemy create, in his mind, a monster that must be annihilated. Rather than having respect for his enemy, the man of *ressentiment* is defined by fear and hatred of him. As a result, what the master merely considered to be the 'enemy' becomes, for the slave, '"the evil enemy, "the Evil One" . . . from which he then evolves, as an afterthought and pendant, a "good one" – himself!'¹⁰⁵

The man of *ressentiment* brought forth, then, a fundamental alteration in the structure of moral categories. First, there was a movement away from the good/bad dichotomy of noble morality to the good/*evil* one of the slaves. The conclusion offered is that the moral category 'evil' is not ahistoric or one that has always existed, but was brought into existence by a particular social group at a particular historical point to construct and defend a worldview more beneficial to them than others.

Second, the meaning of 'good' altered away from those characteristics that defined 'the noble, powerful man, the ruler'¹⁰⁶ towards those needed by the slave: pity, care, an obliging helpfulness, a warm heart, patience, and so on. There was, in other words, a reversal of meaning, which confirms that 'what an age perceives as evil is usually an untimely after-effect of something that used to be perceived as good – the atavism of an older ideal'.¹⁰⁷

Third, whereas the 'bad' of noble morality was an unimportant by-product of the noble's autonomous affirmation, the slave not only replaces 'bad' with 'evil' to bring the latter into existence, but, by linking evil to the character of concrete individuals, turns it into a fixed thing. Evil is, then, based not on an abstract moral judgement, but on an actual thing. As such, reality is now understood to be full of 'evil' things and so becomes far more sinister. Frithjof Bergmann captures this nicely when he explains that

> what renders something 'evil' is not as plain and visible as was true with the former 'bad'. ['Evil'] conjures up a sense of threat, connotes dark, demonic forces set out to define all purity. 'Evil', from the start, introduces a hidden and mysterious element – sinister insinuations, with vile and monstrous spirits in the wings.¹⁰⁸

As Nietzsche puts it: 'evil [came to be] perceived [to be] something powerful and dangerous; it [was] felt to contain a certain awesome quality, a subtlety and strength that block[ed] any incipient contempt'.[109] This fundamentally subverted the individual–world relationship and, indeed, the way in which individuals comported themselves to others and the world they inhabited. Rather than offering something to be purposefully challenged and mastered, the world was understood to be something frightening and dangerous.

And fourth, the aspect privileged in the binary opposition, and so by extension that from which meaning was derived, altered. For the noble morality, it was (their conception of) the 'good' that generated the 'bad'. Meaning emanated from the spontaneous autonomy of the noble. Slave morality, however, not only replaced the 'bad' with 'evil', but derived the 'good' from the negation of 'evil'. Slave morality started from the 'evil' of the noble to negate it and so derive a sense of the 'good' from that reactive act. The 'good', in other words, was always reactive and dependent on that to be overcome.

Nietzsche is highly critical of these changes, seeing in them the creation of moral values and codes that stunt individual vitality. They are held to be instruments that reduce 'the beast of prey "man" to a tame and civilised animal'[110] and, in so doing, 'represent the *regression* of mankind'.[111] It might, however, be wondered why, if the slave morality overcame the noble one, Nietzsche, who values affirmation and overcoming, does not glorify it. This is a complex issue, but, very simply, for Nietzsche it depends on the manner in which overcoming occurs and that which the overcoming affirms. He holds that slave morality, by affirming through a *reaction* to the 'evil' of the noble, is not, in fact, affirmative, even if the affirmation of a different moral code is the consequence of its reaction to the master. The values that are affirmed by slave morality are ones that stunt and tame individuals rather than being those that allow individuals to spontaneously and affirmatively test themselves. In other words, Nietzsche judges the worth of values not by their victory, but by the extent to which moral values permit and affirm the life-growing qualities of struggle, competition, and, in a sense, individual experimentation. These constitute noble morality which, on Nietzsche's telling, strengthened the human race, both biologically and culturally, but not slave morality, which is defined by negativity and a privileging of the abstract and ahistoric.

As such, Nietzsche derives a normative ethics from each individual's ontology as it unfolds immanently. Each has a different ontology and so will live by a different ethic – indeed, this may change throughout an individual's life as the quantum of force constituting him alters – although Nietzsche adds a caveat to this by claiming that only those that affirm the will-to-power to the highest degree are legitimate.[112] That each individual perceives and values events differently means that moral categories do not reveal the truth about phenomena *per se*. Rather, what an individual holds to be true discloses 'truths' about himself. As Nietzsche explains in *Twilight of the Idols*,

> moral judgements can never be taken literally: literally, they always contain nothing but nonsense. But they are *semiotically* invaluable all the same: they reveal, at least to those who are in the know, the most valuable realities of cultures and inner states that did not *know* enough to 'understand' themselves. Morality is just a sign language, just a symptomatology: you already have to know *what* it's all about in order to get any use out of it.[113]

While 'truths' are symbolic constructions, we should not think that this limits their value or reveals that they are simply 'made-up stories'. It is precisely because an event is designated and understood in a particular way that it gains importance; it reveals the thought-processes and values of the individual and/or cultures within which it takes place. Charting how meaning changes and is attributed to events can, therefore, be used to better understand the individuals and/or culture expressing them. This conclusion will subsequently be taken up and developed by the psychoanalytic thinking of Jacques Lacan and Cornelius Castoriadis.

## Concluding Remarks

Nietzsche is an important figure in moral philosophy because he introduces a radical methodology to the study of moral concepts generally, and of evil specifically, that returns to the historical narrative to show how these concepts arose from particular socio-historical circumstances. In so doing, he undermines the notion that moral concepts are fixed, ahistoric, or have *a priori* meaning. Moral concepts are human constructions and have a history that changes and alters 'internally' and in relation to other groups and moralities. They are, however, marked by their genealogy; to speak of evil at all is to always pay homage to the Judaeo-Christian tradition from which it emanated.

The questions that arise from this, however, are whether it is enough to point to the historical changes that a concept has gone through to understand it? Does this produce a sufficiently nuanced understanding, or do we need to complement this historical focus with alternative perspectives? And, if we do, which other perspectives?

These issues became more and more urgent as thinkers struggled to come to terms with the social and political horrors they encountered early in the twentieth century. On the one hand, these horrors gave renewed impetus to the study of the nature and meaning of evil. On the other hand, however, the industrialisation of Western society meant that 'evil' became manifested in different ways and dimensions that appeared to differ substantially from the sufferings of old. In turn, new disciplines, such as sociology, arose that argued that events and meaning are effects of subterranean social processes and structures. On this understanding, societies are not just amalgamations of individuals, but 'have' a 'personality' independent of the entities comprising them. In turn, there was a growing awareness that individuals did not simply exist within society, but were *effects* of the anonymous processes and structures comprising 'it'. The socialisation processes through which individuals came to comprehend what was right or wrong had to be taken into account if moral concepts and meaning were to be properly understood. It is to this that we now turn.

## Notes

1. Arthur Schopenhauer, *The World as Will and Representation*, 2 vols, trans. E. F. J. Payne (New York: Dover, 1966).
2. G. W. F. Hegel, *The Philosophy of History*, trans. J. Sibree (New York: Dover, 1956), p. 33.
3. See, for example, Karl Marx, 'Preface to *A Contribution to the Critique of Political Economy*', p. 425, in *Early Writings*, ed. Lucio Colleti, trans. Rodney Livingstone and Gregor Benton (London: Penguin, 1975), pp. 424–8.
4. Arguably, the fundamental moment in this movement occurred with the publication, in 1859, of Charles Darwin's *On the Origin of Species* (Oxford: Oxford University Press, 2008).
5. Jerrold Siegel also notes this trajectory in his historical account of the self. See his *The Idea of the Self: Thought and Experience in Western Europe since the Seventeenth Century* (Cambridge: Cambridge University Press, 2005), pp. 32–4.
6. For an extensive account of the role that historical analysis played in nineteenth-century thought, see Maurice Mandelbaum, *History, Man, Reason: A Study in 19th Century Thought* (Baltimore: Johns Hopkins University Press, 1974).
7. Friedrich Nietzsche, *On the Genealogy of Morals*, Preface: 3, trans. Walter Kaufman and R. J. Hollingdale, in *On the Genealogy of Morals and Ecce Homo*, ed. Walter Kaufman (New York: Vintage, 1989), pp. 15–198. Conforming to convention, references to this text will correspond first to the essay and then to the aphorism. Unless otherwise stated, citations will be to aphorisms when referencing other texts from Nietzsche.
8. Friedrich Nietzsche, *Daybreak: Thoughts on the Prejudices of Morality*, trans.

R. J. Hollingdale, ed. Maudemarie Clark and Brian Leiter (Cambridge: Cambridge University Press, 1997), Preface: 3.
9. Friedrich Nietzsche, *Beyond Good and Evil: Prelude to a Philosophy of the Future*, trans. Judith Norman, ed. Rolf-Peter Horstmann and Judith Norman (Cambridge: Cambridge University Press, 2002).
10. Friedrich Nietzsche, *Ecce Homo*, trans. Walter Kaufman, p. 312, in *On the Genealogy of Morals and Ecce Homo*, ed. Walter Kaufman (New York: Vintage, 1989), pp. 217–335.
11. Ibid. p. 312.
12. Keith Ansell-Pearson, *An Introduction to Nietzsche as Political Thinker: The Perfect Nihilist* (Cambridge: Cambridge University Press, 1994), p. 126.
13. Nietzsche, *On the Genealogy of Morals*, Preface: 2.
14. Richard Schacht, *Nietzsche* (Abingdon: Routledge, 1985), p. 418.
15. Nietzsche, *On the Genealogy of Morals*, Preface: 5.
16. Ibid. Preface: 6.
17. The latter position is defended by Richard White, 'The Return of the Master: An Interpretation of Nietzsche's *Genealogy of Morals*', p. 65, in *Nietzsche, Genealogy, Morality: Essays on Nietzsche's On the Genealogy of Morals*, ed. Richard Schacht (Berkeley: University of California Press, 1994), pp. 63–75.
18. Nietzsche, *On the Genealogy of Morals*, I: 2.
19. Ibid. Preface: 7.
20. Robert Guay, 'Genealogy and Irony', *Journal of Nietzsche Studies*, 41, 2011, pp. 26–49 (pp. 26–7).
21. Brian Leiter, *Nietzsche on Morality*, 2nd edn (Abingdon: Routledge, 2015), p. 145.
22. Ibid. p. 145.
23. Nietzsche, *On the Genealogy of Morals*, I: 7.
24. For a summary of these issues, see David Owen, 'Nietzsche's Genealogy Revisited', *Journal of Nietzsche Studies*, 35/36, Spring/Autumn, 2008, pp. 141–54 (p. 142).
25. Maudemarie Clarke, 'Nietzsche's Immoralism and the Concept of Morality', p. 23, in *Nietzsche, Genealogy, Morality: Essays on Nietzsche's On the Genealogy of Morals*, ed. Richard Schacht (Berkeley: University of California Press, 1994), pp. 35–48.
26. Eric Blondel, 'The Question of Genealogy', p. 306, in *Nietzsche, Genealogy, Morality: Essays on Nietzsche's On the Genealogy of Morals*, ed. Richard Schacht (Berkeley: University of California Press, 1994), pp. 306–17.
27. Michel Foucault, 'Nietzsche, Genealogy, Critique', p. 78, in *The Foucault Reader*, ed. Paul Rabinow (New York: Vintage, 2010), pp. 76–100.
28. Ibid. p. 78.
29. Ibid. p. 79.
30. Ibid. p. 77.
31. Ibid. p. 82.

32. Ibid. p. 83.
33. Ibid. p. 83.
34. Nietzsche, On the Genealogy of Morals, Preface: 7.
35. Blondel, 'The Question of Genealogy', p. 306.
36. Foucault, 'Nietzsche, Genealogy, Critique', p. 94.
37. David Owen, 'The Contest of Enlightenment: An Essay on Critique and Genealogy', Journal of Nietzsche Studies, 25, Spring, 2003, pp. 35–57 (p. 47).
38. Nietzsche, On the Genealogy of Morals, Preface: 3.
39. Ibid. I: 2.
40. Ibid. I: 2.
41. Ibid. I: 2.
42. Ibid. I: 2.
43. Ibid. I: 2.
44. Ibid. I: 2.
45. Simona Forti, New Demons: Rethinking Power and Evil Today, trans. Zakiya Hanafi (Stanford: Stanford University Press, 2015), p. 120.
46. Nietzsche, Beyond Good and Evil, 259.
47. Nietzsche, On the Genealogy of Morals, I: 4.
48. Nietzsche, Beyond Good and Evil, 260.
49. Ibid. 260.
50. Nietzsche, On the Genealogy of Morals, I: 11.
51. Ibid. I: 11.
52. Ibid. I: 11.
53. Ibid. I: 11.
54. Friedrich Nietzsche, Human, All too Human, trans. Marion Faber and Stephen Lehmann (London: Penguin, 1994), 45.
55. Ibid. 45.
56. Ibid. 45.
57. Nietzsche, Beyond Good and Evil, 260.
58. Nietzsche, Human, All too Human, 45.
59. Ibid. 45.
60. Nietzsche, On the Genealogy of Morals, I: 5.
61. Ibid. I: 5.
62. Ibid. I: 5.
63. Ibid. I: 5.
64. Ibid. I: 5.
65. Ibid. I: 5.
66. Ibid. I: 5.
67. Thomas H. Brobjer, 'Nietzsche's Affirmative Morality: An Ethics of Virtue', The Journal of Nietzsche Studies, 26, Autumn, 2003, pp. 64–78 (p. 66).
68. This ties in to Nietzsche's notion of fate, an extensive discussion of which is provided by Béatrice Han-Pile, 'Nietzsche and Amor Fati', European Journal of Philosophy, 19:2, June, 2011, pp. 224–62.

69. Nietzsche, *On the Genealogy of Morals*, I: 13.
70. Ibid. I: 13.
71. For an extensive discussion of the notion of 'purity' in Nietzsche's thought, see Robbie Duschinsky, 'Nietzsche: Through the Lens of Purity', *The Journal of Nietzsche Studies*, 41, Spring, 2011, pp. 50–64.
72. Nietzsche, *On the Genealogy of Morals*, First Essay, 6.
73. Ibid. First Essay, 6. The ascetic ideal forms the basis for the third essay in the *Genealogy of Morals*. For an interesting discussion of the role that this ideal plays in the slave revolt, see Iain Morrison, 'Ascetic Slaves: Rereading Nietzsche's *On the Genealogy of Morals*', *The Journal of Nietzsche Studies*, 45:3, Autumn, 2014, pp. 230–57.
74. Nietzsche, *On the Genealogy of Morals*, I: 6.
75. Ibid. I: 6.
76. Ibid. I: 6.
77. Ibid. I: 7.
78. Ibid. I: 7.
79. Ibid. I: 7.
80. Ibid. I: 16.
81. Ibid. I: 16.
82. Robert C. Solomon, 'One Hundred Years of *Ressentiment*: Nietzsche's *Genealogy of Morals*', p. 103, in *Nietzsche, Genealogy, Morality: Essays on Nietzsche's On the Genealogy of Morals*, ed. Richard Schacht (Berkeley: University of California Press, 1994), pp. 95–126.
83. Simon May, *Nietzsche's Ethics and his War on 'Morality'* (Oxford: Oxford University Press, 1999), p. 42.
84. Mark Migoti, 'Slave Morality, Socrates, and the Bushmen: A Reading of the First Essay of *On the Genealogy of Morals*', *Philosophy and Phenomenological Review*, 58:4, December, 1998, pp. 745–79 (p. 752).
85. For an interesting discussion of Nietzsche's views on Rome, see Richard Bett, 'Nietzsche and the Romans', *The Journal of Nietzsche Studies*, 42, Autumn, 2011, pp. 7–31.
86. Nietzsche, *On the Genealogy of Morals*, I: 16.
87. Ibid. I: 16.
88. Ibid. I: 16.
89. Ibid. I: 16.
90. Nietzsche never mentions it, but presumably this also applies to Islam, given its constitutive relationship to the other monotheistic religions.
91. Friedrich Nietzsche, *The Anti-Christ*, §24, in *Twilight of the Idols and The Anti-Christ*, trans. R. J. Hollingdale (London: Penguin, 1990), pp. 126–99.
92. Nietzsche, *On the Genealogy of Morals*, I: 16.
93. Ibid. I: 7.
94. Ibid. I: 10.
95. Nietzsche, *Beyond Good and Evil*, 260.

96. Nietzsche, *On the Genealogy of Morals*, I: 10.
97. Ibid. I: 10.
98. Ibid. I: 10.
99. Ibid. I: 10.
100. Ibid. I: 10.
101. Ibid. I: 10.
102. Ibid. I: 10.
103. Ibid. I: 10.
104. Ibid. I: 10.
105. Ibid. I: 10.
106. Ibid. I:11.
107. Nietzsche, *Beyond Good and Evil*, 143.
108. Frithjof Bergmann, 'Nietzsche and Analytic Ethics', p. 81, in *Nietzsche, Genealogy, Morality: Essays on Nietzsche's On the Genealogy of Morals*, ed. Richard Schacht (Berkeley: University of California Press, 1994), pp. 76–94.
109. Nietzsche, *Beyond Good and Evil*, 260.
110. Nietzsche, *On the Genealogy of Morals*, I: 11.
111. Ibid. I: 11.
112. For an extended discussion of the relationship between Nietzsche's ethics and his ontology of the will-to-power, see Henrik Rydenfelt, 'Valuation and the Will to Power: Nietzsche's Ethics with Ontology', *The Journal of Nietzsche Studies*, 44:2, Summer, 2013, pp. 213–24.
113. Friedrich Nietzsche, *Twilight of the Idols*, trans. Richard Polt (Indianapolis: Hackett, 1997), §7.1.

# PART III SOCIALISATION AND PSYCHOANALYSIS

# 9
# Arendt on Evil: From the Radical to the Banal

Nietzsche died in 1900, too early to witness the tumultuous events that were to shortly engulf Western society. Within the space of fifty years, Europe suffered two world wars, genocide, terrorism, mass unemployment, the Spanish Flu pandemic of 1918, the ruthless totalitarian doctrines of Fascism, Stalinism, and National Socialism, and the horrors of the Gulag and Holocaust. There had, of course, been suffering before, but these events were particularly shocking. After all, the fundamental promise of the Enlightenment and economic industrialisation was that they would usher in a new age in which humans controlled their destiny and suffering on this scale was to be consigned to history.[1] Not only did these events reveal the emptiness of that narrative, but many felt that there was something 'new' about these horrors: they entailed more expansive forms of cruelty and suffering that were not adequately explained by prior thinking. The ruins of the Second World War brought forth a period of intense reflection aimed at understanding how the horrors of the Holocaust could happen, to prevent them from doing so again. The most famous and extensive of these, especially as it relates to the problem of evil, was provided by Hannah Arendt.

Arendt produced important analyses of totalitarianism, the question of rights, and the relationship between the private and public, but is often associated with her theory of evil. It was first mentioned in her 1929 doctoral dissertation on love in Augustine,[2] and she continued to discuss evil throughout her works. As she admitted, the biggest reason for this was the experience of the Second World War and, specifically, the news about the Holocaust death camps, which meant she encountered a form of suffering and viciousness beyond anything she could imagine.[3] Part of the process of confronting this new reality was to understand it. She found, however, that the conceptual categories available to her were not up to the job: 'the whole problem [of evil] has haunted philosophers [but] their attempts at solving it have never been very successful'.[4] For Arendt, this was because they appealed to 'either human blindness and ignorance or human weakness'.[5] To correct this, she resisted the temptation to ground evil in autonomous reason or adhere to commonly held assumptions about its nature, instead analysing it from the subterranean socio-political processes and structures that inform society.

As Patrick Hayden explains, this is fundamental to Arendt's attempt to rid 'evil of its [metaphysical or] supernatural connotations by treating it as a secular, historical, and political phenomenon mediated not through divine or demonic forces but through the actions of ordinary individuals and the power relations of social institutions within which these actions are inscribed'.[6] Arendt confirmed this in a posthumously published interview with Roger Errera where she explained that her purpose in studying evil was 'to destroy the legend of the greatness of evil, of the demonic force, to take away from people the admiration they have for the great evildoers like Richard III'.[7] To do so, she recognised that she had to break with the long-maintained claim that evil entails the absence of good,[8] the Augustinian notion that it entails a privation,[9] Leibnizian theodicies,[10] and the conflation of evil with violence.[11] In contrast, she held that evil has real being, is an effect of certain socio-political processes and formations, and was most explicitly manifested in the totalitarian regimes of Communism and Fascism, including the horrors of the Holocaust.

Conceptually speaking, however, her analyses of evil are more suggestive than developed. She tends to describe individual behaviours, social practices, and political formations as evil without ever explaining what she means by the term or why those behaviours, practices, and formations qualify for that nomenclature. This is compounded by her habit of distinguishing between different versions of evil, including elemental,[12] absolute,[13] greater,[14] lesser,[15] limited,[16] infinite,[17] radical,[18] or banal[19] forms, without defining them or identifying how they relate to one another. I will, however, focus on her notions of radical and banal evil because they are the most famous, developed, and those under which the other varieties tend to be discussed.

While she initially developed a radical conception of evil to describe the nature and origins of the new forms of totalitarian government, she subsequently ran into difficulty in identifying what was 'evil' about these regimes and, indeed, in describing what was so 'radical' about the atrocities they committed. This brought her to conclude that 'we cannot conceive of a "radical evil"',[20] 'the horror of the concentration and extermination camps can never be fully embraced by the imagination',[21] 'so little is known'[22] of radical evil, and, ultimately, that 'what radical evil is I don't know'.[23] For this reason, she came to reject the notion of radical evil, claiming in a famous letter to Gershom Scholem that 'I changed my mind and . . . no longer speak of "radical evil".'[24] Rather than being radical, evil was rethought to be banal.

Much work has been done on the relationship between both notions, with a number of contemporary thinkers disagreeing with Arendt's claim that they are fundamentally different,[25] but, in this chapter, I will limit the discussion to outlining the main contours of Arendt's analyses of both. To do so, I pay particular attention to the problems that she claims beset the Kantian notion of radical evil as a result of the rise of totalitarian regimes, and, indeed, her fundamental issue with the notion of 'radical evil' *per se*, before showing that banal evil is intimately tied to social-political regimes that fail to develop an individual's capacity to (1) examine an issue from the perspective of others, and (2) engage in substantive thinking about moral ends. For Arendt, then, (banal) evil is not simply linked to individual choice, but is thoroughly socio-political in nature.

## Radical Evil

Arendt first uses the concept 'radical evil'[26] in her 1951 study *The Origins of Totalitarianism*. She does not, however, actually undertake an analysis of the concept *per se*, but proceeds as if its meaning were clear to condemn the 'new' totalitarian regimes in the Soviet Union and Germany as 'evil'. It is not clear, however, whether she thinks that these regimes are predisposed to commit radically evil acts or whether they are radically evil because they are totalitarian. Nevertheless, she clearly thinks that radical evil accompanies certain socio-political formations.

To outline this, Arendt weaves a historical narrative of totalitarianism to show that its defining aspect, especially as it relates to radical evil, is its total bureaucracy. This intrudes into every aspect of daily life with the consequence that a standardised homogeneity, manifested through rigid bureaucracies and 'the rule of nobody',[27] dominates public and private life. By 'intrud[ing] upon the private individual and his inner life with equal brutality',[28] totalitarian bureaucracy shapes individual hopes, fears, and, crucially for the discussion of radical evil, judgement. Whereas Kant tied radical evil to the individual's autonomous choice to affirm the moral law or not, Arendt recognises that totalitarianism has demolished these conditions by virtue of reaching into and controlling every facet of individual life, including that of consciousness. This indoctrination distinguishes totalitarian regimes from authoritarian ones wherein the government simply imposes its ideology on the populace.²⁹ For Arendt, a key way in which this indoctrination was achieved was through juridical law.

While totalitarian regimes appeared to follow legal principles and often stressed this aspect of their policy-making, the legal principle in question was derived from the will of the Führer or emanated from supposed 'laws' of Nature or History that required certain actions. Furthermore, and as noted, the mask of legality was directed against those social groups or classes either deemed to stand in the way of the fulfilment of that Historical or Natural narrative or thought to be superfluous to its realisation.

Arendt uses the example of the Jews under Nazi rule to show that there is a developmental process to this: first, the aim was to 'reduce the German Jews to a nonrecognised minority in Germany, then to drive them as stateless people across the borders, and finally to gather them back from everywhere in order to ship them to extermination camps'.³⁰ There were also different types of concentration camps, which Arendt calls Hades, Purgatory, and Hell, depending on the purpose behind them. Hades corresponds to 'those relatively mild forms, once popular even in non-totalitarian regimes, for getting undesirable elements of all sorts – refugees, stateless persons, the asocial and the unemployed – out of the way'.³¹ Purgatory denotes the labour camps employed in the Soviet Union 'where neglect is combined with chaotic forced labour'.³² Hell 'in the most literal sense was embodied by those types of camp perfected by the Nazis, in which the whole of life was thoroughly and systematically organized with a view to the greatest possible torment'.³³

While there were different forms of concentration camp, once established there was a common movement towards greater cruelty. This was all part of the process through which the individual was broken down. Explaining this, Arendt notes that 'totalitarian concentration camps were first established for people who had committed a "crime"',³⁴ meaning they opposed the regime, 'but . . . they increased as political opposition decreased and . . . expanded when the reservoir of people genuinely hostile to the regime was exhausted'.³⁵ As political opposition decreased, the reliance on concentration camps, somewhat paradoxically, increased because the regime could get away with more and more oppression. It was, for example, only 'after 1936, i.e., after the pacification of the country, that the Nazi movement became more radical and more aggressive on the domestic as well as on the international scene',³⁶ an intensification that continued 'in 1938 with the mass arrests of all male German Jews during the November pogroms'.³⁷ In turn, the concentration camps became more professional and, thus, more efficient killing-machines as time went on: 'The early cruelty of the SA troops, who had been allowed to run wild and kill whomsoever they pleased, was replaced by a regulated death rate and a strictly organized torture, calculated not so much to inflict death as to put the victim in a permanent status of dying.'[38]

Arendt notes, however, that, despite all the pressure imposed on individuals by the totalitarian regimes, 'it is almost impossible to know how many [individuals] . . . will gladly acquiesce to a "population policy" that consists of regular elimination of surplus people'.[39] Even if the numerous social factors she identifies – anti-Semitism, the weakening of the State, imperialism, the First World War, the shifting position of the Jews in relation to other social groups in society, financial crises, and so on – explain the social environment that brought some to affirm totalitarian regimes while others did not, they do not explain *why* some were brought to accept the new norms while others were not.

This, however, was precisely why these regimes held that the concentration camps were so crucial: they served 'as the laboratories in which the fundamental belief of totalitarianism . . . [was] verified'.[40] While they appear to be a mere, albeit cruel, appendage to the regime, one that needlessly eats up scarce economic resources that would seem to be better suited to helping the totalitarian regime in its war efforts, Arendt claims that, in actuality, 'they [were] more essential to the preservation of the regime's power than any of its other institutions'[41] because their purpose was to experiment with how to create a populace that was totally submissive. To achieve this, they treated individuals as if they no longer existed. By creating the social conditions that obliterated individual autonomous conscience, it became increasingly difficult for the individuals involved to question their norms. Furthermore, by incorporating all individuals into the administration of the camps, 'the consciously organised complicity of all men in the crimes of the totalitarian regimes [was] extended to the victims and thus made really total'.[42]

What was so distressing about this situation was, as noted, that the Kantian notion of individual autonomy that could resist such events had been co-opted by the socio-political structures and processes of the totalitarian regimes. There appeared to be no space away from the regime from which individuals could formulate critical perspectives, engage in critical thought, or autonomously evaluate their actions. The *totali*tarian nature of these regimes meant that they invaded every facet of individual life to bend it to the 'will' and ends of the regime.

Again, Arendt points out that this was cultivated in stages: the first entailed 'the moment of arbitrary arrest when the judicial person [was] . . . destroyed'.[43] This continued through the destruction of their 'moral personality',[44] as manifested through 'the separation of the concentration camps from the rest of the world, a separation which ma[de] martyrdom senseless, empty, and ridiculous'.[45] The final stage was 'the destruction of individuality itself and [wa]s brought about through the permanence and institutionalising of torture'.[46] The end result, of course, was 'the reduction of human beings to the lowest possible denominator of "identical reactions"'.[47] This systematic, wholesale, organised destruction of individuality and the consequences that result from it were, for Arendt, 'the appearance of some kind of radical evil previously unknown to us';[48] one based not on individual choice but on anonymous social structures that destroy the autonomy upon which individual choices were long taken to depend.

## From Radical Evil to Banal Evil

On this telling, totalitarian regimes aimed and were able to absolutely dominate their citizens to achieve their ends. The problem with this formulation is that if the totalitarian regimes were so all-pervasive, there would be no way to counteract them from within. Resistance would be not only futile, but also impossible. Recognising this, Arendt, in a 1953 address to RIAS Radio University in Berlin, tempered her earlier analysis by noting that, while totalitarian regimes might aim to extinguish individual spontaneity and, indeed, could even succeed to a large and almost total degree, they would not and could not completely succeed in this endeavour because 'life as such, and surely human life, is dependent upon it'.[49] This is not to say that individuals are always spontaneous, only that each always has the *possibility* to be. For this reason, she notes that

> totalitarian terror does not curtail all liberties or abolish certain essential freedoms, nor does it, at least to our limited knowledge, succeed in eradicating the love of freedom from the hearts of men; it simply and mercilessly presses men, such as they are, against each other so that the very space of free action – and this is the reality of freedom – disappears.[50]

This remorseless pressure, achieved through 'the arbitrary selection of various groups for concentration camps, by constant purges of the ruling apparatus, by mass liquidations',[51] aims to gradually break individuals down so that they become 'superfluous'.[52] It is this that makes these regimes so radically evil and ensures that they go far beyond the Kantian critique of treating humans as means rather than as ends. By making individuals superfluous, these social-political regimes threaten both the individual's existence as such and the spontaneity that Arendt holds to be fundamental to human being. Not only is the goal itself so far beyond what has ever been previously attempted, but the methods used to achieve it are also so extreme as to defy understanding. As Arendt concludes, the monstrosity of the deeds is such that 'we can neither punish nor forgive such offenses [because] they transcend the realm of human affairs and the potentialities of human power, both of which they radically destroy wherever they make their appearance'.[53]

However, by claiming that radical evil (1) cannot be understood through the categories historically used to think and understand evil, (2) entails means and ends that are beyond human comprehension, and (3) cannot be forgiven or punished, Arendt found herself in the philosophically problematic situation of using terms without being able to actually define or explain them. This was not simply due to a failure on her part, but was inherent in the way in which she conceived of radical evil as being, in some sense, beyond human comprehension. Arendt could only admit that, ultimately, we cannot know what radical evil, as that which is beyond our comprehension, entails. It must, therefore, remain a mystery for us.

Arendt was not, however, happy with this conclusion. The main problem she identified with 'radical evil' is that its Latin origin (*radix*) indicates a root or base point. As we saw, for Kant, this was the individual's own autonomous choice. Arendt, initially, agreed that there was a root source for evil, but, rather than follow Kant and ground it in individual will, she grounded it in social-political structures. Gradually, however, she came to reconceptualise her understanding of these social-political structures, in conjunction with her rethinking of evil. Rather than being grounded in a singular, fixed base, social-political structures and norms operate diffusely throughout the entire social body. Properly understanding the nature of evil requires, then, that we conceptualise evil as insidious rather than radical. For this reason, she famously wrote to Gershom Scholem:

> I changed my mind and do no longer speak of 'radical evil' ... It is indeed my opinion now that evil is never 'radical', that it is only extreme, and that it possesses neither depth nor any demonic dimension. It can overgrow and lay waste the whole world precisely because it spreads like fungus on the surface. It is 'thought-defying', as I said, because thought tries to reach some depth, to go to the roots, and the moment it concerns itself with evil, it is frustrated because there is nothing. That is its 'banality'. Only the good has depth and can be radical.[54]

With this, Arendt abandons the notion that evil be thought in terms of roots to claim that, structurally speaking, it is more akin to a fungus, slowly spreading throughout all aspects of society. The depth-metaphor inherent in the notion of radical evil is inappropriate when conceiving of evil. Kant's notion of an autonomous moral agent choosing his moral maxim is then too simplistic, in so far as it ignores the ways in which that choice is influenced by social structures and processes. As a consequence, individual moral actions are not the result of an individual's autonomous choice – as noted, totalitarian regimes have rendered illusory the notion of autonomy upon which this understanding is based; they are effects of the fungus-like social norms that individuals are immersed in. The need for this alteration and, indeed, an explanation of what it entails were confirmed by and outlined through her coverage of the Eichmann trial.

## The Banality of Evil

On 11 May 1960, Adolf Eichmann was kidnapped by Israeli secret agents in a suburb of Buenos Aires, Argentina, and transported to Jerusalem to stand trial for fifteen crimes, including 'crimes against the Jewish people, crimes against humanity, and war crimes during the whole period of the Nazi regime and especially during the period of the Second World War'.[55] As a correspondent for *The New Yorker*, Arendt travelled to Jerusalem to produce a report that would provide 'a factual account of the trial',[56] but which did, in her words, cause a 'furious controversy'.[57]

Arendt found Eichmann's presence in the dock fascinating: it simply contrasted so sharply with the monstrous figure – manifested most clearly in the figure of Satan – that the Christian West has historically associated with evil. It would have been far easier if Eichmann had been a manifestation of the monster we tend to associate with evil. The prosecution certainly did all it could to portray him in this way. The problem was, however, that 'everybody could see that this man was not a "monster"'.[58] He was, rather, a 'man inside a glass booth built for his protection: medium-sized, slender, middle-aged, with receding hair, ill-fitting teeth, and nearsighted eyes'.[59]

Eichmann's insubstantial physical appearance was also matched by a lack of thoughtfulness, the trait that Arendt focuses on. The only thing that stood out about Eichmann was that he failed at almost everything he did: he did not finish high school, was fired from a sales position at the Vacuum Oil Company in Austria for his Nazi membership, and, much to his chagrin, was never promoted past the rank of lieutenant colonel.[60] There was nothing about Eichmann that was exceptional or out of the ordinary. What was out of the ordinary, however, was the administrative role he fulfilled in the Nazi regime.

While he did not have a particularly high rank, he was responsible for the transportation of Jews to the concentration camps and so occupied a role that was absolutely central to the Nazi regime. It was within this role that Eichmann shone. Between 1937 and 1941, he won four promotions for his 'expert[ise] on "the Jewish question," the intricacies of Jewish organizations and Zionist parties, [and] as an authority on emigration and evacuation, as the "master" who knew how to make people move'.[61] As Arendt explains it, Eichmann conducted his activities without malice or even any real sense of hatred for the Jews. For this reason, he 'was perfectly sure that he was not what he called an *innerer Schweinehund*, a dirty bastard in the depth of his heart'.[62] His actions were directed by far more banal motives: career advancement.

Indeed, Eichmann never actually directly killed anyone.[63] He had visited the death camps, but

> did not see much ... He never actually attended a mass execution by shooting, he never actually watched the gassing process, or the selection of those fit for work – about twenty-five per cent of each shipment – that preceded it at Auschwitz. He saw just enough to be fully informed of how the destruction machinery worked.[64]

He was, in Arendt's words, 'a desk murderer',[65] albeit one who worked assiduously to ensure that prisoners avoided 'unnecessary hardships',[66] indicating that State-sponsored murder, not cruelty, was his end. It was not even clear that Eichmann was aware that his actions contributed to the grisly end of so many. It seemed that he was simply focused on ensuring that his own activities were conducted as efficiently and effectively as possible. Indeed, Arendt notes that 'he showed unmistakable signs of sincere outrage when witnesses told of cruelties and atrocities committed by S. S. men',[67] and, on at least one occasion, even actively worked to save Jews, an action that led to censure from his superiors.[68] Obviously, there was more going on here than a monster intent on causing as much harm and suffering as possible. This gave rise to the question of what brought him and others like him, who it must be remembered did not appear to be sadistic monsters, to commit the deeds they did.

Arendt rejects the notion that it was because they were merely following orders. This ignores the fact that there was always a choice to do otherwise.[69] She also rejects the notion of collective responsibility, noting that 'where all, or almost all, are guilty, nobody is'.[70] Nor was it because each individual, having found themselves in that position, was afraid to leave because of fear of punishment for doing so. It was 'surprisingly easy ... for members of the extermination squads to quit their jobs without serious consequences for themselves'.[71]

Arendt explains that Eichmann's commitment to the horrendous task at hand arose from two different, but complementary, factors: first, while it is often ignored by commentators, she notes that the most decisive 'flaw in Eichmann's character was his almost total inability to ever look at anything from the other fellow's point of view'.[72] This inability meant not only that he was unable to empathise with those he was sending to their deaths, but also that he was not even confronted with the problem. Those he was sending to their deaths were not a problem to be countenanced. Everything he did could be subordinated to the task at hand. It is tempting to conclude that this was an individual flaw in Eichmann, but, as Emmanuel Levinas[73] points out, this lack of empathy was a defining feature of Nazi ideology, itself a manifestation of the long-held Western privileging of the same over the other. If we take Levinas's suggestion seriously, Eichmann's lack of empathy for others was not then due to his autonomous individual choice, but was an effect of the moral and social norms inculcated by his socio-political world.

Second, and far more noted in the literature, is Arendt's claim that while Eichmann was not stupid, he was defined by 'a curious, quite authentic inability to think'.[74] This thoughtlessness manifested itself in the wholesale use of stock phrases and clichés. As a consequence, he would continuously utter the most banal statements, most of which seemed designed to simply offer a response to the question asked and which were invariably those that he thought his interlocutor wanted to hear or which were appropriate to the moment. For Arendt, the resultant inconsistencies were comical,[75] although they did not appear to trouble Eichmann, who held that they were merely 'questions of changing moods';[76] as long as he could identify and employ a stock phrase or cliché he was quite happy.

Eichmann's inconsistencies continued into the moral realm so that he could easily change moods, tones, and requirements depending on the social setting. He 'knew that what he had once considered his duty was now called a crime, and he accepted his new code of judgement as though it was nothing but another language rule'.[77] This allowed him to blend in perfectly to whatever environment he found himself in. He was simply untroubled by the contradictions that this threw up. Dealing with those would have meant thinking about them, something that Arendt is adamant he did not do and, indeed, was not capable of doing. As such, 'the longer one listened to him, the more obvious it became that his inability to speak was closely connected to an inability to *think*, namely, to think from the standpoint of someone else'.[78] Rather than a monster, Arendt could not but help conclude that he was a 'buffoon'.[79]

That Eichmann would not or could not think and take responsibility for his actions challenged one of the central tenets of culpability inherent in all modern legal systems. Generally speaking, this is understood to require some intent on the part of individuals, which, in turn, entails an autonomous decision that the individual can be held to be responsible for. This, however, is what Eichmann and other Nazi defendants denied.[80] Moreover, Arendt notes that legal culpability requires 'that human beings be capable of telling right from wrong even when all they have to guide them is their own judgement'.[81] After all, as Christoph Menke explains, 'if it is a condition of justice for any act of legal judgment that the one judged is able in principle to pass this judgement himself, then he must be able to judge in order to be able to be judged'.[82] Eichmann did not meet this standard. He was simply incapable of thinking and so judging autonomously. Even when he invoked Kant's categorical imperative to justify his blind obedience to the law, this entailed not autonomous judgement regarding the moral law but blind submission to the pronouncements and will of the Führer.[83]

However, given that her analysis depends upon the claim that Eichmann was incapable of thinking, it is not surprising that a number of commentators have questioned whether Eichmann really was incapable of this. Coline Covington, for example, argues that Eichmann's care for his family reveals that he was not the unthinking automaton Arendt portrays. He was, rather, able and willing to think in order to better his own position and, by extension, that of his family.[84] Similarly, George Cotkin points out that the Nazi bureaucracy was a highly decentralised, complex system with multiple players all in fierce competition with one another. Eichmann would not have been able to rise to the position he did if he was incapable of thinking. That he did meant that Arendt's image and understanding of Eichmann were simply wrong: 'he was both a brilliant player and a dedicated one'.[85] Even Arendt notes this with her claim that 'Eichmann's position was that of the most important conveyor belt in the whole operation.'[86] It was his office that synchronised departures and arrivals to ensure that the victims arrived at camps that could absorb them, negotiated with railroad authorities and the Ministry of Transport to obtain enough trains, adhered to the multiple rules governing the different classes of Jews, and did all this across an international network with different national laws, rules, and directives. There is no doubt that all of this took substantial skill, energy, drive, and thought. Why, then, does Arendt come to the opposite conclusion?

Perhaps the way to resolve this issue is to follow Arne Johan Veltsen's[87] distinction between substantively orientated and instrumentally orientated thinking. The former deals with the questioning of ends, whereas the latter engages with a questioning or thinking about the means to achieve a predetermined end. Whereas substantive thinking engages with foundational moral questions about what ends an individual and society should be orientated towards, instrumental thinking takes over a predetermined end and determines how best to achieve it. If we interpret Eichmann through this schema, we find that while he was incapable of substantive thinking, he was very capable of instrumental thinking, and it was this that allowed him to be such a good Nazi administrator.

This confirms Arendt's claim that Eichmann was incapable of (substantive) thinking, but explains that his ability to function very well within the predetermined schema of Nazi ideology was a consequence of his highly developed (instrumental) rationality. In turn, this means that Arendt's claim that banal evil is linked to thoughtlessness needs to be refined so that we understand that it refers to substantive thoughtlessness; that is, an inability to think and make an autonomous judgement about moral ends. It does, however, give rise to the question of whether substantive thinking was possible within the Nazi regime; that is, within a social-political structure that not only aimed to condition and manipulate individual moral action but also was apparently successful in doing so.

## Lessons from Eichmann

What was crucial to Arendt was that Eichmann was not an isolated case. She realised that his substantive thoughtlessness was shared by many others. Indeed, 'the trouble with Eichmann was precisely that so many were like him, and that the many were neither perverted nor sadistic, that they were, and still are, terribly and terrifyingly normal'.[88] While many disagreed with the crimes of the Nazis, they went along with them anyway and in so doing displayed 'a remarkable tendency to [simply] fall in line with whoever happened to constitute their surroundings'.[89] By not resisting the regime, even though they did not necessarily share its ends, they provided support for and legitimacy to it. How, then, can we understand these people? If they were not monsters, what were they? And, most importantly, in what ways were those who simply went along with the Nazi regime different from those who actively collaborated with it?[90]

Arendt responds that it appears that the ability and desire to question were what distinguished collaborators from non-collaborators. The latter not only were still able to question themselves, but actually did so. While they were often 'called irresponsible by the majority',[91] they were the only ones who dared to judge themselves. This was not because 'they disposed of a better system of values or because the old standards of right and wrong were still firmly planted in their mind and conscience'.[92] Instead of depending upon or cultivating 'a highly developed intelligence or sophistication in moral matters',[93] each had merely fostered a disposition that brought him 'to live together explicitly with [him]self, to have intercourse with [him]self, that is, to be engaged in that silent dialogue between me and myself which, since Socrates and Plato, we usually call thinking'.[94] Arendt goes on to explain that this thinking is not technical, but entails what I previously called substantive thinking and so involves a questioning of the ends of action.

Importantly, the dividing line between those who wanted to think and judge and those who did not struck 'across all social and cultural or educational differences'.[95] There was no neat division between the two broad groups. If there had been, it would have been relatively easy to identify the *general conditions* that gave rise to their mentality. That it was not restricted to a segment of the population, but was spread throughout the various socio-economic groups, meant that it was not easy to determine the conditions that brought some to acquiesce and others to resist. Nevertheless, for Arendt, we must examine the *mentality*, one that cuts across socio-economic groupings, underpinning the choice to support the regime.

From this, she claims that those who chose to passively support the Nazi regime were those who clung most strongly to social and cultural norms. By clinging to a *formal* conception of norms, each could quite easily believe one norm one day and another the next. After all, 'we now know that moral norms and standards can be changed overnight, and that all that then will be left is the mere habit of holding fast to something'.[96] What was important was not the norm *per se*, but the sense of stability and order that the norm provided. By not thinking about the ends to be adopted, but simply following the dominant social norm, whole swathes of the populace found themselves unproblematically acting in ways they would previously have rejected. It appears therefore that the best way to prevent totalitarian regimes from arising is to get individuals to recognise that, no matter what is deemed to be socially acceptable, they will have to live with themselves. This, however, assumes that people, within totalitarian regimes, who are being remorselessly pressured and squeezed, are capable of such action.

## Concluding Remarks

It is here that the implicit theological underpinnings of Arendt's analysis come to the fore. In particular, she clarifies her previous claim that the influence of totalitarian regimes is *total* by explaining that 'under conditions of terror most people will comply but *some people will not*'.[97] She supports it with the example of Anton Schmidt, a Nazi officer in charge of a patrol in Poland collecting stray German soldiers, who stumbled across Jews trying to escape. Rather than kill or arrest them, Schmidt 'helped the Jewish partisans by supplying them with forged papers and military trucks'[98] and, most importantly, '"he did not do it for money"'.[99] This went against everything that his society told him to do.

To explain how this is possible, Arendt appeals to her notion of 'natality',[100] initially developed in *The Human Condition* (published in 1958). Rather than describing an individual's 'original physical appearance',[101] 'natality' indicates an 'impulse'[102] or 'insertion [that] is like a second birth'[103] and is therefore tied to a 'new beginning'.[104] This 'sense of initiative ... is inherent in all human activities',[105] but cannot be explained. Rather, it appears 'in the guise of a miracle'[106] to permit alternative action and, in so doing, a new birth. As a consequence, the individual is always capable of remaking himself through his actions. Such action is not necessarily based on a prior plan; it is spontaneous and unpredictable,[107] with the consequence that it renders 'helpless'[108] every attempt to control it.

There are two aspects to this that stand out: first, Arendt ties the notion of 'natality' to that of 'miracle' to describe an event that occurs but which cannot be understood or accounted for logically or in accordance with natural laws. With this, she demonstrates her continuing, if implicit, dependence upon the theological tradition that has long insisted on the importance of (God's) miracles.[109] Second, by arguing that individuals can spontaneously choose to act against the social-political norms and values that define their situation and world, Arendt reveals that her analysis continues to be tied to and conducted through a critical appropriation of the Augustinian-Kantian tradition, where, on the one hand, she challenges its claim that evil is grounded in the individual's autonomous will by emphasising the important role that social-political structures play in fostering and supporting an individual's conception of and adherence to moral values, all the while, on the other hand, repeating the basic Augustinian-Kantian claim that the individual can always choose to alter his morality and is therefore ultimately responsible for it. The result is a complication and reorientation of that tradition rather than a fundamental departure from it.

While this ties Arendt's analysis to the tradition that it supposedly aims to depart from, developments in the second half of the twentieth century called into question the theoretical assumptions upon which her inquiry is based, to claim that it does not pay sufficient analytical attention to the *meaning* of evil or to the psychic mechanisms involved in socially conditioned individual action. For all her insights into the impact that totalitarian regimes have on those living within them, there is always a sense in which she simply assumes the existence of evil without being able to pin down exactly what it signifies, while, as noted, her account of individual action is premised on an unexplainable miraculous event. Subsequent thinkers, especially in France in the 1950s and 1960s under the guise of structuralism and latterly post-structuralism, took a different approach. While joining Arendt in continuing to affirm the crucial role that dynamic, pre-personal, subterranean structures play in conditioning individual action, these thinkers argued that, because social interaction is premised on linguistic interaction, we must turn to the linguistic structures and practices that structure individual understanding and actions.

Importantly, these thinkers held that language is not merely a tool used by already-formed individuals; individuals themselves were held to be effects of the differential relations constitutive of language. This decentring of the subject meant that, to understand the meaning of a concept, it was first necessary to identify and understand the pre-personal, subterranean, linguistic processes and configurations that generated that meaning, which in turn required that the psychic processes involved in meaning acquisition were taken into account. In the next two chapters, I explore the different ways in which Jacques Lacan and Cornelius Castoriadis respond to this issue to show that both offer unique and often-ignored approaches to the problem of evil that (1) depend upon insights from psychoanalytic theory that are absent from prior analyses, (2) focus on the role that dynamic, pre-personal, linguistic structures and imaginary processes play in generating meaning, to (3) emphasise the socially *and* linguistically constructed nature of concepts generally and the meaning of 'evil' specifically.

## Notes

1. There was significant debate on this issue. For example, Theodor Adorno and Max Horkheimer (*Dialectic of Enlightenment*, trans. John Cumming [London: Verso, 1997]) claim that these events were not, in fact, anomalies of Enlightenment reason, but the logical outcome of the logic of exclusion and domination inherent in Enlightenment rationality. Alternatively, Emmanuel

Levinas ('Reflections on the Philosophy of Hitlerism', trans. Seán Hand, *Critical Inquiry*, 17:1, 1990, pp. 62–71) holds that the roots of these events lie not in the Enlightenment, but further back in the West's Christian origins, specifically its body/soul division. For a detailed discussion of Levinas's critique, see my *The Problem of Political Foundations in Carl Schmitt and Emmanuel Levinas* (Basingstoke: Palgrave Macmillan, 2016), ch. 6.
2. Hannah Arendt, *Love and Saint Augustine*, ed. Joanna Vecchiarelli Scott and Judith Chelius Stark (Chicago: University of Chicago Press, 1996), p. 10.
3. Hannah Arendt, '"What Remains? The Language Remains:" A Conversation with Günter Gaus', p. 13, in *Essays in Understanding, 1930–1954*, ed. Jerome Kohn (New York: Schocken Books, 1994), pp. 1–23.
4. Hannah Arendt, *The Life of the Mind: Willing*, ed. Mary McCarthy (New York: Harvest, 1978), pp. 33–4.
5. Hannah Arendt, 'Some Questions of Moral Philosophy', p. 79, in *Responsibility and Judgement*, ed. Jerome Kohn (New York: Schocken Books, 2003), pp. 49–146.
6. Patrick Hayden, 'The Relevance of Hannah Arendt's Reflections on Evil: Globalization and Rightlessness', *Human Rights Review*, 11, 2010, pp. 451–67 (p. 454).
7. Hannah Arendt and Roger Errera, 'Hannah Arendt: From an Interview', *New York Review of Books*, 26 October, 1978, p. 18.
8. Arendt, *The Life of the Mind: Willing*, p. 118. For this reason, Shiraz Dossa is mistaken in concluding that 'following Kant and Arendt, evil I shall take to denote (as a secular phenomenon) the dramatic absence of good' ('Hannah Arendt on Eichmann: The Public, the Private, and Evil', *The Review of Politics*, 46:2, 1984, pp. 163–82, [p. 166]).
9. Hannah Arendt, *On Violence* (New York: Harvest, 1970), p. 56.
10. Hannah Arendt, *The Human Condition*, 2nd edn (Chicago: University of Chicago Press, 1998), p. 281.
11. Arendt, *On Violence*, p. 56.
12. Hannah Arendt, *The Origins of Totalitarianism*, (New York: Harvest, 1976), pp. viii–ix; Hannah Arendt, *On Revolution* (London: Penguin, 2006), p. 77.
13. Arendt, *The Origins of Totalitarianism*, p. 459.
14. Ibid. p. 442.
15. Ibid. p. 442; Hannah Arendt, 'The Eggs Speak Up', p. 271, in *Essays in Understanding, 1930–1954*, ed. Jerome Kohn (New York: Schocken Books, 1994), pp. 270–84; and Hannah Arendt, 'Personal Responsibility under Dictatorship', pp. 36–7, in *Responsibility and Judgement*, ed. Jerome Kohn (New York: Schocken Books, 2003), pp. 17–48.
16. Hannah Arendt, 'The Concentration Camps', *Partisan Review*, 15:7, 1948, pp. 43–64 (p. 747).
17. Hannah Arendt, 'Thinking and Moral Considerations', p. 188, in *Responsibility*

and *Judgement*, ed. Jerome Kohn (New York: Schocken Books, 2003), pp. 159–89.
18. Arendt, *The Origins of Totalitarianism*, p. 439, and *The Human Condition*, p. 241.
19. Hannah Arendt, *The Life of the Mind: Thinking*, ed. Mary McCarthy (New York: Harvest, 1978), pp. 3–5; Hannah Arendt, *Eichmann in Jerusalem: A Report on the Banality of Evil* (London: Penguin, 2006), p. 252.
20. Arendt, *The Origins of Totalitarianism*, p. 459.
21. Arendt, 'The Concentration Camps', p. 748.
22. Arendt, *The Human Condition*, p. 241.
23. Hannah Arendt and Karl Jaspers, *Correspondence: 1932–1969*, ed. Lotte Kohler and Hans Sander (New York: Harcourt, 1992), p. 166.
24. Hannah Arendt, 'Letter of 24 July 1963 to Gershom Scholem', pp. 470–1, in *The Jewish Writings*, ed. Jerome Kohn and Ron H. Feldman (New York: Schocken Books, 2007), pp. 465–71.
25. James Phillips, 'From Radical Evil to Banal Evil: Hannah Arendt against the Justification of the Unjustifiable', *International Journal of Philosophical Studies*, 12:2, 2004, pp. 129–158; George Cotkin, 'Illuminating Evil: Hannah Arendt and Moral History', *Modern Intellectual History*, 4:3, 2007, pp. 463–90; Paul Formosa, 'Is Radical Evil Banal? Is Banal Evil Radical?', *Philosophy and Social Criticism*, 33:6, 2007, pp. 717–35; Hayden, 'The Relevance of Hannah Arendt's Reflections on Evil'.
26. Arendt, *The Origins of Totalitarianism*, p. 443.
27. Arendt, *The Human Condition*, p. 45.
28. Arendt, *The Origins of Totalitarianism*, p. 245.
29. Ibid. p. 6.
30. Ibid. p. 290.
31. Ibid. p. 445.
32. Ibid. p. 445.
33. Ibid. p. 445.
34. Hannah Arendt, 'Social Science Techniques and the Study of Concentration Camps', p. 236, in *Essays in Understanding, 1930–1954*, ed. Jerome Kohn (New York: Schocken Books, 1994), pp. 232–47.
35. Ibid. p. 236.
36. Ibid. p. 236.
37. Ibid. p. 237.
38. Ibid. p. 238.
39. Arendt, *The Origins of Totalitarianism*, p. 437.
40. Ibid. p. 437.
41. Arendt, 'The Concentration Camps', p. 760.
42. Arendt, *The Origins of Totalitarianism*, p. 452.
43. Arendt, 'Social Science Techniques and the Study of Concentration Camps', p. 240.

44. Ibid. p. 240.
45. Ibid. p. 240.
46. Ibid. p. 240.
47. Ibid. p. 240.
48. Arendt, *The Origins of Totalitarianism*, p. 443.
49. Hannah Arendt, 'Mankind and Terror', p. 304, in *Essays in Understanding, 1930–1954*, ed. Jerome Kohn (New York: Schocken Books, 1994), pp. 297–306.
50. Hannah Arendt, 'On the Nature of Totalitarianism: An Essay in Understanding', pp. 342–3, in *Essays in Understanding, 1930–1954*, ed. Jerome Kohn (New York: Schocken Books, 1994), pp. 328–60.
51. Arendt, *The Origins of Totalitarianism*, p. 457.
52. Ibid. p. 457.
53. Arendt, *The Human Condition*, p. 241.
54. Arendt, 'Letter of 24 July 1963 to Gershom Scholem', pp. 470–1.
55. Arendt, *Eichmann in Jerusalem*, p. 21.
56. Arendt, 'Personal Responsibility under Dictatorship', pp. 17–18.
57. Ibid. p. 18.
58. Arendt, *Eichmann in Jerusalem*, p. 54.
59. Ibid. p. 5.
60. Ibid. p. 33.
61. Ibid. p. 65.
62. Ibid. p. 25.
63. Ibid. p. 22.
64. Ibid. pp. 89–90.
65. Ibid. p. 241.
66. Ibid. p. 108.
67. Ibid. p. 109.
68. Ibid. p. 95.
69. Arendt, 'Personal Responsibility under Dictatorship', pp. 31–2.
70. Ibid. pp. 31–2.
71. Arendt, *Eichmann in Jerusalem*, p. 91.
72. Ibid. pp. 47–8.
73. Levinas, 'Reflections on the Philosophy of Hitlerism', p. 69, Preface.
74. Arendt, 'Thinking and Moral Considerations', p. 159.
75. Arendt, *Eichmann in Jerusalem*, p. 54.
76. Ibid. p. 55.
77. Arendt, 'Thinking and Moral Considerations', p. 159.
78. Arendt, *Eichmann in Jerusalem*, p. 49.
79. Arendt, '"What Remains? The Language Remains"', p. 16.
80. Arendt, 'Some Questions of Moral Philosophy', p. 111.
81. Arendt, *Eichmann in Jerusalem*, pp. 294–5.
82. Christoph Menke, 'At the Brink of Law: Hannah Arendt's Revision of the Judgment on Eichmann', *Social Research*, 81:3, 2014, pp. 585–611 (p. 599).

83. Arendt, *Eichmann in Jerusalem*, pp. 135–6.
84. Coline Covington, 'Hannah Arendt, Evil and the Eradication of Thought', *International Journal of Psychoanalysis*, 93, 2012, pp. 1215–36 (pp. 1219–20).
85. Cotkin, 'Illuminating Evil', p. 485.
86. Arendt, *Eichmann in Jerusalem*, p. 153.
87. Arne Johan Veltesen, 'Hannah Arendt on Conscience and Evil', *Philosophy and Social Criticism*, 27:5, 2001, pp. 1–33 (p. 9).
88. Arendt, *Eichmann in Jerusalem*, p. 276.
89. Hannah Arendt, 'Auschwitz on Trial', p. 234, in *Responsibility and Judgement*, ed. Jerome Kohn (New York: Schocken, 2003), pp. 226–56.
90. Arendt, 'Personal Responsibility under Dictatorship', p. 43.
91. Ibid. p. 44.
92. Ibid. p. 44.
93. Ibid. p. 44.
94. Ibid. p. 45.
95. Ibid. p. 45.
96. Ibid. p. 45.
97. Arendt, *Eichmann in Jerusalem*, p. 232.
98. Ibid. p. 230.
99. Ibid. p. 230.
100. Arendt, *The Human Condition*, p. 9.
101. Ibid. pp. 176–7.
102. Ibid. p. 177.
103. Ibid. p. 176.
104. Ibid. p. 9.
105. Ibid. p. 9.
106. Ibid. p. 178.
107. Ibid. p. 191.
108. Ibid. p. 191.
109. For more on this relationship, see David Cormer, *The Philosophy of Miracles* (London: Continuum, 2007); and David Basinger, *Miracles* (Cambridge: Cambridge University Press, 2018).

# 10
# Lacan and the Symbolic Function of Evil

The so-called 'linguistic turn' that marked twentieth-century philosophical thinking brought the question of language to the fore, finding expression in analytic philosophy through the works of J. L. Austin, Donald Davidson, Gottlob Frege, Bertrand Russell, and Ludwig Wittgenstein, and in continental philosophy through the thinking of Jacques Derrida, Jürgen Habermas, and Martin Heidegger.[1] One area where the turn to linguistics was particularly pronounced was in the structuralist paradigm that arose in France in the 1950s and 1960s. Within a cultural and historical orbit that valued scientific rationality, structuralism's turn to scientific linguistics promised to guide the social sciences towards respectability.

This turn also had revolutionary implications. As François Dosse notes in his acclaimed history of the topic, structuralism arose from

> a certain degree of self-hatred, of the rejection of traditional Western culture . . . Antique values were no longer glorified; structuralism demonstrated an extreme sensitivity to everything that had been repressed in Western history. Indeed, it is no accident that the two leading sciences of the period – anthropology and psychoanalysis – privilege the unconscious, the nether side of manifest meaning, the inaccessible repressed of Western history.[2]

Uncovering the hidden and implicit structures subtending thought showed that meaning was far from being unproblematic or *a priori*; it was an effect of the dynamic structural relations sustaining reflective thought. That meaning was generated from relations meant that each aspect was as important as the other. What had previously been overlooked or downgraded to subordinate status was suddenly elevated to an equal footing with that which had previously dominated.

Initially, this found expression in the fields of anthropology and psychoanalysis: the former sought to understand cultures through the structural relations of their symbolic codes, while the latter's notion of the unconscious was particularly important in revealing that these structures operated at a 'hidden', implicit level of human organisation. Anthropology and psychoanalysis came together in the thought of Jacques Lacan, who took insights from Claude Lévi-Strauss[3] and Ferdinand de Saussure[4] and combined them with a particularly innovative reading of Freudian psychoanalytic theory. The result was a powerful, if controversial, theory about the role that language plays in the construction of human reality.

This chapter focuses on Lacan's account of the symbolic, before relating it to the question of evil. When we turn to his work, however, we immediately encounter two problems. First, there is the issue of Lacan's writing style, which is famously disjointed, partial, suggestive, and difficult to read. There is no detailed, worked-out analysis and certainly no line-by-line, point-by-point logical demonstration of the hypothesis he proposes. It is a matter of piecing together statements made across different texts to, in a sense, construct his thinking. This is compounded by Lacan's intransigence, and, to a degree, glee in not making himself better understood, manifested most clearly and ominously in *Seminar I*: 'if you think you have understood, you are bound to be wrong'.[5]

Bruce Fink has, however, pointed out that 'the ambiguities in Lacan's speech and work are often very deliberate';[6] a conclusion mirrored by Louis Sass, who notes that paradox plays a large role in Lacan's thought and writings because it allows him to demonstrate that there is 'something inherently paradoxical in the human condition itself'.[7] That Lacan presents his work in this disjointed fashion mirrors, even magnifies, the content of his theory, which insists on the partial, constructed, open-ended nature of human reality. The disjointedness of Lacan's writing style is, therefore, somewhat paradoxically, perfectly consistent with the content of his thinking.

More problematically for our purposes, Lacan never provides a theory of evil *per se*, rarely talks about evil, and when he does his comments are partial and suggestive rather than developed and thought out. For example, in *Seminar III*, he mentions that it is not possible to distinguish between greater and lesser evil because evil '*always* entails a greater evil'.[8] This is not developed further. In *Seminar VII*, he returns to the topic to claim that, while 'the question remains open',[9] evil is both material and non-material. Again, it is not clear what this might mean.

This chapter will, therefore, treat Lacan as offering a particular *approach* to the issue of how meaning is generated that emphasises the role that the pre-personal, differential relations of the symbolic order play in this process, before, briefly, developing what a Lacanian theory of evil might entail from his comments on the symbolic–real relation (which is where he locates ethics). From this, I show the important role that Lacan gives to the symbolic order in generating meaning, demonstrate that the differential nature of its symbolic grounding ensures that the meaning of 'evil' cannot be unitary or stable – which helps to explain why there has been such historical contestation over its meaning – before engaging with the role that 'evil' plays in symbolic orders to suggest that it is the signifier that aims, but, due to the nature of the Lacanian (non-signifiable) real, always fails to designate the unknowable real *within* the symbolic order.

More specifically, according to Lacan, 'evil' is the symbol that (1) stands at the liminal point between the symbolic and the real, the knowable and unknowable; (2) designates the ineffable, excessive aspect of existence that, because it cannot be symbolically comprehended, is associated with the strange, indescribable, and threatening other; but which (3) by naming that which is beyond comprehension plays a particular and important role in ordering and giving meaning to each individual's (psychic) life. At this stage, however, the unfamiliar reader is likely to be wondering what Lacan means by concepts such as 'symbolic', 'real', and so on. It will therefore be helpful to provide a schematic overview of the conceptual co-ordinates informing his thinking.

## The Three Registers

Freud's thinking on the *subject's psyche* famously distinguishes between and was conducted through two schemas: unconscious, preconscious, and conscious *and* id, ego, and super-ego. While Lacan returned to Freud, he developed a new schema, composed of the real, symbolic, and imaginary, to describe the *subject's experience*.[10] Lacan focused on each one of the registers in three different periods: from approximately 1936 to 1953 the emphasis was on the imaginary; from 1953 to the early 1960s the symbolic came to the fore; and from the mid-1960s onwards, the real was highlighted.

Taking them in that order, the famous 'The Mirror Stage as Formative of the *I* Function as Revealed in Psychoanalytic Experience'[11] explains the formation of the imaginary register in the following fashion. From the age of around six to eighteen months, the child comes to recognise himself in the mirror, which does not have to be an actual mirror, simply an object that represents him to himself; *identifies* with the image obtained through the mirror; and so comes to assume a fictitious identity in the form of the ego.[12]

The mirror stage describes, then, the moment in the psyche's development when it passes from a fragmented, differential notion of itself to the *fantasy* of identity.[13] The problem, of course, is that the *I* constructed is a projection of identity, not an actual one, and, as a consequence, always entails the adoption 'of an alienated identity that will mark his entire development with its rigid structure'.[14]

If the imaginary is associated with an alienating, fantastic identity, the symbolic entails the differential relations that subtend that fantasy. We will explore this in more detail throughout the chapter, but suffice it to say that the increasing importance that Lacan gave to the symbolic order in the 1950s brought him to focus on the differential linguistic matrix that gives rise to subjective meaning and the fantasy identity of the imaginary. The symbolic is that through which meaning, signification, law, and order come to the world. It is the 'motor' that generates the illusion of imaginary identity, as this operates through and on the individual. For this reason, Lacan ties it to 'the notion of machine',[15] which captures the dynamicism inherent in symbolic production. Indeed, he goes on to explain that 'the symbolic world is the world of the machine'.[16]

The third registry Lacan introduces, the real, gradually comes to assume more and more importance in his thinking. As he explains in *Seminar I*, 'the real, or what is perceived as such, is what resists symbolisation absolutely'.[17] Lorenzo Chiesa identifies three senses in which the real can be understood. In the early writings, it denotes 'objects as they are given to us in everyday reality'[18] and 'a rather vague notion of undifferentiated matter as it is in itself before the advent of the symbolic'.[19] In the later writings, however, Chiesa explains that Lacan comes to hold that the real does not exist 'outside' of the symbolic, but 'exists' at the heart of the symbolic as the 'hole' or 'lack' that resists symbolic structures and imaginary identity.[20] There is a lack or mystery at the heart of the symbolic that prevents identity or full disclosure. This reaffirms Lacan's earlier claim that identity is an imaginary construct. No matter the symbolic register, there is always an aspect that cannot be symbolised and so escapes comprehension. It is this 'lack' that ensures that a system is never total and closed and which allows for movement, reconfiguration, and the creation of the new. Because the real cannot be symbolised, any comments about the real are always from the perspective of the symbolic and are always retrospectively imposed on the real from the symbolic register.

Having briefly described the three registers, we now have to identify the relationship between them. This is, however, somewhat complicated and differs depending on whether it is thought logically or experientially.

*Logically*, Lacan distinguishes between the three registers to define each in turn, but goes to great pains to insist that they are, in fact, intimately related. As early as *Seminar I*, he explains that the individual 'acts in several registers at a time, in the symbolic, the imaginary, and the real',[21] which eventually leads him in *Seminar XX* to develop the notion of the Borromean knot to show the ways in which the three registers are entwined.[22] Importantly, the registers are not complementary and so, while they interlock, they are always in conflict with one another.

*Experientially*, a child appears to develop to 'normalcy' by passing through the three registers in a particular order. As the material 'stuff' composing reality, the real is always there. The child is always born into a symbolic order – language is, after all, all around – but to develop the capacity to 'use' symbolic language, he must first pass through the imaginary register into the symbolic. The imaginary is then the first register through which the individual passes, which, as noted, gives rise to the notion of identity and the ego. Subsequent to this, the child learns how to express himself through language, at which point he can be said to 'enter' fully into the symbolic. As Lacan notes, however, 'the domain of the symbolic does not have a simple relation of succession to the imaginary domain whose pivot is the fatal intersubjective domain. We do not pass from one to the other in one jump from the anterior to the posterior.'[23] Once the child has entered the symbolic, it conditions all else, including the imaginary.[24] Indeed, strictly speaking, it is only once the child has passed into the symbolic that the imaginary *I* is born in that it is only through the symbolic that the child can describe himself in those terms.[25]

Lacan admits that, like any theory, his has 'limits',[26] but claims that 'its usefulness [lies] in being critical',[27] specifically with regard to 'where the empirical efforts or researchers meet with a difficulty in handling pre-existing theory'.[28] Lacan is talking here of the clinical experience of psychoanalytic theory, but, in focusing on the linguistic processes through which meaning is developed and assigned, he introduces a new methodology to the study of evil. To develop this and explain what it specifically means for 'evil', I will first outline what the symbolic realm entails before linking it to the real.

## The Symbolic

Lacan's turn to the symbolic was inaugurated with the presentation of the text 'The Function and Field of Speech and Language in Psychoanalysis' to the Rome Congress in 1953. It has, therefore, come to be known as the Rome Report. In it, Lacan writes that he considers psychoanalysis to be important because it 'rediscovered in man the imperative of the Word as the law that has shaped him in its image'.[29] He notes, however, that psychoanalysis had developed 'a growing aversion regarding the functions of speech and language'.[30] For Lacan, this showed how far psychoanalysis had departed from Freud, who, on Lacan's telling, recognised that

> a dream has the structure of a sentence or, rather, to keep to the letter of the work, of a rebus – that is, of a form of writing, of which children's dreams are supposed to represent the primordial ideography, and which reproduces, in adults' dreams, the simultaneously phonetic and symbolic use of signifying elements found in the hieroglyphs of ancient Egypt and in the characters still used in China.[31]

According to Lacan, psychoanalysis needed to return to Freud, meaning it needed to return to the linguistic analysis that Lacan held to be at the heart of Freud's thinking. As a consequence, Lacan warned that for psychoanalysis 'to be constituted as the science of the unconscious, one must set out from the notion that the unconscious is structured like a language'.[32]

While aware that the human is born with biological parameters, Lacan downplays their importance for, at least, two reasons: first, he implicitly distinguishes between the *human being* and the *subject* to claim that while 'human beings are born with all kinds of extremely heterogeneous dispositions . . . whatever the fundamental lot is, the biological lot, what analysis reveals to the subject is its signification'.[33] For Lacan, the human being is a rather uninteresting concept. It is only once the human being enters the symbolic register that it 'fully' enters the human community and turns into a subject capable of expressing and analysing 'itself'. For this reason, he explains that 'everything which is human has to be ordained within a universe constituted by the symbolic function'.[34]

Second, given that the symbolic order provides meaning, any discussion that appeals to biology to explain something does not really discuss a biological event or thing, but is, in actuality, an effect of a particular symbolic order that brings consciousness to think of the matter in biological terms. Not only is there a lack to our self-knowledge, but meaning does not *correspond* to events; meaning is always a *construction* resulting from a particular pre-existing symbolic order. For this reason, it is not the case that a baby cries because it is hungry. Rather, as Bruce Fink explains,

> Lacan's view is more radical in that one cannot even say that a child *knows* what it wants prior to the assimilation of language: when a baby

cries, the *meaning* of that act is provided by the parents or caretakers who attempt to name the pain the child seems to be expressing (e.g., 'she must be hungry'). There is perhaps a sort of general discomfort, coldness, or pain, but its meaning is imposed, as it were, by the way in which it is interpreted by the child's parents. If a parent responds to its baby's crying with food, the discomfort, coldness, or pain will retroactively be determined as having 'meant' hunger, as hunger pangs. One cannot say that the true meaning behind the baby's crying was that it was cold, because meaning is an ulterior product: constantly responding to a baby's cries with food may transform all of its discomforts, coldness, and pain into hunger. Meaning in this situation is thus determined not by the baby but by other people, and on the basis of the language they speak.[35]

Lacan does, however, note that there is one biological issue that escapes the symbolic order: procreation or 'that one being is born from another'.[36] That procreation occurs is beyond doubt, but 'nothing in the symbolic explains the fact of their individuation, the fact that beings come from beings'.[37] While this emphasises the gap between the biological and the symbolic, it also reaffirms Lacan's point that there are always gaps or lacks to explanations. These are not failures of explanation, but are integral to the symbolic order that conditions human understanding. The biological and the symbolic are not then opposed in Lacan's thinking. The former provides the base from where the latter emerges.

Indeed, in *Seminar XI*, Lacan collapses the distinction between matter and the symbolic by claiming that the human is born into certain oppositional relations that form the natural background to its being:

> symbols in fact envelop the life of man with a network so total that they join together those who are going to engender him 'by bone and flesh' before he comes into the world; so total that they bring to his birth, along with the gifts of the stars, if not with the gifts of the fairies, the shape of his destiny; so total that they provide the words that will make him fanciful or renegade, the law of the acts that will follow him right to the very place where he is not yet and beyond his very death; and so total that through them his end finds its meaning in the last judgment, where the Word absolves his being or condemns it – unless he reaches the subjective realisation of being-toward-death.[38]

Signifiers are not then free-floating, abstract entities or relations, but are inherently material. For Lacan, matter only has meaning because it is based on the opposition immanent in the symbolic order, while the symbolic order is intrinsically material. It is this that brings him to explain that 'the least you can afford me concerning my theory of language is, should it interest you, that it is materialist. The signifier is matter transcending itself in language.'[39]

As Louis Sass explains, this symbolic matrix shapes 'a realm that is understood to lie beyond our conscious grasp ... yet which, in contrast with the illusions of the "imaginary" realm ... constitutes the actual matrix and motor of much of our experience and action'.[40] The subject is, then, an effect of language: 'the play of the symbol represents and organises, independently of the peculiarities of its human support, this something which is called a subject. The human subject doesn't foment this game, he takes his place in it, and plays the role of the little *pluses* and *minuses* in it.'[41]

One consequence of this is that, rather than control language, subjectivity is an effect of linguistic structures that, in effect, condition it. As Lacan maintains in *Seminar I*, 'all human beings share in the universe of symbols. They are included in it and submit to it, much more than they constitute it. They are much more its supports than its agents.'[42] Bruce Fink develops this by explaining that 'the unconscious is nothing but a "chain" of signifying elements, such as words, phonemes, and letters, which "unfolds" in accordance with very precise rules over which the ego or self has no control whatsoever'.[43] As an effect of the symbolic order, the subject is nothing but a component piece of it; that is, a signifier. In being given a name, the subject comes forth.

But, importantly, the subject does not come forth as any*thing*. The creation of the signifier-subject 'reduce[s] the subject in question to being no more than a signifier, to petrify the subject in the same movement in which it calls the subject to function, to speak, as subject'.[44] The subject is never a thing:

> the subject is nothing other than that which slides in a chain of signifiers, whether he knows which signifier he is the effect of or not. That effect – the subject – is the intermediary effect between what characterizes a signifier and another signifier, namely, the fact that each of them, each of them is an element.[45]

With this, Lacan radically disrupts the egoistic premises of modern philosophy, claiming that, rather than being in control of itself and its environment, the subject is, in actuality, an effect of the symbolic Other. Indeed, he affirms that 'the promotion of consciousness as essential to the subject in the historical aftermath of the Cartesian cogito is indicative, to my mind, of a misleading emphasis on the transparency of the *I* in action at the expense of the opacity of the signifier that determines it'.[46] The I, for Lacan, is not the foundation of consciousness, but the imaginary construct created by consciousness's attempt to impose order and unity on its fundamental dependence on others and, hence, differential relations.[47] To focus on the ego is to misunderstand the fundamental dependency that consciousness has on signifiers and the symbolic relation. This occurs not at the reflective level of the *I*, but at the unconscious pre-*I* level. For this reason, Lacan explains that 'the true subject [is] the subject of the unconscious'.[48] Because it occurs at the unconscious level, the subject and, by extension, meaning can never be fully present: 'the discovery of the unconscious, such as it appears at the moment of its historical emergence, with its own dimension, is that the full significance of meaning far surpasses the signs manipulated by the individual'.[49] This realisation demands 'a new attitude to man',[50] one that recognises the fundamental role that the unconscious and language play in human existence.

## Lalangue, Language, Communication, and Speech

There is, however, some ambiguity in Lacan's account regarding the exact relationship between the unconscious and language. In *Seminar III*, he holds that 'the unconscious is fundamentally structured, woven, chained, meshed *by* language',[51] which indicates that there is a distinction between the two, with language playing a causative role in the genesis of consciousness. In *Seminar XX*, however, Lacan rejects his earlier formulation, claiming that 'the unconscious is structured *like* a language',[52] before going on to clarify that 'I say *like* so as not to say – and I come back to this all the time – that the unconscious is structured *by* a language.'[53]

Lorenzo Chiesa argues that this clarification is important because it means that Lacan perceives

> the signifiers of the unconscious [to] possess a symbolic (oppositional/ differential) *meaning* that causes signification to emerge in consciousness, but they do not possess, *per se*, any signification. Signification can only be conscious, and the unconscious is, by definition, not conscious. In other words . . . there is no archetypal unconscious signified for Lacan.[54]

Claiming that the unconscious is structured *like*, not *by*, language is important because it allows Lacan to distinguish his position from traditional conceptions of language, which he understands to entail a combination of a signifier and that which is signified; the latter ensuring that the sliding of signifiers is stopped and fixed meaning attributed to the signifier. For Lacan, the signified is an imaginary construct emanating from the dynamic, differential, symbolic matrix. Whereas *consciousness* is structured around the identity of the I and, by extension, the imaginary identity of signifieds, the *unconscious* – the 'true' locus of subjectivity – contains no signified, only a sliding chain of signifiers. For this reason, the unconscious is structured *like* language, in that it comprises signifiers, but not *by* language, because it 'lacks' signifieds. Because it is composed of differential relations between signifiers, there is no fixed meaning inherent in the unconscious. Meaning is a second order *imaginary* phenomenon resulting from the attempt to make sense of the unconscious's differential symbolic relations.

To clarify the relationship between the language of the unconscious and that of consciousness, Lacan initially distinguishes between language, communication, and speech, before, in the later seminars, introducing the notion of *lalangue*.[55] *Lalangue* is understood to be the non-objective, non-signifying source of language. 'It is the introduction of difference as such into the field [of *lalangue*], which allows one to extract from [*lalangue*] the nature of the signifier *(ce qu'il en est du significant)*',[56] and that subsequently permits the 'signifier [to] be called upon to constitute a sign *(faire signe)*'.[57] Delineating this further, Lacan explains in another text that

> the signifier differs from the sign in that its inventory is already given of *lalangue*. To speak of code doesn't work, precisely because it presupposes meaning. The signifying inventory of *lalangue* supplies only the cipher of meaning. According to context, each word takes on an enormous and disparate range of meaning [which] is often attested to by the dictionary.[58]

*Lalangue* is then the 'material' from where the symbolic order of language(s) is generated and always exceeds its expression in a particular language.[59]

With the *lalangue*/language distinction, Lacan re-enforces his earlier thesis that the unconscious is structured *like* language, in that the unconscious contains signifiers without signifieds, without conforming to the signifier–signified relation of language. As Samo Tomšič explains, 'the distinction between language and [*lalangue*] . . . covers the difference between linguistic meaning and the autonomy of the signifier. *Lalangue* stands entirely on the side of this autonomy, negating the primacy of communication and relationality (dialogue).'[60] For this reason,

> *lalangue* is real, not symbolic; it is made up of a multiplicity of elements that convey no meaning in particular, and that are merely the non-sufficient

condition of meaning, each being able to receive a plethora of meanings depending on the different linguistic constructions in which they are used.[61]

While *lalangue* is the source of language, both are expressed through communication and speech. Whereas speech 'links the subjects together into this pact which transforms them, and sets them up as human subjects communicating',[62] communication 'involves a tendency to reach an agreement on the object'.[63] Thus, even if speech and communication are social, Lacan suggests that the latter is focused on the object mediating the relation, while speech is focused on the other subject of the conversation. Summarising Lacan's position, we can say that the formal process of meaning acquisition entails an 'initial' *lalangue* (= real), which is transformed by the symbolic order into language (= symbolic order of the unconscious), which subsequently generates meaning that is communicated through speech (= symbolic/imaginary orders of consciousness). Of course, in actuality, there is not a straightforward linear trajectory from the real, through the symbolic, to the imaginary. The three registers always exist in conflictual entwinement with one another.

Importantly, the naming of things paves the way for their entrance into the symbolic order, all the while demonstrating the formative impact that the symbolic order has on them. After all, the name is an effect of the already-existing symbolic order. Through this act, the object, which as an effect of the symbolic order is always differential and differentiating, is given an identity and so enters the imaginary realm. This naming is never, however, a unilateral act by an autonomous agent:

> naming constitutes a pact, by which two subjects simultaneously come to an agreement to recognise the same object. If the human subject didn't name – as Genesis says it was done in earthly Paradise – the major species first, if the subjects do not come to an agreement over this recognition, no world, not even a perception, could be sustained for more than one instant. That is the joint, the emergence of the dimension of the symbolic in relation to the imaginary.[64]

All of this occurs unconsciously. The subject is born, enters the symbolic, and is conditioned by the differential relations upon which the symbolic depends. From this conditioning, the 'two' of the symbolic relation unconsciously 'agree' on a particular name for an object, with this naming subsequently triggering an imaginary field of meaning for them. 'Meaning' does not then emanate from the autonomous decisions of monadic individuals, but depends on 'discourse, in other words, a mode of functioning or a utilisation of language qua link'.[65] This is why the symbolic order, which is precisely the rules, order, and regulations governing and generating language, is so important.

This gives rise to the question of whether there is a metalanguage governing language; that is, whether language is a closed or open system. Lacan vacillates on this issue, initially claiming in *Seminar III* that 'all language implies a metalanguage'.[66] Because all language can be potentially translated, there must be a metalanguage – a Rosetta stone of sorts – that permits and facilitates the movement between languages. In *Seminar XVII*, however, Lacan, having turned to emphasise the real, explicitly rejects this, affirming that 'I still [sic] maintain that there is no metalanguage. Anything that one might think is of the order of a search for the meta in language is simply, always, a question about reading.'[67] The lacuna(e) that always exist(s) 'in' the symbolic as a consequence of the real's role therein means that there can be no metalanguage that encompasses language or languages. Any search for one is, in a sense, the attempt to impose an imaginary identity on and between languages to gain the closure that always eludes symbolic structures because of the 'presence' of the real 'in' them.

With regard to the problem of translation, Lacan comes to recognise that translations do not, as the existence of a metalanguage would suggest, require *correspondences* between languages, but are always *creations* from one symbolic register to the other. Translations are never exact replicas of the original. This also reaffirms Lacan's thesis that human understanding cannot fall back on a fixed, ahistoric point of reference that generates a singular, universal meaning. As Joan Copjec explains, 'to say that there is no metalanguage is to say, rather, than society *never stops realising* itself, that it *continues* to be formed over time'.[68] Meaning is developed socially and so changes based on alterations to the symbolic order that generates it.

## Meaning through the Symbolic Relation

The symbolic order is composed of two aspects: signifiers and the differential relations that support and give meaning to them. As Lacan explains in the Rome Report, 'in a language, signs take on their value from their relations to each other in the lexical distribution of semantemes as much as in the positional, or even flectional, use of morphemes',[69] a position that ensures that 'each term is sustained only in its topological relation with others'.[70] There are two ways to interpret this relationality: first, it could indicate that two independent monadic signifiers gain *meaning* through their relation. Second, and more radically, it could mean that the *existence* and the *meaning* of the signifiers emanate from their relation. Lacan affirms this second option. 'Prior' to the existence of signifiers lies a pre-signifying field of differential relations that generate and sustain the existence and meaning of each signifier. This 'prior' is not temporal, but logical. The differential matrix is not *transcendent* to the signifiers generated from it, but *transcendental* to them. It is the condition of signifiers that only exists from and through its creation of signifiers.

With this, Lacan takes over Ferdinand de Saussure's description of the differential nature of language:

> *In the language itself, there are only differences.* Even more important than that is the fact that, although in general a difference presupposes positive terms between which the difference holds, in a language there are only differences, *and no positive terms.* Whether we take the signification or the signal, the language includes neither ideas nor sounds existing prior to the linguistic system, but only conceptual and phonetic differences arising out of that system. In a sign, what matters more than any idea or sound associated with it is what other signs surround it. The proof of this lies in the fact that the value of a sign may change without affecting either meaning or sound, simply because some neighbouring sign has undergone a change.[71]

For Saussure, language is based on linguistic differences. There is no fixed identity or point of reference that generates meaning. He, therefore, rejects positivist conceptions of language based on a strict correspondence to the physical world. Rather, as Lionel Bailly explains, 'the relationship *between words* is of greater importance than the relationship between words and objects'.[72] More specifically, Saussure insists that 'it is the relation of the Sign (the word) to the code of signification (the language) that accords it meaning, rather than a simple correspondence with an external object',[73] a position that emphasises the immateriality, or abstract nature, of the linguistic signifier. 'Thus, the signifier (sound imagine/acoustic image) is not the *material* sound but the hearer's impression it makes on our senses.'[74] Further, 'the signified (concept) is not the object (the chair in front of you) but *the idea of the object* (any chair – the property of being a chair – of which an example may or may not be before you at the time of speaking)'.[75] For Saussure, language is an immaterial differential system whereby the individual's existence is always conditioned and constituted by signs, each of which gains meaning through its differential relation to others.

Lacan agrees with Saussure's claim that language is constituted by differential relations, but departs from him in two ways. First, Lacan emphasises the diachronic nature of the signifier–signified relationship to maintain that the signifier always 'slides under' any signified to disrupt any perceived fixed meaning. Second, he holds, *pace* Saussure, that the signifier is *material*. Whereas Saussure insists on the distinction between the immaterial, linguistic world, conditioned by the differential relations of signifiers, and the physical, material one, Lacan implicitly asks for the basis that allows Saussure to continue to affirm the existence of a physical, material world. Because Saussure's assertion about the materiality of the physical world is a linguistic claim, it emanates from the supposed immateriality of the symbolic order. This, for Lacan, reveals that Saussure cannot discuss the nature of the physical world *per se* because any statement he makes can only ever be from the perspective of what he understands to be the immaterial symbolic order.

While this appears to collapse the materiality of the physical world into the immateriality of the signifier, Lacan's innovation is to suggest that, because the subject only ever exists through the symbolic order, the signifier *is* the subject's material world. In doing so, Lacan agrees with Lévi-Strauss that 'symbols are more real than what they symbolise, the signifier precedes and determines the signified'.[76] As the basis of the individual's existence, the so-called 'immateriality' of the signifier is, in actuality, that from which the individual's so-called 'material' existence is created, sustained, and generated. For Lacan, this is only possible because symbols and the symbolic order are material. Any attempt to claim otherwise is the effect of a particular symbolic order. This, of course, gives rise to the problems of what justifies Lacan's thesis that all knowledge passes through the symbolic order and, indeed, whether his account is not itself a symbolic construction. These issues form the basis of Cornelius Castoriadis's critique of Lacan and so will be returned to in the next chapter.

To emphasise that differential relations generate the existence and meaning of signifiers, Lacan provides numerous examples, the most famous of which is his analysis of Edgar Allan Poe's 'The Purloined Letter'. Lacan describes two scenes, but, for the sake of brevity, I will focus only on the first. Lacan notes that the Queen, located in the royal boudoir, receives a letter. At this point, the King enters, thereby causing the Queen some discomfort as she does not want her husband to discover the contents of said letter. It appears that she is aided in this endeavour by the entrance of a third man, Mister D, whose appearance in the room distracts the King and so allows the Queen to hide the letter. Lacan explains, however, that Mister D has noticed the Queen's attention to the letter and having dealt with the business of the day proceeds to 'draw from his pocket a letter similar in appearance to the one before his eyes and, after pretending to read it, places it next to the other'.[77] After a little more conversation to distract attention from the letter he dropped, 'he picks up the embarrassing letter without flinching and decamps, while the Queen, on whom none of his manoeuvre has been lost, remains unable to intervene for fear of attracting the attention of her royal spouse, who is standing at her elbow at that very moment'.[78]

There are many facets to this story, but helpfully, Lacan returns to it in *Seminar II* to explain that the

> letter, which doesn't have the same meaning everywhere, is a truth which is not to be divulged. As soon as it gets into the pocket of the minister, it is no longer what it was before, whatever it was that it had been. It is no longer a love letter, a letter of trust, the announcement of an event, it is evidence, on this occasion a court exhibit. If we imagine that this poor King, seized by some great enthusiasm which would make of him a king of greater grace, one of those kings who isn't easy-going, who isn't capable of letting something go past, and is capable of sending his worthy spouse in front of the judges . . . we realise that the identity of the recipient of the letter is as problematic as the question of knowing to whom it belongs. In any case, from the moment it falls into the hands of the minister, it has in itself become something else.[79]

The meaning of the letter and, by extension, the desire of each participant alters depending on the perspective and relations through which it is examined. Meaning is not, then, *a priori*, but that which is generated through the diachronic relations of the parts (themselves effects of diachronic relations) of the symbolic order.

## Master Signifiers, Meaning, and the Symbolic

That meaning is generated from relations leads to, at least, four consequences: first, it implies that a symbolic order

> differs for different people and . . . is capable of transformation. It is also culturally specific. One can, for example, speak of the symbolic order of a particular country and, while there will be variations between individuals, there will also be a large amount of common constitutive material

that each individual shares. There is a symbolic order of the Western world, where once again there are certain core characteristics that are common.[80]

The symbolic order creates a worldview. Within this order, there are core components linking seemingly disparate positions. After a point, however, one that cannot be determined externally or beforehand, the disparate positions become too dissimilar and give way to a fundamentally different symbolic order.

Second, the differentiating nature of the symbolic order means that it is self-generating. There is no ego or transcendent point generating the differentiation. As Lacan emphasises, we have to understand that 'language is a system of positional coherence and . . . that this system reproduces itself within itself with an extraordinary, frightful, fecundity'.[81]

Third, because each aspect gains significance through its relation to others, which in turn are defined relationally from others still, each signifier is tied to the entirety of the symbolic order. Finally, the relationality inherent in the symbolic order makes 'the empty spaces . . . as signifying as the full ones'.[82] Understanding a symbolic order requires that we focus not just on its signifiers, but on the way in which these signifiers are generated and linked to one another. It requires that we examine the logic underpinning the signifiers employed, how they are joined, how they are defined relationally, any privileging that takes place, the relative importance placed on a signifier at the expense of others, and so on.

A key aspect of Lacan's conception of the symbolic order is the absolute lack of fixed, *ahistoric* points that ground the differential relations from which signifiers and their meaning emanate. If there were fixed points of reference, the movement between relations would eventually stop and a fixed meaning would be determined. For Lacan, the differential relations underpinning signification are interminable. Meaning emanates from the movement along the chain of signifiers, each of which, it will be remembered, does not, on its own, have meaning. Rather, 'it is in the chain of signifiers that meaning *insists*, but . . . none of the chain's elements *consists* in the signification it can provide at that very moment. The notion of an incessant sliding of the signified under the signifier thus comes to the fore.'[83]

This is not to say that each signifier has equal value within the system. Lacan recognises that certain signifiers are more important than others in that they are the keys around which the symbolic order is structured. These master signifiers, otherwise called the Name-of-the-Father – although we have to be clear that they do not entail anything biological or paternal –

are the reference points of each symbolic order. As the orientation from which the incessant sliding of signifiers takes place, the master signifier 'takes on the value of the privileged object that puts a stop to the infinite sliding'.[84] As Bruce Fink explains,

> The Name-of-the-Father is thus our Rock of Gibraltar. Lacan says that it is a signifier, but it is quite clearly different from most, if not all, others. If one word in a language becomes antiquated or goes out of style, other related terms tend to take up the slack; in other words, their meanings broaden to include those of the word that has disappeared. The Name-of-the-Father, on the contrary, is neither fungible nor pronounceable.[85]

Master signifiers remain ineffable; they are a strange combination of presence and absence that differs with each symbolic order. They cannot be defined, nor can their role in generating and bringing coherence to the symbolic order be clearly identified. Aron Dunlap argues that 'this hermeneutical opacity makes them stupid',[86] in so far as their self-grounding denotes that master signifiers lack justification. Their privileged role is 'ultimately based only on themselves',[87] with the consequence that 'they are literally idiotic, self-referential, which is what the Greek root signifies (cf. *idiosyncratic*)'.[88]

While this highlights the groundlessness of master signifiers and may be correct from an etymological perspective, there is something troubling about calling them stupid. If we want to use this language, they could only be considered 'stupid' from the perspective of another symbolic order. This is why, to an outsider, certain social customs of different societies can appear to be so strange and, for want of a better word, stupid. For those within the symbolic order conditioned by those master signifiers, they may be groundless and so incapable of being fully explained, but they are certainly not stupid. There is a sense, a 'feeling', one that is typically used to justify their privileging, that this is simply how things are. As such, master signifiers are not the fixed, ahistoric ground of symbolic orders; master signifiers are the constructed *groundless ground* of symbolic orders: the former because they are arbitrary, subject to change, and unique to each symbolic order; the latter because they are the constructed ground that brings coherence to the differential relations constituting each symbolic order.

The stop function that master signifiers perform is not permanent; if it were, the differential relations generating meaning would be halted, with the consequence that meaning would be permanent. Master signifiers do not provide a static, ahistoric sense or meaning; they only *temporarily* 'stop' the sliding chain of signifiers by *orientating* the signifiers around a particular point of reference which (1) conditions the differential relations that generate signifiers and (2) leads the signifiers generated from the sliding of signifiers to be interpreted in a particular way. Lacan's insistence that the signifier always 'slides under' any signified implies that any signified generated is only temporary; the sliding chain always 'starts' again to undermine it. Master signifiers are the means through which each symbolic order comes to generate and privilege a particular meaning out of the multiple possibilities inherent in the differential relations that compose it. Any meaning created, however, is always imaginary and based on the attempt to impose a fixed identity on the diachronic, differential symbolic relations. While each symbolic order portrays itself as a closed system that reveals the truth, Lacan's notion of the real and its relationship to the symbolic (and imaginary) indicates that there are always lacunae within it.

## Evil as the Real in the Symbolic

By showing that our social worlds are the consequence of symbolic constructions, Lacan undercuts the universal, ahistoric pretensions upon which much Western thought has been based. In their place, he argues that reflective understanding occurs through symbolic orders or worldviews, which are constructed, dynamic, and, ultimately, groundless linguistic registers. Two consequences result: first, by 'grounding' meaning in a constantly shifting symbolic order, he departs dramatically from the foundational metaphysics underpinning Judaeo-Christian thought. This is not, however, to say that Lacan severs all theological connections from his thought; on his telling, this is an impossibility.

Famously, in *Seminar XI*, he explains that 'the true formula of atheism is not *God is dead* – even by basing the origin of the function of the father upon his murder, Freud protects the father – the true formula of atheism is *God is unconscious*'.[89] Even if the subject explicitly and consciously denies a belief in God, his actions convey that he still undoubtedly and unconsciously believes in and depends upon such a being or a more general ordering principle, which, for Lacan, is the same thing. To deny the Judaeo-Christian figure and conception of God is not then to deny order and hence God *tout court*; it is simply to deny the way in which order is constructed within the Judaeo-Christian symbolic framework. One conception of God (= ordering principle) is simply replaced by another.

Kant and Arendt, for example, reject the notion that morality is grounded in the Judaeo-Christian notion of God but replace it with individual will or, in the latter's case, the miracle of individual action. Schelling and Nietzsche replace the God of Judaeo-Christianity with a differential foundational principle; for the former, this is a different conception of God, for the latter, it is the will-to-power. While these thinkers may claim to depart from God, they continue to implicitly depend upon another foundational principle to produce order and so continue to unconsciously depend upon a God. Even Lacan's insistence that meaning is a temporary, imaginary construct based on the differential symbolic relations subtending it depends upon an ordering logic to both designate the three registers and outline their interaction. With this, Lacan reiterates one of the central claims of this book: supposedly secular analyses continue to implicitly and unconsciously depend upon and affirm theological motifs, figures, and concepts. Their explicit rejection of Judaeo-Christian conceptions of God masks a continuing implicit dependence on the content or logical structure of that tradition.

The second issue resulting from Lacan's claim that meaning is a symbolic construction relates to the consequences it has for the meaning of evil. Resolving this issue cuts across three lines: what does Lacan himself say about ethics, what does Lacan say about evil, and, given the paucity of his comments on the topic, is it possible to *think with* Lacan to develop a Lacanian conception of evil?

In relation to the first question, ethics, for Lacan, has a two-fold significance. It is not primarily a normative schema delineating what an individual *should* do, but describes the

> 'elementary structures of kinship' – the elementary structures of property and of the exchange of goods as well. And it is as a result of these structures that man transforms himself into a sign, unit, or object of a regulated exchange in a way that Claude Lévi-Strauss has shown to be fixed in its relative unconsciousness.[90]

At its most general, ethics is closely bound to the symbolic order in that it delineates the structure of social bonds of each society. On this understanding, the symbolic order is an ethical system because it regulates and conditions social relations. Lacan notes, however, that this general sense of ethics is accompanied by a specific sense that outlines the moral law of each symbolic order. The symbolic order establishes what 'good' and 'evil' mean based on the differential relations constituting it. Given the heterogeneity of symbolic relations, numerous conceptions of good/evil are possible and what good/evil mean for each symbolic order can change.

This gives rise to the question of what the symbolic moral law aims to achieve; or, put differently, what the purpose of the moral law is. Lacan addresses this in *Seminar VII*, explaining that 'my thesis is that the moral law, the moral command, the presence of the moral agency in our activity, [in so far] as it is structured by the symbolic, is that through which the real is actualised – the real as such, the weight of the real'.[91] The moral law is a symbolic construction of and from the unknowable real. Indeed, for Lacan, 'the question of ethics is to be articulated from the point of view of the location of man in relation to the real'.[92] For this reason, ethics is the field of the symbolic that engages with and outlines how the real will be incorporated into its structure.

As noted, the Lacanian real is that aspect of existence that escapes the symbolic order. It is, as Louis Sass puts it,

> that which lies beyond not just our *actual* knowledge but beyond the very *possibility* of our knowing, yet which, all the while, we also know to be there: we approach it, if at all, only in states of ecstasy or madness. In this sense the [r]eal is also felt to be that which is most certain and most undeniable – even as we cannot grasp that which we cannot deny.[93]

The subject's relationship to the real is, then, somewhat contradictory. The real is always present, but 'presents' itself through its absence. It can never be articulated, but, at the same time, it is that which can never be escaped.

One commentator warns, however, that, despite superficial similarities, we should not think that the real is 'an unknowable deity (as in Christian apophatic/negative theology), nor a type of Kantian noumenon. It is the part of us which resists language; it either resists symbolisation or is non-symbolisable.'[94] In a sense, the question becomes one of trying to incorporate the real into the symbolic order, while at the same time respecting the absence of the real therein. It is for this reason that Alenka Zupančič calls Lacan's ethics an 'ethics of the real'.[95] This does not mean that Lacan focuses on the real, an impossible task given that the real escapes symbolisation, but means that he offers 'an attempt to rethink ethics by recognising and acknowledging the dimension of the Real (in the Lacanian sense of the term) as it is already operative in ethics'.[96]

In effect, Lacan is criticising closed, normative, universalist accounts of ethics, by pointing out that

> ethics is by nature excessive, that excess is a component of ethics which cannot simply be eliminated without ethics itself losing all meaning. In relation to the 'smooth course of events', life as governed by the 'reality

principle', ethics always appears as something excessive, as a disturbing 'interruption'.[97]

Lacanian ethics is not normative or prescriptive, but descriptive in that it aims to understand how various symbolic orders incorporate the real 'within' its functioning. It is here that the question of 'evil' arises.

Lacan's comments on evil are, however, limited. Besides his claims in *Seminar III* that it is not possible to distinguish between greater and lesser evil because evil '*always* entails a greater evil',[98] and the insistence in *Seminar VII*[99] that evil is both material and non-material, both of which are not developed or fully explained, the only other time that he reflects upon a topic directly linked to evil is the discussion of privation in *Seminar XVII*, where he rejects the notion that privation accurately describes a lack and so distinguishes his position from the Augustinian tradition. Specifically, Lacan explains that

> it is clear that privation can only be situated with respect to the symbolic, for as far as anything real is concerned, nothing can be lacking – what is real is real, and it has to be from elsewhere that this introduction, which is nevertheless essential, be made, for without it we would not be in the real ourselves, namely that something in it is lacking – and this is what initially characterises the subject.[100]

Privation is not an accurate description of an object in-itself, but is a symbolic construction that conceptualises the object in terms of a lack of something that it supposedly should possess. Lacan inquires into what brings us to conceive of the object in the way that subsequently allows for the introduction of the concept 'privation'. After all, as he notes in *Seminar X*, 'it is clear that a woman hasn't got a penis, but, if you don't symbolise the penis as the essential element that one either has or has not, she shall know nothing of this privation'.[101] The question that Lacan's theory pushes us to address is why we think of things in the manner we do. Rather than simply accepting a definition of an object, he asks that we question the categories and logic that generated that conception of the object.

Augustine and the Augustinian tradition do not do this, instead simply adopting a position based on Christian dogma to subsequently account for the existence of evil within that order. Basing its conclusions on fixed foundations and aiming to produce closed, hermetically sealed schemas has been, for Lacan, the dominant trend in Western thinking. As a consequence, the lack of the real has simply been denied. The Kantian tradition comes close to engaging with the real by accepting that there are limits to human knowledge, but, for Lacan, it continues to place too much emphasis on the ego. Nietzsche's historical account recognises that the meaning of moral concepts changes, but does not go far enough in engaging with how meaning arises in the first place. Nietzsche's historical perspective would presumably be too indeterminate, a fate that Arendt's socialisation account also suffers from, with the added problem that she continues to think from egoistic premises. It might be objected that Schelling is an exception to this in that, like Lacan, he appeals to a pre-personal, unconscious, differentiating field to explain the ontogenesis of individuality. While this affirms Matt Ffytche's[102] claim that Schelling plays a crucial role in the development of psychoanalysis, it not only downplays the substantial differences that exist between Lacan's and Schelling's linguistically and metaphysically orientated explanations, but also fails to appreciate that Lacan's linguistic analysis undercuts Schelling's by accounting for the linguistic structures that bring Schelling to think of the issue in the way he does.

## Concluding Remarks

Lacan's approach does not, however, simply entail a critique of past approaches. It also points to a positive conception of ethics generally and, by extension, of evil, although his comments on both are not particularly developed. This is mirrored in the Lacanian literature, which has paid scant attention to the notion of 'evil' within his thought. One exception is Clayton Crockett, who focuses on the issue through the mediation of Lacan's concept of *Das Ding* in *Seminar VII*. Crockett confirms that, for Lacan, ethics is located at the symbolic–real boundary, with *Das Ding* being another name for the real.[103] He makes four claims from this: (1) ethics deals with the relationship between the symbolic and the real;[104] (2) *Das Ding*, which escapes symbolic representation, always appears to symbolic thought as something 'strange';[105] (3) the un-representability of *Das Ding* does not make 'it' synonymous with God, who, within the Judaeo-Christian-Islamic tradition, also tends to be thought of as un-representable;[106] and (4) 'good' and 'evil' belong to the symbolic realm, whereas *Das Ding* 'is beyond good and evil'.[107] The conclusion drawn is that *Das Ding* is the source of ethics without being susceptible of representation, while the meanings of 'good' and 'evil' are by-products of attempts to symbolically represent the un-representable *Das Ding*. In general outline, there is much to agree with in this; Lacanian ethics is concerned with the real–symbolic relationship and, specifically, attempts to represent the former. However, Crockett's account does not sufficiently explain the relationship between *Das Ding* and the good/evil dichotomy; specifically, how the latter arises from the former.

To resolve this issue, we have to move beyond *Seminar VII* to recognise the significant alterations that take place in Lacan's thought, specifically as they relate to the relationship between the symbolic and the real. Once we do, we find that, shortly after *Seminar VII*, the notion of *Das Ding* is dropped from Lacan's vocabulary. One reason for this is that Lacan turns from the symbolic to the real, which leads him to reformulate the symbolic–real relationship.

Lacan always emphasised the entwined relationship between the real and the symbolic, but some of his earlier formulations regarding the real made it appear as if it was defined by something. In *Seminar VII*, this is manifested in the claim that 'the emptiness at the centre of the real . . . is called the Thing [*Das Ding*]'.[108] The danger of this formulation is that, *on a literal reading*, it leads to the conclusion that at the heart of the real lies a thing. This, however, would mean that the real was defined by an essential presence. Correcting this potential misunderstanding brought Lacan to explain that the 'real' is not defined by a centre, even one of absence, but is the excess that always exists '*within*' the 'symbolic'.

This brings forth the question of the liminal point that joins, but separates, the real and symbolic. Following Lacan's suggestion that ethics deals with this liminal relation, we can say that the good/evil symbolic dichotomy arises from attempts to symbolise the un-representable real. More specifically, 'evil' is a concept that exists 'within' the symbolic order and is, therefore, subject to, conditioned by, and an effect of the diachronic, pre-personal, unconscious, differential linguistic structures comprising the symbolic order. But it is also a 'concept' that points to 'something' – the real – 'beyond' the ordered structures of the symbolic. It is the symbolic construction that attempts to delineate and so incorporate the excess of the real within the constraints of the symbolic.

This is different from other supposedly ethical concepts, such as 'freedom', 'justice', and 'the good', which aim to construct a particular notion of these to be implemented socially. As ethical concepts, they emanate from the real–symbolic relation, but are also linked to the imaginary by advocating the adoption of a particular identity. 'Evil' does not signal the adoption of an (imaginary) identity – it is, as we have seen, notoriously difficult to identify – and so stays at the liminality of the real–symbolic relation. Because of the diachronic nature of the real–symbolic relationship, the symbolic must continuously deal with the absence within it. This 'dealing-with' must pass through language, which has to develop a name for that which resists its order. My suggestion is that, from a Lacanian perspective, 'evil' is the signifier that the Western tradition has developed to fulfil this role. As a signifier, 'evil' is part of the symbolic, but, as we have seen from the multiple conceptions of it in previous chapters, there is something about it that escapes comprehension. Even if the symbolic order somehow removed the signifier 'evil' from its lexicon, this symbolic placeholder delineating the real would be taken up by another signifier. Returning to Lacan's claim that the symbolic is machinic, we find that, on his telling, 'evil' is the constructed conceptual release valve connecting the symbolic to the real, the knowable to the unknowable, constraint to excess.

## Notes

1. For an overview of these strands and the 'linguistic turn' more generally, see Michael Losonsky, *Linguistic Turns in Modern Philosophy* (Cambridge: Cambridge University Press, 2006).
2. François Dosse, *History of Structuralism, vol. 1: The Rising Sign, 1945–1966*, trans. Deborah Glassman (Minneapolis: University of Minnesota Press, 1997), p. xx.
3. On the relationship between Lacan and Lévi-Strauss, see Marcos Zafiropoulos, *Lacan and Lévi-Strauss or the Return to Freud (1951–1957)*, trans. John Holland (London: Karnac, 2010).
4. Ferdinand de Saussure, *Course in General Linguistics*, ed. Charles Bally, Albert Sechehaye, and Albert Riedlinger, trans. Roy Harris (Chicago: Open Court, 1986).
5. Jacques Lacan, *Seminar I: Freud's Papers on Technique*, ed. Jacques-Alain Miller, trans. John Forrester (New York: W. W. Norton, 1991), p. 158.
6. Bruce Fink, *A Clinical Introduction to Lacanian Psychoanalysis: Theory and Technique* (Cambridge, MA: Harvard University Press, 1997), p. 220.
7. Louis Sass, 'Lacan: The Mind of the Modernist', *Continental Philosophy Review*, 48, 2015, pp. 409–43 (p. 418).
8. Jacques Lacan, *Seminar III: The Psychoses*, ed. Jacques-Alain Miller, trans. Russell Grigg (New York: W. W. Norton, 1997), p. 322.
9. Jacques Lacan, *Seminar VII: The Ethics of Psychoanalysis*, ed. Jacques-Alain Miller, trans. Dennis Porter (New York: W. W. Norton, 1997), p. 124.
10. In *Seminar VIII*, Lacan recognises the innovation of this schema, explaining that 'classical psychoanalytical theory did not distinguish between the symbolic, the imaginary, and the real'. See Jacques Lacan, *Seminar VIII: Transference*, ed. Jacques-Alain, trans. Bruce Fink, (Cambridge: Polity, 2015), pp. 349–50. Tracy McNulty explains that Lacan felt that he had to develop a new conceptual apparatus because he found that 'psychoanalysis after Freud ha[d] appealed increasingly to behavioural and social norms to repress the

unconscious, and therefore to buttress – rather than dismantle – the defences the subject erects against the real that are at stake in the fantasy and her own unconscious desire' (*Wrestling with the Angel: Experiments in Symbolic Life* [New York: Columbia University Press, 2014], pp. 51–2).
11. Jacques Lacan, 'The Mirror Stage as Formative of the *I* Function as Revealed in Psychoanalytic Experience', in *Écrits*, trans. Bruce Fink (New York: W. W. Norton, 2006), pp. 75–81.
12. Ibid. p. 76.
13. Ibid. p. 78.
14. Ibid. p. 78.
15. Jacques Lacan, *Seminar II: The Ego in Freud's Theory and in the Technique of Psychoanalysis*, ed. Jacques-Alain Miller, trans. Sylvana Tomaselli (New York: W. W. Norton, 1991), p. 38.
16. Ibid. p. 47.
17. Lacan, *Seminar I*, p. 66.
18. Lorenzo Chiesa, *Subjectivity and Otherness: A Philosophical Reading of Lacan* (Cambridge, MA: MIT Press, 2007), p. 126.
19. Ibid. p. 126.
20. Ibid. p. 127.
21. Lacan, *Seminar I*, p. 113.
22. Jacques Lacan, *Seminar XX: On Feminine Sexuality, The Limits of Love and Knowledge*, ed. Jacques-Alain Miller, trans. Bruce Fink (New York: W. W. Norton, 1999), pp. 122–3. A Borromean knot consists of three rings that are linked in such a way that if any one of them is severed, all three become separated.
23. Lacan, *Seminar I*, p. 223.
24. Ibid. p. 219.
25. Lacan, *Seminar II*, p. 52.
26. Lacan, *Seminar I*, p. 113.
27. Ibid. p. 113.
28. Ibid. p. 113.
29. Jacques Lacan, 'The Function and Field of Speech and Language in Psychoanalysis', p. 264, in *Écrits*, trans. Bruce Fink (New York: W. W. Norton, 2006), pp. 197–268.
30. Ibid. p. 201.
31. Ibid. p. 221.
32. Jacques Lacan, *Seminar XI: The Four Fundamental Concepts of Psychoanalysis*, ed. Jacques-Alain Miller, trans. Alan Sheridan (New York: W. W. Norton, 1981), p. 203.
33. Lacan, *Seminar II*, p. 326.
34. Ibid. p. 29.
35. Bruce Fink, *The Lacanian Subject: Between Language and Jouissance* (Princeton: Princeton University Press, 1995), p. 6.

36. Lacan, *Seminar III*, p. 179.
37. Ibid. p. 179.
38. Lacan, 'The Function and Field of Speech and Language in Psychoanalysis', p. 231.
39. Jacques Lacan, *Television*, ed. Joan Copjec, trans. Denis Hollier, Rosalind Krauss, and Annette Michelson (New York: W. W. Norton, 1990), p. 112.
40. Louis Sass, 'Lacan, Foucault, and the "Crisis of the Subject": Revisionist Reflections on Phenomenology and Post-Structuralism', *Philosophy, Psychiatry, Psychology*, 21:4, 2014, pp. 325–41 (p. 333).
41. Lacan, *Seminar II*, p. 192.
42. Lacan, *Seminar I*, p. 157.
43. Fink, *The Lacanian Subject*, p. 9.
44. Lacan, *Seminar XI*, p. 207.
45. Lacan, *Seminar XX*, p. 50.
46. Jacques Lacan, 'The Subversion of the Subject and the Dialectic of Desire in the Freudian Unconscious', p. 685, in *Écrits*, trans. Bruce Fink (New York: W. W. Norton, 2006), pp. 672–702.
47. Lacan, *Seminar I*, p. 193.
48. Jacques Lacan, 'Introduction to Jean Hyppolite's Commentary on Freud's "Verneinung"', p. 310, in *Écrits*, trans. Bruce Fink (New York: W. W. Norton, 2006), pp. 308–17.
49. Lacan, *Seminar II*, p. 122.
50. Ibid. p. 122.
51. Lacan, *Seminar III*, p. 119 (emphasis added).
52. Lacan, *Seminar XX*, p. 15
53. Ibid. p. 48.
54. Chiesa, *Subjectivity and Otherness*, p. 52.
55. In a translator's note, Bruce Fink explains that *lalangue* is a neologism combining the feminine article *la* with the noun *langue*, which means language and specifically spoken language. From this, Fink points out that *lalangue* describes 'the acoustic level of language . . . It is the level at which an infant (or songwriter) may endlessly repeat one syllable of a word (for example, "la la la"), the level at which language may "stutter" – hence the translation provided here, borrowed from Russell Grigg, "llanguage"' (Lacan, *Seminar XX*, p. 44, n. 15). However, given that not all translations or commentators employ this term, I will, for the sake of simplicity and consistency, use the original French *lalangue*.
56. Lacan, *Seminar XX*, p. 142.
57. Ibid. p. 142.
58. Lacan, *Television*, p. 9.
59. Lacan, *Seminar XX*, p. 139.
60. Samo Tomšič, *The Capitalist Unconscious: Marx and Lacan* (London: Verso, 2015), p. 37.

61. Colette Soler, *Lacanian Affects: The Function of Affect in Lacan's Work* (Abingdon: Routledge, 2016), p. 43.
62. Lacan, *Seminar I*, p. 108.
63. Ibid. p. 108.
64. Lacan, *Seminar II*, pp. 169–70.
65. Lacan, *Seminar XX*, p. 30.
66. Lacan, *Seminar III*, p. 226.
67. Jacques Lacan, *Seminar XVII: The Other Side of Psychoanalysis*, trans. Russell Grigg (New York: W. W. Norton, 2007), p. 190.
68. Joan Copjec, *Read my Desire: Lacan against the Historicists* (London: Verso, 2015), p. 9.
69. Lacan, 'The Function and Field of Speech and Language in Psychoanalysis', p. 246.
70. Lacan, *Seminar XI*, p. 89.
71. Saussure, *Course in General Linguistics*, p. 118.
72. Lionel Bailly, *Lacan* (London: OneWorld, 2009), p. 23.
73. Ibid. p. 23.
74. Ibid. p. 43.
75. Ibid. p. 43.
76. Claude Lévi-Strauss, *Introduction to the Work of Marcel Mauss*, trans. Felicity Baker (London: Routledge & Kegan Paul, 1987), p. 37.
77. Jacques Lacan, 'Seminar on "The Purloined Letter', p. 8, in *Écrits*, trans. Bruce Fink (New York: W. W. Norton, 2006), pp. 6–48.
78. Ibid. p. 8.
79. Lacan, *Seminar II*, pp. 198–9.
80. Paul Murphy, 'Jacques, Jacques and Jacks: The Shifting Symbolic in Derrida and Lacan', *Textual Practice*, 19:4, 2005, pp. 509–27 (p. 519).
81. Lacan, *Seminar III*, pp. 226–7.
82. Jacques Lacan, 'Response to Jean Hyppolite's Commentary on Freud's "Verneinung"', p. 327, in *Écrits*, trans. Bruce Fink (New York: W. W. Norton, 2006), pp. 318–33.
83. Ibid. p. 419.
84. Lacan, *Seminar VIII*, p. 170.
85. Fink, *The Lacanian Subject*, p. 74.
86. Aron Dunlap, *Lacan and Religion* (Durham: Acumen, 2014), p. 82.
87. Ibid. p. 82.
88. Ibid. p. 82.
89. Lacan, *Seminar XI*, p. 59.
90. Lacan, *Seminar VII*, p. 7.
91. Ibid. p. 20.
92. Ibid. p. 11.
93. Sass, 'Lacan: The Mind of the Modernist', p. 431.
94. Nicos Mouzelis, 'Lacan and Meditation: From the Symbolic to the

Postsymbolic?', *Psychoanalysis, Culture, and Society*, 19:2, 2014, pp. 127–36 (p. 128).
95. Alenka Zupančič, *Ethics of the Real: Kant and Lacan* (London: Verso, 2011), p. 4.
96. Ibid. p. 4.
97. Ibid. p. 5.
98. Lacan, *Seminar III*, p. 322.
99. Lacan, *Seminar VII*, p. 124.
100. Lacan, *Seminar XVII*, pp. 124–5.
101. Jacques Lacan, *Seminar X: Anxiety*, ed. Jacques-Alain Miller, trans. A. R. Price (Cambridge: Polity, 2014), pp. 135–6.
102. Matt Ffytche, *The Foundation of the Unconscious: Schelling, Freud, and the Birth of the Modern Psyche* (Cambridge: Cambridge University Press, 2012), pp. 2–3.
103. Clayton Crockett, *Interstices of the Sublime: Theology and Psychoanalytic Theory* (New York: Fordham University Press, 2007), p. 57. For an interesting discussion of this concept, see Simon Critchley, '*Das Ding*: Lacan and Levinas', in *Ethics–Politics–Subjectivity: Essays on Derrida, Levinas, and Contemporary French Thought* (London: Verso, 1999), pp. 198–216.
104. Ibid. p. 57.
105. Ibid. p. 57.
106. Ibid. pp. 57–8.
107. Ibid. p. 143.
108. Lacan, *Seminar VII*, p. 121.

# 11

# Castoriadis: Evil and the Social Imaginary

The originality of Lacan's thinking was almost immediately recognised but its radicality was subject to much criticism. His clinical practice was frequently attacked and ultimately led to his expulsion from two psychoanalytical associations.[1] It is the theoretical critique that interests us, though. Cornelius Castoriadis provided one of the most polemic of these.

Born in Constantinople in 1922, Castoriadis was brought up in Greece before, as a consequence of his Marxist political leanings, moving to Paris to escape Fascist persecution. There he initially worked as an economist and agitated as a Marxist, before breaking with Marxism and training and working as a psychoanalyst. Castoriadis recognised that Lacan had renewed psychoanalytic theory by not only breaking 'up the stagnation of [its] pool',[2] but also disturbing its 'institutionalised drowsiness and ... pseudo-"specialist" cretinism'[3] through the incorporation of insights from other disciplines. He recognised too that Lacan had 'revitalised the reading of the Freudian texts ... restored to life their enigmatic movement, and ... introduced some substantial extensions into psychoanalytic research'.[4] He did, however, charge that Lacan had been 'maleficent'[5] in fostering a personality cult that stifled independent thought[6] and produced 'sheeplike followers'[7] who simply repeated ideas that, upon closer inspection, fell into empty abstractions.

Castoriadis's major problem with Lacan's thinking was that, on his telling, it is unable to account for the radically new. This charge is based on two premises: first, Lacan's symbolic account entails a closed system that simply produces a finite number of meanings from the limited permutations possible within its parameters.[8] Second, this closed system of symbolic production is not – as Castoriadis reads Lacan as holding – foundational and auto-generating, but depends upon a prior moment of creation. In combination, Castoriadis concludes that Lacan's thinking leaves no room for *creation*, which, on Castoriadis's definition, is open-ended, unconstrained within prior boundaries, and breaks with that which precedes it.

In response, Lacan would no doubt defend himself by pointing out that this reduces his thought to a conception of the symbolic relation that ignores its relationship to the lack of the real. That the real always exists within the symbolic ensures that the production of the symbolic order is always random, open-ended, and radically creative. Nevertheless, Castoriadis concludes that the closed production inherent in Lacan's notion of the symbolic is only possible because it is grounded in a prior moment of creativity that Castoriadis calls 'the radical imaginary'.[9]

Both Castoriadis and Lacan agree then that thought cannot simply proceed on the assumption that the meaning of a concept (such as evil) is clear or uncontested; understanding the meaning of a concept requires an engagement with the (pre-personal) processes that generate it. Castoriadis departs from Lacan in maintaining that this occurs not through anonymous, differential, linguistic, symbolic relations, but through the anonymous, collective, social-historical *imaginary* of each society. Beyond this, however, Castoriadis has little to say on the actual meaning of concepts, including evil. This is not due to a failing on his part, but results from the nature of his ontogenetic account of meaning: given that moral meaning is an effect of an anonymous social imaginary, it will be different for each society, with the consequence that we cannot treat it as if it had universal or ahistorical significance. His account does, however, offer an innovative way of thinking about the ontogenesis of moral concepts generally and of 'evil' specifically because it holds that they are socio-political, rather than merely individual, constructions that are embedded within the social imaginary of each society. To explain how Castoriadis arrives at this conclusion requires a brief description of his ontology.[10]

## The Natural and the Historical

In the 1992 lecture 'False and True Chaos', Castoriadis states that 'chaos is the ultimate depth of being; more, it is the bottomless depth of being; it is the abyss behind everything that exits'.[11] This does not entail a division between being and its chaotic ground: 'it is precisely through the creation of forms, qua determination, that chaos is always present also as cosmos, that is, as an organised world in the broadest sense of the term, as order'.[12] It is difficult to miss the Schellingian undertones here. Like his predecessor, Castoriadis holds that being is a chaotic abyss which, through an autopoietic process of differentiation, expresses itself in entities. This continuous, creative process brings into existence 'radically new'[13] forms of being through the destruction and reconfiguration of that which already exists.

On Castoriadis's telling, entities are manifestations of the chaos of being. They are split between natural beings and those composing what he calls the social-historical domain.[14] The difference between the natural and the social-historical is that 'autonomy emerges in the latter'.[15] Whereas creativity is an ontological characteristic of natural being, autonomy refers to the way of being adopted by individuals and/or society.[16] However, 'to be autonomous, for an individual or a collectivity, does not signify doing "what one likes" or whatever pleases one at the moment, but rather *giving oneself one's own laws*'.[17] This is not a Kantian notion of autonomy because it 'does not consist in acting according to a law discovered in an immutable Reason and given once and for all. It is the unlimited self-questioning about the law and its foundations as well as the capacity, in light of this interrogation, *to make, to do*, and *to institute* (therefore also, *to say*).'[18]

For Castoriadis, creation is what being is. Autonomy is a form of creativity based on a continuous and explicit questioning of the laws adopted by each individual and society, the aim of which is to stimulate constant renewal:

> The *autonomy* of society presupposes, obviously, explicit recognition that the institution of society is self-institution. Autonomy signifies literally and profoundly: positing one's own law for oneself. Here self-institution is explicit and is recognised: recognition by society of itself as source and origin, acceptance of the absence of any extrasocial Norm or Law that would impose itself on society.[19]

The law is not given, but is created through the autonomous participation of individuals, which, in turn, largely rests on the norms adopted by the anonymous social collective that each exists within.[20]

That the natural and social-historical domains are distinguished does not mean that they are entirely distinct. The social-historical continues to lean on the natural world,[21] which 'merely' provides the 'material' from which the social-historical world exerts its autonomy. Indeed, the meaning of the natural substratum is 'recreated, isolated, chosen, filtered, brought into relation, and, above all, *endowed with meaning* by the institution and the imaginary significations of the given society'.[22]

These imaginary significations are not abstract or timeless, but are intimately linked to history, which is understood as the temporal horizon from and within which the 'self-alteration of society'[23] occurs. History does not determine the social, but is that which joins the various alterations of each society together. This does not mean that history is transcendent to the social or that there is a transcendent position from which to analyse history. 'History is essentially *poiesis*, not imitative poetry, but creation and ontological genesis in and through individuals' doing and representing/saying.'[24] It is 'the world of human *doing*'[25] – which is inherently social – that gives rise to meaning. None of the meanings established is 'ever complete and closed in on itself; each always refers to something else, and no thing, no particular historical fact can deliver a meaning that in and of itself would be inscribed on it'.[26] Societies attribute different meanings to events based on their distinct social-historical configurations and so have, for example, alternative conceptions of time based on 'tempo, significant articulations, anchorages, prospects, and promises'.[27]

With this, Castoriadis rejects the Lacanian assertion that the meaning of history is simply a linguistic construct. While accepting that 'history exists only in and through "language" (all sorts of language)',[28] he explains that 'history gives itself this language, constitutes it and transforms it'.[29] While *explaining* history, language does not *create* history. History exists prior to the advent of language, even if it must wait for language to account for it. This brings forth the conclusion that 'language and understanding are social-historical creations'.[30]

Having examined the history–language relationship, Castoriadis turns to the role that the social plays in the formation of both. Noting that there is no such thing as a singular, universal linguistic order, he explains that language is tied to particular societies. While recognising that language is a '*transhistorical*'[31] condition for all societies, Castoriadis maintains that each society expresses itself through a particular language which '*establishes, creates its own world*, within which, of course, it includes "itself"'.[32] This creates not only representations and values, but also the framework through which events are perceived, including what counts as an event. In turn, this establishes 'a *mode* of representing, a categorisation of the world, an aesthetics and a logic, as well as a *mode* of valuation'.[33]

Castoriadis warns, however, that a society is not a family,[34] an amalgamation of individuals,[35] 'mere intersubjectivity',[36] 'a "social contract" or a "gathering up" of hypothetically pre-existing individuals'.[37] It is

> the always already instituted anonymous collective in and through which 'subjects' can appear, it goes indefinitely beyond them (they are always replaceable and being replaced), and it contains in itself a creative potential that is irreducible to 'cooperation' among subjects or to the effects of 'intersubjectivity'.[38]

As Castoriadis puts it, 'the social is what is everyone and what is no one, what is never absent and almost never present as such, a non-being that is more real than any being, that in which we are wholly immersed yet which we can never apprehend "in person"'.[39] The basic point is that the social is real, diffuse, and ineffable.[40] This ineffability is, however, manifested through the entities that comprise society: institutions.

While there is a tendency to reduce the meaning of institutions to objective structures, whether this be nations, companies, universities, governments, or the like, Castoriadis has a particularly wide definition of the concept. It refers not only to those objective structures mentioned, but also to the 'norms, values, language, tools, procedures and methods of dealing with things and doing things, and, of course, the individual itself both in general and in the particular type and form (and their differentiation: e.g., man/woman) given to it by the society considered'.[41] Institutions shape, structure, and define each society through a diachronic process whereby the changing composition of institutions is reflected through the particular society they express. The social does not encompass its institutions as an overarching unity. The social 'fills in the institution, what is formed by it, what continually overdetermines its functioning, and what in the final analysis founds it: creates it, maintains it in existence, alters it, destroys it'.[42] There is an immanent relationship between the social and its institutions, although the former always exceeds the latter.

Crucially, the unity of society is not derived from the collection of objective structures and institutions that express it. It is 'the unity and internal cohesion of the immensely complex web of meanings that permeate, orient, and direct the whole life of the society considered, as well as the concrete individuals that bodily constitute society'.[43] To understand what unifies the various meanings, how it occurs, where it emanates from, and what it entails, we need to turn to Castoriadis's notion of the imaginary.

## The Radical Imaginary and the Social

The imaginary is *the* fundamental concept of Castoriadis's thinking and, in particular, his attempt to describe the creative processes inherent in any social-historical domain. It comprises the operations that bring forth radically new configurations, entities, and meanings. Castoriadis suggests that it is 'quite natural'[44] that this 'faculty of radical innovation'[45] be called the imaginary and, in its human form, 'imagination' because both are typically associated with the creation of the radically new.

His notion of the imaginary is not, however, the same as Lacan's. In fact, he is highly critical of Lacan's conception, concluding that such are its 'gross inadequacies'[46] that it is simply 'ridiculous'.[47] The basic point behind the polemical language is Castoriadis's insistence that Lacan reduces the imaginary to 'the specular – that is, what can be seen in the mirror'.[48] In contrast to Lacan's *representational* understanding of the imaginary, Castoriadis posits a *creative* one. This 'power'[49] is not a transcendent or transcendental one, but immanent in its expression. It is the process through which the anonymous collective creates its social imaginary.

Castoriadis explains that he chose the term 'social imaginary' because imaginary significations 'are neither rational (they cannot be "constructed logically") nor real (they cannot be derived from things); they do not correspond to "rational ideas" any more than to natural objects'.[50] Further, they are the result not of individual agents, but of society at large. The collective is not a substance or object, but is in flux. This seems like a simple point, but it is obscured by everyday talk of *this*, *that*, or *a* society, which tends to posit society as, in some way, completed. For Castoriadis, societies are always open-ended processes of creation and re-creation. 'We must therefore recognise that there is, in human collectivities, a power of creation, a *vis formandi*, which I call the instituting social imaginary',[51] that is concerned with 'the creation of significations and the creation of the images and figures that support these significations'.[52]

Importantly, there is no external ground to the process through which social imaginaries are created:

> The questions of origin, foundation, cause, and end are posed in and through society, but society, like signification, 'has' no origin, foundation, cause, or end other than itself. It is its own origin – that is what self-creation means; it does not have its genuine, essential origin in *something* that would be external to it, and it has no end other than its own existence as society positing *these* ends – which is merely a formal and ultimately an abusive use of the term *end*.[53]

As a process of self-creation, the social imaginary is, somewhat paradoxically, a *groundless ground*. It is not founded on anything other than its own continuous flux, but grounds all else and so supports and perpetuates the particular imaginary significations of the society. As Castoriadis explains,

> each society creates its own forms. These forms in turn bring into place a world in which this society inscribes itself and gives itself a place. It is by means of them that society constitutes a system of norms, institutions in

the broadest sense of the term, values, orientations, and goals (*finalités*) of collective life as well as of individual life. At their core are to be found, each time, social imaginary significations, which also are created by each society and which are embodied in its institutions.[54]

By defining what counts as knowledge, delineating the concepts to be used and the meaning attributed to each, the questions that can be legitimately asked and the ways in which they can be answered, as well as outlining the form of social institutions and the permitted relationships between them and the nature of individuality, the social imaginary constitutes the creative processes through which society makes and defines itself.

The social imaginary is, then, the process through which society is *instituted*. It 'provides continuity within society, the reproduction and repetition of the same forms, which henceforth regulate people's lives and persist as long as no gradual historical change or massive new creative occurs, modifying them or radically replacing them by others'.[55] There are two fundamental aspects to this institutionalisation: *teukhein* and *legein*. The former describes 'the ensemblist-ensemblising dimension of social doing'.[56] It denotes the functional processes through which institutions and societies fulfil tasks, including what those tasks will be in the first place. *Legein* delineates 'the (implicit) institution of understanding *and* of something else – of the signitive relation which is, in truth, unanalysable and without which nothing is possible'.[57] As that which produces signification, *legein* cannot be signified, but delineates the specific, if implicit, rules for bringing together signifiers to produce meaning. Each society does this differently, thereby giving rise to different significations and significatory regimes. Pointing out that the signification of *legein* is an effect of the social imaginary supports the conclusion that the symbolic order is not foundational. For Castoriadis, Lacan's closed symbolic binary schema is instantiated by the anonymous, open, creative spontaneity of the radical imaginary.

Emphasising that the instantiation of a symbolic order is grounded in a creative, imaginary act leads to the conclusion that the imaginary takes precedence over the symbolic. The imaginary is fundamentally radical because it is not encumbered by precedents, actuality, logic, or significations; it is that which generates all of these. It is also radical in the sense in which Kant used the term; that is, Castoriadis refers to the Latin etymology of the term 'radical' (*radix* = root or base) to suggest that the imaginary is that which generates and supports individual and social-historical existence.[58] We do not, however, tend to recognise this, thinking that social and individual existence is grounded in a fixed foundation, whether this is God, a founding myth, or some other ahistorical premise.[59]

Importantly, the *radical imaginary* manifests itself through two forms: the 'social imaginary'[60] of each society and the 'radical imagination'[61] of each human psyche. I will examine the first here, before turning to the second in the next section. The social imaginary is the instituting power that produces the significations that delineate each particular society. This occurs through an instituting-instituted process whereby each anonymous collective creates a social world 'constituted and articulated as a function of . . . a system of significations, and these significations *exist*, once they have been constituted, in the mode of what we called the *actual imaginary* (or the *imagined*)'.[62]

The instantiation of an actual social imaginary is the consequence of the responses given to a variety of questions fundamental to the establishment of a society, including 'who are we as a collectivity? What are we for one another? Where and in what are we? What do we want; what do we desire; what are we lacking?'[63] These questions and the answers provided are never made explicit. Rather,

> society constitutes itself by producing a *de facto* answer to these questions in its life, in its activity. It is in the *doing* of each collectivity that the answer to these questions appears as an embodied meaning: this social doing allows itself to be understood only as a reply to the questions that it implicitly poses itself.[64]

Through the practical responses given to these questions, society defines its identity, 'its articulation, the world, its relations to the world and to the objects it contains, its needs and its desires'.[65] With this, the *instituting* radical social imaginary turns into the *instituted* social imaginary.

There is not, however, a simple linear movement from the instituting of a society to one instituted. Because 'society is intrinsically history',[66] which means self-alteration, 'instituted society is not opposed to instituting society as a lifeless product to an activity which brought it into being'.[67] Instituted society simply 'represents the relative and transitory fixity/stability of the instituted forms-figures in and through which the radical imaginary can alone exist and make itself exist as social-historical'.[68] As a consequence, 'the instituted society is always subject to the subterranean pressure of instituting society. Beneath the established social imaginary, the flow of the radical imaginary continues steadily.'[69] This flow not only supports existing structures, processes, norms, and values, but, due to its creative power, can always express itself in new ways.

Castoriadis likens the relationship between the radical imaginary and its expression in social structures to 'magma'.[70] While 'there are flows that are denser, nodal points, clearer or darker areas, bits of rock caught in the whole ... the magma never ceases to move, to swell and to subside, to liquefy what was solid and to solidify what was almost inexistent'.[71] Similarly, the instituting-instituted structure of society is always conditioned by movements that are not smooth or undifferentiated, but heterogeneous and uneven. Like an eruption of magma, the instituting radical imaginary subtending each social-historical formation can always explode through existing institutions to instantiate a radically new world. The continuous, uneven movement of magma mirrors the fundamental diachronic nature of society: it is always 'to-be'[72] and, as a consequence, is not and cannot ever be anything in the sense of a fixed thing or substance.

The creation of social imaginary significations gives rise to a whole network of values, frameworks, conceptualisations, and norms that reveal 'the *orientation* of a society'.[73] Castoriadis explains that 'the imaginary isn't the production of images; it is the *creation of a human world*, and not only at the level of the individual psyche, but in the social-historical field'.[74] It is not the case that 'each society contains a system for interpreting the world ... each society *is* a system for interpreting the world'.[75] As effects of the social imaginary, the meaning constructed and attributed to values reflects and so reveals the parameters of the society.[76] Analysing moral concepts, such as evil, does not, then, inform us about the nature of the concept *per se*. It reveals the ways in which the 'collective-anonymous imaginary'[77] 'of' each society understands itself and its world.

Importantly, Castoriadis rejects the notion that creation is an effect of an ego or can be 'thought solely in relation to the *subject*, within a psychological or ego-logical horizon'.[78] The ego does not control or determine the creation of social-historical imaginary significations since it is an effect of them. For this reason, social imaginary significations cannot 'be thought on the basis of an alleged relation to a "subject" which would "carry" them or "intend" them'.[79] This holds whether the 'subject' in question is an individual or something designated as '"group consciousness" [or] "collective unconscious"'.[80] It also cannot be thought in terms of a transcendental faculty.[81] Each social-historical imaginary is the creation of the 'anonymous collective'[82] of each society. It is a spontaneous self-creation that cannot be located within or from a specific point, but 'is a constitutive faculty of human collectivities, and more generally of the social-historical sphere'.[83] Individuals are effects of these anonymous, social imaginary significations, which is not to say that individuals are simply and passively determined by them. To explain this, Castoriadis turns to examine the radical imaginary from the perspective of the human psyche, including the relationship between the psyche and the social imaginary.

## The Radical Imagination of the Psychic Monad

Castoriadis reminds us that individuals are born into a pre-existing society defined by social imaginary significations. This counters the notion that each human is, in some way, an unencumbered monad divorced from its social-historical position. This becomes more complicated when he introduces the notion of the 'psychic monad',[84] but the basic point is that the psychic monad is a moment of transcendence *within* rather than *from* society.[85] Each human is born into a social-historical formation, meaning that each is '*in and of* history [and] *in and of* society'.[86] Because individual thought occurs through language, which is dependent upon the structures of *legein*, Castoriadis explains that thought is necessarily representative of the social imaginary significations within which each individual exists. While this makes it clear that the *individual* is an effect of its society, Castoriadis notes that there is not a straightforward linear development from the social imaginary to the individual. Social imaginary significations 'can be effective, and effectively alive, only as long as they are invested ("cathected") and lived by human beings'.[87] If individuals no longer 'buy into them' and so express them through their actions, the social imaginary changes to one that is more acceptable to those inhabiting it.[88] Humans can, therefore, always do other than their social imaginary, although they cannot exist without one.

Castoriadis develops a particular ontology of the human based on a psyche that undergoes a process of socialisation through which it is turned into an individual. He starts by explaining that 'we know ... that human beings are born with a given biological constitution (which is extremely complex, rigid in certain respects, and endowed with an incredible plasticity in others) and that its make-up includes a psyche so long as it is functioning'.[89] The psyche is a basic *part* of human biology that exists as long as the human does. But Castoriadis does not reduce the human's biology to the psyche. This would entail an idealism that contradicts the emphasis he places on the concreteness of the social-historical domain. The 'essential characteristic of the human psyche [is] afunctionality',[90] meaning that it is not conditioned by a predetermined goal. For this reason, the psyche exists

> as a level of being that differs both from the central nervous system and even from the biological psyche [because] in comparison with the central

nervous system, there is the emergence of meaning for the self [*pour soi*]; in comparison with the biological psyche, the meaning that the human psyche creates or that it is by creating is defunctionalised.[91]

In contrast to the central nervous system and the biological psyche, the human psyche is not defined by a prior end or goal such as 'the preservation of the individual [or] the reproduction of the species'.[92] It is pure, spontaneous, 'autonomous imagination'.[93] This consists of 'the ability to formulate what is not there, to perceive, in just anything, what is not there'.[94] While always existing *within* a social-historical context, one that conditions it to a substantial degree, the human psyche is never determined by its social-historical environment.

The 'psychic monad'[95] describes the unconscious 'monadic core of the psyche'.[96] It is a 'simple unity, in which difference has not yet emerged'.[97] Castoriadis links it to Leibniz's windowless monad, although he warns that, in contrast to his predecessor's view, there is no pre-established harmony between monads. 'The monad's "perception" is a perception of self, its conatus is directed toward itself and is in no way harmonised with that of other monads.'[98] This permits the psychic monad to always do other than its social imaginary demands. The psychic monad is not, however, to be thought of in terms of a substance. It 'is an unceasing flux or stream of representations, desires, and affects'.[99]

With this, Castoriadis rejects Lacan's claim that the unconscious is structured like a language; 'such a standpoint . . . suppresses the radical implications of Freud's discovery of the unconscious, reducing passion and creativity to a binary code of signifiers'.[100] The psyche's desire is not *of* or *for* anything in particular. It simply constitutes an unceasing, unintentional striving and, for this reason, is linked to pure creation.

Importantly, 'creation is *ex nihilo* but it is not *in nihilo* or *cum nihilo*; it arises somewhere and it surges forth by means of some things'.[101] The psyche must always work *from* the materials provided to it by its social-historical setting, even though its autonomy means that it can always radically reconfigure its social-historical world. This can entail a 'minute' alteration that is so imperceptible that it gives rise to the appearance of continuity with that which went before. Alternatively, it can manifest itself as a 'large' alteration that gives rise to the appearance of fundamental rupture.[102]

The binary opposition between the psyche and its social-historical world that this viewpoint depends upon has been questioned,[103] but Castoriadis claims that it is necessary to secure the autonomy of the psychic monad and so permit the creation of the radically new. He recognises, however, that this autonomy causes problems for social life. By adhering to its egoistic desires to the detriment of its interactions with others, the psychic monad soon finds itself in conflict with others. To forestall this, it must develop the skills, outlook, and values that permit it to live with others. This requires socialisation.

## The Socialisation of the Psychic Monad

Having divorced itself from the natural world (on which it nevertheless continues to lean) through the creation of 'a fantastically complex (and amazingly coherent) edifice of significations which vest any and every thing with *meaning*',[104] the social imaginary finds expression through individuals who perpetuate its significations. As such, the anonymous collective socialises and incorporates 'the wild, raw, antifunctionally mad psyche of the newborn [by imposing] on it a formidable complex of constraints and limitations'.[105] This socialisation process creates and opens up *individuals* by 'giving them access to a *world* of social imaginary significations whose instauration as well as incredible *coherence* . . . goes unimaginably beyond everything that "one or many individuals" could ever produce'.[106] This occurs unconsciously, which allows it to succeed to 'an unbelievable degree';[107] although, as noted, an aspect of the psyche 'escapes' this process, thereby securing the continuing fundamental autonomy of the psyche 'within' the socialised individual.

The socialisation process does, however, require the participation of the psyche involved.[108] Specifically, the psyche must renounce its 'absolute egocentrism and omnipotence of imagination, recognise "reality" and the existence of others, subordinate desires to rules of behaviour, and accept sublimated satisfactions and even death for the sake of "social" ends'.[109] This is not a pleasant experience for psyche, requiring that it 'abandon – or better . . . bury – what it identifies as meaning for itself, in exchange for the possibility, the quasi-necessity, of internalising and cathecting that which society offers to it by way of meaning: its social imaginary significations'.[110]

For this reason, the socialisation process is initially something that is forcibly *done to* the child, who cannot give his permission because he lacks the linguistic skills to do so.[111] As Castoriadis explains,

> the new-born will *always* have to be torn out of *his* world, without asking him for an opinion he cannot give, and forced . . . to renounce his imaginary omnipotence, to recognise the desire of others as equally legitimate with his own, and taught that he cannot make the words of language signify what he may want them to, made able to enter the world as such,

the social world and the world of significations as everyone's world and as no one's world.[112]

From the perspective of the psyche, socialisation is a process of altering, by way of sublimating, '(although never fully) its initial ways and objects'[113] to those that are socially meaningful and acceptable. From the perspective of society, 'it is the social fabrication (nurturing, rearing) of the individual'.[114] Regardless of the perspective through which it is analysed, the result is the same: 'society . . . succeeds to an unbelievable degree (though never exhaustively) in diverting, orienting, and channelling the psyche's egotistic, asocial (and, of course, fully "arational") drives and impulses into coherent social activities, more or less "logical" diurnal thinking, etc.'.[115]

Lest we underestimate how powerful the social imaginary is, Castoriadis explains that

> people think they have 'their personal way of thinking'. The truth is that even the most original thinker owes everything but a minute particle of what she says to society, to what she learned, her surroundings, the opinion and mood of the times, or a trivial reworking of all that, which is to say, the conclusions that may be drawn, or the underlying postulates that may be uncovered.[116]

To illustrate his point, he argues that 'were we to quantify, metaphorically, the truly novel kernel in Plato, Aristotle, Kant, Hegel, Marx, or Freud, it would represent, possibly, one per cent of what they said or wrote'.[117]

We see then that the socialisation process turns the psyche into the individual who understands and adheres to what that society considers to be morally acceptable and unacceptable. Depending on whether they form part of the social imaginary within which the individual exists, it is at this point that the terms 'good' and 'evil' are first encountered. Having explained how meaning is generated from the social imaginary, the next stage in the argument would, ideally, be to analyse what concepts mean for different social imaginaries. Castoriadis rarely does this and certainly does not do so in relation to 'evil'. Nonetheless, by extrapolating from his theory, we can start to demonstrate what it means for our understanding of 'evil'. When we do, we find that (1) moral concepts are constructed by the anonymous collective from the radical imaginary subtending each; (2) moral concepts may not be part of a social imaginary; and (3) the *meaning* of moral concepts changes depending on the social-historical context within which they are located. Evil may not then be part of the symbolic order of a social imaginary, but, if it is, its meaning is not fixed or *a priori*; it is open, historical, and contestable.

Crucially, Castoriadis holds that it is politics that decides 'the institution of society and its contents'.[118] Politics is not based on a representational model of truth or determined by universal, *a priori* meaning. There is no *a priori* standard against which to determine the validity of various positions. Politics is an inherently conflictual process whereby different imaginaries compete for dominance. Through this process, the social imaginary is shaped and reshaped. As a consequence, the meanings attributed to 'Auschwitz', which as we saw from Arendt is often taken to be the paradigm of evil in post-Second World War Western thinking, and 'the Gulag' 'are not to be refuted, they are to be combated'.[119]

With this, Castoriadis follows the Augustinian-Kantian tradition by affirming a role, through the psychic monad, for autonomous choice, all the while departing from that tradition by emphasising 'a politics of autonomy'[120] rather than an ethics of autonomy. Contrary to the Augustinian-Kantian tradition, evil is not an individual, ethical issue; it is a *collective, political* one that pushes us to more closely examine why we describe certain events and not others in the ways we do, which, in turn, requires an examination of the significations inherent in the social imaginary within and from which we exist. Only this will bring the anonymous collective of the social-historical to explicitly recognise and affirm the instituting power of the radical imaginary. In turn, this will create individuals that reflectively and continuously choose laws, values, and significations that express this autonomy and the solidarity it entails. Presumably, this will prevent another Auschwitz or Gulag from occurring.

## Concluding Remarks

Regardless of whether we agree with Castoriadis's political prescriptions, he certainly provides a particularly innovative framework from which to explain how meaning is attributed to concepts. He breaks decisively with any notion that meaning is ahistoric and universal. Instead, he follows Nietzsche in holding that the meaning of moral concepts is a construction, but combines this with the emphasis that Arendt places on social processes. By suggesting that these social processes are anonymous, historical, and located in and from the imaginary, Castoriadis explicitly points to the role that radical (imaginary) creativity plays in generating moral meaning.

The strength of this approach is that it reminds us that our moral judgements are fundamentally grounded in and reflect our social and historical situations and contexts. Nevertheless, Castoriadis salvages a degree of individual autonomy by pointing out that the psyche's fundamental autonomy ensures that it can always alter the meanings its social imaginary attributes to concepts and events. In so doing, he continues the Augustinian line that holds that individual autonomy is fundamental to individual moral action. Rather than simply being a passive recipient of social meaning, the radical imagination allows the individual to resignify acts and, by extension, its world.

The great weakness of Castoriadis's approach is that while it can describe, in general terms, how meaning is generated from particular social imaginaries, it is unable to explain what moral concepts signify. Each social imaginary will have a different sense of the term, assuming that each uses the term in the first place. Insisting that the meaning of concepts is, ultimately, an effect of an anonymous collective has led, at least, one commentator to wonder whether Castoriadis's analysis of creativity falls into the very empty abstraction it aims to overcome.[121] Indeed, on Axel Honneth's assessment, the claim that meaning is a consequence of anonymous social processes ensures that 'creative achievements entirely forego the character of practice as social action, and increasingly take on the characteristics of an impersonal occurrence'.[122]

While it might be questioned whether this downplays the role that the independent psychic monad plays in Castoriadis's political project, there is something in the claim that, ultimately, he privileges the conforming tendencies inherent in the social imaginary over the disruptive autonomy of the psychic monad. As he explains,

> creation, as the work of the social imaginary, of the *instituting* society (*societas instituans*, not *societas instituta*), is the mode of being of the social-historical field. To recognise this and to stop asking meaningless questions about 'subjects' and 'substances' or 'causes' requires, to be sure, a radical ontological conversion.[123]

For Jürgen Habermas, this exposes the fundamental problem with Castoriadis's approach. By making meaning and individual actions effects of the anonymous, pre-personal, social-historical field, it is unable to hold socialised individuals to account for 'their' actions. After all, strictly speaking, 'their' actions are not 'theirs;' they are effects of 'the anonymous hurly-burly of the institutionalization of ever new worlds from the imaginary dimension'.[124] A single individual cannot, then, be held '*accountable*'[125] for specific actions, which raises questions about whether Castoriadis's account can adequately deal with the perpetrators of actions deemed evil.

For this reason, subsequent thinking on evil, especially within Anglo-American analytic philosophy, moved away from the constructivist approach adopted by Castoriadis (and Lacan). Rather than focus on how meaning is constructed, but say little on what it means for particular humans, proponents of this style of thought tended to ignore the question of how meaning is generated to simply adopt an axiomatic definition of evil to examine evil from the perspective of those involved. This gave rise to what have become known as perpetrator-based and victim-based accounts of evil.

## Notes

1. Lacan's use of short sessions and disdain for orthodox psychoanalytic practices motivated his expulsion from the Société Française de Psychanalyse (SFP) in 1953. This was repeated in 1963 when the Société Parisienne de Psychanalyse (SPP), the group established by those who broke from the SFP with Lacan, negotiated entrance into the International Psychoanalytical Association (IPA). A condition of its entrance was Lacan's removal from the approved list of training analysts. Lacan subsequently left the SPP to establish the École Freudienne de Paris (EFP), which existed outside the framework of the IPA. For Lacan's comments on his 'excommunication', see *Seminar XI: The Four Fundamental Concepts of Psychoanalysis*, ed. Jacques-Alain Miller, trans. Alan Sheridan (New York: W. W. Norton, 1981), pp. 1–16. The definitive biographical account of Lacan remains Elisabeth Roudinesco's *Jacques Lacan: Esquisse d'une vie, histoire d'un système de pensée* (Paris: Librairie Arthème Fayard, 1993).
2. Cornelius Castoriadis, 'Psychoanalysis: Project and Elucidation', p. 99, in *Crossroads in the Labyrinth*, trans. Kate Soper and Martin H. Ryle (Cambridge, MA: MIT Press, 1984), pp. 46–115.
3. Ibid. p. 99.
4. Ibid. p. 99.
5. Ibid. p. 53.
6. Ibid. p. 99.
7. Cornelius Castoriadis, 'Remarks on Space and Number', p. 245, in *Figures of the Thinkable*, trans. Helen Arnold (Stanford: Stanford University Press, 2007), pp. 244–59.
8. Castoriadis explains that 'contrary to what Lacan believed, the Unconscious is not a machine' ('From Monad to Autonomy', p. 185, in *World in Fragments*, ed. and trans. David Ames Curtis [Stanford: Stanford University Press, 1997], pp. 172–95).
9. Cornelius Castoriadis, *The Imaginary Institution of Society*, trans. Kathleen Blamey (Cambridge, MA: MIT Press, 1998), p. 127.
10. This will focus on the relationship between the natural world, the histor-

ical, and the social and will pave the way for a discussion of Castoriadis's notion of the imaginary. For an excellent analysis of Castoriadis's ontology, see Suzi Adams, *Castoriadis's Ontology: Being and Creation* (New York: Fordham University Press, 2011).
11. Cornelius Castoriadis, 'False and True Chaos', p. 241, in *Figures of the Thinkable*, trans. Helen Arnold (Stanford: Stanford University Press, 2007), pp. 236–43.
12. Ibid. p. 241.
13. Cornelius Castoriadis, 'Psychoanalysis: Its Situation and Limits', p. 190, in *Figures of the Thinkable*, trans. Helen Arnold (Stanford: Stanford University Press, 2007), pp. 188–202.
14. Castoriadis, *The Imaginary Institution of Society*, p. 204.
15. Cornelius Castoriadis, 'Imaginary Significations', p. 56, in *A Society Adrift: Interviews and Debates, 1974–1977*, ed. Enrique Escobar, Myrto Gondicas, and Pascal Vernay, trans. Helen Arnold (New York: Fordham University Press, 2010), pp. 45–68.
16. Castoriadis's thought gradually navigates away from this binary opposition to the extent that his later work comes to explicitly engage with the creative processes at work in nature. See Suzi Adams, 'Castoriadis' Shift towards *Physis*', *Thesis Eleven*, 74, 2003, pp. 105–12.
17. Cornelius Castoriadis, '*Phusis* and Autonomy', p. 332, in *World in Fragments*, ed. and trans. David Ames Curtis (Stanford: Stanford University Press, 1997), pp. 331–41.
18. Cornelius Castoriadis, 'Power, Politics, Autonomy', p. 164, in *Philosophy, Politics, Autonomy: Essays in Political Philosophy*, ed. David Ames Curtis (Oxford: Oxford University Press, 1991), pp. 143–74.
19. Cornelius Castoriadis, 'Institution of Society and Religion', p. 329, in *World in Fragments*, ed. and trans. David Ames Curtis (Stanford: Stanford University Press, 1997), pp. 311–30.
20. Autonomy is the concept through which the *philosophical* and *political* aspects of Castoriadis's thinking most clearly and explicitly meet. Thus, we find him explaining that 'what I want is for society to . . . acquire its peculiar dimension as a society, a network of relationships among autonomous individuals' (Castoriadis, *The Imaginary Institution of Society*, p. 94). For a critical discussion of Castoriadis's notion of autonomy and its relationship to politics, see Natalie Doyle, 'Autonomy and Modern Liberal Democracy: From Castoriadis to Gauchet', *European Journal of Social Theory*, 15:3, 2012, pp. 331–47.
21. Cornelius Castoriadis, 'The Imaginary: Creation in the Social-Historical Domain', p. 10, in *World in Fragments*, ed. and trans. David Ames Curtis (Stanford: Stanford University Press, 1997), pp. 3–18.
22. Castoriadis, 'Power, Politics, Autonomy', p. 147.
23. Ibid. p. 34.
24. Castoriadis, *The Imaginary Institution of Society*, pp. 3–4.
25. Ibid. p. 72.

26. Ibid. pp. 22–3.
27. Cornelius Castoriadis, 'The "End of Philosophy"?', p. 34, in *Philosophy, Politics, Autonomy: Essays in Political Philosophy*, ed. David Ames Curtis (Oxford: Oxford University Press, 1991), pp. 13–32.
28. Castoriadis, *The Imaginary Institution of Society*, p. 138.
29. Ibid. p. 138.
30. Cornelius Castoriadis, 'The Ontological Import of the History of Science', p. 372, in *World in Fragments*, ed. and trans. David Ames Curtis (Stanford: Stanford University Press, 1997), pp. 342–73.
31. Cornelius Castoriadis, 'Primal Institution of Society and Second-Order Institutions', p. 100, in *Figures of the Thinkable*, trans. Helen Arnold (Stanford: Stanford University Press, 2007), pp. 91–101.
32. Castoriadis, 'The Imaginary', p. 9.
33. Cornelius Castoriadis, 'Reflections on Racism', p. 23, in *World in Fragments*, ed. and trans. David Ames Curtis (Stanford: Stanford University Press, 1997), pp. 19–31.
34. Castoriadis, 'Psychoanalysis: Project and Elucidation', p. 89.
35. Cornelius Castoriadis, 'Individual, Society, Rationality, History', p. 77, in *Philosophy, Politics, Autonomy: Essays in Political Philosophy*, ed. David Ames Curtis (Oxford: Oxford University Press, 1991), pp. 47–80.
36. Castoriadis, *The Imaginary Institution of Society*, p. 108.
37. Castoriadis, 'Imaginary Significations', p. 46.
38. Castoriadis, 'Individual, Society, Rationality, History', p. 77.
39. Castoriadis, *The Imaginary Institution of Society*, p. 111.
40. Ibid. p. 144.
41. Castoriadis, 'The Imaginary', p. 6.
42. Castoriadis, *The Imaginary Institution of Society*, p. 112.
43. Castoriadis, 'The Imaginary', p. 7.
44. Cornelius Castoriadis, 'Imaginary and Imagination at the Crossroads', p. 72, in *Figures of the Thinkable*, trans. Helen Arnold (Stanford: Stanford University Press, 2007), pp. 71–90.
45. Ibid. p. 72.
46. Castoriadis, 'From Monad to Autonomy', p. 182.
47. Cornelius Castoriadis, 'The Psyche and Society Anew', p. 205, in *Figures of the Thinkable*, trans. Helen Arnold (Stanford: Stanford University Press, 2007), pp. 203–20.
48. Ibid. p. 205.
49. Castoriadis, 'Imaginary and Imagination at the Crossroads', p. 72.
50. Castoriadis, 'Imaginary Significations', p. 48.
51. Castoriadis, 'Imaginary and Imagination at the Crossroads', p. 72.
52. Castoriadis, *The Imaginary Institution of Society*, p. 238.
53. Castoriadis, 'Institution of Society and Religion', p. 315.
54. Cornelius Castoriadis, 'The Greek and the Modern Political Imaginary', p. 84,

in *World in Fragments*, ed. and trans. David Ames Curtis (Stanford: Stanford University Press, 1997), pp. 84–107.
55. Castoriadis, 'Imaginary and Imagination at the Crossroads', pp. 73–4.
56. Castoriadis, *The Imaginary Institution of Society*, p. 238.
57. Ibid. p. 259.
58. Nathalie Karagiannis and Peter Wagner miss this aspect of Castoriadis's thought when they affirm that his use of the term 'radical' suggests 'a distinction between radical and non-radical uses or modes of imagination'. They do, however, recognise that 'there is no explicit discussion of this distinction' ('Imagination and Tragic Democracy', *Critical Horizons*, 13:1, 2012, pp. 12–28 [p. 16]). However, there is no discussion of it because 'radical' is used in terms of its etymological sense: *radix*, meaning root or base. 'Radical imaginary' simply means the grounding imaginary or that the imaginary grounds all else. Given this, there cannot be, for Castoriadis, an imaginary that is non-radical or non-grounding.
59. Castoriadis, 'Imaginary and Imagination at the Crossroads', p. 73.
60. Castoriadis, *The Imaginary Institution of Society*, p. 3.
61. Ibid. p. 274.
62. Ibid. p. 146.
63. Ibid. pp. 146–7.
64. Ibid. p. 147.
65. Ibid. p. 147.
66. Ibid. p. 372.
67. Ibid. pp. 372–3.
68. Ibid. p. 372.
69. Castoriadis, 'Power, Politics, Autonomy', p. 153.
70. Castoriadis, *The Imaginary Institution of Society*, p. 182.
71. Ibid. pp. 243–4.
72. Castoriadis, 'Institution of Society and Religion', p. 315.
73. Castoriadis, *The Imaginary Institution of Society*, p. 150.
74. Cornelius Castoriadis, 'Response to Richard Rorty', p. 81, in *A Society Adrift: Interviews and Debates, 1974–1977*, ed. Enrique Escobar, Myrto Gondicas, and Pascal Vernay, trans. Helen Arnold (New York: Fordham University Press, 2010), pp. 69–82.
75. Castoriadis, 'Imaginary Significations', p. 50.
76. Castoriadis, 'Psychoanalysis: Its Situation and Limits', pp. 195–6.
77. Castoriadis, 'The Greek and the Modern Political Imaginary', p. 84.
78. Castoriadis, 'The Discovery of the Imagination', p. 245, in *World in Fragments*, ed. and trans. David Ames Curtis (Stanford: Stanford University Press, 1997), pp. 213–45.
79. Castoriadis, *The Imaginary Institution of Society*, p. 364.
80. Ibid. p. 366.
81. On this point, Castoriadis famously claims that 'there is nothing more deprived

of imagination than the transcendental imagination of Kant' ('The Discovery of the Imagination', p. 245).
82. Cornelius Castoriadis, 'Psychoanalysis and Politics', p. 131, in *World in Fragments*, ed. and trans. David Ames Curtis (Stanford: Stanford University Press, 1997), pp. 125–36.
83. Castoriadis, 'Imaginary and Imagination at the Crossroads', p. 73.
84. Castoriadis, *The Imaginary Institution of Society*, p. 298.
85. Ibid. p. 33.
86. Ibid. p. 33.
87. Cornelius Castoriadis, 'Heritage and Revolution', p. 105, in *Figures of the Thinkable*, trans. Helen Arnold (Stanford: Stanford University Press, 2007), pp. 105–17.
88. Castoriadis makes the same point in relation to instituted States, explaining that 'there is no omnipotence of instituted States. Their power is nothing but the reverse side of people's belief in that power' ('On the Possibility of Creating a New Form of Society', p. 116, in *A Society Adrift: Interviews and Debates, 1974–1977*, ed. Enrique Escobar, Myrto Gondicas, and Pascal Vernay, trans. Helen Arnold [New York: Fordham University Press, 2010], pp. 103–16).
89. Castoriadis, 'Individual, Society, Rationality, History', p. 61.
90. Castoriadis, 'The Psyche and Society Anew', p. 204.
91. Castoriadis, 'False and True Chaos', p. 241.
92. Ibid. p. 241.
93. Castoriadis, 'The Psyche and Society Anew', p. 203.
94. Ibid. p. 203.
95. Castoriadis, *The Imaginary Institution of Society*, p. 298.
96. Ibid. p. 298.
97. Ibid. p. 294.
98. Cornelius Castoriadis, 'Psyche and Education', p. 171, in *Figures of the Thinkable*, trans. Helen Arnold (Stanford: Stanford University Press, 2007), pp. 165–87.
99. Castoriadis, 'Imaginary and Imagination at the Crossroads', p. 74.
100. Anthony Elliot, 'The Social Imaginary: A Critical Assessment of Castoriadis's Psychoanalytic Social Theory', *American Imago*, 59:2, 2002, pp. 141–70 (pp. 154–5).
101. Castoriadis, 'False and True Chaos', pp. 240–1. For more on Castoriadis's notion of creation, see Jeff Klooger, 'From Nothing: Castoriadis and the Concept of Creation', *Critical Horizons*, 12:1, 2010, pp. 29–47.
102. Castoriadis thinks that, while the latter is possible, the former tends to dominate, to the extent that he points to only two *fundamental alterations* in Western history: 'There is neither progress nor regression between the Parthenon and Notre-Dame de Paris, between Plato and Kant. But *there are* breaks: in Ancient Greece, between the eighth and fifth century BCE, with the creation of democracy and philosophy, or in Western Europe, starting

in the tenth and eleventh centuries, with an enormous quantity of new creations, and culminating in the modern period' (Cornelius Castoriadis, 'The Project of Autonomy is not Utopia', p. 7, in *A Society Adrift: Interviews and Debates, 1974–1977*, ed. Enrique Escobar, Myrto Gondicas, and Pascal Vernay, trans. Helen Arnold [New York: Fordham University Press, 2010], pp. 3–10). Castoriadis expands on the changes that have taken place in Western Europe since the tenth century in 'The Imaginary', p. 15.

103. Jürgen Habermas, 'Excursus on Cornelius Castoriadis: The Imaginary Institution', pp. 333–4, in: *The Philosophical Discourse of Modernity: Twelve Lectures*, trans. Frederick Lawrence (Cambridge: Polity, 1987), pp. 328–35.
104. Cornelius Castoriadis, 'The Social-Historical: Mode of Being, Problems of Knowledge', p. 41, in *Philosophy, Politics, Autonomy: Essays in Political Philosophy*, ed. David Ames Curtis (Oxford: Oxford University Press, 1991), pp. 33–46.
105. Ibid. p. 41.
106. Ibid. p. 42.
107. Ibid. p. 42.
108. Toula Nicolacopoulos and George Vassilacopoulous, 'The Time of Radical Autonomous Thinking and Social-Historical Becoming in Castoriadis', *Thesis Eleven*, 120:1, 2014, pp. 59–74 (p. 60). For a detailed discussion of how the psyche participates in its own socialisation, see Gavin Rae, 'Taming the Little Screaming Monster: Castoriadis, Violence, and the Creation of the Individual', in *The Meanings of Violence: From Critical Theory to Biopolitics*, ed. Gavin Rae and Emma Ingala (Abingdon: Routledge, 2019), pp. 171–90.
109. Castoriadis, 'The Social-Historical', pp. 41–2.
110. Castoriadis, 'Psychoanalysis: Its Situation and Limits', p. 201.
111. That the socialisation process rips the psyche from its initial autism means that the human always harbours a deep-seated, if unconscious, hatred for society. Society must, then, find ways to release this deep-seated hatred, with competition and war being the two historically dominant forms through which this has been achieved. See Cornelius Castoriadis, 'On Wars in Europe', p. 93, in *A Society Adrift: Interviews and Debates, 1974–1977*, ed. Enrique Escobar, Myrto Gondicas, and Pascal Vernay, trans. Helen Arnold (New York: Fordham University Press, 2010), pp. 83–102.
112. Castoriadis, *The Imaginary Institution of Society*, p. 311.
113. Castoriadis, 'The Social-Historical', p. 42.
114. Ibid. p. 42.
115. Castoriadis, *The Imaginary Institution of Society*, p. 42.
116. Castoriadis, 'Imaginary Significations', p. 47.
117. Ibid. p. 47.
118. Castoriadis, 'Psychoanalysis: Its Situation and Limits', p. 194.
119. Cornelius Castoriadis, 'Preface', p. xxviii, in *Crossroads in the Labyrinth*, trans. Kate Soper and Martin H. Ryle (Cambridge, MA: MIT Press, 1984), pp. ix–

xxx. This was written in November 1977. Castoriadis reaffirmed it ('You don't refute Auschwitz or the Gulag; you combat them') two weeks later in a talk first published in *Le Monde* and translated under the title 'On the Possibility of Creating a New Form of Society' (p. 116).
120. Castoriadis, *The Imaginary Institution of Society*, p. 101.
121. Claudia Strauss, 'The Imaginary', *Anthropological Theory*, 6:3, 2006, pp. 322–44 (p. 323).
122. Axel Honneth, 'Rescuing the Revolution with an Ontology: On Cornelius Castoriadis' Theory of Society', *Thesis Eleven*, 14, 1986, pp. 62–78 (p. 71).
123. Castoriadis, *The Imaginary Institution of Society*, pp. 13–14.
124. Habermas, 'Excursus on Cornelius Castoriadis', p. 330.
125. Ibid. p. 330.

# PART IV  THE SUBJECTS OF EVIL

# 12

# The Perpetrators of Evil

Perpetrator accounts of evil can be divided into soft and hard versions. The former focus on the *act* committed by the perpetrator to determine whether it qualifies as an evil. The latter makes the stronger claim that the act committed by the perpetrator *also* reveals the moral worth of the perpetrator of that act. The conclusion reached is that some individuals are simply evil. In *Facing Evil*,[1] published in 1990, John Kekes outlines and defends this hard version, before subsequently publishing a follow-up volume in 2005 titled *The Roots of Evil*.[2] In the second volume, Kekes provides new arguments supporting his previous views and uses his initial framework to analyse a number of historical examples. Due to space constraints and because his later book is an extension of the framework developed in the former, I will focus on *Facing Evil*.

The analysis of evil found in *Facing Evil* is part of a larger project affirming what Kekes calls 'character-morality'[3] over the historically dominant 'choice-morality'.[4] The former claims that moral actions are the consequence of an individual's character, which is unchosen and based on habits learnt from others, whereas choice-morality follows the Augustinian line that moral actions are the result of the autonomous choices that individuals make regarding the good/evil. Character-morality holds that an agent's action reveals the agent's moral character and hence moral worth. In contrast, Kekes understands that choice-morality defends a soft perpetrator account of evil that is 'reluctan[t] to allow evil actions to count as evidence for their agent's being evil'.[5]

Although he accepts that choice-morality has been the dominant, historical form of morality defining Western 'sensibility',[6] Kekes affirms character-morality to conclude that: (1) if evil results from an individual's actions, then, regardless of his intentions, the agent should be held responsible for that evil; and (2) an individual's actions reveal his moral character.[7] Those who habitually commit evil acts are evil individuals. With this, he contributes to historical debates on evil by suggesting that it refers to their actions *and* the moral worth of individuals. Evil individuals exist and, on Kekes's telling, are far more prominent than typically realised.

To defend this, Kekes does not engage in a substantive historical analysis of the concept, but mentions a number of predecessors who are taken to be representative of opposing positions, typically produces a short summary of their positions, before developing a critique based on the assumptions of character-morality. He also bases his analysis on a number of presuppositions, such as 'there are no gods',[8] which he takes to mean that he does not have to engage with theological accounts of evil. Psychoanalytical approaches are also rejected because he 'find[s] the theoretical assumptions ... untenable'.[9] He does not, however, explain what is untenable about them or what justifies such an approach. He also rejects what he calls 'the transcendental temptation',[10] which explains this world through recourse to another.

Two reasons are given for this, both from the premises of character-morality: first, the existence of another world cannot be verified experientially, which reveals his unexamined privileging of empiricism;[11] and, second, he understands that arguments that rely on another world suppose that good will eventually overcome evil. This, however, violates his 'tragic view of life',[12] which holds that good and evil, as he understands them, are built into the human condition. The human condition is, for him, defined by an ongoing tension between the two. Evaluating alternative conceptions of evil against his assumptions allows Kekes to clearly position and defend his account of character-morality. It does, however, mean that his treatment of alternative positions is always brought back to and analysed from the assumptions that ground character-morality, including its understanding of evil.

The assumptions that Kekes relies upon take two different, but ultimately complementary, forms. First, he postulates objective and universal foundations that find expression in his understanding of (1) human beings, which are defined by an objective, universal, human nature;[13] (2) perception, which allows him to insist on non-controversial interpretations of actions;[14] and (3) language, in so far as words are conceived to have a fixed, objective, and determinate meaning. This is re-enforced by a reliance on everyday meaning, as manifested through dictionary definitions,[15] an appeal to what 'reasonable people'[16] would agree to or to what 'is obvious'.[17]

Second, he demands causal explanations wherein an action can be causally traced back to an agent, whose motivations can, in turn, be causally understood. His rejection of transcendent/al and psychoanalytical explanations prevents him from explaining these actions by appealing to an unconscious or non-experiential realm, so, instead, he argues that an agent's actions are expressions of habitual modes of behaviour that have been learnt through experience.

The combination of both sets of assumptions brings Kekes to conclude that (1) evil has a definitive meaning, (2) evil actions are the consequence of the actions of agents, (3) an agent's actions demonstrate the moral worth of his character, and (4) much, if not most, evil acts are unchosen by agents, but this does not prevent the perpetrator from being held responsible for them.

## The Nature of Morality

According to Kekes, morality is a 'human invention'[18] 'designed to make the world as hospitable to our interests as possible'.[19] These interests are not subjective, but entail the objective and universal conditions necessary for human welfare. How the individual acts in relation to the conditions necessary for human welfare reveals his moral character. If he predominantly promotes human welfare, he is judged to have turned towards the good and, on Kekes's telling, is of good moral character; if not, he is of evil moral character.[20] Human welfare consists of 'particular virtues and vices, with various conceptions of good lives, and so on'.[21]

This description is, of course, ambiguous. Kekes admits as much, but defends it by stating that 'the interpretation of what commitment to human welfare involves is left deliberately vague to allow for moral disagreements'.[22] Nevertheless, he goes on to explain that there are two general types of good necessary for the promotion of human welfare. *Internal* goods 'are satisfactions involved in living according to our conceptions of good lives'.[23] *External* goods 'are satisfactions derived from possessing the means required for living in the ways we do and from receiving appropriate rewards for it'.[24] Kekes clarifies that 'typically, understanding, good judgement, clarity, and sensitivity are internal goods, while physical, psychological, and financial security, honour, prestige, and influence are external goods'.[25]

The fundamental difference between internal and external goods is that 'in the case of internal goods, the human agency is primarily oneself, while external goods are benefits conferred on us by others, and frequently by others acting on behalf of institutions'.[26] He warns, however, that internal goods are not wholly within our power. They are a consequence of human effort, but 'the effort presupposes that we have the talents or the capacities to cultivate, and whether we do depends on the outcome of the genetic lottery. So, internal goods are not the pure products of human endeavour.'[27]

Kekes's overall point is that human welfare is a complex combination of agency, biological endowment, and social environment, in so far as, while each individual strives to exist in accordance with an individual conception of the good life, the satisfaction of this depends upon the attainment of the (1) internal goods necessary for this, which depend upon each individual's effort and genetic predisposition, and (2) external goods necessary for a good life, which are dependent on the actions of others. The good is not, then, a purely individualistic pursuit, but one that takes place in the concrete world inhabited by others, each of whom also strives for a conception of the good life dependent on the actions of and his interactions with others. Living a good life is, therefore, a continuous process that is often frustrated by our own and others' actions.

The achievement of a good life is made even more difficult by Kekes's claim that there is a structural flaw in the human condition that prevents internal and external goods from being realised. This results from what he calls *'the essential conditions of life'*.[28] Kekes identifies three: contingency, indifference, and destructiveness.

'Contingency' refers to the vulnerability of human life, in so far as 'there are vast areas of our lives in which we lack understanding and control'.[29] Again, rejecting theological accounts, Kekes explains that even if 'we may not be playthings of gods . . . we are often at the mercy of natural forces'.[30] His point is that the contingency of human life means that we may find ourselves in situations where we are forced, through no fault of our own, to act in ways that produce evil. This links to Kekes's insistence that 'much evil is beyond human control. Often it is not ignorance or destructiveness that causes undeserved harm but natural forces.'[31]

'Indifference' refers to the absence of moral justice in the cosmos. With this, Kekes rejects theodicies that see evil as being part of a grand cosmic order orientated to the good or which hold that the good will eventually be rewarded and evil punished. For Kekes, 'there is no cosmic justice; the good may suffer, and the wicked may flourish'.[32] This is because

> the order of nature is not a moral order; it is not evil, rather than good, nor is it Manichean. It is indifferent. Indifference is worse than neutrality, for the latter implies the presence of an umpire, or perhaps some spectators, who are there as witnesses but stand above the fray and remain uncommitted.[33]

To justify this, Kekes appeals to 'our common experience',[34] which shows that 'vicious dictators live out their lives in comfort, continuing to wield their evil power amid the adulation of people they have duped'.[35] Similarly, 'good causes supported by good people lose out to unscrupulous defenders of deplorable conditions. Crimes, accidents, and disease befall us, regardless of our merit.'[36] The cosmos's indifference to the lives of good, deserving people ensures that there is no guarantee that the good will prevail. There is simply no moral order to nature, although as we saw, the contingency of the natural order means that it frequently prevents the good from being realised.

'Destructiveness' refers to 'the barbaric and life-diminishing force of evil [that] is an active force in us'.[37] Kekes rejects the suggestion that destructiveness only enters an individual's life due to the actions of others. For him, destructiveness does not refer to the influence of external forces on us because 'corrupting influences can take hold only if we are ready to receive them'.[38] Without mentioning him, Kekes appears to be appealing to something akin to Kant's notion of a propensity to evil (*Hang zum Bösen*) within human being as a species. Rather than the actualisation of this propensity requiring an individual choice, Kekes argues that destruction is integral to the ontological structure of human being because failure, suffering, and lack of fulfilment are, on Kekes's telling, integral to the conditions of human life.

Nevertheless, Kekes does not think that all forms of suffering are equal. Undeserved suffering is more closely linked to evil than is deserved suffering, but Kekes goes further by claiming that 'the problem is not merely undeserved suffering but a broader one of undeserved harm'.[39] The difference between suffering and harm is never laid out, but we might think of it in the following terms: suffering derives from a specific harm that is explicitly experienced, whereas harm is defined in terms of the absence of the internal and external goods necessary to facilitate and secure human welfare.

Crucially, evil entails not just harm, but '*undeserved* harm inflicted on human beings'.[40] This harm could be to oneself or to another person, or the consequence of natural events. Because undeserved harm is constitutive of ordinary life, evil (= undeserved harm) is everyday and banal.[41] This is not to say that there are not moral monsters. Kekes thinks, however, that these types of people are incredibly rare historically and, by extension, the majority of us never encounter them in our everyday day. As he states, 'we have to look far and wide to find the likes of Stalin and Hitler'.[42]

Kekes maintains that once we conceive of evil in terms of undeserved harm and complement this with the realisation that the essential conditions of life often cause such harm, we will learn to understand and accept that evil is 'not rare and freakish concatenations of unfavourable circumstances but daily occurrences in the lives of us all'.[43] To deal with these daily occurrences and so better approximate the ideal lives we aspire to, Kekes suggests that we must face evil and accept that it is a banal phenomenon rooted in the everyday, undeserved harms that are caused, sometimes intentionally, but more often than not from unreflective habit, as individuals go about their lives. He goes on to clarify the link between evil and undeserved harm by analysing the meanings of 'harm' and 'desert' and the judgement necessary to determine when harm is and is not deserved.

## Evil as Undeserved Harm

Kekes maintains that harm can be complex or simple: 'torture is simple harm, emotional blackmail is much more complex'.[44] Complex harms are built on the foundation of simple harm, which occurs when people are deprived 'of the minimum requirement of their welfare'.[45] To explain the 'minimum requirements of human welfare',[46] Kekes returns to the distinction between internal and external goods. Significantly, he argues that his description of the requirements of human welfare is non-controversial and that he 'only repeat[s] what everyone knows'.[47] With this, he appeals to forms of welfare that 'are universally human, culturally invariant, and historically constant features of human life'.[48] We are, then, told that 'our physiology imposes requirements on all of us: we need to eat, drink, and breathe to survive; we need protection from the elements'.[49] Furthermore, 'if uninjured, we perceive the world in the same sense modalities; and within a narrow range, we are capable of the same motor responses'.[50]

Kekes therefore identifies common biological needs shorn of any cultural or linguistic significance or symbolism to focus on the brute fact that humans need specific, minimum conditions for life. By distinguishing between the biological and symbolic in this fashion, he does not need to take into consideration socio-cultural meanings when describing the basic considerations of human life. These are second order phenomena built on the foundation of biological needs. As a consequence, implicit to his schema is a nature/culture, biology/symbolic division wherein the former terms are privileged over the latter. His conclusion is that 'part of human nature is that all healthy members of our species have many of the same physiological needs and capacities for satisfying them'.[51]

Noticing the simplicity of his attempt to associate human welfare with mere biological needs, Kekes subsequently recognises that humans do not only have physiological needs; they also have psychological ones. These are based on specific aspirations that 'differ, of course, from person to person, culture to culture, age to age'.[52] While this heterogeneity would appear to pose problems for any attempt to delineate the requirements of human welfare, upon which his account of evil depends, Kekes immediately reduces this heterogeneity to a homogeneous principle. Although we may desire different goals and seek to fulfil these in different ways based on our individual capacities, 'there is no difference in the psychological aspiration to go beyond necessity and enjoy the luxury of satisfying our needs in whatever ways happen to count as desirable to us'.[53] Kekes's basic point is that, even if our desires and means are heterogeneous, that we desire at all is not: *all* humans, regardless of culture, history, or upbringing, have an inbuilt desire for things beyond those that are strictly necessary for biological survival.

Kekes continues to identify the universal conditions of human existence:

> We all prefer the civilized state to the primitive one. Furthermore, we are alike in having the capacities to learn from the past and plan for the future; we have a view, perhaps never articulated, about what we want to make of our lives; we have likes and dislikes, and we try to have much of the former and little of the latter; we have capacities to think, remember, imagine, use language, have feelings, emotions, moods, and emotions, make efforts, go after what we want, or restrain ourselves.[54]

Whereas constructivist accounts would object that what individuals like and dislike, feel, and communicate are socio-cultural constructions, Kekes thinks that this only applies to the *content* of what we like and dislike. This specific content can only, however, be constructed if there are innate *capacities* that can be realised through the acculturation process that constructivist accounts rely on.

It appears that Kekes is pointing to, what might be called from a Kantian perspective, the transcendental conditions of experience: the structures of cognition that shape individual phenomenal experiences. Kekes, however, conflates *transcendental* with *transcendent*, meaning that he associates transcendental conditions with another world that escapes the natural one. From this, and without discussing it explicitly, he appears to hold that transcendental arguments are based on a two-world, rather than a two-aspect, interpretation that sees objects split between the phenomenal world and another world that conditions, but remains hidden from, the phenomenal one.[55]

The reduction of transcendental accounts to the two-world interpretation lies behind his rejection of what he calls the 'transcendental temptation'.[56] Given his critique of transcendental accounts, Kekes's own analysis cannot use that language, even though he appears to be arguing for something similar when he claims that there are universal conditions of human cognition/being that are given content phenomenally. Rather than employ the language of transcendental idealism, Kekes uses essentialist language, with the consequence that he suggests that there are essential conditions for human being that are expressed differently depending on the concrete conditions within which each individual exists. We find, therefore, that the items previously mentioned are 'commonplace facts and others like them form a universal and unchanging aspect of human nature'.[57]

That the necessities for human welfare are universal and innate provides Kekes with a universal standard against which an agent's actions can be judged. Those actions that allow the essential conditions of human life to be fulfilled contribute to human welfare and so are morally good. Those that prevent the satisfaction of the conditions necessary for human welfare are simple harms, which, we are told, 'are caused by frustrating the needs and curtailing the exercise of the capacities [that] I have included in the description of human nature'.[58]

Kekes is aware that harm is part of everyday life. The contingency, indifference, and destructiveness of human life mean that each individual is subjected to suffering and harm on a daily basis. Harm morphs into evil if it is undeserved. Judgement about whether an action is deserved or not depends upon the presence of moral reasons for it.[59] For example, Kekes recognises the suffering of prisoners who are locked up to punish a crime they committed, but holds that that their suffering is deserved because of their past crime. Thus, 'if there are no moral reasons for [suffering], it is evil to deprive people of the opportunity to direct their lives, assess what they regard as important, develop their capacities, and do what they can to make good lives for themselves'.[60]

It is not clear, however, how this fits in with Kekes's claim that internal goods 'are satisfactions involved in living according to our conceptions of good lives'.[61] This appears to accept that each individual will have a different conception of the good life, meaning that there are multiple conceptions of what constitutes a good life, which seems to be in tension with the notion that to live a good life requires that individuals direct their lives, assess what is important, develop their capacities, and act to affirm the good life. What happens if there is a conception of the good life that does not affirm these activities, but individuals claim that it is a good life?

Presumably Kekes would fall back on his objectivity claim to explain that, despite an individual's assurances to the contrary, a conception of the good life is simply not good if it fails to meet the objective conditions of human welfare that Kekes identifies. Alternatively, he might argue that the requirements that individuals direct their lives, assess what is important, develop their capacities, and act to affirm the good are what reasonable people would agree to. What happens, however, when two 'reasonable' people disagree on this point or when two 'reasonable' individuals disagree on what it is to be able to direct their own lives, assess what is important, or develop their capacities?

Recognising this issue, Kekes distinguishes between 'simple and complex evil. *Simple evil* is to cause simple harm to people who do not deserve it. *Complex evil* derives from particular conceptions of good lives.'[62] The latter is 'historically, culturally, and individually variable, and . . . presuppose[s], but also go[es] beyond, the minimum requirements of human welfare'.[63] Given that he wants to provide a theory of evil that is objective and universal, the admission that the full notion of the good life, upon which his evaluation of evil depends, is culturally and historically specific causes his theory substantial problems. In response, Kekes states that he will simply bypass the problem of complex evil to 'concentrate on simple evil from now on'.[64] To do so, he proceeds 'from truisms about human nature to the moral presumption against causing simple evil'.[65] Returning to our simple, universal, natural needs will provide the criterion from and against which actions can be judged. Those that fulfil those innate needs are morally good; those that do not (and inflict undeserved harm) are evil.

Importantly, Kekes maintains that no judgement is required to determine whether a simple harm has occurred. The objectivity of perception and the simplicity of the act and harm caused, as well as of whether the suffering was deserved or not, mean that determining when simple harms are evil is obvious and easy. Three theses back up this position. The first, titled '*the objectivity of simple evil*',[66] insists that 'simple evil provides morality with some objective content'.[67] Because there are objective and universal conditions of human welfare and because 'morality is concerned, among other things, with minimising simple evil, there are some objectively true or false moral judgements'.[68] Kekes reaches this conclusion because he holds that whether an act satisfies or violates the conditions necessary for human welfare is an objective fact. As such, the moral worth of an action 'is independent of the moral attitudes of the person judging'.[69]

This leads to the second thesis: '*the irrelevance of choice to simple evil*'.[70] By this, Kekes means that the value of an action is independent of the intent behind it. This affirms a consequentialist, action-based approach, whereby the value of that action is defined by its consequences: 'the moral evaluation of simple evil depends not on its agents' being in the appropriate mental state but on the undeserved simple harm they cause'.[71] If an action caused simple harm that was undeserved, it is evil even if the agent committing it intended to help the one harmed. The first thesis – the objectivity of simple harm – ensures that the judgement about whether simple harm was caused and deserved or undeserved is objective and obvious.

The third thesis, called '*the reflexivity of simple evil*',[72] ties into Kekes's belief that evil is the consequence not of reflective choice, but of habits, which are manifested in and expressive of an individual's character. As a result, 'an action causing simple evil may be chosen or unchosen, characteristic or uncharacteristic, part of a pattern or an isolated episode'.[73] Remembering the second thesis, the intention behind an act is not important for the moral evaluation of that act; if an action causes simple harm, it is evil.

Complementing this, Kekes holds that the majority of actions are not thought out or reflective, but are spontaneously committed because the individual thinks that they are correct or acceptable. Given the objectivity of simple evil, the moral worth of those actions and habits can be determined. Once character traits are habitual, Kekes maintains that they can be understood to reveal the moral worth of the individual. When this occurs, he argues that we must go beyond claiming that the *act* is evil to accept that the *agent* committing it is: 'if vices achieve dominance in the character of moral agents, then it is proper to characterize such agents as, derivatively, evil'.[74] The conclusion reached is that there are evil individuals, and they are evil because they habitually commit acts that produce undeserved harms that prevent others from obtaining the general conditions necessary for human welfare. Having outlined the relationship between evil and harm, Kekes goes on to develop his analysis by engaging with the meaning and nature of desert.

## The Nature of Desert

The starting point for Kekes's analysis of desert is the claim that 'life should be such that moral merit receives the appropriate benefit and moral demerit results in the appropriate harm'.[75] Just desert is not based on the moral goodness of the cosmic order. As we have seen, Kekes explicitly rejects the notion that the natural world is a moral one. Rather, 'the essential feature of desert is that it is fitting, proper, or appropriate that individuals should receive their due. But it is also essential that the entitlement created by desert should be based on some characteristics or actions of the individuals to whom it is due.'[76]

An individual's character is then 'at least to some extent, formed',[77] meaning that it is due to a process of acculturation. This acculturation process depends upon the individual's innate characteristics and stops at a certain point of development, namely when he has internalised certain traits and developed a determinate character. The character developed strongly shapes his actions, but does not determine them: 'from the fact that people have at least some minimal moral concern, it does not follow that it prevents them from causing evil, for they may not act on the moral concern they have'.[78] Conversely, that some people have evil characters does not mean that they necessarily act in that manner; they may choose not to.

Despite admitting that an individual's character traits are not determinative of his actions, Kekes maintains that we should, nevertheless, judge an individual based on his habits. That he might fail to act in accordance with them does not and should not prevent us from describing an agent as evil. This is an integral part of Kekes's argument: moral worth is not determined by the choices that individuals make; it is determined by the extent to which their moral characters habitually affirm human welfare as this is revealed through their actions. An agent does not always act in accordance with the good or cause the undeserved harm of evil, but, on average, Kekes thinks that each tilts one way. This reveals the agent's dominant moral traits and so allows for a judgement about the moral worth of his character. As a consequence, an individual's character determines his desert.

Kekes suggests that action can cause either 'benefit or harm'.[79] If an individual has been a consistent proponent of moral welfare, Kekes thinks that this reveals a morally good character that should be rewarded. Attributes of a morally good character include 'some intelligence, the capacity for self-control, a mental equilibrium that makes it possible to pay attention to others, the absence of brutalising influences, and not being victimised by extreme poverty, discrimination, or exploitation'.[80] The benefits to be distributed are not just economic. Kekes has a more expansive understanding of desert 'that includes, in addition to material goods, many other kinds of goods, such as moral, political, psychological, and personal. The goods I regard as relevant to moral desert are the external and internal goods required by good lives.'[81]

In contrast, if an individual habitually causes harm that is considered to be undeserved, that individual must be censured for his negative character traits. Harm is 'undeserved if there is no morally acceptable justification for causing it'.[82] A morally justifiable harm would be one inflicted to punish an undeserved simple harm caused by an agent. As Kekes explains, 'harming evildoers is deserved harm, and so it is not evil'.[83] Given the objectivity of simple harm, there is no controversy regarding what does and does not count as undeserved harm. If 'reasonable people'[84] objectively look at the act and do not 'psychologise'[85] what they see, it will be easy for them to determine whether undeserved harm has occurred.

Despite Kekes's claim that identifying simple evils is an objective and simple exercise, he recognises that desert is far from objective and straightforward. The nature of desert is complex and not something that can be worked out *a priori*. It depends upon a myriad of causes, including biological, social, psychological, and moral judgements based on worth as this relates to the notion of 'good life' underpinning the society. Indeed, he admits that 'establishing proportionality between desert and merit is often impossibly difficult'.[86] If this is true, it is terminal for Kekes's theory because the practical judgement needed to determine if evil has occurred is not possible.

Kekes tries to resolve this problem by turning to the structure of the notion 'desert'. While recognising that it is heterogeneous, he claims that this plurality is underpinned by an objective, homogenous core meaning:

> There is no doubt that plurality is a pluralistic notion. But underlying the plurality, there is a unity established by the necessary concern of character-morality with promoting human welfare. Good actions contribute to it, and evil actions detract from it, but both reflect on the moral merits of their agents, and so they contribute both the basis and justification of claims about desert.[87]

The problem with this formulation, of course, is that it does not actually describe what desert entails. It provides a basis for delineating desert, but does not demonstrate how we are to judge the worth of an action.

Kekes's thinking on desert seems, then, to pull in two directions: the first affirms the objectivity of simple evil and maintains that determining an individual's desert is an objective judgement. The second recognises that desert is a complex and multi-dimensional concept that is far from being objective and universal. It is not clear how these two fit together, although one way would be to reaffirm his insistence that morality is a 'practical',[88] not theoretical, activity, so the determination of desert would lie in its practical application, not *a priori* determination.

Nevertheless, the claim that an agent's actions emanate from and reveal the moral worth of his character fits into and is re-enforced by Kekes's overall conclusion that morality refers to what an individual *is*, not what he *does*. Kekes holds that this is a radical departure from the understanding of morality and, by extension, evil that has dominated Western thinking. To show why, we need to turn to the distinction between choice-morality and character-morality.

## Evil as Choice

On Kekes's assessment, Western thought has been dominated by what he calls 'choice-morality'. This is defined by three conditions: (1) there is an emphasis on autonomous choice with regard to an individual's morality; (2) each human has a basic, innate worth; and (3) it is the intention behind an action, not the action itself, that determines whether the agent will be held morally responsible for it.[89] The key historical proponent of this form of morality was Kant. Indeed, for Kekes, 'Kant's *Religion within the Limits of Reason Alone* is the only work by a major philosopher devoted to a consideration of evil.'[90] As I have shown throughout this book, this statement is inaccurate, a point borne out by Kekes himself when he notes and takes issue with a number of other philosophers on evil. Nevertheless, it bolsters Kekes's privileging of Kant as a particularly important student of evil.

Aspects of Kant's treatment are met with approval: 'part of the strength of Kant's position is that it . . . recognises that there are people who habitually subordinate the moral law to self-love'.[91] However, Kekes charges that Kant does not go far enough, because he was unwilling to draw the conclusion that there exist moral monsters, in so far as a moral monster is someone who has 'become so corrupt as to extinguish in [himself] the predisposition to obey the moral law'.[92] Kant rejects this because he insists that the choice of good and evil is grounded in human noumenal freedom. It must, therefore, be possible for a moral agent to alter his fundamental moral maxim. As a consequence, there is no such thing as an absolutely and irretrievably evil moral monster. For Kekes, this ignores the connection between an agent's actions and his character. While they are rare, actions can be so monstrous that they point to monstrous characters.[93]

Kekes also criticises the metaphysical underpinnings of Kant's thinking on evil. Depending on a two-world interpretation, Kekes rejects Kant's account of noumenal freedom, calling it 'a castle in the air'[94] and 'a metaphysical fiction'.[95] In turn, he rejects Kant's claim that the individual can simply choose to alter his moral maxim, to suggest that once a set of habits have become entrenched, the individual cannot choose to alter them. Choice does not play a role in the formation of an individual's character. An agent's actions emanate from his character, which is developed not through choice, but through habits acquired from experience. This is one of the key differences between choice-morality and character-morality: 'in the first action is primary, and character, being formed by action, is secondary; in the second character is primary, and action, being a consequence of character, is secondary'.[96]

Kekes does, however, make contradictory statements about the relationship between choice and character. When discussing the formation of character, he takes a much more Kantian-inspired line, claiming that 'in the distant past, as their characters were being formed, they may or may not have had choices'.[97] This not only raises questions about when character-formation stops, but also seems to create and depend upon an absolute division between a pre-character period, when choice appears to be able to influence character, and a post-character-formation point, where choice is an effect of the character that emanated, in part, from choice.[98] Kekes also seems to take a Kantian line when he recommends that those with evil characters should simply question and change their outlooks 'to avoid the bad end to which they are likely to come as a result of their unreflective actions'.[99]

Despite being closer to Kant's position than his polemic would suggest, Kekes continues to distance himself from Kant in two ways. First, he suggests that 'Kant has not accounted for all the relevant facts'[100] about evil. The thesis driving this judgement derives from an appeal to 'common human experience',[101] which is understood to show that evil involves not a falling away from the good, but a positive action that affirms 'the vices of selfishness, greed, malice, envy or cruelty'.[102] Harm, for example, is not the absence of anything, but actually hurts. Furthermore, Kekes maintains that, for Kant, the human is fundamentally good, with evil resulting from a falling away from that original predisposition to the good. Kekes argues, however, that Kant has not justified his claim that human being has an original predisposition to the good. This is simply stated without being justified. Kekes suggests that other options are available, which feeds into his thesis that human being exists between good and evil, both of which have positive being.[103]

Second, Kekes criticises the notion of autonomy that underpins Kant's account of moral choice. He correctly points out that Kant understands that the will is associated with autonomy; it is this that allows the individual to choose. He questions, however, 'how it is possible for the will to be autonomous? How can it be a law to itself and escape the influence of causes outside of itself?'[104] To do so, he again relies upon common sense:

> ordinarily, we think that this power is influenced by many factors over which the choosing agents have no control, such as past experiences, the circumstances in which the choice has to be made, the likely consequences, the native abilities agents bring to their choices, the presence or absence of threats, bribes, temptations, and so on.[105]

To say that the will is autonomous is to hold that it chooses independently of these factors. Kekes explains that Kant gets round this by appealing to the noumenal/phenomenal distinction, so that 'freedom is possible because external influences belong to the world of appearances, while the law that the will is to itself belongs to another world, the world of things in themselves'.[106] Kekes objects, however, that Kant's *positing* of another world to account for this one offers not an explanation, but a postulation that must be based on trust or a willingness to simply follow Kant. It does not, therefore, live up to rational scrutiny.

Kekes also objects that even 'if we overlook the arbitrariness of Kant's postulation of freedom',[107] we find that it is inconsistent with his epistemology. Pointing out that Kant suggests that knowledge must be based on experience rather than on pure understanding or reason, Kekes concludes that since noumenal freedom can only be postulated from, and not explained by, experience, 'we must suppose that it is [one of the] "sheer illusion[s]"'[108] that Kant's critical philosophy rejects. Rather than account for our actions through recourse to another world, we must understand them in terms of 'the context of the only world we know and can know'.[109] Once we do so, we will realise that the autonomy that Kant depends upon does not exist. Choices are influenced by and made in accordance with the concrete, historical conditions within which the individual exists.

Kekes's objections are unlikely to convince a Kantian, mainly because Kekes seems content to ground his analysis in a number of empirical phenomena without explaining how those phenomena are possible. It, therefore, relies on a number of assumptions, such as appealing to common sense or ordinary thinking, the truth of which have not been demonstrated. Kekes recognises this and so claims that if we are not 'deterred by the arbitrariness and inconsistency of Kant's view, we have to contend with its extreme implausibility'.[110] Specifically, he suggests that Kant asks us to assume that the actions we perform are subject to the 'natural necessity operating in the world of appearances and that our choices to perform them are based on the law that the will is to itself in the world of things in themselves'.[111] Kekes asks 'how these sets of causes are related to each other'.[112] Kant maintains that there is an absolute division between the two realms and that the categories of the phenomenal are not applicable to the noumenal. How then can a noumenal occurrence, which as pure freedom is devoid of causality, causally impact on the phenomenal realm? Kekes finds no possible answer and so concludes that 'the only reason for accepting this incredible idea is that it is a consequence of Kant's argument'.[113] It has, in other words, no experiential force, but results from dogmatically accepting Kant's fallacious assumptions about the noumenal/phenomenal distinction. Given that 'Kant's analysis of freedom is untenable . . . his analysis of morality as the exercise of free will and of rationality as the free choice of the categorical imperative must be seen as equally flawed'.[114]

The conclusion drawn is that the metaphysical structures that Kant and, by extension, choice-morality grounds his/its understanding of freedom in are fundamentally unsound, fail to understand the embedded, habitual nature of moral choices, and so are unable to adequately face evil. To rectify these problems, Kekes outlines his alternative notion of character-morality, before describing what it means for evil. This leads to three conclusions: (1) individual morality is based on character, not choice; (2) evil actions are usually habitual rather than chosen; and, (3) because evil actions are signs that demonstrate the moral character of individuals, we must adopt a hard stance towards evil that holds individuals accountable for the harm caused regardless of the intent to do evil.

## Habits, Character, and Unchosen Evil

Up to this point, Kekes has implicitly relied upon his own account of character-morality when criticising alternative positions. The task now is to make *explicit* what was previously *implicit*. This leads him to outline the nine theses of character-morality.[115] Rather than go through each in turn, I will focus on providing an overview of the central argument of character-morality: morality refers to the character of agents, not just the actions they commit.

Kekes claims that each individual is born with a certain number of predispositions that, through various social interactions and individual actions, develop into character traits. Each individual's predispositions are different, as is each individual's place in society, the resources available to them, cultural requirements, and the social norms governing behaviour. 'The development of character is the long process of trying to find a fit between our predispositions and the available forms for translating them into action.'[116] This does not involve choice or reflection, but the spontaneous affirmation of the individual's predisposition to specific traits. If the traits that affirm human welfare become dominant, the individual develops a morally good character; if vices become dominant, he develops a morally evil one. Once developed, an individual's character is the framework through which he interacts with his world and understands himself. This creates a particular sensibility through which he lives. For this reason, the individual lives with a particular '*moral intuition*'[117] that requires 'no conscious reflection'.[118] After all, 'many of our morally relevant actions are the unexamined consequences of our characters, rather than the results of choices, and the choices themselves reflect the characters of the choosing agents'.[119]

Importantly, the acculturation process through which character is developed is based on mimesis. We copy what those around us do, how they think, and what they appreciate and devalue, and, in so doing, internalise it and identify with it:

> The moral lives of most people most of the time consist in the routine transactions of everyday life. Family, neighbourhood, work, hobbies, friends, colleagues, and acquaintances establish the context of our conduct. The rights and duties, the rewards and punishments, the supererogatory and backsliding actions, and the norms observed or deviated from are familiar to everybody through custom, habit, convention, and moral education.[120]

If we reflect the values of those around us, internalise and identify with them, the danger is that we end up unreflectively perpetuating them. Kekes writes of the case of the dogmatist who commits evil and explains that, while we may wonder why he did not critically reflect on the harm he is doing, the reality is that 'the need for critical examination is not felt, because the belief is unquestionably accepted by all'.[121] He returns to the case of Adolf Eichmann, who, on Arendt's telling, made exactly this point: 'the most potent factor in the soothing of his own conscience was the simple fact that he could see no one, no one at all, who actually was against the Final Solution'.[122] Both Kekes and Arendt are critical of this unreflective stance, but they appreciate that social pressure and the failure to experience contrary positions mean that it was very easy for individuals to simply do as others around them do. They become habituated to perpetuating the dominant norms.

That individual interactions are driven by habit, not reflective choice, has significant implications for the meaning and understanding of evil: it brings Kekes to claim that much evil is unchosen.[123] The notion of unchosen evil is nonsensical to choice-morality given its emphasis on reflective choice. How, then, can evil be unchosen?

Kekes's response rests on two premises: first, it is actions, not intentions or choice, that determine whether an action is evil. If an action causes harm and that harm is undeserved, then, regardless of the intention or reflection of the agent behind it, that agent is to be held responsible for it. Second, there is a distinction between choice, which is associated with reflection, and habit, which is associated with non-reflection. Having rejected the basic assumptions of psychoanalytic theory, Kekes dismisses the notion that an individual can unconsciously choose. Instead, he operates with an implicit binary opposition between reflective choice and unreflective (unchosen) habit. Claiming that human action is normally habitual, Kekes concludes that 'much evil is caused by unchosen actions . . . [so if] morality is to be faithful to its concern, it must attend to unchosen evil'.[124]

Unchosen evil is, on Kekes's telling, far more prevalent than we typically realise. It does not just emanate from individuals with morally evil characters acting spontaneously and so causing others undeserved simple harm. It is also a consequence of the essential conditions of life: contingency, indifference, destructiveness.[125] There is no escaping these essential conditions, with the consequence that human being is frequently subject to suffering and harm that it has not chosen. If this harm is undeserved, then evil occurs. Similarly, that the natural order is not a moral one means that individuals who have good character may not receive the desert their action entitles them to. For example, Kekes points out that evil can result from the scarcity of resources.[126] These are not just material, but also emotional, psychological, and social. The distribution of resources in the natural world may ensure that individuals simply do not have the required resources to allow them to obtain the internal and external goods necessary for their human welfare. Assuming that the harm that results is undeserved, agents suffer evil without that evil being caused by another agent.

## Facing Evil

If evil is so widespread, is often unchosen, and, indeed, results from the essential conditions of life and nature itself, what can be done about it? The tragic view of life that Kekes initially depends upon ultimately falls into despair. For this reason, he advocates a modification of it that accepts that evil is part of existence, but insists that agents must work to alleviate the conditions that cause it. There are three aspects to this: first, Kekes adopts the hard reaction to evil: 'moral agents [are to be held] accountable for their vices, even if they are not chosen'.[127] With regard to why we should adopt this perspective, Kekes explains that 'the justification of the hard reaction is that it is the most reasonable way of coping with evil'.[128]

Second, he maintains that we have to re-orientate our understanding of the good–evil relationship away from one that views evil as a temporary occurrence to be overcome by the former. The essential conditions of life and the non-morality of the natural order mean that evil, in the form of undeserved harm, is an inherent and inescapable part of life.[129]

Despite claiming that choice is an effect of character, Kekes's third solution to the problem of evil is that individuals should alter their behaviour so that they do not habitually do evil actions. He does, however, recognise that this causes an issue: 'If what [individuals] do is often influenced by forces beyond their control, whether forces for the good, such as morality ought to be, or forces for the evil, such as the essential conditions of life tend to be, then the very attempt to reflect critically on these forces is itself subject to their control.'[130] His solution is to fall back on the line of thought developed by Arendt and Castoriadis, but rooted in Augustine: while character *tends* to *shape* an individual's response to events, it does not *determine* it. The individual is always sufficiently autonomous to choose his action.

It is not clear, however, that this is consistent with the central tenet of character-morality: character determines the moral worth of actions, meaning that we must adopt a hard reaction to evil and judge the moral worth of agents rather than just their acts. This only seems to follow if there is a strict causal connection between an agent's dominant character traits and his actions. If, however, an agent can choose his actions to mitigate the evil that may result from his character, this not only indicates that choice precedes character, but also cuts the determinate causal link between character and action that underpins Kekes's justification for the hard reaction to evil.

Despite this, Kekes explains that we also need to change institutions so that they become more scientific. This is because 'science is our greatest achievement. It has done a very great deal to enlarge the area of our control.'[131] By engaging with the natural world scientifically, we will be better able to understand it, control it, and so mitigate the harms that result from the essential conditions of life.

Kekes complements this institutional-cultural focus with a personal one: individuals need to develop a particular mindset based on the cultivation of a 'reflective temper'.[132] This requires: (1) '*an enlarged understanding of the essential conditions of life*',[133] meaning the acceptance and recognition of how 'contingency, indifference, and destructiveness jeopardise human aspirations in general';[134] (2) '*a particular kind of reflection*',[135] the aim of which is to 'modify our psychological states and thereby control the actions that follow from them';[136] (3) '*the motivation to increase control over ourselves*',[137] wherein we try to increase control of our lives while recognising and accepting that we cannot control everything; and (4) '*the capacity to restrain our emotional reactions*',[138] so that 'we shall not be led by them to falsify our situation and thus ... respond to it inappropriately'.[139] By advocating the cultivation of a rational, reflective, and controlled approach to evil, Kekes argues that the spontaneous, habitual actions of character-morality should be replaced by a response informed by the reflective, rational, non-emotional actions and behaviours that underpin choice-morality. This will not abolish evil, but will change our approach to it.

## Concluding Remarks

Kekes offers a novel approach to morality generally and the problem of evil specifically that challenges many of the assumptions upon which Western thinking on these topics has historically been based. His explicitly secular account rejects the notion that God grounds moral choice, to base moral worth and hence guilt on individual action. But, by insisting that some individuals are more morally worthy than others, he offers an account of morality that asks us to judge individuals, not just their actions, and, in so doing, concludes that there are evil individuals.

Furthermore, by arguing that it is habits, not choices, that determine moral action and, by extension, worth, he makes individuals morally responsible for *all* their actions, not just the ones they reflectively choose. But no sooner has he rejected the Augustinian notion that moral action is based on autonomous choice than he implicitly returns to Augustine to outline how we must choose to face evil. Basing his conclusions and arguments on what he takes to be definitive, ahistoric, universal meanings, and an axiomatic definition further ties Kekes to the Judaeo-Christian tradition by virtue of demonstrating that his 'secular'[140] thinking on the topic is grounded in the same foundational logic as that which grounds theological analyses. The difference, of course, is that he calls this ground 'habit', rather than God, but the *logic* continues to depend upon a singular, foundational source. In so doing, and despite his rejection of psychoanalytical approaches, Kekes affirms Lacan's point that supposedly secular analyses always implicitly presume an ordering point of reference and so take over and continue to depend upon the foundational logic of the theological tradition.

Nonetheless, grounding his analysis in axiomatic definitions allows Kekes to offer an evaluative schema from and against which moral actions can be compared to determine their moral worth. In so doing, he brings a specificity to the topic that is missing from the socio-historical and symbolic-imaginary accounts previously engaged with. This does, however, mean that the validity of his approach relies upon the reader being willing to accept the assumptions that drive his argument. In particular, his dependence on 'objectivity', 'facts', and 'absolute, ahistoric standards', simply ignores the critique of these terms found in much of the last hundred or so years of philosophical inquiry. By justifying this through recourse to common sense or what 'reasonable' people would think, Kekes severely downplays the socio-historical-symbolic processes that construct meaning. He also rejects the idea that what is considered 'reasonable' is itself a construction that differs significantly from populace to populace, culture to culture, and historical period to historical period.

Perhaps the biggest issue that arises from Kekes's approach is the conclusion that he derives from his action-based account. Having defined evil in terms of actions that cause undeserved harm, Kekes draws conclusions about the moral worth of the *perpetrators* of those actions. However, if evil entails causing or suffering undeserved harm, should we not focus on the victims of that action? It is, after all, only if there is a victim that suffers undeserved harm that Kekes can claim that his suffering is a consequence of evil perpetrators. For this reason, Claudia Card rejected Kekes's perpetrator-based approach to suggest that we must never forget and, indeed, can only ever understand evil by focusing on its victims.

## Notes

1. John Kekes, *Facing Evil* (Princeton: Princeton University Press, 1990).
2. John Kekes, *The Roots of Evil* (Ithaca: Cornell University Press, 2005), p. xii.
3. Kekes, *Facing Evil*, p. 3.
4. Ibid. p. 7.
5. Ibid. p. 6.
6. Ibid. p. 11.
7. Ibid. p. 8.
8. Ibid. p. 22.
9. Ibid. p. 86, n. 2.
10. Ibid. p. 27.
11. Ibid. p. 46.
12. Ibid. p. 116.
13. 'These commonplace facts and others like them form a universal and unchanging aspect of human nature' (ibid. p. 52).
14. For example, he explains that 'evil is undeserved harm, and some occurrences of it are as hard, factual, observable, and empirical as other items in the furniture of the world' (ibid. p. 50), a position that supports his later claim that 'whether moral truths about simple harm are true or false . . . is independent of the mental states of the agent whose action is being judged' (ibid. p. 54).
15. Ibid. p. 45.
16. Ibid. pp. 9, 29, 167, 215, 224.
17. Ibid. p. 50.
18. Ibid. p. 126.
19. Ibid. p. 195.
20. Ibid. p. 9.

21. Ibid. p. 56.
22. Ibid. p. 56.
23. Ibid. p. 13.
24. Ibid. p. 13.
25. Ibid. p. 13.
26. Ibid. p. 15.
27. Ibid. p. 15.
28. Ibid. p. 26.
29. Ibid. p. 23.
30. Ibid. p. 23.
31. Ibid. p. 23.
32. Ibid. p. 24.
33. Ibid. p. 24.
34. Ibid. p. 24.
35. Ibid. p. 24.
36. Ibid. p. 24.
37. Ibid. p. 25.
38. Ibid. p. 25.
39. Ibid. p. 3.
40. Ibid. p. 4 (italics added).
41. In *The Roots of Evil*, Kekes praises Arendt's analysis of evil in *Eichmann in Jerusalem*, explaining that 'there are reasons against accepting her explanation, but of all the ones I have so far discussed, hers comes closest, in my opinion, to being right' (Kekes, *The Roots of Evil*, p. 176).
42. Kekes, *Facing Evil*, p. 6.
43. Ibid. p. 29.
44. Ibid. p. 51.
45. Ibid. p. 51.
46. Ibid. p. 51.
47. Ibid. p. 51.
48. Ibid. p. 51.
49. Ibid. p. 51.
50. Ibid. p. 51.
51. Ibid. p. 51.
52. Ibid. p. 51.
53. Ibid. p. 51.
54. Ibid. p. 51.
55. Scholarship on the two-world versus the two-aspect interpretation of Kant is enormous. For a defence of the former, see P. F. Strawson, *The Bounds of Sense: An Essay on Kant's Critique of Pure Reason* (Abingdon: Routledge, 1975); and of the latter, see Henry Allison, *Transcendental Idealism: An Interpretation and Defence* (New Haven: Yale University Press, 2004). For a compatibilist account, see Michael Oberst, 'Two Worlds *and* Two Aspects: on Kant's

Distinction between Things in Themselves and Appearances', *Kantian-Review*, 20:1, 2015, pp. 53–75.
56. Kekes, *Facing Evil*, p. 27.
57. Ibid. p. 52.
58. Ibid. p. 53.
59. Ibid. p. 53.
60. Ibid. p. 53.
61. Ibid. p. 13.
62. Ibid. p. 53.
63. Ibid. p. 53.
64. Ibid. p. 53.
65. Ibid. p. 53.
66. Ibid. p. 53.
67. Ibid. p. 53.
68. Ibid. pp. 53–4.
69. Ibid. p. 54.
70. Ibid. p. 54.
71. Ibid. p. 54.
72. Ibid. p. 55.
73. Ibid. p. 55.
74. Ibid. p. 55.
75. Ibid. p. 57.
76. Ibid. p. 57.
77. Ibid. p. 7.
78. Ibid. p. 60.
79. Ibid. p. 57.
80. Ibid. p. 115.
81. Ibid. p. 61.
82. Ibid. p. 65.
83. Ibid. p. 63.
84. Ibid. p. 167.
85. Ibid. pp. 230–1.
86. Ibid. p. 153.
87. Ibid. p. 62.
88. Ibid. p. 50.
89. Ibid. p. 88.
90. Ibid. p. 124.
91. Ibid. p. 131.
92. Ibid. p. 132.
93. Ibid. p. 6.
94. Ibid. p. 138.
95. Ibid. p. 138.
96. Ibid. p. 92.

97. Ibid. p. 7.
98. In a later text, Kekes side-steps the question about when character-formation stops, which would clarify who is the agent that informs his analysis, by limiting the discussion to 'normal human adults' ('The Reflexivity of Evil', *Social Philosophy and Policy*, 15:1, 1998, pp. 216–32 [p. 218]). This does not, however, resolve the problem, for it does not clarify when adulthood begins, and it continues to depend upon a binary opposition between a character-forming childhood constituted by limited choices and a determined, character-formed adulthood.
99. Kekes, *Facing Evil*, p. 181.
100. Ibid. p. 129.
101. Ibid. p. 126.
102. Ibid. p. 126.
103. Kekes is correct to point out that Kant never accounts for his claim that human being has an original predisposition (*Anlage*) to the good. As we saw in Chapter 6, however, Kant's insistence that human being as a species is predisposed to the good does not mean that the individual is initially good. The Kantian individual is caught between the predisposition (*Anlage*) to the good and the propensity (*Hang*) to evil constitutive of the human species. He must choose which to follow, with this choice determining his moral disposition (*Gesinnung*). A Kantian response might then be to suggest that the choice of evil is not a negative action, in the sense that the individual denies what he initially is, but is a positive choice between two competing options available to him from his membership of the human species.
104. Ibid. p. 138.
105. Ibid. p. 138.
106. Ibid. p. 138.
107. Ibid. p. 139.
108. Ibid. p. 139.
109. Ibid. p. 140.
110. Ibid. p. 139.
111. Ibid. p. 139.
112. Ibid. p. 139.
113. Ibid. p. 140.
114. Ibid. p. 140.
115. These are (1) the objectivity of simple evil, (2) the irrelevance of choice to simple evil, (3) the reflexivity of simple evil, (4) the importance of character to moral judgement, (5) the unavoidability of moral agency, (6) the significance of moral achievement, (7) the centrality of moral desert, (8) the dependence of moral desert on moral merit, and (9) the mixed view of human nature (ibid. pp. 155–6).
116. Ibid. p. 104.
117. Ibid. p. 167.

118. Ibid. p. 167.
119. Ibid. p. 224.
120. Ibid. p. 104.
121. Ibid. p. 87.
122. Hannah Arendt, *Eichmann in Jerusalem: A Report on the Banality of Evil* (London: Penguin, 2006), p. 116.
123. Kekes, *Facing Evil*, p. 124.
124. Ibid. p. 124.
125. Ibid. p. 146.
126. Ibid. pp. 151–2.
127. Ibid. pp. 161–2.
128. Ibid. p. 162.
129. Ibid. p. 225.
130. Ibid. p. 181.
131. Ibid. p. 188.
132. Ibid. p. 221.
133. Ibid. p. 221.
134. Ibid. p. 222.
135. Ibid. p. 222.
136. Ibid. p. 222.
137. Ibid. p. 222.
138. Ibid. p. 222.
139. Ibid. p. 222.
140. Ibid. pp. 4, 44.

# 13

# Remembering the Victims

The start of the new millennium sparked renewed and significant interest in the question of evil.[1] One of the key debates pitted 'evil sceptics' – who, as the name suggests, were sceptical that we should retain the concept 'evil', instead claiming that, given the historical difficulties in identifying what precisely it entails, we would be better served by focusing on other (negative) moral concepts – against 'evil revivalists', who not only insisted that we should continue with the term but affirmed that this required new, more substantial engagements with the notion.[2] Given that the former argue that the concept 'evil' should be abandoned, I will focus on the latter to show how thinking on evil developed at the start of the twenty-first century. In particular, I will engage with Claudia Card's attempt – one of the most influential and widely discussed analyses of recent times – to outline an atrocity paradigm, first in *The Atrocity Paradigm* (published in 2002) and subsequently in *Confronting Evils* (published in 2012).[3]

Card explicitly rejects the psychoanalytical/symbolic approach derived from Nietzsche that asks 'what inclines people to make judgements of evil in the first place, what functions such judgements have served',[4] and instead 'presupposes that there are defensible norms of right and wrong'.[5] This allows her to claim that certain actions are objectively evil regardless of the perception of agents. From this foundation, *The Atrocity Paradigm* aims to 'articulate an ethical analysis of what makes deeds, people, relationships, practices, intentions, and motives evil and use that to begin a more general pursuit of ethical questions regarding what to do about evils and how best to live with them'.[6] This aspires not to provide 'a comprehensive theory of ethics',[7] but 'to articulate a conception of evil that captures the ethically most significant, most serious publicly known evils of [her] lifetime'.[8] Importantly, she explicitly emphasises that her analysis of evil should be regarded 'as a conception of evil, not the only conception'.[9] It does not aim to settle the debate once and for all, but offers the far more modest goal of 'rehabilitat[ing] the concept of evil in the face of widespread scepticism, especially among intellectuals, given the ongoing history of political abuses of the label "evil"'.[10]

To do so, she takes over many of the methodological assumptions informing Kekes's thinking: the outlook of the 'ordinary-language tradition of analytical philosophy',[11] appeals to dictionary definitions,[12] 'common sense',[13] 'folk-wisdom',[14] and what 'normal adults'[15] would do and think. From this, she claims to offer a 'secular'[16] analysis that starts 'with a simple abstract definition, not expected to be controversial, which is developed by amplifying its basic concepts, and placing the theory in relation to others influential in the history of moral philosophy, and considering some case studies'.[17] We are initially told, therefore, that 'evils are foreseeable intolerable harms produced by culpable wrongdoing'.[18] By emphasising the intolerable harm caused by evil actions, Card insists that evil must be judged from the perspective of the victim, not the perpetrator, although she does note that the latter's culpable wrongdoing must also be taken into account. In this respect, she offers a corrective to Kekes's perpetrator account of evil.

To defend this, *The Atrocity Paradigm* first clarifies the analytical definition of evil, before justifying it through an engagement with key historical moral theories, such as Stoicism, Utilitarianism, Nietzsche's genealogical analysis, and Kant's moral thought, and a number of concrete events, including rape in war, domestic abuse or gender violence, and the *Sonderkommando* of the Nazi concentration camps.

Card therefore covers much ground, all of which is premised on the validity of the axiomatic definition guiding the analysis. That definition proved to be more controversial than she anticipated, with the consequence that she came to realise that it needed to be revised. In *Confronting Evils*, these alterations take three forms: '(1) that evils are *inexcusable*, not just culpable, (2) that evils need not be extraordinary (probably most are not), and (3) that not all institutional evil implies individual culpability'.[19] This alters the definition guiding the analysis from 'evils are foreseeable intolerable harms produced by culpable wrongdoing'[20] to 'evils are reasonably foreseeable intolerable harms produced by *inexcusable* wrongs'.[21] Starting from this revised foundation, Card significantly develops the analytic of its various parts to clarify the meaning of 'reasonably foreseeable', 'intolerable', 'harm', 'inexcusable', and 'wrong', including the relationship between evils and lesser wrongs. She also emphasises that her analysis of atrocities is not meant to imply that evil is reducible to those horrors. She studies those atrocities to identify the main features of evil, to show how it is manifested in everyday deeds and actions such as 'domestic violence, prison rape, and other forms of terrorism and torture suffered daily by people whose names most of us will never know (although each of us probably knows some), and of the torture of animals'.[22]

Following Arendt's claim that evil is far more everyday and banal than has historically been appreciated, Card rejects three dominant myths about evil: (1) 'evil-doers are monstrous and cannot be reasoned with';[23] (2) 'the Manichean fantasy that humanity can be divided into good . . . and the evil';[24] and (3) 'the idea that evil is a metaphysical power or force that possesses some individuals'.[25] Agents are not simply faced with a binary opposition of good or evil. Morality is far more complex than this binary opposition implies. This is developed through a critical engagement with Kant's rigorism, which holds that individuals can only ever be good or evil. Pointing to a third option, between good and evil, Card develops Primo Levi's notion of 'grey zones',[26] which are extremely stressful spaces or relationships wherein victims become perpetrators of evil against other victims. This brings her analysis into the socio-political realm, which, by linking grey zones to diabolical evil, leads her to defend a form of absolute evil that Kant rejected.

## Evil from Atrocities

For Card, 'evil' is the most serious ethical judgement possible. It is also a judgment that is 'cross-cultural and transhistorical, if not global'.[27] That it is serious, denoting behaviour or actions that are judged to be the worst of the worst, and exists in multiple cultures and histories indicates, for Card, that 'evil' is an important aspect of human being. This brings forth further questions such as: why do we use the term 'evil' and not 'wrong' or 'severely wrong'? At what point do actions become evil from being merely bad? And what actions or traits delineate evil from wrong? These motivate Card's analysis and support her statement that 'we need a theoretical account of what makes wrongdoing serious enough to count as evil or in what ways it is serious'.[28]

Generally speaking, evil is held to be 'what anyone can be presumed to want to avoid and what no one should have to suffer'.[29] Card will, however, substantially refine this. To do so, she identifies particular actions or events that capture 'the ethically most significant, most serious publicly known evils of [her] lifetime'.[30] These include

> the Holocaust, the bombings of Hiroshima, Nagasaki, Tokyo, Hamburg, and Dresden; the internment of Japanese Americans and Japanese

Canadians during World War II; the My Lai massacre; the Tuskegee syphilis experiments; genocides in Rwanda; Burundi, and East Timor; the killing fields of Cambodia; the rape/death camps of the former Yugoslavia; and the threat to life on our planet posed by environmental poisoning, global warming, and the destruction of rain forests and other natural habitats.[31]

There is no discussion or analysis of what makes an event an atrocity because Card takes these events to be 'uncontroversially evil'.[32] She also claims that they have been relatively neglected and that 'they deserve priority of attention (more than philosophers have given them so far)'.[33] This is not just a matter of correcting the historical record, but has analytical importance because 'the core features of evils tend to be writ large in the case of atrocities, making them easier to identify and appreciate'.[34]

Card rejects the religious narrative that sees evils as being the fault of a cosmic battle between the forces of good and those of evil. If evil was the consequence of demonic forces, it could not 'be reasoned with or understood'.[35] Nor, given that 'demons are monolithic, malevolent through and through',[36] could they and hence evil ever be changed. Indeed, blaming 'inhuman'[37] forces for evil abrogates the responsibilities that individual human agents have for atrocities. Atrocities are perpetrated not by cosmic forces but 'by agents who have epistemological limitations and emotional attachments. They are ambivalent, deluded, changeable, fickle.'[38] Evil always 'wears a human face'.[39]

That evil is intimately connected to human agents means that natural events are not atrocities; they are catastrophes.[40] A catastrophe is an unfortunate event for which no one is responsible. In contrast, 'there is no such thing as an atrocity that just happens or an atrocity that hurts no one'.[41] Card does, however, warn against thinking of evil in terms of a binary opposition between natural disasters that lack agency and agent-caused atrocities. After all, 'human failure to respond can turn a natural catastrophe into an atrocity. Much of the involvement of human agency in atrocities is a matter of aggravating the suffering brought about by nonhuman causes or tolerating it unnecessarily.'[42] She does not discuss this further, but, for Card, atrocities are a consequence of either human action aimed at inflicting evil on others or inaction on the part of human agents to mitigate the horrors that result from natural catastrophes.

## Analysing Evil

Card initially defines evil as 'foreseeable intolerable harms produced by culpable wrongdoing',[43] before altering this in *Confronting Evils* to 'evils are reasonably foreseeable intolerable harms produced by *inexcusable* wrongs'.[44] This revision 'preserves and clarifies culpability in the evil deeds of individuals, and ... allows an improved account of evil in institutions'.[45] She accepts that evils can happen to non-humans and, indeed, in *Confronting Evils* discusses this,[46] but focuses primarily on human victims and exclusively on human perpetrators.[47]

There are, at least, three questionable aspects to this definition, referring to the meanings of 'reasonably foreseeable', 'intolerable harms', and 'inexcusable'. To start to resolve these controversies, Card situates her atrocity paradigm within the history of moral theory, first claiming that it resides between Stoicism and modern Utilitarianism, before subsequently replacing the latter with Epicureanism.[48] Stoicism 'takes evil to reside solely in wrongful intentions',[49] whereas Epicureanism 'takes it to reside solely in the experience of harm'.[50] For Card, each is too one-sided: 'evils, on my view, have both a Stoic and an Epicurean component, neither reducible to the other'.[51] The intention of the perpetrator is an important factor in determining the type of evil committed, while the harm caused by an action is key to determining whether an action is intolerable and so evil.

These do not have equal standing. Rather, Card 'encourages a focus first on suffering. Harm is what is most salient about atrocities.'[52] Victims have tended to be ignored in historical discussions of evil. By focusing on them, Card aims to correct this and introduce a new perspective from which to understand evil. This feeds into and supports the atrocity paradigm's attempt 'to broaden our theoretical interests ... by giving victims' perspectives more of their due [to consider] how perpetrators might respond to what they have done and to the continuing needs of victims'.[53]

This is different from Kekes's perpetrator-based account, which holds that an action is evil based on the harm it causes and that such action permits a judgement about the *perpetrator's character*. One way of judging this is to identify the harm caused to the victim as it is described by its victim, and from this work back to the perpetrator. Card rejects this approach, claiming that victims are frequently unable to accurately identify the motives of the perpetrator. Appealing to psychologist Roy F. Baumeister's notion of 'the magnitude gap',[54] which explains that victims and perpetrators distort what happens in different ways and so come to different conclusions about the event that joins them, she 'conjecture[s] ... that perpetrators are likely to underestimate the harm, whereas victims are likely to exaggerate the responsibility of the perpetrators' motives'.[55] Because victims' testimonies tend to exaggerate the harm caused by an action and fail to correctly identify the motives of the perpetrators of the act, they cannot be relied upon to accurately describe the intentions and moral worth of perpetrators.

The problem is not simply a matter of judgement. Card goes further by maintaining that there is no strict causal connection between the harm that a victim identifies that an action has caused and the moral worth of the perpetrator's character. Kekes admits this, affirming that the harm caused by an action does not definitively reveal the moral worth of the perpetrator's character. An agent could, for example, always choose to act against the habits constitutive of his character. Nevertheless, Kekes argues that the connection *tends* to hold and insists that this is sufficient to use the harm caused by a perpetrator's act to judge the moral worth of the perpetrator's character. Card, however, objects that 'evil people need not be evildoers (intentions may fail) and that evildoers need not be evil people (evil intentions or gross oversights may be anomalous)'.[56]

This depends upon a distinction between intentions and motives: the former describes 'a choice to act'[57] whereas 'a motive (such as compassionate or sadistic desire) [is] not a choice but ... a basis for possible choices'.[58] Motives provide the inclination for a choice, but need to be actually affirmed through intentions. Because they *tend* to outline the responses that will be given in each situation, motives appear to be associated with what Kekes calls character. They do not, however, *determine* action. 'Under moderately favourable circumstances, we can resist an inclination, feel the attraction of a possible choice without forming the intention to act on it.'[59] For this reason, an agent's act may not necessarily reflect his underlying motives and, by extension, character.

Card also dismisses the idea that some are born evil: 'we are not all potentially evil simply because we are human beings, although many of us might acquire that potentiality under circumstances we would not choose'.[60] By 'potentially evil', she means 'more than the mere [logical] possibility of becoming evil and more than the mere capacity to experience the attraction of evil incentives or even to form evil intentions'.[61] Even if an individual develops this potentiality for evil, it is not a consequence of unreflective habit or action. It results from having 'something real (a persistent desire, habits of gross inattention) in one's character, in virtue of which one's evildoing would be no accident'.[62] If the potential for evil exists, it is a direct consequence of human action, which presumably means reflective or explicit action that can be tied to an agent. It is the action, not the individual, that is key to understanding evil and, crucially, it is from the victim's perspective that we should start.

Card also points out that 'the atrocity paradigm does not focus on victims' deserts or innocence'.[63] In relation to the former, she sets her theory against 'the classical treatment of the theological problem of evil'[64] in which God punishes, typically with natural evils, those who committed moral evils. In so doing, she further distances her thought from Kekes's perpetrator approach, which posits that desert is an important factor in determining moral worth; some individuals are more worthy than others by virtue of their past deeds.[65] Given that Kekes focuses on the perpetrators of evil, he tends not to discuss the situation of victims. His argument would, however, seem to indicate that some victims are worthy of suffering evil. In contrast, Card works with 'the presumption . . . that no one should have to suffer atrocities, regardless of individual character or deserts'.[66] Regardless of what they have previously done, all victims of evil have equal worth in that they all suffered evils and should be respected as such.

This ties in to Card's rejection of the notion that 'innocence' should play a role in moral judgement: 'innocence is neither necessary nor sufficient for suffering to count as evil'.[67] It is not necessary because whether a perpetrator's action entails inexcusable wrongdoing is not dependent on the innocence of the victim. An action is excusable or inexcusable based on its morality; that is, whether it is good or not. The victim's worth does not enter into the equation. Innocence is also not sufficient for an action to count as evil because 'the suffering may not be intolerable'.[68] For Card, not all suffering is evil; only *intolerable* suffering is. That a perpetrator's action causes suffering is not sufficient to judge that action 'evil'. While 'there are special evils in harming the innocent, who are commonly defenceless and naïve . . . there is no general presumption of innocence among atrocity victims, who may include habitual criminals, as they commonly do in the case of genocide'.[69] The atrocity paradigm defines an *action* as evil. This judgement neither depends upon nor incorporates the moral worth of the victims.

Card recognises that there is a potential problem with focusing on the victims of evil, namely that many survivors of evil 'avoid the term "victim" because of its suggestion of passivity and embrace the term "survivor" instead'.[70] She explains that out of respect 'for victims who do not survive . . . I prefer to emphasise that victims are also, often, capable of agency'.[71] With this, Card reminds us that not all victims of evil are physically annihilated. Some are, of course, and the many atrocities she mentions are proof of that, but her point is that evil is not synonymous with death or physical annihilation. Some, if not most, victims continue to live after suffering evil and frequently do so through tremendous resilience and powers of recuperation.

Claiming that victims are capable of agency also feeds into Card's attempt to bring to our attention the blurred line between victims and perpetrators. Working against the logic that pits an aggressive perpetrator against a passive victim, Card points out that this binary opposition is too simplistic: 'the terms "victims" and "perpetrators" mislead . . . if they suggest that individuals are simply one or the other, if either. For it is not unusual for victims of evils (perhaps as a result) to perpetrate others.'[72] Especially in social evils, such as atrocities, there is no straightforward, clear-cut line dividing victims and perpetrators. This is one of the reasons why atrocities are suitable means for the study of evils. They call into question long-standing assumptions about evil as a conceptual category and the actual practices and actions constitutive of evils. That victims can also be perpetrators of evil is an important insight that underpins Card's later analysis of grey zones.

Before getting to that, it is necessary to further engage with Card's claim that 'evils are reasonably foreseeable intolerable harms produced by *inexcusable* wrongs'.[73] That the meaning of evil depends upon a number of components reveals that it is a higher order concept that 'presuppose[s] other, more basic'[74] concepts. The complexity of higher order concepts gives rise to multiple conceptions of evil, which explains why, historically speaking, there have been so many conceptions of it. She notes, however, that evil is different from, but intimately linked to, wrongdoing. Distinguishing evil from wrongs offers an important conceptual contribution to the literature on the topic, which has traditionally tended to conflate them.[75] One of the main purposes of Card's atrocity paradigm is to stop this conflation of bad or wrong with evil by identifying the differences between them. In this, she takes her lead from common sense, which reserves the term 'evil' 'for the worst wrongs, those that we think no one should have to suffer. Genocide is an evil. Premeditated murder is an evil. Petty theft and tax evasion is not.'[76] What then marks the difference between evil and other wrongs?

In response, Card engages with the main aspects of the definition of evils as 'reasonably foreseeable intolerable harms produced by *inexcusable* wrongs'[77] to determine what 'reasonably foreseeable' means, what counts as an intolerable harm, and what makes a wrong inexcusable. In turn, defining what is 'reasonably foreseeable' requires responses to questions including: what is 'reasonable?' Is it possible to foresee the consequences of an action? And who makes this judgement?

Card tackles these issues most fully in *Confronting Evils* by distinguishing between what is 'reasonably foreseeable' from the perspective of individuals and from that of institutions or social practices. In relation to the former, she explains that 'from the perspective of the doer . . . "reasonably foreseeable" means "would be foreseen if that agent were to exercise reasonable care"'.[78] There are two obvious problems with this definition: first, how do we know that the doer is actually describing a state of ignorance? And how can we know what the perpetrator understood or foresaw at the time of the act? Second, both the definitions of 'foreseeable' and 'care' depend upon a notion of 'reasonable'. This is never discussed, nor is the perspective that is to be used to identify what is reasonable outlined: is it from the perspective of the perpetrator, the victim, and/or some other third party?

This is compounded for institutions or social practices. Within these, 'agents stand in many relationships to practice',[79] meaning that it is not possible to identify who within an institution knew what was happening in that institution, let alone what could be reasonably foreseen given the complexity involved. For this reason, Card suggests that 'perhaps it is not necessary to specify a position from which the harm is foreseeable. It may suffice to say that a morally indefensible rule or practice or institution is evil if *anyone* can reasonably foresee its intolerably harmful consequences.'[80]

This, however, seems to assume that others can identify the position of the perpetrator, including what he knew at the time. It also assumes that the judgement of others can accurately assess the position and knowledge of the perpetrator at the time of the act. This risks imposing an understanding on the perpetrator, especially given what Card subsequently calls 'the problem of relevant act-descriptions'.[81] As the name suggests, this points out that 'an act can be described in a multitude of ways'.[82] The danger is that the individual judging the act describes not the actual situation of the perpetrator, but what the one judging thinks the perpetrator should have known.

This is compounded by Card's claim that we can extend that idea over time, so that we are able to say 'that a practice was an evil even at times when no one *then* could foresee or appreciate the harm that it does, if others at later times can appreciate that it does intolerable harm for which there is no moral excuse'.[83] However, if there are problems with identifying what our immediate others could foresee, how can we know what others from history could? The risk is that we attribute culpability to them from our own perspective rather than from what could be expected then. One way to get round this problem is to insist on what they could 'reasonably foresee', but this brings us back to the issue of what 'reasonable' means; an issue never discussed by Card.

'Harm' is defined by the act, not the intention or will of the perpetrators. Evil can occur from an action even if the perpetrator did not mean it to have those consequences. In this instance, the culpability of the perpetrator would depend on whether he could have reasonably foreseen that those consequences would have arisen from his actions, whether the harm caused was intolerable, and whether he had a valid moral excuse that mitigated his responsibility. A harm is intolerable if it leads to 'setbacks [that] are irreversible, incompensable, and cannot be survived at a decent level of well-being'.[84] This gives rise to two different, but related, issues: (1) who decides the nature of the setback or indeed that one has occurred, and (2) what counts as a 'decent' level of well-being.

Card's response is that the nature of the setback must be decided from the perspective of the victims. But this 'is not an entirely subjective matter, even if what is worth tolerating is somewhat relative to time and place, available resources, available knowledge, and so on'.[85] She also claims that '"intolerable" . . . refers not to what individuals cannot in fact tolerate but to what a decent life cannot include'.[86] There are objective criteria that must be met for a minimally decent life to be met and which, if not met, allow the harm caused to be intolerable. Examples include

> lack of access to non-toxic food, water, or air; lack of freedom from prolonged and severe pain, humiliation, or debilitating fear; prolonged inability to move one's limbs or to stand, sit, or lie down; lack of affective bonds with others; and the inability to make choices and act on at least some of them effectively.[87]

These 'are basics that all humans, as members of a common species and regardless of cultural differences, need for our lives to be not just possible but decent, and for our deaths to be decent'.[88] This leads to two questions: (1) what does 'decent' entail? And (2) who decides that an individual has the requirements needed for a decent life?

By 'decent' Card 'do[es] not mean "morally decent"'.[89] Nor does she mean 'modest' in the sense that it has been used to describe 'feminine decorum'.[90] She means 'simply meeting minimal standards of quality'.[91] 'Decent' implies not a high standard of living, but one that is 'just not bad. It will do, is acceptable, passes muster for the kind of thing it is.'[92]

To elucidate what this involves, she turns to the concept of degradation. 'To degrade, in its general sense, is to reduce in rank or diminish in capacity or value.'[93] Importantly, degradation can take the form of 'disabling or diminishing'.[94] It has degrees, so that 'serious degradation pushes a being below the level of a decent life, severely impairing capacities central to the meaning or value of that life'.[95]

Card holds that 'understanding intolerable harms as major degradations is promising with respect to the aim of preserving the moral gravity of evils and retaining contrast with lesser wrongs'.[96] However, if what counts as a decent life is defined through analogy with what is degrading, and what is seriously degrading is that which 'pushes a being below the level of a decent life',[97] then 'decent' is that which does not degrade life below the level necessary for a decent life. This circularity does not clarify the nature of decent or, by extension, degradation.

In relation to the question of who decides that an individual has met the basic requirements for a decent life, Card explains that it is not necessary to appeal to whether 'the sufferer necessarily *minds*'[98] an imposition. This would make harm dependent on the victim's perception, which would potentially conflate his perception with actuality. Card wants to keep the perception of an event apart from its actuality to maintain the objectivity that her theory of evil demands. She claims that this is possible if we focus on the *functionality* of individuals. The guiding contention is that the tolerance of pain occurs within parameters that differ for each individual. Within these parameters individuals can function well. After a certain point, however, which is different for each, 'we do not function at all'.[99] Whether or to what degree an individual functions reveals the extent to which his basic needs are being met.

Crucially, this brings forth the question of the nature of 'functionality'. Does it refer to a normative conception of that which is required to function in a particular society or does Card have in mind a more universal understanding, so that an individual stops functioning well only if they are unable to 'function at all[?]'[100] Card does not clarify this issue. Indeed, problematically for her theory, she recognises that the exact nature of what makes a life decent is 'not precisely specifiable'.[101] This does not, however, sit well with her insistence that evil entails intolerable harms, which result when the basic requirements for a decent life are not satisfied. If it is not possible to determine what the basics of a decent life are, it is not possible to identify whether an action produced intolerable harms and, by extension, whether evil occurred.

Having outlined Card's understanding of 'reasonably foreseeable' and 'intolerable harm', the final issue is the meaning of 'inexcusable wrongdoing'. The nature of wrong is not dealt with in her analysis. Presumably, it is an act that violates the good, although the nature of the good is also not engaged with. She does, however, deal extensively with the nature of 'inexcusable'. This is important because it is only if the wrong committed by an act is inexcusable that it can be held to be an evil: 'what is shocking about evils is not only that the harm is intolerable but also that the deed producing it is utterly without moral excuse'.[102] If there is a valid excuse for the action, the wrongdoing cannot be considered to be evil. What, then, counts as a valid excuse?

Card responds by distinguishing between *metaphysical* and *moral* excuses, before further explaining that the nature of the excuse is different if it relates to an individual or institutional act. A *metaphysical* excuse refers to 'the ontology of agency',[103] specifically whether the agent is justifiably capable of 'pleading reduced responsibility or even no responsibility'.[104] This alludes to whether the agent was capable of making an informed judgement, not whether that judgement was actually made. It only applies to individuals and to a lesser extent organisations; never to social practices, as these are not agents and so cannot plead diminished capacity to act. Forms of metaphysical excuse include compulsion and ignorance brought about by ontologically deficient cognition. If the individual or organisation was so constituted that he/it was unable to understand the likely consequences of his actions, then his or its culpability and responsibility were mitigated or removed.

Whereas *metaphysical excuses* mitigate culpability and hence responsibility, *moral excuses* mitigate 'culpability *without* reducing responsibility'.[105] This kind of excuse does not plead diminished ontological capacity. 'Rather, its argument is that there was a morally appropriate and defensible reason in favour of the deed or practice, a reason that carries more weight even though not enough weight to justify the deed or the practice on the whole.'[106] Wholly justifiable actions need no excuse. Diabolically evil actions have no excuse. Card is, however, pointing to actions that produce foreseeable intolerable harms, but where the culpability for the act is mitigated by a valid moral reason. Importantly, 'it is not sufficient that the agent *thinks* there is a good reason. There must *be* one (and it must be the agent's reason), a reason defensible on reflection and in terms of moral values.'[107]

The problem, of course, is that it is not clear what a good reason entails, what justifies it, and who would judge it. This is part of a larger problem within Card's account relating to the nature and possibility of judgment. She admits that 'we need to be able to make judgements of right and wrong in order to apply the atrocity theory of evil',[108] but remains quiet on this fundamentally important topic. It is simply taken for granted that we can identify and accurately judge when an action brings about 'reasonably foreseeable intolerable harms produced by *inexcusable* wrongs'.[109] On the one hand, this reveals a troubling lacuna in her theory. But, on the other hand, it is a consequence of her insistence that the atrocity paradigm does not offer 'a comprehensive theory of ethics'.[110] It aims to spark debate about the nature of evil through the definition provided. This debate will include discussion about the meaning and nature of reasonable foreseeability, intolerable harm, and inexcusable wrongdoing.

## Evil and Lesser Wrongs

One of the main benefits of Card's atrocity paradigm is that it explicitly distinguishes evil from lesser forms of wrongdoing. The fundamental difference between evil and other wrongs is based on the harm caused. Card explains that 'both evils and lesser wrongs are culpable. But only evils do intolerable harm.'[111] In contrast, 'wrongs that do extreme harm, wrongs that foreseeably do no harm (or little harm) do not warrant the gravity of the judgment "evil"'.[112] That evils are inexcusable wrongdoings indicates that they are types of wrong. However, not all wrongs are equal. Wrongs exist on a sliding scale based on the harm caused and whether the wrongdoing was morally or metaphysically excusable. At a certain point, when the harm inexcusably caused becomes intolerable, the wrong turns into evil. Harming individuals to the point that they cannot function is the most harm and, by extension, most evil that can be imposed on a victim. To capture this absolute sense of evil, Card altered her definition of evil away from the notion of 'culpable wrongdoing', to that of 'inexcusable wrongdoing'. Whereas 'culpability' admits of degrees, inexcusable does not. 'Inexcusable' is then better able to grasp the notion of what distinguishes evil from lesser wrongs.[113]

However, if evil were limited to this absolute standard of intolerability, the ability to use the term 'evil' would be severely restricted to major events where the threat of physical annihilation exists. This would contravene Card's attempt to draw attention to lower-profile atrocities suffered by people in everyday existence. To account for this, she needs a criterion that allows her to describe as evil actions that are more intolerable than everyday tolerable harms, but not as harmful as harms that threaten the physical existence of the victim. She needs, in other words, a way to distinguish between absolute evils that threaten the physical annihilation of victims, less serious evils that cause harms that are intolerable but do not entail physical annihilation, and non-evil wrongs.

With this goal in mind, she returns to the notion of 'intolerable' to point out that there is also a relative aspect to it: what each individual is able to tolerate varies. This relates not to the bare minimum requirements for human functionality, but to what each individual, based on his unique physical and mental configurations and capacities, is able to tolerate to function.

What is intolerable for one will differ from what is intolerable for another. By extension, what counts as an evil for one will not count for another with a higher tolerance level.

Card's conclusion is that 'not only are evils worse than other wrongs (such as minor injustices), but some evils are worse than others'.[114] This allows the atrocity paradigm to grade and rank different atrocities based on the degree of evil each entails. Card is hesitant about doing so, however, because 'an atrocity is already so evil that in some contexts it seems disrespectful of victims to point out that another was even worse'.[115]

Evils are not only distinguished from lesser wrongs by the nature of the harm inflicted on victims. Card's definition of 'evils a[s] reasonably foreseeable intolerable harms produced by *inexcusable* wrongs'[116] brings her to also distinguish them based on the culpability of the wrong committed. Lesser wrongs may produce intolerable harm to the victims but not be judged to be evils because 'either there is no reasonably foreseeable intolerable harm, or the agent willing to inflict it has some good (morally defensible) reason'.[117] Card thinks that this outcome is far more common:

> Everyone who is not a saint does inexcusable things, not always with harmful results. Many of us can easily recall having done inexcusable wrongs, or we can recall that members of our families have. Not all inexcusable wrongs are evils but only those that do reasonably foreseeable intolerable harm.[118]

That everyone has caused intolerable harms that have not been called evils because they were either not reasonably foreseeable or inexcusable reveals that individuals, in their everyday lives, are far closer to committing evil acts than is typically realised. In some cases, it is just luck that the line separating lesser wrongs from evil is not crossed.[119]

However, it is not just the line dividing lesser wrongs from evils that is far more fragile than typically acknowledged. Card claims that so is an individual's relationship to good and evil. Rather than adopt the binary opposition between good and evil that has defined the Western moral tradition, she insists that our moral lives are amalgamations of good *and* evil. To justify this as a precursor to explaining what it entails through her notion of grey zones, Card engages with Kant's moral theory and, in particular, his rigorism.

## Kant's Moral Theory

Kant is a particularly important figure for Card, to the extent that she devotes a chapter to his thought in both *The Atrocity Paradigm* and *Confronting Evils*. Rather than provide a close textual reading, she outlines what she considers to be the salient features of his moral thought. Her conclusion is that it contains three problematic aspects: (1) his lack of treatment of victims; (2) his rejection of diabolical evil; and (3) his rigorism. The aim here is not to evaluate her reading of Kant, but to show how she uses it to develop her own conclusions.

While the question guiding Kant's analysis of evil was something akin to 'how is evil possible?', Card claims that the question used to evaluate Kant's analysis should actually be 'whether Kant's understanding of evil takes adequate account of victims'.[120] From this premise, she suggests that 'we need to consider whether the Categorical Imperative directs us to think about relationships between our conduct and the satisfaction of basic human needs or the avoidance of harms that would make life intolerable'.[121] Given that she previously asserted that Kant's moral thought 'is basically stoic in values'[122] because it judges the moral merit of an action based on the will of the perpetrator, it is clear that her conclusion will be that it is not orientated towards the harm an action produces in its victims. Indeed, she finds Kant at fault on this issue: 'the sufferings of victims are just incidental'.[123] This is compounded by her insistence that 'Kant's theory of evil draws helpful distinctions among perpetrators but is deeply deficient in its recognition of harms'.[124] This derives from the inadequacies of Kant's conceptual schema: he simply 'does not have enough distinctions to be able to contrast grave wrongs (such as murder), ethically, from relatively trivial ones (such as petty theft). Kant (like so many other moral philosophers) does not distinguish evils from lesser wrongs.'[125]

Card thinks that this is a result of Kant's claim that the moral worth of an action is judged not by the consequences of that action, but by the will that commits it. If the will has as its moral maxim the universal moral law, it is good; if not, it is evil. This contravenes common sense, which 'distinguishes evils from relatively minor wrongs not just by the agent's motives or strength of commitment but by the depth of the harm that is wrongfully but willingly done'.[126]

Furthermore, while Kant differentiates between kinds of evil based on the will's commitment to the moral law, this prevents him from focusing on the harms that such choices cause; a focus that, on Card's telling, would allow him to distinguish between evil and lesser wrongs. As it stands, however, according to Kant's grades of an evil will, culpable wrongs that are similarly motivated are ethically (although not juridically) on a par, regardless of differences in foreseeable harm. More harmful offences can make one deserving of more severe punishments. But they are not, for Kant, ethically worse.[127]

Ethically speaking, 'an evil, petty theft is on a par with murder, for Kant, when the incentive of both is self-love'.[128] Card insists that this is ethically and conceptually unacceptable: 'in contrast to wrongs that do extreme harm, wrongs that foreseeably do no harm (or little harm) do not warrant the gravity of the judgment "evil"'.[129] Kant's argument only makes sense, on Card's telling, if 'he reasons that an individual who would commit petty theft from calculated self-interest is also prepared to commit murder should it become profitable since, barring fundamental character change, the underlying principle would be the same: prioritising self-love'.[130]

It is not necessarily the case, however, that a petty thief shares the same underlying motive as a murder, that theft leads to murder, or that the thief is, ethically speaking, potentially prepared to murder. 'A self-loving thief could have scruples against murder or torture, drawing the line not from fear of detection (self-love) but because of the depth of the harm to victims.'[131] Card posits the example of 'a Robin Hood who would *steal* from the rich but would not *murder or torture* even the rich, not because he is squeamish but because of the seriousness of the wrong'.[132] The binary logic underpinning Kant's moral theory, wherein an agent acts in accordance with the moral law or self-love, is unable to account for those situations in which an agent's actions emanate from 'a principle of self-love that makes concessions to morality'.[133] Moral agents are far more complex and multi-dimensional than Kant's rigorism can capture. We need therefore an account of morality that distinguishes between different types of evils and the harms inherent in lesser wrongs.

To develop this, Card turns to Kant's gradated account of the evil will. As outlined in Chapter 6 above, Kant distinguishes between three types of evil will:

> *First*, [there] is the general weakness of the human heart in complying with the adopted maxims, or the *frailty* of human nature; *second*, the propensity to adulterate moral incentives with immoral ones (even when it is done with good intention, and under maxims of the good), i.e. *impurity*; *third*, the propensity to adopt evil maxims, i.e. the *depravity* of human nature, or of the human heart.[134]

These exist in a descending order of seriousness. Frailty points to the possibility that the individual may choose a good moral maxim, but in its application may not always follow it. Impurity entails the individual choosing a good moral maxim with the intent of following it, but 'not, as ... should be [the case, adopting] the law *alone* as its *sufficient* incentive'.[135] He, therefore, 'often (and perhaps always) needs still other incentives besides it in order to determine the power of choice for what duty requires'.[136] Depravity is the most serious, entailing 'the *corruption* (*corruptio*) of the human heart'[137] and the subordination of the moral law to other, non-moral ends.

Card focuses on frailty, insisting that it contradicts Kant's rigorism because it points to a middle ground between good and evil. In frailty, the agent remains committed to the moral law, but does not always live according to it. This, however, appears to be excluded by Kant's rigorism, which holds that the individual affirms the moral law or does not. Rather than conclude that this reveals a contradiction within Kant's account, Card uses the example of frailty to draw a different conclusion: individuals can be both good and evil at the same time. She backs this up by appealing to 'a widely shared common-sense view ... that good and evil, unlike right and wrong, are not contradictories. They are contraries. It is not possible to be both good and evil in the same respect at the same time. But it is at least logically possible to be neither.'[138]

This offers two options: (1) 'someone's will is neither good nor evil but something in-between',[139] and/or (2) 'someone's will is partly good and partly evil'.[140] While recognising that Kant rejects both options, Card claims that 'common sense acknowledges the validity of both kinds of judgment'.[141] She does not develop this further or explain why she is justified in privileging common sense over Kant's thought. Instead, she identifies people 'who appear systematically to exercise good (even exemplary) moral judgment in certain contexts or on certain types of issues and, during the same time period, astonishingly poor moral judgment in others. They seem to have a good side and an evil side, which is what we commonly say.'[142]

Card describes the example of Sue William Silverman, who in a memoir about her father, published after his death, describes his moral dualism. On the one hand, he was Chief Counsel to the United States Secretary of the Interior from 1933 to 1953 and played key roles 'in establishing statehood for Alaska and Hawaii, Philippine independence, in creating the Puerto Rican Commonwealth, in home rule for the Virgin Islands, Guam, and Samoa, and in the establishment of civilian rule of Japanese possessions after [the Second World War]'.[143] From 1954, he was the president of large banks, and was photographed with President Harry Truman, Adlai Stevenson, and other influential political figures. Card is aware that many of these political projects do not, strictly speaking, affirm his moral worth, but claims that 'it seems unlikely that he would have developed such a record of trust and responsibility if he had not impressed others as morally reliable'.[144] She takes this to confirm his good moral judgement.

The problem was that, at the same time as he affirmed his moral worth at work during the day, he went home at night and 'for many years, he assaulted his daughter sexually, severely, locking her bedroom door at night, beginning when she was less than five'.[145] These actions raise a number of troubling questions: 'were those who placed this man in positions of public trust *totally* deceived about his character? Or did he have a good side and an evil side?'[146] Card notes that 'he appears ... to embody the contradiction that Kant thought impossible: being committed to both good and evil, prioritizing duty in some contexts but prioritizing his sexual inclination in other contexts'.[147] If this 'is a correct description, [he] has more than one higher-order will. If he is responsible for both patterns, his character is not at its *most* basic level defined by either of them.'[148] This is not a case of frailty; it would not require much effort to abstain from doing those actions to his daughter. Card thinks that there was no moral slippage. 'There is a policy here, not a lapse.'[149] The man lived with good and evil inclinations *at once*.

Card recognises one possible Kantian response to this: the man 'does not exhibit a good will and a bad will at the *same* time'.[150] Strictly speaking, his actions at work and those at home occur at two different time periods. Kant's insistence that an individual's moral maxim can be changed indicates that he could choose one moral maxim based on the moral law when at work and one that departs from the moral law at home. Card asks, however, whether Kant is 'right to assume that at any given time we must have a fundamental principle, whether we know it or not'.[151] This also brings forth the question of duration: how long does the choice of moral maxim last? Can it be changed in each instant or must it last over a period of time?

While Card recognises that, for Kant, the choice of moral maxim does not occur in time, 'the choice of a commitment needs a stretch of time for its realisation'.[152] She affirms that Kant sees this, especially in the cases of frailty and impurity, but that he does not 'acknowledge that the time required to translate commitment into action opens a space for ambivalence or indecisiveness *in regard to particular commitments or even whether to become committed at all*, not just space for weakness in regard to a particular commitment'.[153] While Kant's rigorism explains how individuals 'can exhibit a good will and a bad will at *different* times',[154] it is unable to account for 'conflicting *patterns* of behaviour ... in the same stretch of time and in the same contexts [which] suggest a will that is fundamentally *un*decided, *un*committed'.[155] This lack of commitment permits the will to change moral positions quickly and without trouble within the same time period and context. Card states that 'such ambivalence seems common among children, adolescents, adults with troubled pasts, and those who live under stressful conditions'.[156] She develops this notion of moral ambivalence through the diabolical evils of grey zones.

## Diabolical Evil

Card links diabolical evil to grey zones in both *The Atrocity Paradigm*[157] and *Confronting Evils*.[158] Kant rejected the possibility of diabolical evil since it required that an individual 'incorporate evil *qua* evil for incentive into one's maxim'.[159] It demanded that the individual want to do evil for the sake of evil. Kant thought that no individual would want this, even though evil may result from a failure to understand the moral law or be true to it. In that case, the intention was the good, but the individual chose or implemented the moral law in a flawed manner.

Card rejects this, arguing that diabolical evil is not only a possibility but, as evidenced by the sheer number of atrocities committed, an all too common occurrence. In particular, she challenges two assumptions underpinning Kant's rejection of diabolical evil: first, his insistence that the good is possible but its opposite – absolute diabolical evil – is not. Card finds this puzzling. If Kant dismisses the notion that 'beings never do evil *simply for its own sake* ... we must also conclude that we never do good simply for its own sake either'.[160] If Kant affirms the good, he must also affirm diabolical evil.

Card also challenges Kant's claim that the will chooses independently of the phenomenal world. Kant's theory, on Card's telling, is premised on the truth of the noumenal realm, which, in relation to the ego, presupposes an I unencumbered from the constraints of space and time found in the phenomenal world. Kant's noumenal ego decides how it will interact with its phenomenal world; it is not, strictly speaking, part of the phenomenal world. Card, in contrast, argues for an embedded understanding of the ego that sees the individual as being influenced by its social relations and, in particular, its attachments to others. These attachments are understood to be particularly important to the development of an individual's morality.

Appealing to psychoanalyst Lorna Smith Benjamin's notion of 'Important Persons and their Internalised Representations (IPIR)',[161] Card explains that affiliation with someone considered to be important leads to a sense of psychic proximity that brings the individual to identify with and internalise the norms of that person.¹⁶² Card's aim is to make explicit the IPIRs that shape an individual's moral outlook, to subsequently permit individuals to choose whether to continue to affirm them or not. Her point is underpinned by the assumption that 'one who became aware of having a racist IPIR might wish to disengage or renegotiate, even though the IPIR is supportive in many ways and hostile only to other racial groups'.¹⁶³ It is not clear, though, how an individual who has adopted a hostile IPIR would simply choose to alter it. Kant posited the notion of a noumenal will divorced from the phenomenal world to explain it. Card rejects that approach, insisting instead that the ego can simply alter its IPIR and, by extension, self-conception, despite also holding that the IPIR conditions the ego's moral values and self-conception.

In any case, Card suggests that 'if unfortunate attachments can be renegotiated or rejected, they can also be reflectively endorsed, leading in some cases to the wilful perpetration of evils'.¹⁶⁴ This would mean that individuals appear to choose evil for evil's sake. The problem is that 'one may value support from a cruel IPIR not *for the sake of* the cruelty but because the person internalised is or once was an important source of support, perhaps one's only source of support'.¹⁶⁵ The evil committed would not then be for the sake of evil, but to gain approval from the important person.

Card does not respond to this possibility, but changes tack to suggest that Kant's conception of diabolical evil 'is a very simple and not the most interesting account of diabolical evil'.¹⁶⁶ Whereas Kant locates diabolical evil entirely in the perpetrator's will, Card states that 'if we consider also the harm that evil does, another interpretation of diabolical evil suggests itself that is all too human and much more interesting'.¹⁶⁷ In *The Atrocity Paradigm*, this takes the form: 'I find diabolical evil in the knowing or deliberate corruption of the character of others, especially if it is done not for prudential reasons, such as economic gain, but for the satisfaction of being able to look down on them or, at least, of not having to look up at them.'¹⁶⁸ This notion of corrupting the character of others is important to her conception of grey zones.

In *Confronting Evils*, Card complements this by appealing once more to common sense, in combination with insights from international human rights law, to explain that 'diabolical evils are especially *cruel, inhuman, or degrading*'.¹⁶⁹ She links this with an understanding of 'doing evil for evil's sake' that interprets it as 'doing one evil as a means to another',¹⁷⁰ and concludes that 'diabolical evil [is] extremely cruel, inhuman, or degrading treatment as means to an evil end'.¹⁷¹ Whereas 'ordinary evils are excusable',¹⁷² this simply 'means that the agent's reasons do not begin to justify the deed.

Those reasons do not have to be grounded in interests in promoting an evil end.'[173] In diabolical evil, however, 'the agent's reasons are so grounded'.[174] In other words, the agent's actions are evil and are done for the sake of evil. Card goes on to claim that conceiving of diabolical evil in this way 'comes closer than Kant's . . . to the classic view of Satan as corrupter, as one who tempts others to abandon morality or demote it to a low position on their scale of value'.[175] Presumably the figure of Satan pointed to here is the figure of the New Testament, embodying absolute evil opposed to the good.

In spite of this reference, Card insists that her notion of diabolical evil is not cosmic, but thoroughly human.[176] Furthermore, diabolical evil is not simply the result of the harm caused; the motives for it must also be incomprehensible. Examples provided include 'the invention and use of such a device as the brass bull designed by Perillos of Athens for Phalaris, tyrant of Akragas, Sicily',[177] which 'was designed with flutes in the bull's mouth so that the screams of victims roasting inside emerged sounding like music',[178] and the Rwandan genocide of the 1990s where men, women, and children identified as belonging to a particular ethnicity were 'hack[ed] to death with a machete, from sunup to sundown, day after day'[179] simply because they were thought to belong to that particular ethnicity. Claiming that these actions are so evil and incomprehensible that they qualify for diabolical status brings Card to take over and depend on the *concept* and *logic* underpinning the Christian conception of Satan (good versus absolute [diabolical] evil) without endorsing its cosmic narrative.

Card returns to the figure of Satan when describing the three paradigms of diabolical evil: the Torture paradigm, the Nero paradigm, and the Serpent paradigm. The *Torture* paradigm, 'symbolised by a devil with pitchforks torturing sinners in hell for eternity, is a paradigm of cruel and inhuman diabolical treatment'.[180] Rather than appeal to theological texts, Card relies on the religious teaching she grew up with to assert that the devil loves company and so tortures others 'eternally for no better end than not to endure torment alone'.[181] This 'is doing evil for an evil end'.[182]

The *Nero* paradigm complements this because it is 'marked by profound betrayal coupled with great callousness and lack of proportion'.[183] While it is named after the famous cruelty of the Roman Emperor, Card points to contemporary examples such as 'the murder committed by the serial rapists Jeffrey Dahmer and Ted Bundy',[184] who, in order to be able to temporarily satisfy their sexual urges, 'lured vulnerable and trusting victims to their deaths'.[185] This 'is evil conduct for an evil end: murder for the sake of being able to continue raping'.[186] Specifically, 'their grotesque betrayals and the bizarre disproportion between the harm they did and what they got out of it make their deeds sufficiently inhuman to warrant the judgement "diabolical".[187]

The cruelty of the Nero paradigm is linked to the *Serpent* paradigm, 'which couples deception and manipulation with hostile envy'[188] to ensure the 'destruction of what is good in others'.[189] Card again models this understanding 'on the Christian reading of the serpent in the Genesis story of Eve's temptation in the Garden of Eden as Satan in disguise'.[190] Satan, in the form of the serpent, 'lures Eve into first destroying her own innocence and then becoming complicit in the destruction of Adam's'.[191] The only 'benefit' the serpent receives from this is 'to no longer have to feel that Adam and Eve were so much better off or so much more beloved of God'.[192] This counts as diabolical evil because 'one evil (the serpent's inexcusable deception that results in death and pain) is done for the sake of another (to rob Adam and Eve of God's favour . . .)'.[193]

From these three paradigms, Card concludes that diabolical evil refers to endless torture for its own sake, profound betrayal, callousness, lack of proportion, and the purposeful destruction of what is good in others. These three forms come together in the case of grey zones, which are understood to be the paradigmatic example of diabolical evil.

## Grey Zones

Card takes the notion of 'grey zones' from Primo Levi, who used it to describe the 'special hells'[194] of the Nazi concentration camps. Admitting that Levi does not provide a definition of it, Card focuses on his description of the death-camp *Sonderkommando* to draw out its main features. The *Sonderkommando* were a group of 'prisoners, already victims themselves, [who] were selected for positions of authority over other prisoners'.[195] Chosen for their physical health and numbering from seven hundred to one thousand,

> it was their task to maintain order among the new arrivals (often completely unaware of the destiny awaiting them) who must be sent into the gas chambers; to extract the corpses from the chambers, pull gold teeth from jaws, cut the women's hair, sort and classify clothes, shoes, and the contents of the luggage; transport the bodies to the crematoria and oversee the operation of the ovens; extract and eliminate ashes.[196]

In exchange, the *Sonderkommando* received preferential treatment: extra food, healthcare, living space, and exemption from being summarily executed. This is not to say that they escaped every other prisoner's fate. Given their intimate knowledge of the workings of the death camps, the Nazis considered the *Sonderkommando* to be *Geheimnisträger*: the bearers of secrets. As such, 'the SS exerted the greatest diligence to prevent any man who had been part of it from surviving and telling'.[197] Their average length of service was three months. For this reason, Levi explains that 'twelve squads succeeded each other in Auschwitz; each one remained operative for a few months, then it was supressed, each time with a different trick to head off possible resistance, and as its initiation the next squad burnt the corpses of its predecessors'.[198]

These prisoners were in a horrendous moral situation: if they did not agree to become *Sonderkommando* or, as the last group did in 1944, fought back, they were immediately murdered. If they agreed to become *Sonderkommando* (although they were not informed of what it entailed prior to agreeing), they received some temporary relief from some of the horrors other inmates had to endure, but suffered other horrors: namely, the work they were required to do. This was combined with the psychological tolls such work took: 'many of these unfortunates bore, in addition to the harms and the suffering inflicted on them, the burdens of shame and guilt for what they did to others'.[199] The only way out was suicide. For the deeds they were forced to commit and the situation they found themselves in, Levi describes the creation of the *Sonderkommando* as 'National Socialism's most demonic crime'.[200] It 'represented an attempt to shift on to others – specifically the victims – the burden of guilt, so that they were deprived of even the solace of innocence'.[201]

While it is tempting to judge the actions of the *Sonderkommando*, Levi is quick to warn against doing so: 'It must be clear that the greatest responsibility lies with the system, the very structure of the totalitarian state, the concurrent guilt on the part of the individual big and small collaborators (never likeable, never transparent!) is always difficult to evaluate.'[202] The only ones who are able to judge the *Sonderkommando* are 'those who found themselves in similar circumstances, and had the possibility to test on themselves what it means to act in a state of coercion'.[203]

Card follows this exhortation and so does not aim to judge the horrendous deeds perpetrated by the *Sonderkommando*. Her 'interest is ultimately more in the evil done to [the concentration camp] inhabitants than in any evils they do'.[204] From this, she uses the example of the *Sonderkommando* to identify three defining features of a grey zone: 'First, its inhabitants are victims of evil. Second, these inhabitants are implicated through their choices in perpetrating some of the same or similar evils on others who are already victims like themselves. And third, inhabitants of the gr[e]y zone act under extraordinary stress.'[205]

The most striking aspect of grey zones is the second feature: victims become perpetrators against other victims. They are both victim and perpetrator at once. Good (represented presumably by the victim) and evil (represented by the perpetrator) can exist simultaneously 'in' the same person at the same time.[206] This backs up Card's earlier critique of Kant's rigorism. Rather than being good or evil, the *Sonderkommando* 'lends substance to the idea of "gr[e]y areas" between good and evil, areas of neither indifference nor mere ambivalence'.[207]

While, in *Confronting Evils*, Card claims that the *Sonderkommando* meet the conditions of the Torture, Nero, and Serpent paradigms of diabolical evil, meaning that they are the most severe historical form of diabolical evil,[208] she also points out that grey zones are found in less extreme circumstances than the Holocaust, particularly if 'they set up victims of oppression to pass along oppressive practices to the next generation'.[209] Examples given include 'the evils of everyday misogyny, racism, homophobia, and anti-semitism'.[210] They do not tend to be one-off events, but are shaped over a lifetime of influences and decisions, meaning that it is not easy to produce clear-cut analyses of culpability and, by extension, of right and wrong regarding them. This confusion reveals that, rather than there being a straightforward binary opposition between good and evil, the moral status of individuals is often highly ambiguous and multi-dimensional.

Card warns, however, that we cannot reduce grey zones to situations where individuals are both victims and perpetrators of evil. Doing so would produce 'too wide'[211] an analysis that would include 'those who survive to take revenge, for example, by doing to former torturers – or to persons suspected of being former torturers – some of what was done to themselves, even though the retaliators are no longer in danger of suffering torture'.[212] Card gives the historical example of 'former prisoners of National Socialist camps who were hired in 1945 by Russians to staff camps for German inmates who were accused or suspected of having been members of the National Socialist Party or of having served it'.[213] 'It would [also] include those who wrong[ed] others in order to advance their own positions when what they gain[ed] [bore] no comparison with what those they victimized lost or suffered.'[214] Card has in mind 'the thousands of white Protestant women in the United States who joined the Ku Klux Klan in the 1920s not only to promote racist, intolerant, and xenophobic policies but for a social setting in which to enjoy friendship and solidarity among like-minded women'.[215] She claims that this behaviour 'is evil, not gr[e]y'.[216] Just because 'a person's life as a whole evokes in us a mixed emotional response – sympathy in so far as they are wrongly victimized by others but also anger in so far as they wrong others – does not imply that any of their choices possessed the moral complexity or ambiguity of a gr[e]y zone'.[217]

Grey zones are socio-political spaces and/or practices in which all inhabitants are initially victims before becoming perpetrators against other victims to facilitate the continuation of the rules or structures governing that space. They are purposefully created to place individuals under tremendous existential stress. This occurs when 'agents must choose under such conditions as intense or prolonged fear for basic security or their very lives or for the lives or basic security of loved ones'.[218] In so doing, grey zones complicate the moral options available to individuals by making their 'choices . . . morally problematic'[219] in a way that 'jeopardises the character and self-respect of survivors'.[220] In so far as they place individuals in morally problematic situations, grey zones ask their inhabitants to decide what to do when there are no clear right or wrong answers or when there might be numerous equally 'right' answers.

> Thus 'gr[e]y' suggests many things. Sometimes it invokes a complex judgment whose elements are mixed, although individually they are clear enough. It may be impossible to do justice to the case with an overall summary such as 'good on the whole' or 'bad on the whole'. At other times, 'gr[e]y' evokes a deed whose very elements are morally unclear or ambiguous.[221]

Therefore, grey zones have an epistemological aspect referring to 'what is unclear or ambiguous (to the agent, an observer, or both), whether it be degree of responsibility, motive, or rightness of action'.[222] This epistemological aspect also points to and depends upon an ontological one, relating to questions such as:

> Are there really always right and wrong choices in such situations (where voluntariness is not an option)? Are there always responsible or excusable choices (where rightness or wrongness is not the issue)? Is there always such a thing as the agent's real motive? Does our moral vocabulary fail to mark distinctions that we should want to make, to capture the ways things really are? Would gr[e]y zones cease to be gr[e]y, if we had more fine-tuned concepts? Or are some gr[e]y zones ineliminable?[223]

Card does not provide answers on these issues. Given the 'greyness' in question, it is uncertain whether she would ever be able to. They are designed to stimulate debate and thought on the subject. That is the point of her notion of moral grey zones: it not only demonstrates the complexity of moral judgements and the difficulty of making clear-cut judgements about what is good and evil, but also calls into question many of the simplistic oppositions that moral thought has tended to work with – individual actions versus social actions, victim versus perpetrator, individual will versus political organization, good versus evil, and so on.[224]

## Concluding Remarks

Card's atrocity paradigm offers a number of important additions to the study of evil. Her focus on large-scale atrocities and the victims of evils introduces a *methodological* innovation, which is complemented by a number of *conceptual* ones, including her distinctions between evil, wrongdoing, and harm; insistence that there is a fundamental rupture between evil and lesser wrongs; recognition that evil and lesser wrongs are differentiated; and defence of the notions of diabolical evil and grey zones. These emphasise the complexity of evil and our moral categories more generally, while introducing examples of everyday evils that tend to be passed over: rape, domestic abuse or gender violence, racial discrimination, and so on.

Questions do, however, remain over Card's analysis. Methodologically, she relies on everyday common sense, ordinary language, and dictionary definitions to limit what is controversial and provide clear-cut definitions that can be applied to concrete circumstances. These definitions are not, however, as uncontroversial as she assumes. Indeed, at one point, she recognises this, explaining that 'philosophers trained as I was in the ordinary-language tradition of analytical philosophy should be cautious about relying on what "people" say is or is not evil. We should form the habit of asking, which people? Whose voices (if any) are dominating the conversation?'[225] Yet, she never does this; a task that would bring her to question how language is created, the power structures underpinning this creation, while, in so doing, also problematising her attempt to ground the atrocity paradigm in an axiomatic definition.

Operationalising her definition of evil is also challenging because it relies on a notion of judgement that is not outlined. An analysis of judgement is required to identify the motives and intentions of the perpetrator, what he could reasonably foresee, whether the victim's description of the harm suffered is accurate, and what counts as intolerable, decent, and inexcusable. Card never makes explicit what she means by 'judgement'. It is simply assumed that it can occur properly. On the one hand, this is one of the most significant and troubling failings of her atrocity paradigm. On the other hand, this 'failing' re-enforces what we have seen throughout: thinking on evil is tied to and dependent on a range of other philosophical issues, including epistemological, metaphysical, and ontological questions relating to the nature and possibilities of human cognition. It is this that makes 'evil' such a complex and multi-faceted moral concept.

Perhaps the most complicated issue that arises from Card's thinking on evil, especially as it relates to the history of evil, refers to her defence of diabolical evil. While the notion of grey zones challenges the traditional binary opposition between good and evil, Card's defence of diabolical evil continues to posit an absolute form of evil opposed to the good. By linking diabolical evil to the Biblical narrative of Satan and claiming that it is absolutely opposed to the good, Card's secular theory of evil continues to be tied to a conception of absolute evil, itself underpinned by a logic of moral foundations, that was first introduced by (and, indeed, continues to shape) Christian thinking on the topic. Despite aiming to offer a secular analysis of the problem of evil, Card continues to appeal to and so depend upon a trace of the logic, narrative, and concepts inherent in the theological approach that she supposedly rejects.

# Notes

1. See, for example, Maria Pia Lara (ed.), *Rethinking Evil: Contemporary Perspectives* (Berkeley: University of California Press, 2001); Susan Neiman, *Evil in Modern Thought: An Alternative History of Philosophy* (Princeton: Princeton University Press, 2002); Richard Bernstein, *Radical Evil: A Philosophical Investigation* (Cambridge: Polity, 2002); Brian Davies, *The Reality of God and the Problem of Evil* (London: Continuum, 2006); Phillip Cole, *The Myth of Evil* (Edinburgh: Edinburgh University Press, 2006); Maria Pía Lara, *Narrating Evil: A Postmetaphysical Theory of Reflective Judgement* (New York: Columbia University Press, 2007); Peter Dews, *The Idea of Evil* (Oxford: Blackwell, 2008); Terry Eagleton, *On Evil* (New Haven: Yale University Press, 2010); Robert Meister, *After Evil: A Politics of Human Rights* (New York: Columbia University Press, 2011); Simona Forti, *New Demons: Rethinking Power and Evil Today*, trans. Zakiya Hanafi (Stanford: Stanford University Press, 2015).
2. For an overview of these positions and this debate, see Luke Russell, 'Evil-Revivalism v Evil-Skepticism', *Journal of Value Inquiry*, 40:1, 2006, pp. 89–105.
3. Claudia Card, *The Atrocity Paradigm: A Theory of Evil* (Oxford: Oxford University Press, 2002), and *Confronting Evils: Terrorism, Torture, Genocide* (Cambridge: Cambridge University Press, 2010). At the time of her death in 2015, Card was working on a third volume on surviving atrocities. It is unclear

whether the notes for it will be published. A collection of responses to Card's initial formulation of the atrocity paradigm was published in Andrea Veltman and Kathryn J. Norlock (eds), *Evil, Political Violence, and Forgiveness* (Lanham: Lexington Books, 2009).
4. Card, *The Atrocity Paradigm*, p. 28.
5. Card, *Confronting Evils*, p. 6.
6. Card, *The Atrocity Paradigm*, p. xiii.
7. Card, *Confronting Evils*, p. 6.
8. Card, *The Atrocity Paradigm*, p. 5.
9. Ibid. p. 5.
10. Card, *Confronting Evils*, p. 7.
11. Ibid. p. 25.
12. Ibid. pp. 136, 177.
13. Ibid. pp. 34, 36, 38.
14. Ibid. p. 51.
15. Ibid. p. 23.
16. Card, *The Atrocity Paradigm*, p. 4.
17. Ibid. p. 3.
18. Ibid. p. 3.
19. Card, *Confronting Evils*, p. 4.
20. Card, *The Atrocity Paradigm*, p. 3.
21. Card, *Confronting Evils*, p. 18.
22. Ibid. p. xi.
23. Ibid. p. 8.
24. Ibid. p. 8.
25. Ibid. p. 8.
26. Card, *The Atrocity Paradigm*, p. 212.
27. Ibid. p. 31.
28. Ibid. p. 7.
29. Ibid. p. 114.
30. Ibid. p. 5.
31. Ibid. p. 8. In *Confronting Evils*, she augments this list with a new one: 'the Holocaust, carpet-bombings in World War II, and the Tuskegee syphilis experiments . . . Stalin's gulags, the 1937 rape of Nanking, the 1995 Oklahoma City bombing, the 1964 murder of the three civil rights workers, James Cheney, Michael Goodman, and Andrew Schwerner, in Mississippi, and the dragging murder of James Byrd in Jasper, Texas, 1998' (p. 6).
32. Card, *The Atrocity Paradigm*, p. 9.
33. Ibid. p. 9.
34. Ibid. p. 9.
35. Card, *Confronting Evils*, p. 16.
36. Ibid. p. 16.
37. Ibid. p. 16.

38. Ibid. p. 16.
39. Ibid. p. 16.
40. Card, *The Atrocity Paradigm*, p. 5.
41. Ibid. p. 9.
42. Ibid. p. 5.
43. Ibid. p. 3.
44. Card, *Confronting Evils*, p. 18.
45. Card, *The Atrocity Paradigm*, p. 16.
46. Card, *Confronting Evils*, ch. 4.
47. Card, *The Atrocity Paradigm*, p. 9.
48. In *The Atrocity Paradigm*, Card places her atrocity paradigm between Stoicism and modern Utilitarianism, specifically that of Bentham and Mill (ch. 3). In *Confronting Evils*, she replaces the latter with Epicureanism (p. 8). While she does not discuss it explicitly, it appears that she takes Epicureanism and Utilitarianism to agree that an action is evil based solely on the harm caused.
49. Ibid. p. 8.
50. Ibid. p. 8.
51. Ibid. p. 8.
52. Ibid. p. 9.
53. Ibid. p. 10.
54. Ibid. p. 9.
55. Ibid. pp. 9–10.
56. Ibid. p. 22.
57. Ibid. p. 22.
58. Ibid. p. 22.
59. Ibid. p. 22.
60. Ibid. p. 22.
61. Ibid. p. 22.
62. Ibid. p. 22.
63. Ibid. p. 13.
64. Ibid. p. 13.
65. John Kekes, *Facing Evil* (Princeton: Princeton University Press, 1990), p. 57.
66. Card, *The Atrocity Paradigm*, p. 13.
67. Ibid. p. 13.
68. Ibid. p. 13.
69. Ibid. p. 13.
70. Ibid. p. 11.
71. Ibid. p. 11.
72. Ibid. p. 9.
73. Card, *Confronting Evils*, p. 18.
74. Card, *The Atrocity Paradigm*, p. 12.
75. Card, *Confronting Evils*, p. 6.
76. Ibid. p. 7.

77. Ibid. p. 18.
78. Ibid. p. 28.
79. Ibid. pp. 28–9.
80. Ibid. p. 29.
81. Ibid. p. 49.
82. Ibid. p. 49.
83. Ibid. p. 29.
84. Ibid. p. 101.
85. Ibid. p. 8.
86. Ibid. p. 8.
87. Ibid. p. 8.
88. Ibid. p. 9.
89. Ibid. p. 105.
90. Ibid. p. 106.
91. Ibid. p. 106.
92. Ibid. p. 106.
93. Ibid. p. 106.
94. Ibid. p. 106.
95. Ibid. p. 106.
96. Ibid. p. 106.
97. Ibid. p. 106.
98. Ibid. p. 105.
99. Ibid. p. 105.
100. Ibid. p. 105.
101. Ibid. p. 105.
102. Ibid. p. 9.
103. Ibid. p. 16.
104. Ibid. p. 16.
105. Ibid. p. 16.
106. Ibid. p. 17.
107. Ibid. p. 17.
108. Card, *The Atrocity Paradigm*, p. 5.
109. Card, *Confronting Evils*, p. 18.
110. Ibid. p. 6.
111. Ibid. pp. 10–11.
112. Ibid. p. 48.
113. Ibid. p. 17.
114. Card, *The Atrocity Paradigm*, p. 13.
115. Ibid. p. 15.
116. Card, *Confronting Evils*, p. 18.
117. Ibid. p. 13.
118. Ibid. p. 26.
119. Ibid. p. 26.

120. Card, *The Atrocity Paradigm*, p. 79.
121. Ibid. p. 79.
122. Ibid. p. 73.
123. Ibid. p. 73.
124. Ibid. p. 82.
125. Card, *Confronting Evils*, p. 43.
126. Ibid. p. 45.
127. Ibid. p. 45.
128. Ibid. p. 45.
129. Ibid. p. 48.
130. Ibid. p. 48.
131. Ibid. p. 48.
132. Ibid. p. 48.
133. Ibid. p. 48.
134. Immanuel Kant, *Religion within the Boundaries of Mere Reason and Other Writings*, trans. and ed. Allen Wood and George di Giovanni (Cambridge: Cambridge University Press, 1998), 6:29.
135. Ibid. 6:30.
136. Ibid. 6:30.
137. Ibid. 6:30.
138. Card, *Confronting Evils*, p. 36.
139. Ibid. p. 40.
140. Ibid. p. 40.
141. Ibid. p. 40.
142. Ibid. p. 46.
143. Ibid. p. 52.
144. Ibid. p. 52.
145. Ibid. p. 52.
146. Ibid. p. 52.
147. Ibid. p. 52.
148. Ibid. p. 52.
149. Ibid. p. 53.
150. Ibid. p. 51.
151. Ibid. p. 51.
152. Ibid. p. 51.
153. Ibid. p. 51.
154. Ibid. p. 51.
155. Ibid. p. 51.
156. Ibid. p. 51.
157. Card, *The Atrocity Paradigm*, p. 94.
158. Card, *Confronting Evils*, p. 57.
159. Kant, *Religion within the Boundaries of Mere Reason*, 6:37
160. Card, *The Atrocity Paradigm*, pp. 93–4.

161. Ibid. p. 90.
162. Ibid. p. 93.
163. Ibid. p. 91.
164. Ibid. p. 91.
165. Ibid. pp. 91–2.
166. Ibid. p. 94.
167. Ibid. p. 94.
168. Ibid. p. 94.
169. Card, *Confronting Evils*, p. 58.
170. Ibid. p. 58.
171. Ibid. p. 58.
172. Ibid. p. 58.
173. Ibid. p. 58.
174. Ibid. p. 58.
175. Card, *The Atrocity Paradigm*, p. 212.
176. Ibid. p. 212.
177. Card, *Confronting Evils*, p. 58.
178. Ibid. p. 58.
179. Ibid. p. 58.
180. Ibid. p. 59.
181. Ibid. p. 59.
182. Ibid. p. 59.
183. Ibid. p. 59.
184. Ibid. p. 59.
185. Ibid. p. 59.
186. Ibid. p. 59.
187. Ibid. p. 59.
188. Ibid. p. 59.
189. Ibid. p. 59.
190. Ibid. p. 59.
191. Ibid. p. 60.
192. Ibid. p. 60.
193. Ibid. p. 60.
194. Card, *The Atrocity Paradigm*, p. 212.
195. Ibid. p. 212.
196. Primo Levi, *The Drowned and the Saved*, trans. Raymond Rosenthal (New York: Vintage, 1989), p. 48.
197. Ibid. pp. 48–9.
198. Ibid. p. 49.
199. Card, *The Atrocity Paradigm*, p. 212.
200. Levi, *The Drowned and the Saved*, p. 52.
201. Ibid. p. 52.
202. Ibid. p. 40.

203. Ibid. pp. 40–1.
204. Card, *The Atrocity Paradigm*, p. 213.
205. Ibid. p. 224.
206. Card, *Confronting Evils*, p. 56.
207. Ibid. p. 56.
208. Ibid. pp. 60–1.
209. Card, *The Atrocity Paradigm*, p. 233.
210. Ibid. p. 233.
211. Ibid. p. 231.
212. Ibid. p. 231.
213. Ibid. p. 231.
214. Ibid. p. 231.
215. Ibid. pp. 231–2.
216. Ibid. p. 232.
217. Ibid. p. 232.
218. Ibid. p. 224.
219. Ibid. pp. 212–13.
220. Ibid. p. 213.
221. Ibid. p. 226.
222. Ibid. p. 226.
223. Ibid. p. 226.
224. To my knowledge, Card never mentions or references Jacques Derrida's work specifically or deconstruction generally, but this recalls Derrida's notion of what he calls the 'crisis of *versus*'; that is, the idea that the binary oppositions historically used to structure Western thought are inadequate and should be replaced with a more nuanced and fluid logic. See Jacques Derrida, *Dissemination*, trans. Barbara Johnson (London: Continuum, 2004), p. 21.
225. Card, *Confronting Evils*, pp. 25–6.

# Conclusion

The history of evil outlined in the previous chapters has, amongst other things, shown that in the Western philosophical tradition the question of evil was initially framed within an explicitly theological, predominantly Christian, metaphysical framework, before moving to secular premises with the advent of Kant's critical philosophy. At first glance, it appears then that Western thinking on evil has undergone a historical process of secularisation.

I have argued, however, that this is only apparent. From Arendt's, Castoriadis's, and Kant's continuing dependence on the connection that Augustine makes between autonomous will and moral choice, Schelling's rejection of Judaeo-Christian conceptions of God and affirmation of an alternative, Nietzsche's claim that 'evil' is an inherently Judaeo-Christian concept, Lacan's insistence that God is always an unconscious part of semiotic systems, Kekes's and Card's dependence – through their affirmation of a fixed, ahistoric definition of evil – on the foundational logic underpinning Judaeo-Christian metaphysics, and Card's reference to and use of the figure of Satan and the concept of absolute evil, thinkers who have professed to offer an explicitly secular response to the problem of evil have continued to implicitly depend upon the logic, imagery, and figures of the theological tradition that they supposedly oppose.

This conclusion is, however, premised on a number of theoretical assumptions, regarding the nature of transformation and the issue of whether a position can be completely divorced from that which it opposes, that have remained implicit to this point. To bolster my conclusion and, indeed, engage with what it might mean for future thought on the subject, it might be helpful to make explicit my main assumptions.

Put schematically, I have been working with the assumption that there are two criteria that have to be met for an account to be considered fully 'secular'. The first is *linguistic* and holds that, to be fully secular, an analysis must not use the concepts (besides the term 'evil', which is the issue under discussion) found in the theological tradition. So if a supposedly secular analysis employs terms found initially within the theological tradition – regardless of whether the meaning of the term used by the 'secular' analysis is the same as that of the theological tradition – that is sufficient to conclude that it remains bound to the theological tradition. By simply using the same concepts – even if the history of them is not always understood by those employing them – a connection remains between the secular tradition and the theological tradition that it seeks to escape from.

However, that a secular approach successfully removes the linguistic categories of the theological tradition from its analysis does not automatically mean that it has broken decisively with that tradition. It must also fulfil a second criterion that refers to the *logic* underpinning the inquiry to determine whether it continues to depend upon the foundationalism that sustains theological accounts, wherein the analysis is generated from a singular point called 'God' – conceived of as an all-powerful, all-knowing, and supremely good being – that grounds all else. There are two related aspects to this: (1) a dependence on a unitary foundation (2) that is called 'God'. For a secular position to break entirely with the theological approach, I have been guided by the contention that it must remove both aspects from its schema. However, while secular approaches have tended to remove references to God, we have seen that they have continued to, at least implicitly, depend on a foundational point or principle. The obvious exception to this – one that makes his thinking stand out in the tradition – is Schelling, who, in affirming a differential ground, appears to break with (1), but continues to call this 'God', thereby affirming (2).

That attempts to offer a purely secular analysis have, to this point, failed does, however, bring forth the question of whether it might be achieved in the future. This will obviously be for future analyses to determine, but I am initially sceptical for, at least, three reasons. First, it would appear that any secular approach must continue to depend upon a certain foundational logic to simply *establish* the problem of evil prior to providing a response to it. Whereas theological approaches hold that evil is a problem because it reveals a disjunction between empirical existence and certain metaphysical premises held to be true (namely the existence of an all-powerful, all-knowing, supremely good God), secular approaches have continued – and, so I would argue, must continue – to pose the problem in terms of empirical actions contradicting the premises not of an all-powerful, all-knowing, supremely good God, but of another foundational principle, such as a privileged fixed criterion or axiomatic definition of the good, or simply individual decision or choice.

As I have shown, this foundational principle has normally simply been assumed by proponents of secular analyses, but if an attempt has been made to justify it, this has had to be done, and indeed must be done, in non-theological terms through an appeal to what is 'natural', 'common-sensical', 'rational', or demonstrable through formal logic. Each of these, however, ultimately, rests on an implicit foundationalism as to what is natural or common-sensical, or tends to assume an end-point or foundation that must be appealed to for that demonstration to be considered rational or logical.

Second, secular positions tend to be implicitly premised on the idea that an absolute *rupture* from the theological tradition is possible and even desirable, with the consequence that they operate by way of a binary opposition between the secular and the theological. The history outlined in the previous chapters has, however, called that model of transformation into question. By showing that supposedly secular analyses continue to be bound to the theological ones rejected, the relationship between the two has been shown to be one of *transition*, wherein the movement from one position to another never fully departs from that which is rejected.

This depends upon two additional sub-claims: first, rather than being *a priori*, meaning is generated relationally, so that, for a secular analysis to have meaning, it must define itself against what it is not; namely, the theological. Second, the act of distinguishing between two positions – the secular and the theological – is diachronic, not synchronic. A synchronic act describes a one-off negation that subsequently affirms a completely distinct position. If this described the secular–theological relation – and assuming the absence of theological concepts and foundationalism – it would respect the notion that meaning is generated relationally and so account for why secular accounts of evil typically discuss theological ones, all the while allowing secular approaches to insist that their subsequent (positive) accounts of evil are totally distinct from and devoid of any theological influences.

In contrast, if meaning is generated from a diachronic act of negation, the negation must be continually reaffirmed. The secular must then return continuously to the theological tradition to negate it and, in so doing, show how it – the secular – is distinguished from that tradition. By having to continually make this return to the theological to establish and maintain itself, the secular continues to be (implicitly) bound to and so defined by its relationship to the theological.

So, putting the various pieces together, we see that if, as I have argued, transformation is transitional and meaning is relational and diachronic, any attempt to depart from the theological tradition to offer a purely secular account of evil will always have to constantly distinguish itself from that tradition and so be returned to it. Rather than conforming to a relationship of binary opposition, the secular and the theological exist and must exist in a relationship of continuous (uneasy) *logical* entwinement.

Third, the attempt to offer a 'purely' secular account of evil is implicitly premised on the notion that thought can remove itself completely from its historical setting. It is, after all, only by completely transcending its history that a 'purely' secular account of evil, devoid of any theological influences, could be provided. However, if the history outlined here has taught us anything, it is that no matter how hard it tries, thought is always thoroughly embedded within a socio-historical setting that it cannot become wholly disencumbered of. Rather than divorce itself from its history, thought can, at most, twist itself *through* its history to reconceptualise the contours defining its past. This is not to escape from that history, but to subtly alter it, all the while remaining tied to it. If this supposition is correct, there cannot be a purely secular approach devoid of and wholly distinct from the theological approaches that constitute and have long dominated Western thinking on the topic.

The fundamental problem with purely secular approaches is not therefore that they incorrectly implement correct assumptions; it is the assumptions themselves that are problematic because they are based on a flawed rupture-model of transformation that depends upon and perpetuates a straightforward binary opposition and movement between the theological and secular. I do not, however, want to claim that this demonstrates the inevitable dominance of theological approaches or that we should simply revert to theological explanations. Such a conclusion would remain trapped within and perpetuate the logic of binary oppositions – the secular versus the theological – that the transitional model of transformation I have affirmed undermines. Instead, the history of evil charted here points to the need for a far more nuanced and non-binary rethinking of the relationship between the secular and theological, so that secularity is not pitched as entailing the absence of theology, but is understood to be engaged in a complex, entwined, ongoing, and subtle relationship with the theological tradition that it emanates from and defines itself against; a relationship that will, no doubt, take on new forms as Western philosophy continues to grapple with its theologically dominated history generally and the problem of evil specifically.

# Bibliography

Adams, Suzi, 'Castoriadis' Shift towards *Physis*', *Thesis Eleven*, 74, 2003, pp. 105–12.
—, *Castoriadis's Ontology: Being and Creation* (New York: Fordham University Press, 2011).
Adorno, Theodor, and Max Horkheimer, *Dialectic of Enlightenment*, trans. John Cumming (London: Verso, 1997).
Aertsen, Jan A., 'Aquinas's Philosophy in its Historical Setting', in *The Cambridge Companion to Aquinas*, ed. Norman Kretzmann and Eleonore Stump (Cambridge: Cambridge University Press, 1993), pp. 12–38.
Alexander, Jeffrey C., 'Toward a Sociology of Evil: Getting beyond Modernist Common Sense about the Alternative to "the Good"', in *Rethinking Evil: Contemporary Perspectives*, ed. Maria Pia Lara (Berkeley: University of California Press, 2001), pp. 153–72.
Allen, Wayne, 'Hannah Arendt's Foundation for a Metaphysics of Evil', *The Southern Journal of Philosophy*, 38, 2000, pp. 183–206.
Allison, Henry E., *Kant's Theory of Freedom* (Cambridge: Cambridge University Press, 1990).
—, 'Ethics, Evil, and Anthropology in Kant: Remarks on Allen Wood's *Kant's Ethical Thought*', *Ethics*, 111, 2001, pp. 594–613.
—, 'On the Very Idea of a Propensity to Evil', *The Journal of Value Inquiry*, 36, 2002, pp. 337–48.
—, *Transcendental Idealism: An Interpretation and Defence* (New Haven: Yale University Press, 2004).
Ameriks, Karl, *Kant and the Historicist Turn: Philosophy as Critical Interpretation* (Oxford: Oxford University Press, 2006).
Anderson-Gold, Sharon, 'Kant's Rejection of Devilishness: The Limits of Human Volition', *Idealistic Studies*, 14:1, 1984, pp. 35–48.

Ansell-Pearson, Keith, *An Introduction to Nietzsche as Political Thinker: The Perfect Nihilist* (Cambridge: Cambridge University Press, 1994).

Antognazza, Maria Rosa, 'Metaphysical Evil Revisited', in *New Essays on Leibniz's Theodicy*, ed. Larry M. Jorgensen and Samuel Newlands (Oxford: Oxford University Press, 2014), pp. 112–34.

Aquinas, Thomas, *Summa Theologiae*, trans. Fathers of the English Dominican Province (Einsiedeln: Benziger Bros, 1947).

—, *On Evil*, trans. Richard Regan (Oxford: Oxford University Press, 2003).

Arendt, Hannah, 'The Concentration Camps', *Partisan Review*, 15:7, 1948, pp. 43–64.

—, *On Violence* (New York: Harvest, 1970).

—, *The Origins of Totalitarianism* (New York: Harvest, 1976).

—, *The Life of the Mind: Thinking*, ed. Mary McCarthy (New York: Harvest, 1978).

—, *The Life of the Mind: Willing*, ed. Mary McCarthy (New York: Harvest, 1978).

—, '"What Remains? The Language Remains": A Conversation with Günter Gaus', in *Essays in Understanding, 1930–1954*, ed. Jerome Kohn (New York: Schocken Books, 1994), pp. 1–23.

—, 'Social Science Techniques and the Study of Concentration Camps', in *Essays in Understanding, 1930–1954*, ed. Jerome Kohn (New York: Schocken Books, 1994), pp. 232–47.

—, 'The Eggs Speak Up', in *Essays in Understanding, 1930–1954*, ed. Jerome Kohn (New York: Schocken Books, 1994), pp. 270–84.

—, 'Mankind and Terror', in *Essays in Understanding, 1930–1954*, ed. Jerome Kohn (New York: Schocken Books, 1994), pp. 297–306.

—, 'On the Nature of Totalitarianism: An Essay in Understanding', in *Essays in Understanding, 1930–1954*, ed. Jerome Kohn (New York: Schocken Books, 1994), pp. 328–60.

—, *Love and Saint Augustine*, ed. Joanna Vecchiarelli Scott and Judith Chelius Stark (Chicago: University of Chicago Press, 1996).

—, *The Human Condition*, 2nd edn (Chicago: University of Chicago Press, 1998).

—, 'Personal Responsibility under Dictatorship', in *Responsibility and Judgement*, ed. Jerome Kohn (New York: Schocken Books, 2003), pp. 17–48.

—, 'Some Questions of Moral Philosophy', in *Responsibility and Judgement*, ed. Jerome Kohn (New York: Schocken Books, 2003), pp. 49–146.

—, 'Thinking and Moral Considerations', in *Responsibility and Judgement*, ed. Jerome Kohn (New York: Schocken Books, 2003), pp. 159–89.

—, 'Auschwitz on Trial', in *Responsibility and Judgement*, ed. Jerome Kohn (New York: Schocken, 2003), pp. 226–56.
—, *Eichmann in Jerusalem: A Report on the Banality of Evil* (London: Penguin, 2006).
—, *On Revolution* (London: Penguin, 2006).
—, 'Letter of 24 July 1963 to Gershom Scholem', in *The Jewish Writings*, ed. Jerome Kohn and Ron H. Feldman (New York: Schocken Books, 2007), pp. 465–71.
Arendt, Hannah, and Roger Errera, 'Hannah Arendt: From an Interview', *New York Review of Books*, 26 October, 1978, p. 18.
Arendt, Hannah, and Karl Jaspers, *Correspondence: 1932–1969*, ed. Lotte Kohler and Hans Sander (Harcourt: New York, 1992).
Aslam, Adnan, 'The Fall and Overcoming of Evil and Suffering in Islam', in *The Origin and the Overcoming of Evil and Suffering in the World Religions*, ed. Peter Koslowski (Dordrecht: Kluwer, 2001), pp. 24–47.
Augustine, *The City of God against the Pagans*, ed. and trans. R. W. Dyson (Cambridge: Cambridge University Press, 1998).
—, *Confessions*, trans. Henry Chadwick (London: Penguin, 2008).
—, *On the Free Choice of the Will, On Grace and Free Choice, and Other Writings*, ed. and trans. Peter King (Cambridge: Cambridge University Press, 2010).
Bailly, Lionel, *Lacan* (London: OneWorld, 2009).
Baker, Patrick, *Italian Renaissance Humanism in the Mirror* (Cambridge: Cambridge University Press, 2015).
Basinger, David, *Miracles* (Cambridge: Cambridge University Press, 2018).
Beiser, Frederick C., *German Idealism: The Struggle against Subjectivity 1781–1801* (Cambridge, MA: Harvard University Press, 2002).
Bergmann, Frithjof, 'Nietzsche and Analytic Ethics', in *Nietzsche, Genealogy, Morality: Essays on Nietzsche's On the Genealogy of Morals*, ed. Richard Schacht (Berkeley: University of California Press, 1994), pp. 76–94.
Bernstein, Richard, *Radical Evil: A Philosophical Investigation* (Cambridge: Polity, 2002).
Bett, Richard, 'Nietzsche and the Romans', *The Journal of Nietzsche Studies*, 42, Autumn, 2011, pp. 7–31.
Blondel, Eric, 'The Question of Genealogy', in *Nietzsche, Genealogy, Morality: Essays on Nietzsche's On the Genealogy of Morals*, ed. Richard Schacht (Berkeley: University of California Press, 1994), pp. 306–17.
Boureau, Alain, *Satan hérétique: Naissance de la démonologie dans l'Occident Médiéval, 1280–1330* (Paris: Éditions Odile Jacob, 2004).

Bowie, Andrew, *Schelling and Modern European Philosophy* (Abingdon: Routledge, 1993).
Broadie, Frederick, *An Approach to Descartes' Meditations* (London: Athlone Press, 1970).
Brobjer, Thomas H., 'Nietzsche's Affirmative Morality: An Ethics of Virtue', *The Journal of Nietzsche Studies*, 26, Autumn, 2003, pp. 64–78.
Brown, Robert, *The Later Philosophy of Schelling: The Influence of Boehme on the Works of 1809–1815* (Plainsboro: Associated University Press, 1977).
Brownlee, Timothy, 'Hegel's Moral Concept of Evil', *Dialogues: Canadian Philosophical Review*, 52:1, 2013, pp. 81–108.
Bruce, Steve, *Secularisation: In Defence of an Unfashionable Theory* (Oxford: Oxford University Press, 2011).
Burkert, Walter, *Griechische Religion der archaischen und klassischen Epoche* (Stuttgart: W. Kohlhammer, 1977).
Burns, J. Patout, 'Augustine on the Origin and Progress of Evil', *The Journal of Religious Ethics*, 16:1, Spring, 1988, pp. 9–27.
Burrell, David B., 'Aquinas and Islamic and Jewish Thinkers', in *The Cambridge Companion to Aquinas*, ed. Norman Kretzmann and Eleonore Stump (Cambridge: Cambridge University Press, 1993), pp. 60–84.
Cabrera, Isabel, 'Is God Evil?', in *Rethinking Evil: Contemporary Perspectives*, ed. Maria Pia Lara (Berkeley: University of California Press, 2001), pp. 17–26.
Card, Claudia, *The Atrocity Paradigm: A Theory of Evil* (Oxford: Oxford University Press, 2002).
—, *Confronting Evils: Terrorism, Torture, Genocide* (Cambridge: Cambridge University Press, 2010).
—, 'Kant's Moral Excluded Middle', in *Kant's Anatomy of Evil*, ed. Sharon Anderson-Gold and Pablo Muchnik (Cambridge: Cambridge University Press, 2014), pp. 74–92.
Cary, Phillip, *Inner Grace: Augustine in the Traditions of Plato and Paul* (Oxford: Oxford University Press, 2008).
Castoriadis, Cornelius, 'Preface', in *Crossroads in the Labyrinth*, trans. Kate Soper and Martin H. Ryle (Cambridge, MA: MIT Press, 1984), pp. ix–xxx.
—, 'Psychoanalysis: Project and Elucidation', in *Crossroads in the Labyrinth*, trans. Kate Soper and Martin H. Ryle (Cambridge, MA: MIT Press, 1984), pp. 46–115.
—, 'The "End of Philosophy"?', in *Philosophy, Politics, Autonomy: Essays in Political Philosophy*, ed. David Ames Curtis (Oxford: Oxford University Press, 1991), pp. 13–32.

—, 'The Social-Historical: Mode of Being, Problems of Knowledge', in *Philosophy, Politics, Autonomy: Essays in Political Philosophy*, ed. David Ames Curtis (Oxford: Oxford University Press, 1991), pp. 33–46.

—, 'Individual, Society, Rationality, History', in *Philosophy, Politics, Autonomy: Essays in Political Philosophy*, ed. David Ames Curtis (Oxford: Oxford University Press, 1991), pp. 47–80.

—, 'Power, Politics, Autonomy', in *Philosophy, Politics, Autonomy: Essays in Political Philosophy*, ed. David Ames Curtis (Oxford: Oxford University Press, 1991), pp. 143–74.

—, 'The Imaginary: Creation in the Social-Historical Domain', in *World in Fragments*, ed. and trans. David Ames Curtis (Stanford: Stanford University Press, 1997), pp. 3–18.

—, 'Reflections on Racism', in *World in Fragments*, ed. and trans. David Ames Curtis (Stanford: Stanford University Press, 1997), pp. 19–31.

—, 'The Greek and the Modern Political Imaginary', in *World in Fragments*, ed. and trans. David Ames Curtis (Stanford: Stanford University Press, 1997), pp. 84–107.

—, 'Psychoanalysis and Politics', in *World in Fragments*, ed. and trans. David Ames Curtis (Stanford: Stanford University Press, 1997), pp. 125–36.

—, 'From Monad to Autonomy', in *World in Fragments*, ed. and trans. David Ames Curtis (Stanford: Stanford University Press, 1997), pp. 172–95.

—, 'The Discovery of the Imagination', in *World in Fragments*, ed. and trans. David Ames Curtis (Stanford: Stanford University Press, 1997), pp. 213–45.

—, 'Institution of Society and Religion', in *World in Fragments*, ed. and trans. David Ames Curtis (Stanford: Stanford University Press, 1997), pp. 311–30.

—, '*Phusis* and Autonomy', in *World in Fragments*, ed. and trans. David Ames Curtis (Stanford: Stanford University Press, 1997), pp. 331–41.

—, 'The Ontological Import of the History of Science', in *World in Fragments*, ed. and trans. David Ames Curtis (Stanford: Stanford University Press, 1997), pp. 342–73.

—, *The Imaginary Institution of Society*, trans. Kathleen Blamey (Cambridge, MA: MIT Press, 1998).

—, 'Imaginary and Imagination at the Crossroads', in *Figures of the Thinkable*, trans. Helen Arnold (Stanford: Stanford University Press, 2007), pp. 71–90.

—, 'Primal Institution of Society and Second-Order Institutions', in *Figures of the Thinkable*, trans. Helen Arnold (Stanford: Stanford University Press, 2007), pp. 91–101.

—, 'Heritage and Revolution', in *Figures of the Thinkable*, trans. Helen Arnold (Stanford: Stanford University Press, 2007), pp. 105–17.
—, 'Psyche and Education', in *Figures of the Thinkable*, trans. Helen Arnold (Stanford: Stanford University Press, 2007), pp. 165–87.
—, 'Psychoanalysis: Its Situation and Limits', in *Figures of the Thinkable*, trans. Helen Arnold (Stanford: Stanford University Press, 2007), pp. 188–202.
—, 'The Psyche and Society Anew', in *Figures of the Thinkable*, trans. Helen Arnold (Stanford: Stanford University Press, 2007), pp. 203–20.
—, 'False and True Chaos', in *Figures of the Thinkable*, trans. Helen Arnold (Stanford: Stanford University Press, 2007), pp. 236–43.
—, 'Remarks on Space and Number', in *Figures of the Thinkable*, trans. Helen Arnold (Stanford: Stanford University Press, 2007), pp. 244–59.
—, 'The Project of Autonomy is not Utopia', in *A Society Adrift: Interviews and Debates, 1974–1977*, ed. Enrique Escobar, Myrto Gondicas, and Pascal Vernay, trans. Helen Arnold (New York: Fordham University Press, 2010), pp. 3–10.
—, 'Imaginary Significations', in *A Society Adrift: Interviews and Debates, 1974–1977*, ed. Enrique Escobar, Myrto Gondicas, and Pascal Vernay, trans. Helen Arnold (New York: Fordham University Press, 2010), pp. 45–68.
—, 'Response to Richard Rorty', in *A Society Adrift: Interviews and Debates, 1974–1977*, ed. Enrique Escobar, Myrto Gondicas, and Pascal Vernay, trans. Helen Arnold (New York: Fordham University Press, 2010), pp. 69–82.
—, 'On Wars in Europe', in *A Society Adrift: Interviews and Debates, 1974–1977*, ed. Enrique Escobar, Myrto Gondicas, and Pascal Vernay, trans. Helen Arnold (New York: Fordham University Press, 2010), pp. 83–102.
—, 'On the Possibility of Creating a New Form of Society', in *A Society Adrift: Interviews and Debates, 1974–1977*, ed. Enrique Escobar, Myrto Gondicas, and Pascal Vernay, trans. Helen Arnold (New York: Fordham University Press, 2010), pp. 103–16.
Chiesa, Lorenzo, *Subjectivity and Otherness: A Philosophical Reading of Lacan* (Cambridge, MA: MIT Press, 2007).
Clarke, Maudemarie, 'Nietzsche's Immoralism and the Concept of Morality', in *Nietzsche, Genealogy, Morality: Essays on Nietzsche's On the Genealogy of Morals*, ed. Richard Schacht (Berkeley: University of California Press, 1994), pp. 35–48.
Cole, Phillip, *The Myth of Evil* (Edinburgh: Edinburgh University Press, 2006).

Copjec, Joan, *Read my Desire: Lacan against the Historicists* (London: Verso, 2015).
Cormer, David, *The Philosophy of Miracles* (London: Continuum, 2007).
Cotkin, George, 'Illuminating Evil: Hannah Arendt and Moral History', *Modern Intellectual History*, 4:3, 2007, pp. 463–90.
Covington, Coline, 'Hannah Arendt, Evil and the Eradication of Thought', *International Journal of Psychoanalysis*, 93, 2012, pp. 1215–36.
Critchley, Simon, '*Das Ding*: Lacan and Levinas', in *Ethics–Politics–Subjectivity: Essays on Derrida, Levinas, and Contemporary French Thought* (London: Verso, 1999), pp. 198–216.
—, *The Faith of the Faithless: Experiments in Political Theology* (London: Verso, 2012).
Crockett, Clayton, *Interstices of the Sublime: Theology and Psychoanalytic Theory* (New York: Fordham University Press, 2007).
—, *Radical Political Theology: Religion and Politics after Liberalism* (New York: Columbia University Press, 2011).
Darwin, Charles, *On the Origin of Species* (Oxford: Oxford University Press, 2008).
Davies, Brian, *The Reality of God and the Problem of Evil* (London: Continuum, 2006).
—, *Thomas Aquinas on God and Evil* (Oxford: Oxford University Press, 2011).
Deleuze, Gilles, and Felix Guattari, *A Thousand Plateaus: Capitalism and Schizophrenia*, trans. Brian Massumi (London: Continuum, 2004).
Derrida, Jacques, *Dissemination*, trans. Barbara Johnson (London: Continuum, 2004).
Descartes, René, *Discourse on the Method*, trans. R. Stoothoff, in *The Philosophical Writings of Descartes*, vol. 1 (Cambridge: Cambridge University Press, 1985), pp. 111–51.
—, *Meditations on First Philosophy*, trans. and ed. John Cottingham (Cambridge: Cambridge University Press, 1986).
Dews, Peter, *The Idea of Evil* (Blackwell: Oxford, 2008).
Dossa, Shiraz, 'Hannah Arendt on Eichmann: The Public, the Private, and Evil', *The Review of Politics*, 46:2, 1984, pp. 163–82.
Dosse, François, *History of Structuralism, vol. 1: The Rising Sign, 1945–1966*, trans. Deborah Glassman (Minneapolis: University of Minnesota Press, 1997).
Doyle, Natalie, 'Autonomy and Modern Liberal Democracy: From Castoriadis to Gauchet', *European Journal of Social Theory*, 15:3, 2012, pp. 331–47.

Dudley, Will, *Hegel, Nietzsche, and Philosophy: Thinking Freedom* (Cambridge: Cambridge University Press, 2002).

Duncan, Samuel, '"There is none Righteous": Kant on the *Hang zum Bösen* and the Universal Evil in History', *The Southern Journal of Philosophy*, 49:2, 2011, pp. 137–63.

Dunlap, Aron, *Lacan and Religion* (Durham: Acumen, 2014).

Duschinsky, Robbie, 'Nietzsche: Through the Lens of Purity', *The Journal of Nietzsche Studies*, 41, Spring, 2011, pp. 50–64.

Eagleton, Terry, *On Evil* (New Haven: Yale University Press, 2010).

Eberl, Jason T., 'Aquinas on the Nature of Human Being', *The Review of Metaphysics*, 58:2, 2004, pp. 333–65.

Elliot, Anthony, 'The Social Imaginary: A Critical Assessment of Castoriadis's Psychoanalytic Social Theory', *American Imago*, 59:2, 2002, pp. 141–70.

Emery, Gilles, and Matthew Levering (eds), *Aristotle in Aquinas's Theology* (Cambridge: Cambridge University Press, 2015).

Erdozain, Dominic, *The Soul of Doubt: The Religious Roots of Unbelief from Luther to Marx* (Oxford: Oxford University Press, 2016).

Evans, G. R., *Augustine on Evil* (Cambridge: Cambridge University Press, 1982).

Farrell-Krell, David, 'The Crisis of Reason in the Nineteenth Century: Schelling's Treatise on Human Freedom (1809)', in *The Collegium Phaenomenologicum: The First Ten Years*, ed. John Sallis, Giuseppina Moneta, and Jacques Taminiaux (Dordrecht: Springer, 1988), pp. 13–32.

Ffytche, Matt, *The Foundation of the Unconscious: Schelling, Freud, and the Birth of the Modern Psyche* (Cambridge: Cambridge University Press, 2012).

Fink, Bruce, *The Lacanian Subject: Between Language and Jouissance* (Princeton: Princeton University Press, 1995).

—, *A Clinical Introduction to Lacanian Psychoanalysis: Theory and Technique* (Cambridge, MA: Harvard University Press, 1997).

Formosa, Paul, 'Is Radical Evil Banal? Is Banal Evil Radical?', *Philosophy and Social Criticism*, 33:6, 2007, pp. 717–35.

—, 'Kant on the Radical Evil of Human Nature', *The Philosophical Forum*, 38:3, 2007, pp. 221–45.

Forsyth, Neil, *The Old Enemy: Satan and the Combat Myth* (Princeton: Princeton University Press, 1987).

—, 'The Origin of "Evil": Classical or Judeo–Christian?', *Perspectives on Evil and Human Wickedness*, 1:1, January, 2002, pp. 17–52.

Forti, Simona, *New Demons: Rethinking Power and Evil Today*, trans. Zakiya Hanafi (Stanford: Stanford University Press, 2015).
Foucault, Michel, 'Nietzsche, Genealogy, Critique', in *The Foucault Reader*, ed. Paul Rabinow (New York: Vintage, 2010), pp. 76–100.
Frieson, Patrick R., *Freedom and Anthropology in Kant's Moral Philosophy* (Cambridge: Cambridge University Press, 2003).
—, 'Character and Evil in Kant's Moral Anthropology', *Journal of the History of Philosophy*, 44:4, 2006, pp. 623–34.
Gaukroger, Stephen, *The Emergence of a Scientific Culture: Science and the Shaping of Modernity 1210–1685* (Oxford: Oxford University Press, 2009).
Gillespie, Michael Allen, *The Theological Origins of Modernity* (Chicago: University of Chicago Press, 2008).
Glasgow, Joshua, 'Kant's Conception of Humanity', *Journal of the History of Philosophy*, 45:2, 2007, pp. 291–308.
Graham, Gordon, *Evil and Christian Ethics* (Cambridge: Cambridge University Press, 2001).
Grimm, Stephen R., 'Kant's Argument for Radical Evil', *European Journal of Philosophy*, 10:2, 2002, pp. 160–77.
Groves, Christopher, 'Ecstasy of Reason, Crisis of Reason: Schelling and Absolute Difference', *Pli*, 8, 1999, pp. 25–45.
Guay, Robert, 'Genealogy and Irony', *Journal of Nietzsche Studies*, 41, 2011, pp. 26–49.
Guerrier, Eric, *Le problème du Mal dans une métaphysique de l'alchimie: Une filiation insolite entre Luther, Böhme et Schelling* (Paris: Éditions L'Harmattan, 2013).
Habermas, Jürgen, 'Excursus on Cornelius Castoriadis: The Imaginary Institution', in *The Philosophical Discourse of Modernity: Twelve Lectures*, trans. Frederick Lawrence (Cambridge: Polity, 1987), pp. 328–35.
Han-Pile, Béatrice, 'Nietzsche and Amor Fati', *European Journal of Philosophy*, 19:2, June, 2011, pp. 224–62.
Hatfield, Gary, *Descartes and the Meditations* (Abingdon: Routledge, 2003).
Hayden, Patrick, 'The Relevance of Hannah Arendt's Reflections on Evil: Globalization and Rightlessness', *Human Rights Review*, 11, 2010, pp. 451–67.
Hegel, G. W. F., *The Philosophy of History*, trans. J. Sibree (New York: Dover, 1956).
Heidegger, Martin, *Schelling's Treatise on the Essence of Human Freedom*, trans. Joan Stambaugh (Athens: Ohio University Press, 1985).
Hernandez, Jill Graper, 'Moral Evil and Leibniz's Form/Matter Defence of Divine Omnipotence', *Sophia*, 49:1, 2010, pp. 1–13.

Honneth, Axel, 'Rescuing the Revolution with an Ontology: On Cornelius Castoriadis' Theory of Society', *Thesis Eleven*, 14, 1986, pp. 62–78.

Houlgate, Stephen, *Hegel, Nietzsche and the Criticism of Metaphysics* (Cambridge: Cambridge University Press, 1986).

Janowski, Zbigniew, *Cartesian Theodicy: Descartes' Quest for Certitude* (Dordrecht: Kluwer, 2000).

Jeffery, Renée, *Evil and International Relations: Human Suffering in an Age of Terror* (Basingstoke: Palgrave Macmillan, 2008).

Jorgensen, Larry M., and Samuel Newlands, 'Introduction', in *New Essays on Leibniz's Theodicy*, ed. Larry M. Jorgensen and Samuel Newlands (Oxford: Oxford University Press, 2014), pp. 1–12.

Josephson-Storm, Jason A., *The Myth of Disenchantment: Magic, Modernity, and the Birth of the Human Sciences* (Chicago: University of Chicago Press, 2017).

Kamen, Henry, *The Spanish Inquisition: A Historical Revision*, 4th edn (New Haven: Yale University Press, 2014).

Kant, Immanuel, 'On the Common Saying: "This may be True in Theory, but it does not Apply in Practice"', in *Political Writings*, ed. Hans Reiss, trans. H. B. Nisbet (Cambridge: Cambridge University Press, 1991), pp. 61–92.

—, *The Metaphysics of Morals*, trans. and ed. Mary Gregor (Cambridge: Cambridge University Press, 1996).

—, *Critique of Practical Reason*, trans. Mary Gregor (Cambridge: Cambridge University Press, 1997).

—, *Critique of Pure Reason*, trans. and ed. Paul Guyer and Allen Wood (Cambridge: Cambridge University Press, 1998).

—, *Groundwork of the Metaphysics of Morals*, trans. Mary Gregor (Cambridge: Cambridge University Press, 1998).

—, *Religion within the Boundaries of Mere Reason and Other Writings*, trans. and ed. Allen Wood and George di Giovanni (Cambridge: Cambridge University Press, 1998).

—, 'On the Miscarriage of all Philosophical Trials in Theodicy', in *Religion within the Boundaries of Mere Reason and Other Writings*, trans. and ed. Allen Wood and George di Giovanni (Cambridge: Cambridge University Press, 1998), pp. 17–30.

Karagiannis, Nathalie, and Peter Wagner, 'Imagination and Tragic Democracy', *Critical Horizons*, 13:1, 2012, pp. 12–28.

Kekes, John, *Facing Evil* (Princeton: Princeton University Press, 1990).

—, 'The Reflexivity of Evil', *Social Philosophy and Policy*, 15:1, 1998, pp. 216–32.

—, *The Roots of Evil* (Ithaca: Cornell University Press, 2005).

Kelsey, David, 'Aquinas and Barth on the Human Body', *The Thomist*, 50:4, 1986, pp. 643–89.

Keys, Mary M., *Aquinas, Aristotle, and the Promise of the Common Good* (Cambridge: Cambridge University Press. 2008).

Klooger, Jeff, 'From Nothing: Castoriadis and the Concept of Creation', *Critical Horizons*, 12:1, 2010, pp. 29–47.

Kosch, Michelle, *Freedom and Reason in Kant, Schelling, and Kierkegaard* (Oxford: Oxford University Press, 2006).

Kremer, Elmer J., 'Leibniz and the "Disciples of Saint Augustine" on the Fate of Infants who Die Unbaptized', in *The Problem of Evil in Early Modern Philosophy*, ed. Elmar J. Kremer and Michael J. Latzer (Toronto: University of Toronto Press, 2001), pp. 119–37.

Lacan, Jacques, *Seminar XI: The Four Fundamental Concepts of Psychoanalysis*, ed. Jacques-Alain Miller, trans. Alan Sheridan (New York: W. W. Norton, 1981).

—, *Television*, ed. Joan Copjec, trans. Denis Hollier, Rosalind Krauss, and Annette Michelson (New York: W. W. Norton, 1990).

—, *Seminar I: Freud's Papers on Technique*, ed. Jacques-Alain Miller, trans. John Forrester (New York: W. W. Norton, 1991).

—, *Seminar II: The Ego in Freud's Theory and in the Technique of Psychoanalysis*, ed. Jacques-Alain Miller, trans. Sylvana Tomaselli (New York: W. W. Norton, 1991).

—, *Seminar III: The Psychoses*, ed. Jacques-Alain Miller, trans. Russell Grigg (New York: W. W. Norton, 1997).

—, *Seminar VII: The Ethics of Psychoanalysis*, ed. Jacques-Alain Miller, trans. Dennis Porter (New York: W. W. Norton, 1997).

—, *Seminar XX: On Feminine Sexuality, The Limits of Love and Knowledge*, ed. Jacques-Alain Miller, trans. Bruce Fink (New York: W. W. Norton, 1999).

—, 'Seminar on "The Purloined Letter"', in *Écrits*, trans. Bruce Fink (New York: W. W. Norton, 2006), pp. 6–48.

—, 'The Mirror Stage as Formative of the I Function as Revealed in Psychoanalytic Experience', in *Écrits*, trans. Bruce Fink (New York: W. W. Norton, 2006), pp. 75–81.

—, 'The Function and Field of Speech and Language in Psychoanalysis', in *Écrits*, trans. Bruce Fink (New York: W. W. Norton, 2006), pp. 197–268.

—, 'Introduction to Jean Hyppolite's Commentary on Freud's "Verneinung"', in *Écrits*, trans. Bruce Fink (New York: W. W. Norton, 2006), pp. 308–17.

—, 'Response to Jean Hyppolite's Commentary on Freud's "Verneinung"', in *Écrits*, trans. Bruce Fink (New York: W. W. Norton, 2006), pp. 318–33.
—, 'The Subversion of the Subject and the Dialectic of Desire in the Freudian Unconscious', in *Écrits*, trans. Bruce Fink (New York: W. W. Norton, 2006), pp. 672–702.
—, *Seminar XVII: The Other Side of Psychoanalysis*, trans. Russell Grigg (New York: W. W. Norton, 2007).
—, *Seminar X: Anxiety*, ed. Jacques-Alain Miller, trans. A. R. Price (Cambridge: Polity, 2014).
—, *Seminar VIII: Transference*, ed. Jacques-Alain Miller, trans. Bruce Fink (Cambridge: Polity, 2015).
Lambert, Gregg, *Return Statements: The Return of Religion in Contemporary Philosophy* (Edinburgh: Edinburgh University Press, 2016).
Lara, Maria Pia (ed.), *Rethinking Evil: Contemporary Perspectives* (Berkeley: University of California Press, 2001).
—, 'Narrating Evil: A Postmetaphysical Theory of Reflective Judgement', in *Rethinking Evil: Contemporary Perspectives*, ed. Maria Pia Lara (Berkeley: University of California Press, 2001), pp. 239–50.
—, *Narrating Evil: A Postmetaphysical Theory of Reflective Judgement* (New York: Columbia University Press, 2007).
Latzer, Michael, 'The Nature of Evil: Leibniz and his Medieval Background', *The Modern Schoolman*, 71:1, 1993, pp. 59–69.
—, 'Leibniz's Conception of Metaphysical Evil', *Journal of the History of Ideas*, 55:1, January, 1994, p. 1–15.
—, 'Descartes's Theodicy of Error', in *The Problem of Evil in Early Modern Philosophy*, ed. Elmar J. Kremer and Michael J. Latzer (Toronto: University of Toronto Press, 2001), pp. 35–48.
Lee, Patrick, 'The Goodness of Creation, Evil, and Christian Teaching', *The Thomist*, 64, 2000, pp. 239–69.
Leibniz, G. W., *Discourse on Metaphysics, Correspondence with Arnauld, and Monadology*, trans. George R. Montgomery (Chicago: Open Court, 1950).
—, *Theodicy: Essays on the Goodness of God, the Freedom of Man, and the Origin of Evil*, trans. E. M. Huggard (Chicago: Open Court, 1985).
—, *Confessio Philosophi: Papers Concerning the Problem of Evil, 1671–1678*, trans. Robert C. Sleigh Jr. (New Haven: Yale University Press, 2005).
Leiter, Brian, *Nietzsche on Morality*, 2nd edn (Abingdon: Routledge, 2015).
Lennon, Thomas M., 'The Fourth Meditation: Descartes' Theodicy *Avant la Lettre*', in *The Cambridge Companion to Descartes' Meditations*, ed. David Cunning (Cambridge: Cambridge University Press, 2014), pp. 168–85.

Levi, Primo, *The Drowned and the Saved*, trans. Raymond Rosenthal (New York: Vintage, 1989).

Levinas, Emmanuel, 'Reflections on the Philosophy of Hitlerism', trans. Seán Hand, *Critical Inquiry*, 17:1, 1990, pp. 62–71.

Lévi-Strauss, Claude, *Introduction to the Work of Marcel Mauss*, trans. Felicity Baker (London: Routledge & Kegan Paul, 1987).

Loncar, Samuel, 'Converting the Kantian Self: Radical Evil, Agency, and Conversion in Kant's *Religion within the Boundaries of Mere Reason*', *Kant-Studien*, 104:3, 2013, pp. 346–66.

Losonsky, Michael, *Linguistic Turns in Modern Philosophy* (Cambridge: Cambridge University Press, 2006).

McCabe, Herbert, *God and Evil in the Theology of St Thomas Aquinas*, ed. Brian Davies (London: Continuum, 2010).

McGrath, S. J., 'Schelling on the Unconscious', *Research in Phenomenology*, 40:1, 2010, pp. 72–91.

McNulty, Tracy, *Wrestling with the Angel: Experiments in Symbolic Life* (New York: Columbia University Press, 2014).

Maker, William, 'Augustine on Evil: The Dilemma for the Philosophers', *International Journal for Philosophy of Religion*, 15:3, 1984, pp. 149–60.

Mandelbaum, Maurice, *History, Man, Reason: A Study in 19th Century Thought* (Baltimore: Johns Hopkins University Press, 1974).

Mann, William E., 'Augustine on Evil and Original Sin', in *The Cambridge Companion to Augustine*, ed. Eleonore Stump and Norman Kretzmann (Cambridge: Cambridge University Press, 2001), pp. 40–8.

Marenbom, John, *Pagans and Philosophers: The Problem of Paganism from Augustine to Leibniz* (Princeton: Princeton University Press, 2015).

Marion, Jean-Luc, *In the Self's Place: The Approach of Saint Augustine*, trans. Jeffrey L. Kosky (Stanford: Stanford University Press, 2012).

Maritain, Jacques, *St. Thomas and the Problem of Evil*, trans. Gordon Andison (Milwaukee: Marquette University Press, 1942).

Marshall, John, *Descartes's Moral Thought* (Ithaca: Cornell University Press, 1998).

Marx, Karl, 'Preface to *A Contribution to the Critique of Political Economy*', in *Early Writings*, ed. Lucio Colleti, trans. Rodney Livingstone and Gregor Benton (London: Penguin, 1975), pp. 424–8.

May, Simon, *Nietzsche's Ethics and his War on 'Morality'* (Oxford: Oxford University Press, 1999).

Meister, Robert, *After Evil: A Politics of Human Rights* (New York: Columbia University Press, 2011).

Menke, Christoph, 'At the Brink of Law: Hannah Arendt's Revision of the Judgment on Eichmann', *Social Research*, 81:3, 2014, pp. 585–611.

Michalson, Gordon, *Fallen Freedom: Kant on Radical Evil and Moral Regeneration* (Cambridge: Cambridge University Press, 1990).

Migoti, Mark, 'Slave Morality, Socrates, and the Bushmen: A Reading of the First Essay of On the Genealogy of Morals', *Philosophy and Phenomenological Review*, 58:4, December, 1998, pp. 745–79.

Morrison, Iain, 'Ascetic Slaves: Rereading Nietzsche's On the Genealogy of Morals', *The Journal of Nietzsche Studies*, 45:3, Autumn, 2014, pp. 230–57.

Mouzelis, Nicos, 'Lacan and Meditation: From the Symbolic to the Postsymbolic?', *Psychoanalysis, Culture, and Society*, 19:2, 2014, pp. 127–36.

Murphy, Paul, 'Jacques, Jacques and Jacks: The Shifting Symbolic in Derrida and Lacan', *Textual Practice*, 19:4, 2005, pp. 509–27.

Murray, Michael J., '*Vindicatio Dei*: Evil as a Result of God's Free Choice of the Best', in *New Essays on Leibniz's Theodicy*, ed. Larry M. Jorgensen and Samuel Newlands (Oxford: Oxford University Press, 2014), pp. 153–71.

Nadler, Steven, *The Best of All Possible Worlds: A Story of Philosophers, God, and Evil in the Age of Reason* (Princeton: Princeton University Press, 2010).

Neiman, Susan, 'What's the Problem with Evil?', in *Rethinking Evil: Contemporary Perspectives*, ed. Maria Pia Lara (Berkeley: University of California Press, 2001), pp. 27–45.

—, *Evil in Modern Thought: An Alternative History of Philosophy* (Princeton: Princeton University Press, 2002).

Neuhouser, Frederick, *Fichte's Theory of Subjectivity* (Cambridge: Cambridge University Press, 1990).

Newlands, Samuel, 'Leibniz on Privations, Limitations, and the Metaphysics of Evil', *Journal of the History of Philosophy*, 52:2, April, 2014, pp. 281–308.

Nicolacopoulos, Toula, and George Vassilacopoulous, 'The Time of Radical Autonomous Thinking and Social-Historical Becoming in Castoriadis', *Thesis Eleven*, 120:1, 2014, pp. 59–74.

Nietzsche, Friedrich, *On the Genealogy of Morals*, trans. Walter Kaufman and R. J. Hollingdale, in *On the Genealogy of Morals and Ecce Homo*, ed. Walter Kaufman (New York: Vintage, 1989), pp. 15–198.

—, *Ecce Homo*, trans. Walter Kaufman, in *On the Genealogy of Morals and Ecce Homo*, ed. Walter Kaufman (New York: Vintage, 1989), pp. 217–335.

—, *The Anti-Christ*, in *Twilight of the Idols and The Anti-Christ*, trans. R. J. Hollingdale (London: Penguin, 1990), pp. 126–99.

—, *Human, All too Human*, trans. Marion Faber and Stephen Lehmann (London: Penguin, 1994).

—, *Daybreak: Thoughts on the Prejudices of Morality*, trans. R. J. Hollingdale, ed. Maudemarie Clark and Brian Leiter (Cambridge: Cambridge University Press, 1997).

—, *Twilight of the Idols*, trans. Richard Polt (Indianapolis: Hackett, 1997).

—, *Beyond Good and Evil: Prelude to a Philosophy of the Future*, trans. Judith Norman, ed. Rolf-Peter Horstmann and Judith Norman (Cambridge: Cambridge University Press, 2002).

Oberst, Michael, 'Two Worlds *and* Two Aspects: On Kant's Distinction between Things in Themselves and Appearances', *Kantian-Review*, 20:1, 2015, pp. 53–75.

O'Grady, Paul, *Aquinas's Philosophy of Religion* (Basingstoke: Palgrave Macmillan, 2014).

Owen, David, 'The Contest of Enlightenment: An Essay on Critique and Genealogy', *Journal of Nietzsche Studies*, 25, Spring, 2003, pp. 35–57.

—, 'Nietzsche's Genealogy Revisited', *Journal of Nietzsche Studies*, 35/36, Spring/Autumn, 2008, pp. 141–54.

Pagels, Elaine, *The Origin of Satan* (London: Penguin, 1995).

Perez, Joseph, *Brève Histoire de L'Inquisition en Espagne* (Paris: Faynard, 2002).

Peters, F. E., *Aristotle and the Arabs: The Aristotelian Tradition in Islam* (New York: New York University Press, 1968).

Phillips, James, 'From Radical Evil to Banal Evil: Hannah Arendt against the Justification of the Unjustifiable', *International Journal of Philosophical Studies*, 12:2, 2004, pp. 129–58.

Pinkard, Terry, *German Philosophy 1760–1860: The Legacy of Idealism* (Cambridge: Cambridge University Press, 2002).

Platinga, Alvin, *God, Freedom, and Evil* (Cambridge: William B. Eerdmans, 1974).

Plato, *Euthyphro*, trans. G. M. A. Grube, in *Complete Works*, ed. John M. Cooper (Indianapolis: Hackett, 1997), pp. 1–16.

—, *Republic*, trans. G. M. A. Grube and C. D. C. Reeve, in *Complete Works*, ed. John M. Cooper (Indianapolis: Hackett, 1997), pp. 971–1223.

Rae, Gavin, 'Alienation, Authenticity, and the Self', *History of the Human Sciences*, 23:4, 2010, pp. 21–36.

—, *Ontology in Heidegger and Deleuze* (Basingstoke: Palgrave Macmillan, 2014).

—, *The Problem of Political Foundations in Carl Schmitt and Emmanuel Levinas* (Basingstoke: Palgrave Macmillan, 2016).

—, 'Taming the Little Screaming Monster: Castoriadis, Violence, and the Creation of the Individual', in *The Meanings of Violence: From Critical*

Theory to Biopolitics, ed. Gavin Rae and Emma Ingala (Abingdon: Routledge, 2019), pp. 171–90.

Rateau, Paul, 'The Theoretical Foundations of the Leibnizian Theodicy and its Apologetic Aim', in *New Essays on Leibniz's Theodicy*, ed. Larry M. Jorgensen and Samuel Newlands (Oxford: Oxford University Press, 2014). pp. 92–111.

Robbins, Jeffrey W., *Radical Democracy and Political Theology* (New York: Columbia University Press, 2011).

Römer, Thomas, *L'Invention de Dieu* (Paris: Éditions du Seuil, 2014).

Roney, Patrick, 'Evil and the Experience of Freedom: Nancy on Schelling and Freedom', *Research in Phenomenology*, 39:3, 2009, pp. 374–400.

Rosenthal, Abigail L., 'Defining Evil Away: Arendt's Forgiveness', *Philosophy*, 86, pp. 155–74.

Roudinesco, Elisabeth, *Jacques Lacan: Esquisse d'une vie, histoire d'un systéme de pensée* (Paris: Librairie Arthème Fayard, 1993).

Russell, Jeffrey Burton, *The Devil: Perceptions of Evil from Antiquity to Primitive Christianity* (Ithaca: Cornell University Press, 1977).

—, *Satan: The Early Christian Tradition* (Ithaca: Cornell: University Press, 1981).

Russell, Luke, 'Evil-Revivalism versus Evil-Skepticism', *Journal of Value Inquiry*, 40:1, 2006, pp. 89–105.

Rutherford, Donald, *Leibniz and the Rational Order of Nature* (Cambridge: Cambridge University Press, 1995).

—, 'Leibniz and the Stoics: The Consolations of Theodicy', in *The Problem of Evil in Early Modern Philosophy*, ed. Elmar J. Kremer and Michael J. Latzer (Toronto: University of Toronto Press, 2001), pp. 138–64.

Rydenfelt, Henrik, 'Valuation and the Will to Power: Nietzsche's Ethics with Ontology', *The Journal of Nietzsche Studies*, 44:2, Summer, 2013, pp. 213–24.

Sanford, John, *Evil: The Shadow Side of Reality* (New York: Crossroads, 1981).

Sass, Louis, 'Lacan, Foucault, and the "Crisis of the Subject": Revisionist Reflections on Phenomenology and Post-Structuralism', *Philosophy, Psychiatry, Psychology*, 21:4, 2014, pp. 325–41.

—, 'Lacan: The Mind of the Modernist', *Continental Philosophy Review*, 48, 2015, pp. 409–43.

Saussure, Ferdinand de, *Course in General Linguistics*, ed. Charles Bally, Albert Sechehaye, and Albert Riedlinger, trans. Roy Harris (Chicago: Open Court, 1986).

Schacht, Richard, *Nietzsche* (Abingdon: Routledge, 1985).

Schelling, F. W. J., *Philosophie der Offenbarung, 1841–1842*, ed. M. Frank (Frankfurt am Main: Suhrkamp, 1977).
—, *Bruno, or on the Natural and Divine Principle of Things*, trans. Michael G. Vater (Albany: State University of New York Press, 1984).
—, *On the History of Modern Philosophy*, trans. Andrew Bowie (Cambridge: Cambridge University Press, 1994).
—, *Philosophical Investigations into the Essence of Human Freedom*, trans. Jeff Love and Johannes Schmidt (Albany: State University of New York Press, 2006).
—, *Philosophy and Religion*, trans. Klaus Ottman (Putnam: Spring, 2010).
Schopenhauer, Arthur, *The World as Will and Representation*, 2 vols, trans. E. F. J. Payne (New York: Dover, 1966).
Schwarz, Hans, *Evil: A Historical and Theoretical Perspective*, trans. Mark W. Worthing (Minneapolis: Fortress Press, 1995).
Siegel, Jerrold, *The Idea of the Self: Thought and Experience in Western Europe since the Seventeenth Century* (Cambridge: Cambridge University Press, 2005).
Sleigh Jr., Robert C., 'Remarks on Leibniz's Treatment of the Problem of Evil', in *The Problem of Evil in Early Modern Philosophy*, ed. Elmar J. Kremer and Michael J. Latzer (Toronto: University of Toronto Press, 2001), pp. 165–79.
Snow, Dale, *Schelling and the End of Idealism* (Albany: State University of New York Press, 1996).
Soler, Colette, *Lacanian Affects: The Function of Affect in Lacan's Work* (Abingdon: Routledge, 2016).
Solomon, Robert C., 'One Hundred Years of *Ressentiment*: Nietzsche's *Genealogy of Morals*', in *Nietzsche, Genealogy, Morality: Essays on Nietzsche's On the Genealogy of Morals*, ed. Richard Schacht (Berkeley: University of California Press, 1994), pp. 95–126.
Steel, Carlos, 'Does Evil have a Cause? Augustine's Perplexity and Thomas's Answer', *The Review of Metaphysics*, 48:2, 1994, pp. 251–73.
Strauss, Claudia, 'The Imaginary', *Anthropological Theory*, 6:3, 2006, pp. 322–44.
Strawson, P. F., *The Bounds of Sense: An Essay on Kant's Critique of Pure Reason* (Abingdon: Routledge, 1975).
Taylor, Charles, *Sources of the Self: The Making of the Modern Identity* (Cambridge: Cambridge University Press, 1989).
—, *A Secular Age* (Cambridge, MA: Harvard University Press, 2007).
Taylor, Donald, 'Theological Thoughts about Evil', in *The Anthropology of Evil*, ed. David Parkin (Oxford: Blackwell, 1985), pp. 26–41.

Theunissen, Michael, *Hegels Lehre vom absolutem Geist als theologisch-politischer Traktat* (Berlin: De Gruyter, 1970).
Tomšič, Samo, *The Capitalist Unconscious: Marx and Lacan* (London: Verso, 2015).
Torchia, Joseph, 'Creation, Finitude, and the Mutable Will: Augustine on the Origin of Moral Evil', *Irish Theological Quarterly*, 71, 2006, pp. 47–66.
Vanderkam. James C., *Book of Jubilees* (London: Bloomsbury, 2001).
Van Luijk, Ruben, *Children of Lucifer: The Origins of Modern Religious Satanism* (Oxford: Oxford University Press, 2016).
Veltesen, Arne Johan, 'Hannah Arendt on Conscience and Evil', *Philosophy and Social Criticism*, 27:5, 2001, pp. 1–33.
Veltman, Andrea, and Kathryn J. Norlock (eds), *Evil, Political Violence, and Forgiveness* (Lanham: Lexington, 2009).
Voltaire, *Candide* (Paris: Magnard, 2013).
Vries, Hent de, *Philosophy and the Turn to Religion* (Baltimore: Johns Hopkins University Press, 1999).
Wallen, Martin, 'Schelling's Dialogue of Health in *Philosophical Inquiries into the Nature of Human Freedom*', *Studies in Romanticism*, 33:2, 1994, pp. 201–21.
Ware, Owen, 'The Duty of Self-Knowledge', *Philosophy and Phenomenological Review*, 79:3, November, 2009, pp. 671–98.
Wee, Cecelia, 'The Fourth Meditation: Descartes and Libertarian Freedom', in *The Cambridge Companion to Descartes' Meditations*, ed. David Cunning (Cambridge: Cambridge University Press, 2014), pp. 186–203.
White, Richard, 'The Return of the Master: An Interpretation of Nietzsche's *Genealogy of Morals*', in *Nietzsche, Genealogy, Morality: Essays on Nietzsche's On the Genealogy of Morals*, ed. Richard Schacht (Berkeley: University of California Press, 1994), pp. 63–75.
Wirth, Jason, *The Conspiracy of Life: Meditations on Schelling and His Time* (Albany: State University of New York Press, 2003).
Wood, Allen, *Kant's Ethical Thought* (Cambridge: Cambridge University Press, 1999).
Zafiropoulos, Marcos, *Lacan and Lévi-Strauss or the Return to Freud (1951–1957)*, trans. John Holland (London: Karnac, 2010).
Zupančič, Alenka, *Ethics of the Real: Kant and Lacan* (London: Verso, 2011).

# Index

absence, 40, 44, 48, 59, 61, 63, 72, 224, 227, 230, 238, 264–5, 271, 274, 321–2
agency, 168, 264, 292–3
alienation, 4
angels, 24, 30–1, 34
Aquinas, Thomas, 6, 55, 57–72, 78–9, 91, 100, 102–3, 105
Arendt, Hannah, 11, 15, 189–202, 225, 249, 277, 279, 319
Aristotle, 56–7, 248
atrocities, 190, 197, 287–90, 292–3, 299, 304, 311
attributes, 41, 78, 84–6, 271
Augustine, 5–6, 8, 36, 39–52, 57–9, 62, 66–7, 69–70, 72–3, 78–9, 91, 100, 102–5, 110, 279–80
Auschwitz, 197, 249, 308
authority, 26, 56, 78–9, 81, 170, 197, 307
autonomy, 118, 139, 155, 171, 194, 196, 217, 238, 246–7, 249, 274–5
  individual, 13, 193, 250

beings, 42, 44, 64–6, 104–8, 141–2, 145–6, 195, 214–15, 237–40, 263–5, 271–4, 280–2, 295–6, 303–7, 309
  existent, 89, 145–6, 148, 150, 152
  natural, 66, 140, 148–50, 238
belief, 12, 24, 70, 79–81, 89, 225, 277
  religious, 3
birth, 122, 147–8, 152, 155–6, 164, 176, 214
body, 39, 42, 47, 57, 69–72, 307
  human, 70

Card, Claudia, 13–15, 281, 286–94, 296–312
caste, 171, 173–4
Castoriadis, Cornelius, 12–13, 15, 180, 203, 221, 236–42, 244–57, 279, 319
cause, 48–50, 58, 65, 85–9, 92, 106, 110, 122, 124, 241, 269, 271, 278, 281
  intrinsic, 65–6
chaos, 148, 237–8
character, 122, 124, 126–7, 166, 172, 175, 178, 270–4, 276–9, 291, 303, 305, 310
  good, 271, 276, 278
children, 210, 212–14, 247, 304, 306
choice, 45, 47–8, 50, 91–2, 101, 121–2, 125–33, 139, 141, 144, 151–2, 196–7, 273–80, 291, 310
  autonomous, 29, 139, 191, 195–6, 249, 261, 273, 280
  moral, 9, 14, 40, 45–6, 121, 124, 130, 132–3, 139, 156–8, 274, 276, 280, 319
  power of, 121–3, 126, 128–9, 132, 302
  reflective, 270, 277–8
  unconscious, 155
Christ, 32, 34, 56, 70–1, 100
Christian, 7, 14, 24, 29–30, 32, 34, 56, 138, 142, 149, 176, 307, 319
Christianity, 1, 5–6, 22, 27–8, 33–9, 55, 58, 138, 164, 167, 176
cognition, 91, 117–20, 124, 267
community, 26–7, 124, 129, 171
concentration camps, 192–4, 197, 308
consciousness, 155, 191, 213, 215–18
contingency, 264–5, 268, 278–9
corruption, 72, 128, 302

cosmos, 23, 28, 32–3, 78, 102, 142, 150, 237, 264, 306
creativity, 12, 237–8, 246, 249–50
cruelty, 175, 189, 192, 197, 274, 305–7
culture, 2, 11, 55, 166, 180, 266–7, 281

death, 63–4, 150, 198, 214, 247, 292, 295, 302, 306–7
decision, 66, 89–90, 124, 153, 155, 157, 309
demons, 77, 289
Derrida, Jacques, 208
Descartes, Rene, 7, 77–96, 98, 103
destruction, 24, 66, 193–4, 238, 265, 289, 307
devil, 29–30, 32, 48, 66–8, 306
disease, 154, 174
disharmony, 151, 153–4
divine, 47, 50, 63, 68, 89, 111, 143, 149, 190

earth, 30, 33–5, 50, 140, 148
ego, 210, 212, 215–16, 223, 229, 244, 304–5
Eichmann, Adolf, 196–200
enemy, 175, 177–8
Enlightenment, 189
entities, 5, 44, 59, 63–4, 84, 99, 148, 154, 181, 237–8, 240
error, 78–9, 82, 87–8, 91–3
  evil of, 77, 79, 81, 83, 85, 87, 89, 91–3, 96
  human, 7, 88, 90
essence, 44, 59, 83, 90, 99, 103, 106–7, 118, 167–8, 170, 175, 178
ethics, 42, 78, 123, 177, 179, 210, 226–30, 249
evil
  absolute, 15, 63, 288, 298, 306, 319
  actions, 29, 48, 121, 125, 155, 261, 263, 276, 279, 287, 297–8
  -as-such, 60–1, 63–4
  banal, 11, 190–1, 194, 200
  characters, 271, 274, 278
  diabolical, 8, 15, 128, 288, 300, 304–7, 309, 311–12
  efficient cause of, 48, 68
  genealogy of, 163, 165–9, 171, 173, 175, 177, 179–85, 187
  general, 9, 152–3

heart, 125, 128
individuals, 35, 262, 270, 280, 291
  maxims, 121, 124, 128, 132, 301
  metaphysical, 7, 100, 102–7, 120
  metaphysics of, 138–9, 141, 143, 145, 147, 149, 151, 153, 155, 157
  moral, 5–6, 8, 46, 51, 60, 68, 97, 100–2, 104–9, 125, 130–1
  natural, 5–6, 8, 46, 51, 60, 100–2, 292
  origin of, 55, 57, 96, 111, 129, 154, 156, 168
  particular, 9, 152
  physical, 100–2, 105, 107
  principle, 21, 27, 98, 142
  pure, 29, 31–2, 62–3
  radical, 11, 15, 117, 119–21, 123, 125, 127, 129, 131, 156, 190–1, 194–6
  simple, 269–70
  symbolic function of, 208–9, 211, 213, 215, 217, 219, 221, 223, 225, 227, 229
excess, 227, 230–1
existence, 9, 11–12, 40–2, 77–8, 80–4, 86, 98–100, 106, 108–10, 127, 138–40, 147–53, 169–70, 177–8, 219–21

faith, 78–9, 81, 101, 110, 138
field, 11, 209, 212, 217, 227, 229
  social-historical, 244, 250
Foucault, Michel, 166–8
foundation, 6–7, 40, 59–60, 78, 80, 82–3, 89, 130, 133, 164, 166–7, 238, 241, 266
freedom, 91, 96, 99, 118, 122–3, 127–8, 130, 132–3, 138–44, 149–51, 155–7, 194, 275–6
Freud, Sigmund, 210, 213, 225, 248

genocide, 189, 289, 292–3
God, 4–9, 12, 21–35, 39–51, 57–61, 66–71, 77–83, 85–93, 96–111, 120–1, 141–54, 225–6, 280, 319–20
  city of, 40, 43, 47–8
  existence of, 41, 79–80, 98
  ground of, 146, 148–9
goods
  external, 263–6, 278
  internal, 263–4, 268, 271
grey zones, 15, 288, 293, 299, 304–5, 307–11
ground, 64, 66, 120, 122, 124, 127, 130,

132, 139–41, 145–52, 154–5, 275, 280, 287
  abyssal, 140, 151–3
  dark, 148–50, 154
  subjective, 122, 124–7, 130, 156
groups, 10, 180, 194, 201, 307–8
  social, 27, 192–3
guilt, 280, 308

habits, 13, 177, 190, 201, 270–1, 273, 276–8, 280, 291, 311
harm, 13, 34, 197, 265–6, 268–71, 274, 276–9, 287, 290–1, 294–301, 305–6, 308, 311
  intolerable, 14, 287, 290, 293–4, 296–9
  simple, 266, 268–70
  undeserved, 14, 264–6, 269–72, 278
health, 107, 154
heaven, 7, 24, 28, 30, 33–4, 50–1, 140
Hegel, Georg, 10, 248
history, 2, 9–10, 33, 164–8, 180–1, 189, 192, 238–9, 287–8, 290, 320–2
  metaphysical, 167–8
Holocaust, 11, 189–90, 288, 309
human
  beings, 35, 42, 58–9, 62, 98, 107, 124, 126, 131, 154, 194, 199, 245, 262, 265
  cognition, 7, 80, 83, 88–92, 98, 110–11, 117–21, 138–9, 143, 151, 157, 312
  condition, 70–1, 202, 209, 262, 264
  existence, 47, 70–1, 174, 216, 267
  nature, 72, 35
  120, 126–7, 129–31, 262, 268–9
  understanding, 110, 118, 122, 214, 219
  welfare, 263–6, 268–72, 276, 278
  world, 50–1, 244

identity, 145–6, 148, 152, 211–12, 217–18, 222, 230, 243
imaginary, 12, 83, 175, 210–12, 215–18, 225–6, 230–1, 240–2, 244, 249
  radical, 12, 240, 242–5, 249
  significations, 238, 241–2, 244–5, 247
  social, 4, 13, 236–7, 239, 241–5, 247–51, 259
imagination, 91, 190, 240, 247
imperfection, 50, 87–8, 104–5
impurity, 128, 174, 301–3
infinity, 90, 103, 106
Islam, 6, 55–6

Judaism, 5, 22–3, 27, 174, 176
judgement, 83, 88, 91–2, 198–9, 266, 268–71, 274, 286, 288, 290–4, 297–8, 301–2, 307, 311
  autonomous, 199–200
  faculty of, 87–8, 91–2
  good, 92, 263
  moral, 13, 69–70, 156–7, 172, 180, 249, 272, 292, 311
  reflective, 83
justice, 23, 50–1, 57, 96–9, 199, 230, 310
  original, 71–2

Kant, Immanuel, 8–10, 15, 110–11, 117–40, 142–4, 152–3, 156–8, 195–6, 273–6, 287–8, 299–306, 319
Kekes, John, 13–15, 261–85, 290–2, 319
kingdom, 55, 58, 120
knowledge, 41, 50, 56, 58, 79, 81, 83, 91–2, 96, 98, 103, 138–9, 144, 242

Lacan, Jacques, 12–13, 180, 203, 208–37, 240–2, 280
language, 4, 170, 208–9, 212–21, 223–4, 227, 230, 239–40, 245–7, 262, 267–8, 311
law, 24–5, 68, 71, 121, 123, 127–8, 132–3, 139, 143, 211, 213–14, 238, 274–5
  universal, 119, 121, 139, 143, 157
Leibniz, Gottfried, 7–8, 10, 28, 51, 89–90, 96–111, 142–3
Levinas, Emmanuel, 198
life, 63–4, 107, 145, 148, 150, 155, 170, 177, 192, 194, 240, 265–6, 278–9, 295–6
  decent, 295–6
  good, 264, 268–9, 272
  human, 2, 194, 264–6, 268
  individual, 13, 173, 191, 193, 242
light, 21, 24, 26, 31, 42, 62, 121, 145, 148–50, 152–3, 168, 238
  emergence of, 149–50
  of God, 9, 154
  natural, 84–5

madness, 81, 227
magma, 244
Manichaeism, 5, 35, 39–40
metaphysics, 98, 143–4, 150, 156–7, 170
mind, 41–3, 47–8, 78, 81, 88, 117, 191, 195, 201, 215, 296, 298

miracles, 202, 226
monotheism, 4–5, 21–3, 28, 30, 34, 39, 87, 145
monsters, 65–6, 178, 196, 199–200, 265, 273
moral
  actions, 118, 128–9, 132, 261, 280
  agents, 14, 119, 124, 196, 200, 250, 270, 273, 278, 301
  categories, 10–11, 158, 164–5, 169, 172–4, 178, 180, 311
  character, 14, 89, 130, 261, 263, 271, 276
  disposition, 123–4, 127, 132
  law, 8, 101–2, 105, 119–30, 139, 143, 191, 199, 226–7, 273, 300–4
  maxim, 8, 120–33, 139, 143, 152, 156–7, 196, 273, 300, 302–3
  morality, 47–8, 118, 120–1, 139, 141, 164–6, 168, 172–4, 180–2, 261, 263, 269, 272–3, 278–80
  character-, 13, 261–2, 272–3, 276, 279
  choice-, 13, 261, 272–3, 277, 280
  noble, 169–75, 177–9
  slave, 176–7, 179
murder, 101, 225, 300–1, 306

Name-of-the-Father, 223–4
natural
  laws, 118, 143, 202
  world, 69, 77, 140, 163, 238, 247, 270, 278–9
nature, 10–13, 43–7, 59–62, 70, 82–4, 96, 120–2, 130–1, 140, 149–50, 163–4, 190–2, 264–6, 295–9
  divine, 28, 30–1
necessity, 51, 89–90, 100–3, 106, 109–10, 138, 142–4, 155, 267–8
negation, 5, 44, 59, 61–2, 100, 104–6, 177, 179, 321
Nietzsche, Friedrich, 8, 10–12, 163–77, 179–85, 187, 189, 226, 229, 249, 286
norms, 32, 121, 170, 193, 195, 201, 238, 240–1, 243–4, 277, 305
nothing, 8, 40, 42–3, 45, 48, 50, 62–3, 98, 100, 146–7, 195–6, 198, 214–15, 228
nothingness, 88, 146
noumenal, 9, 117–18, 122, 130–1, 138–40, 144, 153, 156–7, 275–6, 304–5
  choice, 9, 130
  freedom, 8, 273, 275

Old Testament, 22, 24, 30–1
omnipotence, 21, 29, 34, 49–50, 63, 67–8, 80, 82, 90–1, 98–9, 106, 141, 247
ontology, 42, 48, 173, 179, 237

pagans, 43, 48, 56, 58
pain, 63, 212, 214, 295–6, 307
paradigm
  Nero, 306–7
  Serpent, 306–7, 309
  Torture, 306
perception, 47, 92, 151, 218, 246, 262, 269, 286, 296
perfection, 8, 50, 58–60, 62–3, 70, 85, 87–8, 90, 97–9, 103–5, 107, 142
perpetrators, 13–14, 250, 261, 263, 281, 287, 290–1, 293–5, 300, 305, 309–11
personality, 125, 172, 181
potentiality, 58, 148, 195, 291
power, 5, 7, 32, 35, 72, 89, 96–8, 125, 127, 132–3, 169–72, 175–6, 241
predisposition, 124–5, 127, 132, 273, 276
  original, 152, 274
priests, 173–5
privation, 5, 44–5, 55, 57, 59–67, 69–71, 87–8, 92, 102, 104–7, 150–1, 190, 228
  of being, 9, 60, 64–5, 67, 104, 107
  moral, 107
  pure, 62–4
procreation, 71, 214
propensity, 45, 124–8, 130, 132, 142, 153, 265, 301
  natural, 45, 48–9, 125–6, 130, 152
psyche, 245–8, 250
  biological, 245–6
  human, 9, 243, 245–6
psychic monad, 245–7, 249–50
psychoanalysis, 11, 187, 20–9, 212–13, 229
punishment, 30, 46, 61–2, 68, 101–3, 109, 197, 277, 301
  evil of, 60–1

reality, 44, 82, 85–6, 103, 108–9, 147, 153–4, 157, 163, 168, 172, 178, 180
  formal, 84–7, 89–90, 103
  human, 152–3, 209
  objective, 84–7, 89, 117
reason, 25–8, 40–2, 65–8, 71, 98–9,

110–11, 118–22, 124–6, 130–2, 138–9, 142–3, 216–17, 245–7, 275–6
autonomous, 8, 10, 115, 129, 163–4, 190
human, 23, 41, 120
practical, 118, 120, 133, 138, 143
responsibility, 25, 33, 39–40, 50, 68, 91, 93, 199, 289, 291, 295, 297, 303, 310
*ressentiment*, 164, 175–8
revenge, 174–5, 309
revolution, 132, 174
rigorism, 128, 288, 299–303, 309

Saussure, Ferdinand de, 209, 220–1
Schelling, Friedrich, 9–10, 138–62, 226, 229, 320
Scholem, Gershom, 191, 195
secular, 1–2, 4, 15, 190, 280, 287, 319, 321–2
self, 147, 201, 215, 246
-love, 129, 273, 301
-revelation, 148–9
semen, 6, 65–6, 72
significations, 211, 213, 216, 220, 223, 241–3, 247–9
signifiers, 12, 210, 214–17, 219–21, 223–5, 242, 246
chain of, 215, 223
master, 222–5
simple harm
objectivity of, 269–71
undeserved, 269, 271, 278
sin, 4, 6, 26–7, 30, 32, 43, 50–1, 60, 62, 66–7, 70, 72, 99–100, 102, 107
original, 6, 55, 57, 59, 61, 63, 65, 67, 69–72, 102–3, 131, 141–2
slaves, 173, 176–8
socialisation, 245, 247–8
society, 3, 13, 181, 193, 195, 200, 202, 224, 226, 237–45, 247–8, 272, 276
instituted, 243
instituting, 243, 250
institution of, 238, 249
*Sonderkommando*, 287, 307–9
soul, 32–3, 39, 58, 69–71, 79, 131, 170, 176
space, 139, 189, 193–4, 303–4, 310
species, 59, 62, 66, 68–70, 108, 122, 124, 126, 129–30, 132, 153, 218, 246, 265–6
human, 130–2

spirit, 30–1, 142–3, 156, 164, 167, 175, 178
Stoicism, 287, 290
Structuralism, 11, 203, 208
structures, 8–9, 11, 107–8, 117–18, 120, 149, 151, 166, 168, 181, 209, 211, 213, 226–7, 243
social-political, 195, 200, 202
subjectivity, 78, 215, 217
substance, 40, 43–4, 64, 78, 84–6, 96, 107, 241, 244, 246, 250, 309
finite, 84–6, 103
infinite, 84–7, 89, 103, 141
suffering, 101–2, 105, 107–10, 175, 181, 189, 197, 265, 268–9, 278, 281, 289–90, 292, 300
symbolic
construction, 180, 221, 226–8, 230
order, 12, 210–15, 217–19, 221–8, 230–1, 237, 242, 248
relations, 12–13, 216, 218–19, 226, 230, 237
system, 35, 84, 96, 118, 142, 145, 201, 211, 220, 223, 241, 243–4, 308
semiotic, 10, 164–5

theodicy, 51, 61, 90, 93, 96–7, 99, 101, 103, 105–7, 109–15, 264
thinking, 41, 69, 78, 81–3, 97, 142–4, 146, 164–6, 168–9, 172, 198–201, 208–11, 237
instrumental, 200
substantive, 11, 191, 200–1
time, 28–9, 33–4, 80–1, 122–3, 130–1, 141, 143, 145, 155, 171, 219–20, 227–8, 294–5, 302–4, 308–9
torture, 14, 194, 266, 288, 301, 306–7, 309
transcendent, 147, 173–4, 220, 239, 241, 267
transformation, 164, 222, 319, 321–2
truth, 7, 26–7, 42–3, 78, 80–3, 89–90, 117–19, 124, 163, 172, 180, 222, 225, 242, 248

unity, 96, 144, 146, 149–51, 153, 216, 240, 272
universe, 46, 50–1, 58, 90, 102–3, 108, 138, 142, 167, 213, 215

values, 132, 164, 169–76, 179–80, 201–2, 219–20, 224, 239–40, 242–4, 247, 249, 269, 277, 295, 306
victims, 13–15, 110, 193, 199, 281, 286–95, 297–301, 303, 305, 307–11
will
  free, 14, 39, 41, 43, 45–7, 49, 51, 66, 68, 91, 108, 139, 172
  -to-power, 170, 172–3, 180, 226
world, 39–40, 50, 67–8, 88–90, 99–103, 140–2, 144, 149, 151, 171–3, 178–9, 243–4, 247–8, 262–3, 275–6
  best possible, 97, 99, 101–2, 109, 111
  external, 83–4, 86, 167
  noumenal, 143
  phenomenal, 118, 120, 267, 304–5
  physical, 220–1
  social-historical, 238, 246
wrongs, 287–8, 293, 298–9, 301
  inexcusable, 14, 287, 290, 293, 297, 299
  lesser, 14, 287, 296, 298–301, 311

Yahweh, 24, 26, 30–1

EU representative:
Easy Access System Europe
Mustamäe tee 50, 10621 Tallinn, Estonia
Gpsr.requests@easproject.com

www.ingramcontent.com/pod-product-compliance
Lightning Source LLC
Chambersburg PA
CBHW052056300426
44117CB00013B/2154